OUTLAWS

Scala Arts & Heritage Publishers

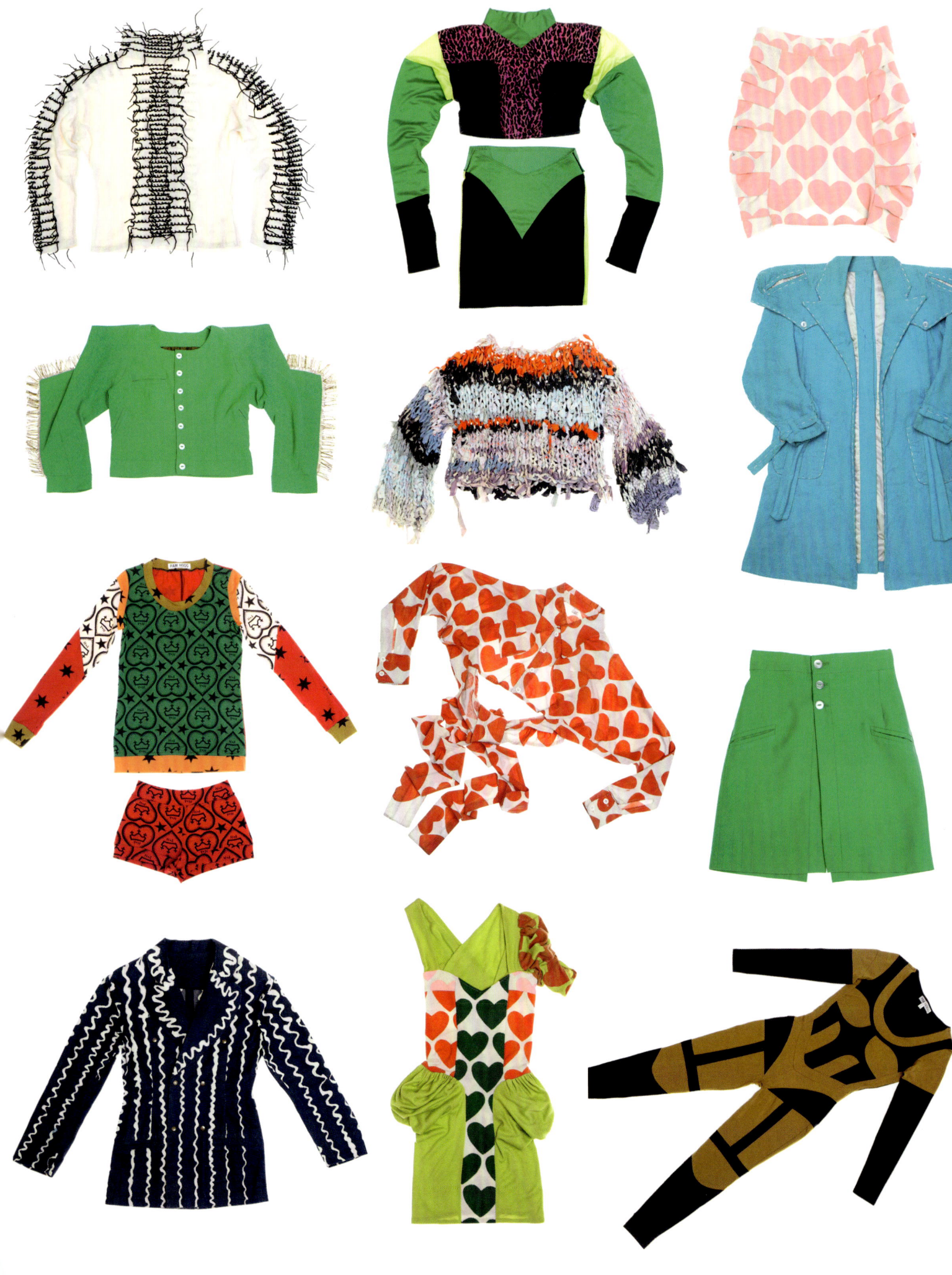

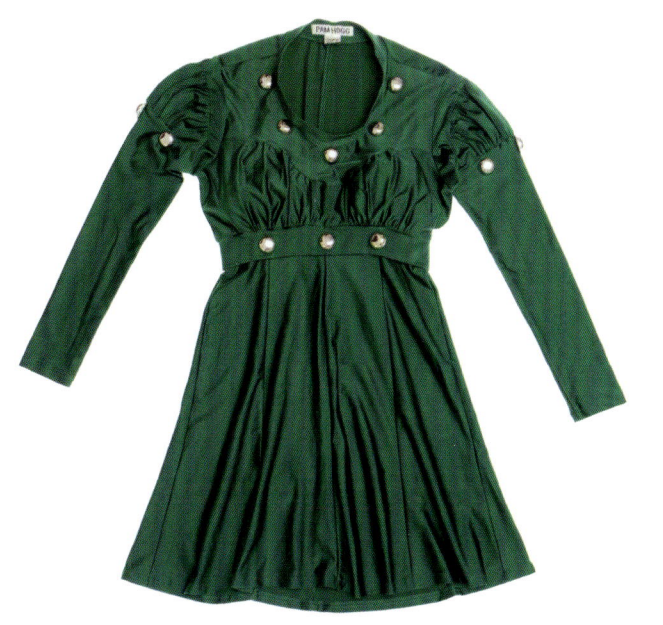
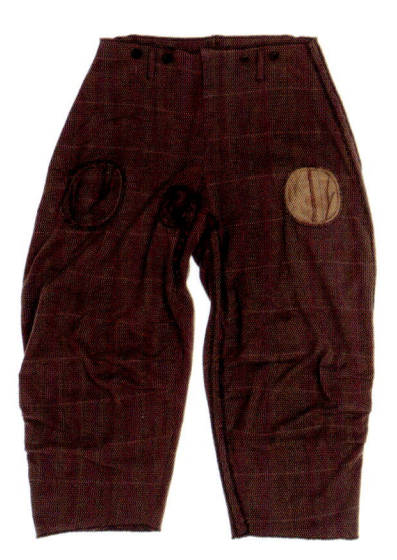
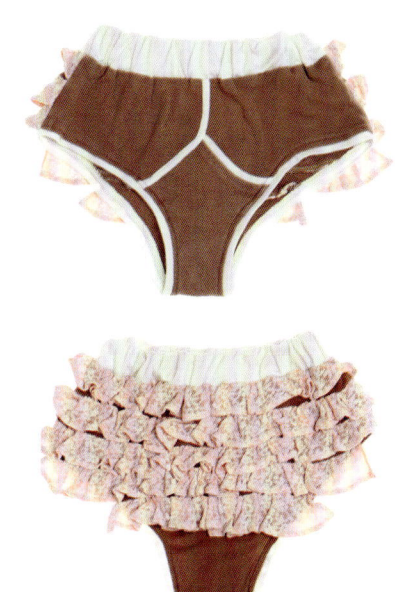

MARTIN GREEN NJ STEVENSON

OUTLAWS

FASHION RENEGADES OF LEIGH BOWERY'S 1980s LONDON

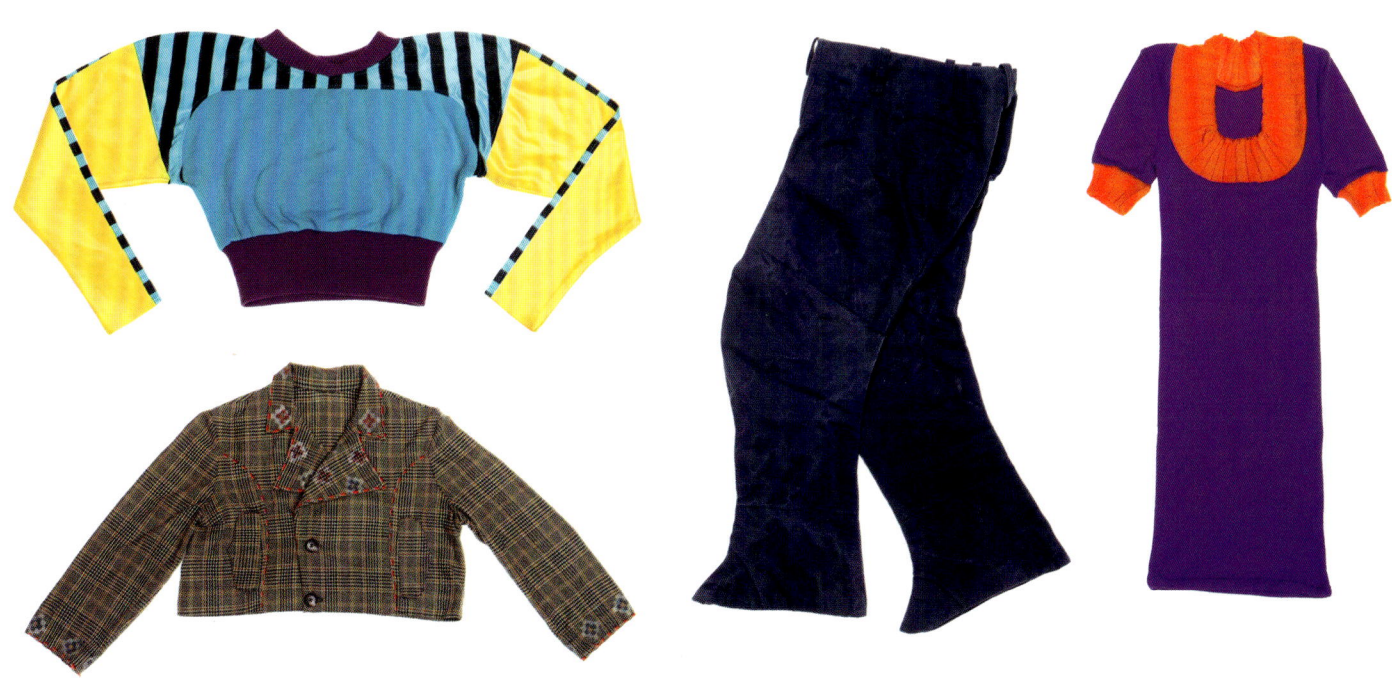

INTO TABOO
MARTIN GREEN

Madonna released 'Into the Groove' on 15 July 1985, and that's how I can date my first trip to Leigh Bowery's notorious club night Taboo.

Maximus was a large, glitzy Romanesque discotheque buried beneath Leicester Square and fairly empty when I arrived at Taboo's second night. The sumptuous space was full of mirrored columns holding up flashing revolving lights above a central dancefloor surrounded by plush red velvet banquettes and a raised viewing platform. I sat with friends Carl Putnam, who would later form indie rock band Cud, and Andrew Downs, a tall, flamboyant teenage dandy, in a large booth near the entrance, sipping drinks we'd smuggled in and waiting for the new glitterati to arrive. But they didn't.

Now, after years of running clubs, I know about second nights. Openings are packed, but it can take a while to build up a regular following. Taboo was no exception, but although it wasn't busy, the people attending were the most dressed-up provocateurs in town and word rapidly spread.

Lads in cropped jackets strutted around in black and white BodyMap leggings and Dr. Martens steel toe-capped boots, while a group of girls danced together in plastic coats, PVC miniskirts, go-go boots and great big Jackie O sunglasses. Then at midnight Leigh made his entrance in a tousled grey wig with big pink spots covering his jacket, trousers and face.

The dancefloor erupted as Leigh threw himself on the ground and the room was filled with smoke, screams and dancers sniffing poppers as DJs Jeffrey Hinton and Rachel Auburn played a crazed concoction of Hi-NRG, Bollywood, Italo disco and 'Into the Groove', which we heard five times throughout the night, sometimes directly after it had already been played. Taboo was unpredictable, unabashed and unforgettable. A new court had taken over London and Leigh Bowery was king.

Taboo closed in 1986 and rapidly became mythical. Then in 1991, erstwhile agitator Matthew Glamorre asked if I would like to start a weekly club night with him at Maximus. Together we launched Smashing and along with Michael Murphy DJed a mix in the spirit of Taboo, so when Leigh first arrived and immediately began pogo-ing to X-Ray Spex, I felt especially honoured. He swiftly became a regular and in 1993 his avant-garde art-rock garage band Minty played their debut gig at Smashing. But that's another story.

When I embarked on co-curating the *Outlaws: Fashion Renegades of 80s London* exhibition with James Lawler and NJ Stevenson, I specifically wanted to put back into history the frequently forgotten figures from that era. I spent over two years contacting people on social media and asking friends of friends while searching through ex-clubber's wardrobes, sheds and attics to find hidden gems. Style writer Ben Cobb called me 'the Indiana Jones of curation'.

This was a difficult task as many designers only produced for a short period and in very small quantities. Mark Lowings and Syrie Panton of Mark & Syrie are a prime example; they only produced collections for four years before disappearing. The impoverished duo slept on floors while tailoring suits from garish rugs and tourist tea towels, which then sold to Barbra Streisand and Madonna. I discovered a few rare pieces and found Syrie, who had left London, changed career and has kindly contributed to this book.

As I discovered more and more pieces during my treasure hunt, I was constantly amazed at the skill, imagination and expertise that produced such a wonderful array of inventive designs. In particular, Elmaz Hüseyin, whose astounding work her sister found in boxes in her parent's loft, unopened for 40 years.

The brilliant Elmaz, who tragically died in 2019, was part of a group of influential graduates from St Martin's School of Art including Stephen Jones and John Galliano. I recently discovered that her fellow student Peter Doig created T-shirt designs before his stellar career as an internationally renowned artist.

It was Peter who suggested we photograph the pieces in this book flat rather on mannequins, which we did thanks to Dominic Harris, who built a giant light box in his studio. Other pieces were shot at Westminster University Menswear Archive thanks to Andrew Groves, who founded the UK's only educational institution dedicated to creating a major collection of contemporary menswear. On the pages that follow, you'll find those photographs along with interviews with their designers – compiled with help from DuoVision co-founder James Lawler – first-hand accounts from those who were part of the scene and stories from those who wore the pieces.

I must thank original club kid David Cabaret, who now works as a specialist costume maker on Hollywood movies, for helping find many pieces, including his own, and restoring them back to their former glory after years of disco damage.

For this book and the *Outlaws* exhibition, I wanted to evoke the thrill I experienced as a teenager observing the world of Taboo and the designers who inhabited the scene; continual surprises, radical glamour and the creative unpredictability of the 1980s, when working-class kids were paid to go to college, accommodation was cheap, squats were accessible and nightclubs were our social centres.

A time when anything seemed possible.

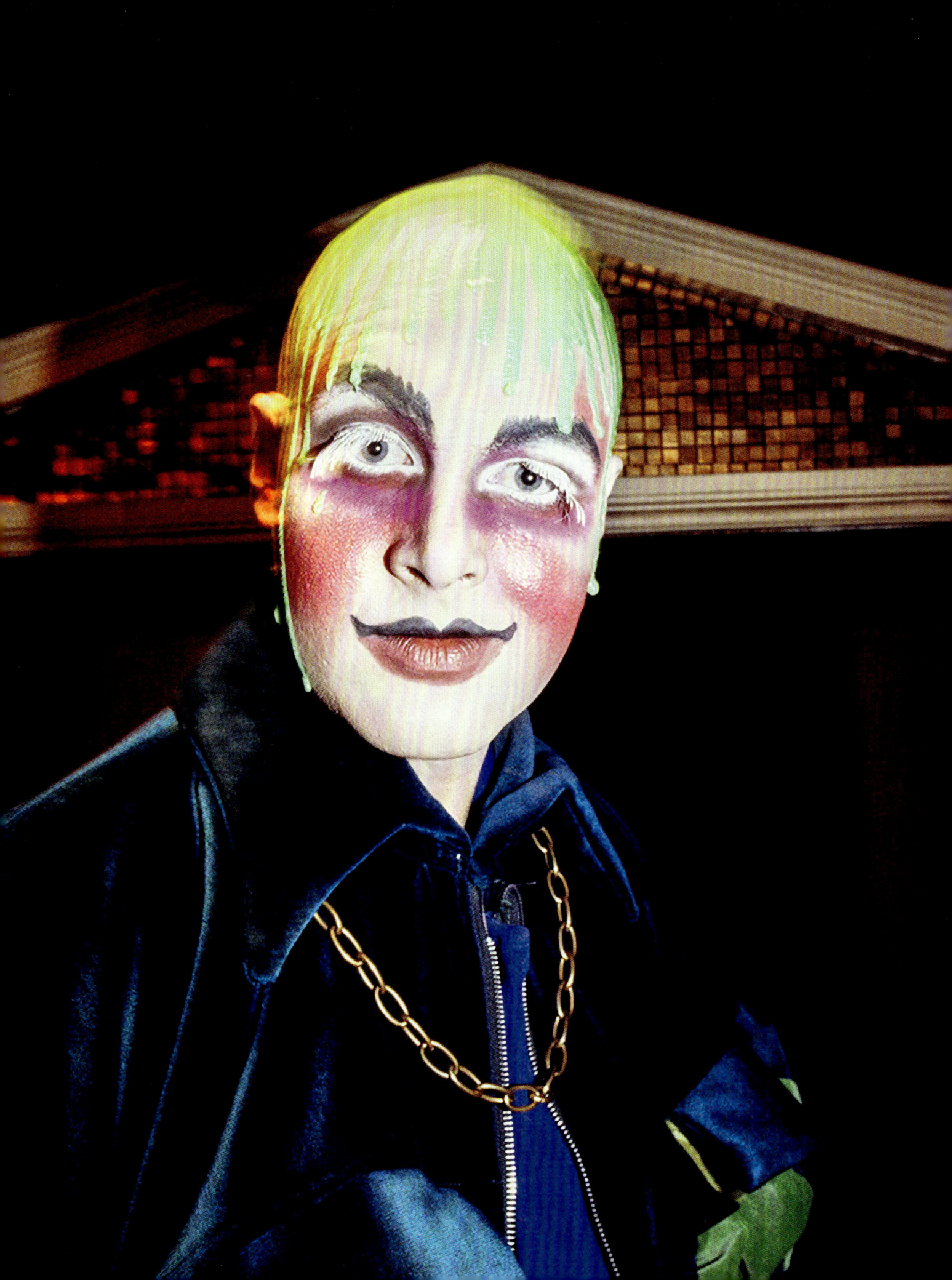

CONTENTS

TIMELINE 8
INTRODUCTION 12

THE DESIGNERS

LEIGH BOWERY	30–41
ANNIE LA PAZ	44–49
RACHEL AUBURN	50–59
JOHN CRANCHER	62–65
PETER DOIG	66–67
GALLAGHER WALLS	70–71
JOHN FLETT	72–73
JULIANA SISSONS	74–75
BODYMAP	80–89
DEAN BRIGHT	90–97
BOYS WONDER	104–107
ENGLISH ECCENTRICS	108–113
PX	114–115
JUDY BLAME	116–119
JOHN GALLIANO	120–123
PAM HOGG	128–135
DEMOB	136–137
CHRISTOPHER NEMETH	140–143
NOCTURNE	144–145
STEPHEN LINARD	146–147
DAVID CABARET	152–155
MARK & SYRIE	156–159
DEGVILLE'S DISPENSARY	162–163
RICHARD TORRY	164–167
RED OR DEAD	170–175
VAUGHAN & FRANKS	178–181
ELMAZ HÜSEYIN	182–189
MARK LAWRENCE	190–195

IN CONVERSATION WITH

Peter Doig	68
Holly Johnson	76
Mark Moore	138
Dave Swindells	148
Wayne & Gerardine Hemingway	176

ESSAYS

Now Everything is New	60
A Year in Fashion (PHOTO ESSAY)	98
The Parish Noticeboard	124
Clothes for London Warriors	160

THE AFTERPARTY 196
AUTHOR BIOGRAPHIES 206
ACKNOWLEDGEMENTS 207

TIMELINE

1962
Education Act passed requiring local authorities to pay tuition fees and provide maintenance grants for first-degree courses.

1967
Kensington Market opens in West London.

Sexual Offences Act passed, decriminalising private homosexual acts between men aged over 21.

1969
The Royal College of Art awards degree status to its fashion course, followed by St Martin's School of Art and Kingston University.

1970
Joan and Sidney Burstein open Browns on South Molton Street.

1971
Vivienne Westwood and Malcolm McLaren open Let It Rock on the King's Road, later rebranded as Too Fast to Live, Too Young to Die followed by SEX, Seditionaries and finally Worlds End.

1972
London's first Gay Pride march.

1974
Camden Market opens.

1978
Steve Strange and Rusty Egan take over Tuesday nights at the Blitz wine bar in Covent Garden. New Romantics are born.

1979
Margaret Thatcher becomes Prime Minister.

1980
The Face, *i-D* and *Blitz* magazines launch.

Leigh Bowery arrives in London from Australia.

1981
Prince Charles and Lady Diana Spencer marry in St Paul's Cathedral. Diana's dress, by the Emmanuels, places the 'romantic' fashion trend firmly in the mainstream.

The Cha Cha club, run by Michael Hardy, Judy Blame and Scarlett Canon, opens at Heaven. Leigh Bowery attends the club.

The Greater London Council (GLC) starts directly funding small LGBT groups and organisations.

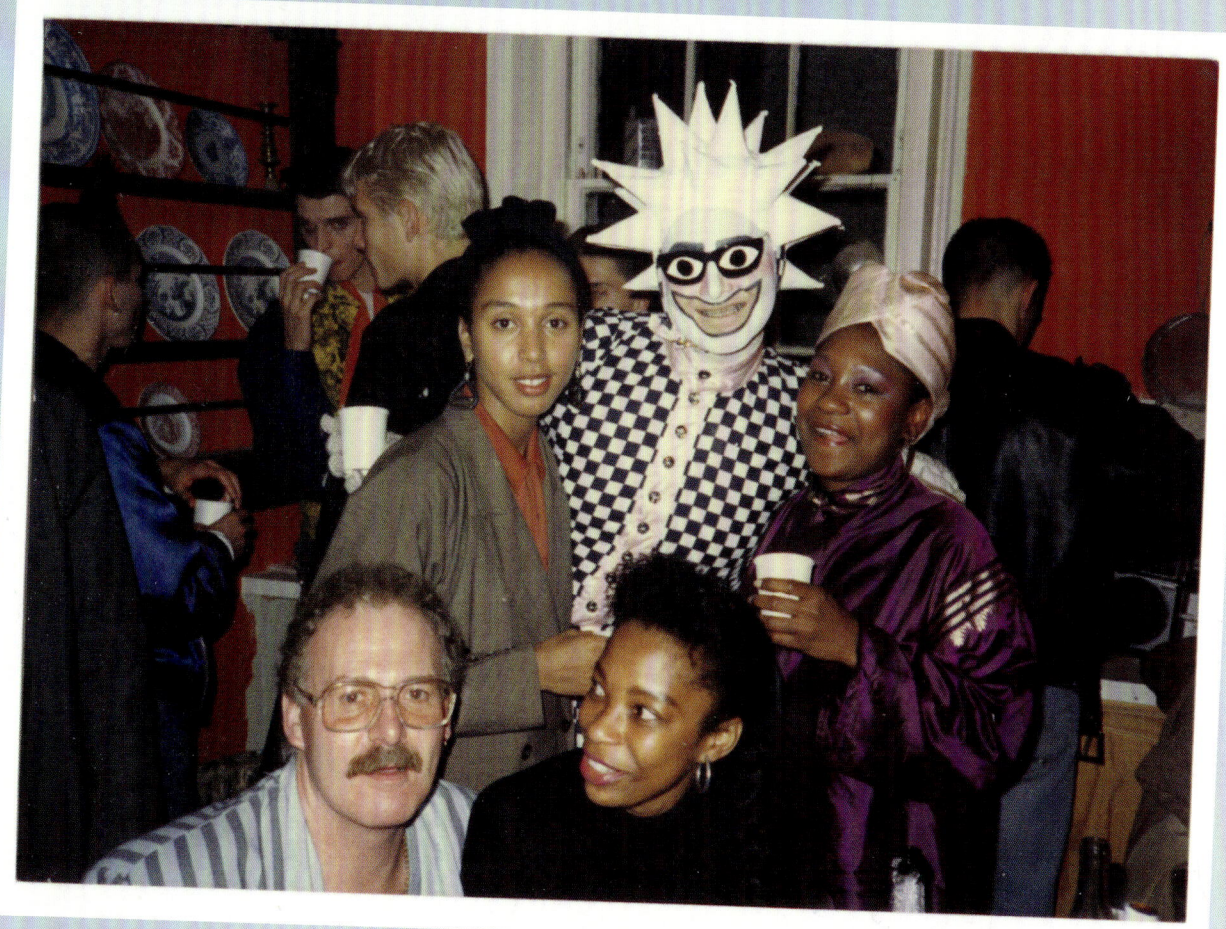

1982

The Terence Higgins trust is set up after Terry Higgins dies of AIDS-related illness at St Thomas' Hospital, London.

Boy George first appears on *Top of the Pops* and 'Do You Really Want to Hurt Me?' tops the UK charts.

Steve Strange takes a group of British designers including Stephen Linard, Stephen Jones and PX to Paris for a fashion show to promote the launch of Visage's album *The Anvil*.

Chris Sullivan, frontman of Blue Rondo à la Turk, and hairdresser Ollie O'Donnell open The Wag Club on Wardour Street. The club hosts the UK's first hip-hop event, with 25 artists from the US.

Olli Wisdom, singer in the band Specimen, opens goth club The Batcave on Dean Street.

Hyper Hyper, a unit providing stall space for new designers, opens on Kensington High Street.

Michael Clark becomes resident choreographer at the Riverside Studios.

Circus, the peripatetic warehouse party run by Annie La Paz, Jeremy Healy, Patrick Lilley and Lucy Morahan, launches and is later featured on the arts TV programme *South of Watford*, where Leigh Bowery is among the interviewees.

Gay pub and alternative venue The Bell opens in King's Cross.

Total Fashion Victims opens at The Wag, hosted by Stephen Linard and with DJs Princess Julia and Jeffrey Hinton.

1983

The Enterprise Allowance Scheme gives unemployed people £40 a week to set up their own businesses.

Susanne Bartsch holds New London in New York fashion show, followed by London Goes to Tokyo a year later.

The British Fashion Council is formed to promote the British fashion industry and support London Fashion Week.

Philip Sallon opens the Mud Club in Leicester Square with Tasty Tim and Mark Moore DJing upstairs. Tasty Tim is interviewed on *South of Watford* about 'gender bending' on the release of his single 'Sugar, Sugar'.

1984

'Relax' by Frankie Goes to Hollywood reaches number one in the UK despite being banned by the BBC.

The Michael Clark Company dances to The Fall playing 'Lay of The Land' live on *The Old Grey Whistle Test* on BBC2, with costumes by Leigh Bowery and make-up by Trojan.

Katharine Hamnett, wearing her '58% Don't Want Pershing' T-shirt, meets Margaret Thatcher at a reception at 10 Downing Street.

John Galliano's St Martin's School of Art graduation collection 'Les Incroyables', inspired by the French Revolution, is bought by Browns.

The UK miners' strike starts in March and lasts almost a year.

1985

Dead or Alive top the UK charts with 'You Spin Me Round'. Pete Burns and the band are dressed in Dean Bright's graduate collection.

Leigh Bowery and Tony Gordon open Taboo at Maximus in Leicester Square, with Jeffrey Hinton and Rachel Auburn as DJs.

Leigh Bowery and Trojan are photographed by Sheila Rock in their 'outer space' look for The New Glitterati featured in *The Face* magazine.

Pyramid opens on Wednesdays at Heaven, one of the first clubs in the country to play house music.

The Africa Centre in Covent Garden hosts Jazzie B's Soul II Soul sound system on Sunday nights.

An estimated 15,000 people, including mining communities showing solidarity in return for gay support during the miners' strike, march at Gay Pride.

The Limelight opens in a disused chapel on Shaftesbury Avenue with decor by Michael Costiff.

ABC tops the US dance charts with 'Be Near Me' wearing clothes by Leigh Bowery, BodyMap, Elmaz Hüseyin and Vaughan & Franks.

Bob Geldof launches Fashion Aid at the Royal Albert Hall.

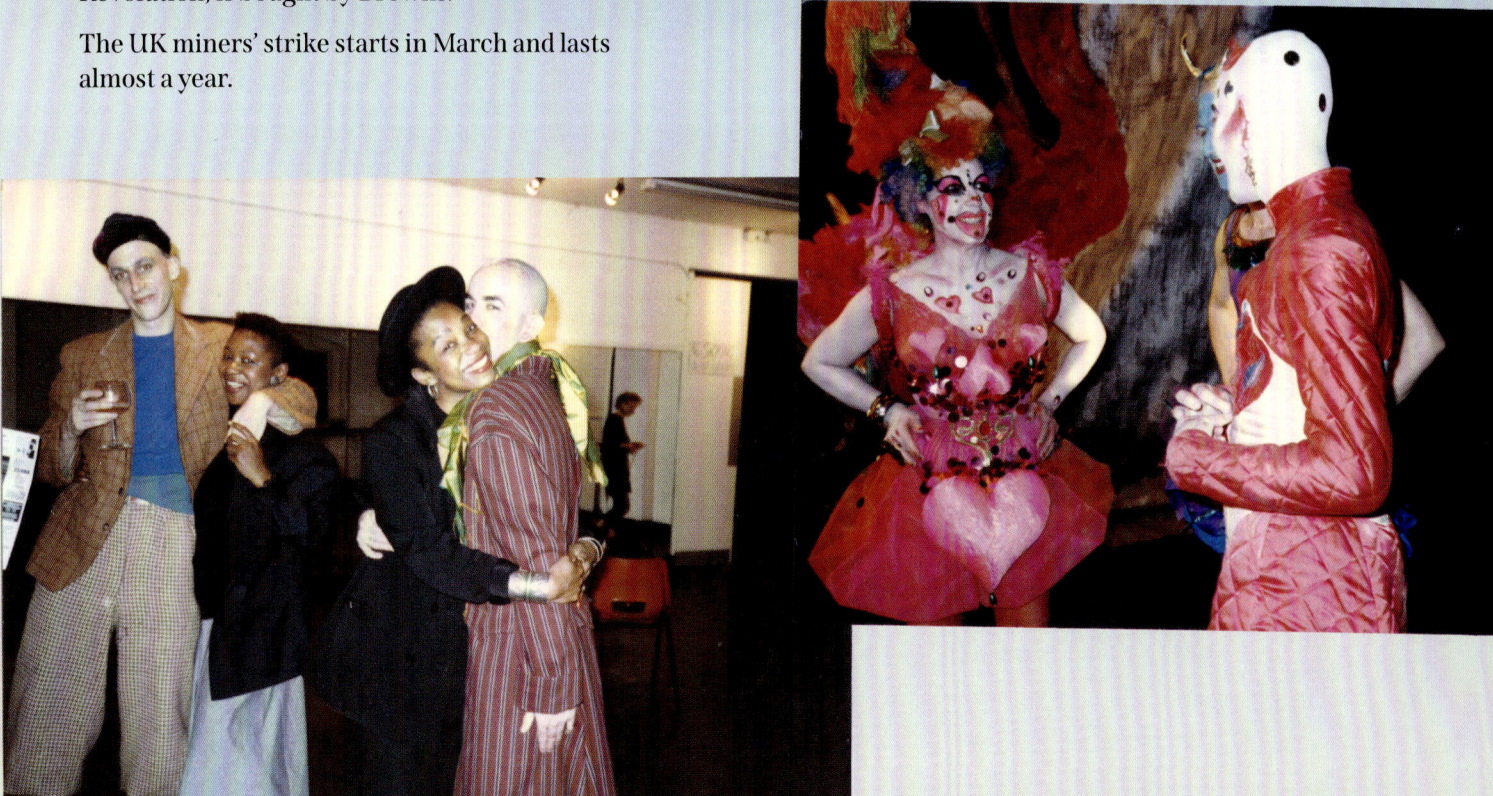

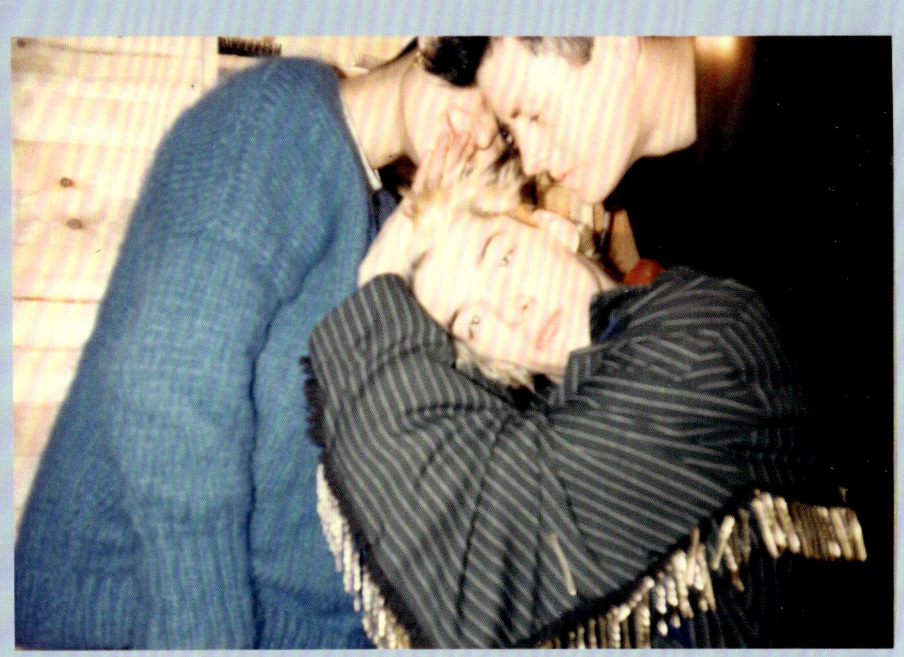
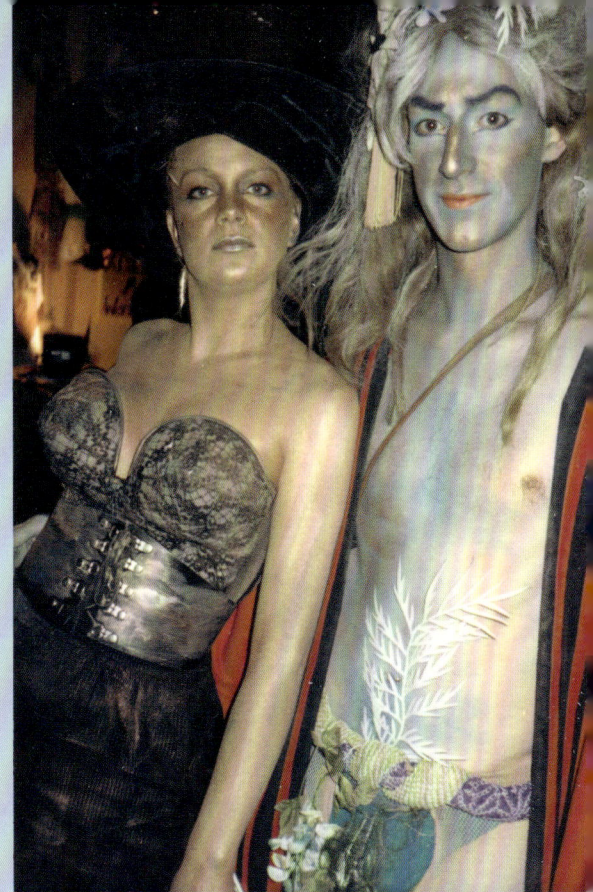

1986

Designer Martin Degville of Kensington Market boutique YaYa scores a hit with debut track 'Love Missile F1-11' by Sigue Sigue Sputnik.

John Crancher opens Anarchy at Studio Valbonne on Kingly Street, Soho with Jeffrey Hinton and Martin Confusion as DJs.

South of Watford devotes an episode to Leigh Bowery with comedian Hugh Laurie shadowing him for a day at home, at a BodyMap show and finishing at Taboo.

Madame Jojo's cabaret club opens on Brewer Street.

Hail The New Puritan, a 'fictional' documentary about dancer and choreographer Michael Clark, is broadcast on Channel Four featuring a scene in Leigh Bowery and Trojan's flat.

The Clothes Show, a weekly fashion programme hosted by Jeff Banks, Selina Scott and Caryn Franklin, begins on BBC1. Leigh Bowery is given regular guest appearances.

The House of Beauty and Culture opens in Dalston.

An article in *The Mail on Sunday* exposes the drug use at Taboo and provokes the club's closure.

1987

Daisy Chain opens at the Fridge, Brixton, run by Jimmy Trindy, with DJs Princess Julia, Mark Lawrence and Jeffrey Hinton.

Princess Diana opens the UK's first purpose-built HIV/AIDS unit at London's Middlesex Hospital.

Government-issued leaflets with the words 'AIDS: Don't Die of Ignorance' are delivered to every household in the UK.

Shoom, the first weekly acid house all-nighter, opens in Southwark hosted by DJ Danny Rampling.

1988

Section 28, prohibiting the 'promotion of homosexuality' by local authorities, is introduced by the Conservative government.

DJ Mark Moore has a UK number one hit with landmark acid house track 'Theme from S'Express' using early sampling techniques.

1989

Kinky Gerlinky drag balls run by Gerlinde and Michael Costiff open at Legends in London's West End, hosted by Winn Austin, with DJ Princess Julia.

INTRODUCTION
NJ STEVENSON

'I remember seeing the 1960s film *Smashing Time* on the telly in the early 1980s, all about coming to London and being famous and getting fabulous clothes. And I remember thinking: "Oh, can that happen to you?" Can you have a life like that where you come from a working-class home and then you can be discovered, and you can make it and suddenly your life could change?'

—David Cabaret
performance artist

The London that Leigh Bowery encountered in 1980, when he first arrived from the Melbourne suburb of Sunshine, was a place where things were starting to happen. Three new magazines, *The Face, i-D* and *Blitz* had launched that year, an indication of a sea-change of style in the capital that was infiltrating popular culture. A post-punk synthesis of youth fashion and subculture had begun to be noticed – most particularly at Steve Strange and Rusty Egan's weekly night at the Blitz wine bar in Covent Garden. The New Romantic look (as its denizens refused to be called) was recognisable in the designs of the St Martin's fashion students who frequented the Blitz, in the street-style photography in the pages of *i-D* and on pop bands such as Spandau Ballet and Strange and Egan's own band, Visage.

Avidly devouring any information on the British New Romantic scene that he could find, it was this that shaped Bowery's expectations as a 19-year-old. Ambition, a grounding in technical fashion education and a sewing machine were his initial resources in the journey to become the central figure in a scene of his own making.

OPPOSITE
Rachel Auburn and Leigh Bowery, 1989

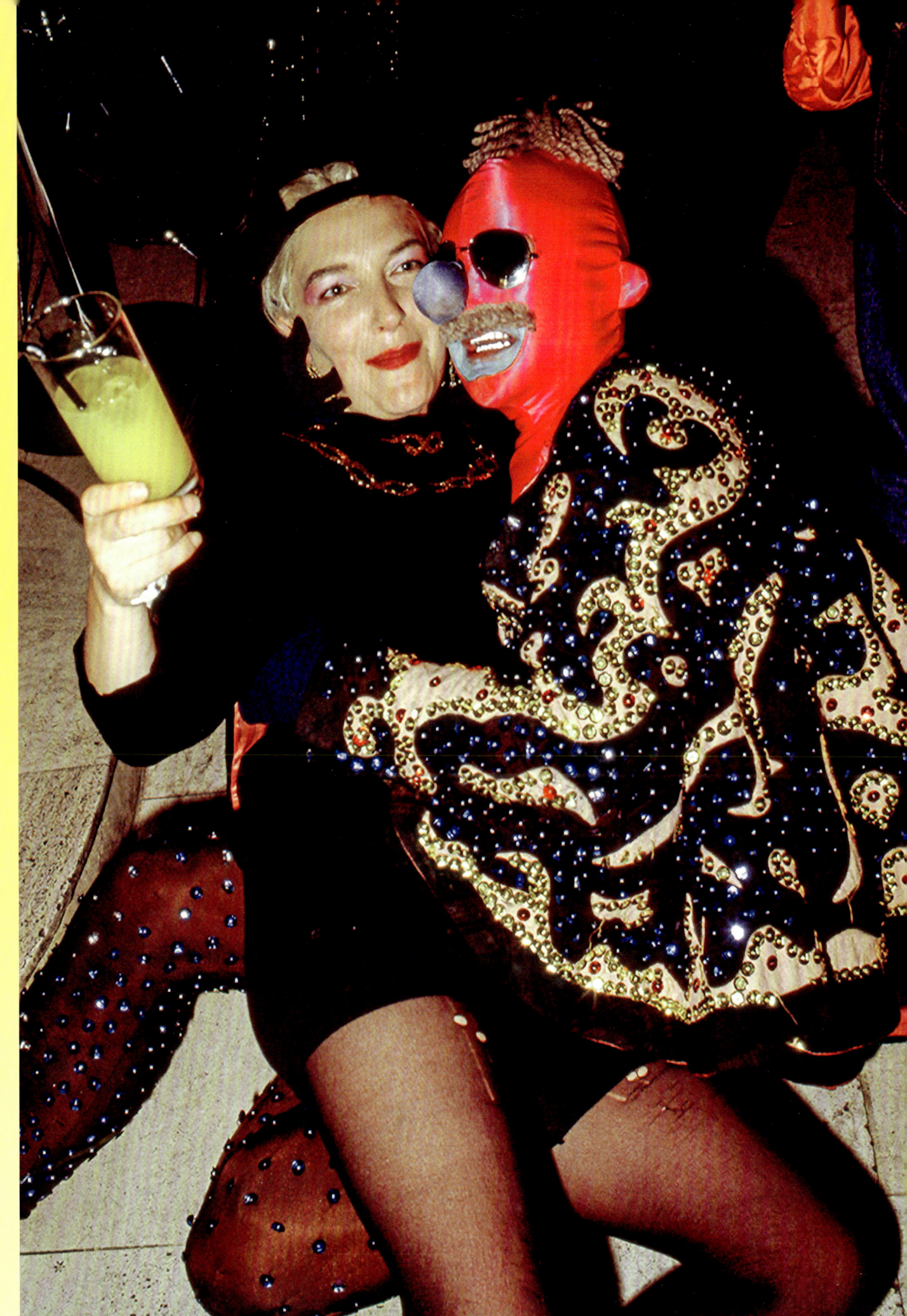

Associating with a group of talented and driven designers, artists, performers and musicians, Bowery was quick to absorb the ever-changing atmosphere of self-expression in clubland. It was not long before his presence and vision infected the creative output of mid-1980s London with the radicalism of Taboo.

MEETING YOUR HEROES

Bowery later told his friend, the designer Richard Torry, that 'the Blitz was over and done with by the time I arrived because news reached Australia a bit too late.' Night shifts at Burger King, 'because my money was running out and I hadn't met any fabulous people', were detrimental to an aspiring nightclub personality, but when Bowery saw an advertisement for sculptor and designer Andrew Logan's Alternative Miss World party in *Time Out* magazine, he asked for the evening off. It was at the fancy-dress ball extravaganza that Logan had been running periodically since 1972 that Bowery first met the drag performer Yvette the Conqueror, which led to a change of fortune.

Yvette took Bowery to Steve Strange and Rusty Egan's new venture, Club for Heroes: a David Bowie-themed night on Baker Street. Since the Blitz, the media had been fascinated with the stars of the new club-centric fashion scene and Bowery finally glimpsed them for himself. This included the exotic Blitz Kid Kim Bowen, 'looking really spectacular, a bit like Elizabeth I', and Strange, 'at that point, my number one idol'. Moving on, the night progressed to the Cha Cha club, run by Judy Blame and Michael Hardy, former coat-check employees at Heaven whose friends were so numerous that it became impossible to get past them to retrieve your jacket. When the management realised the potential of the alternative crowd, they were given the back space at Heaven to run their own club. Bowery encountered Scarlett

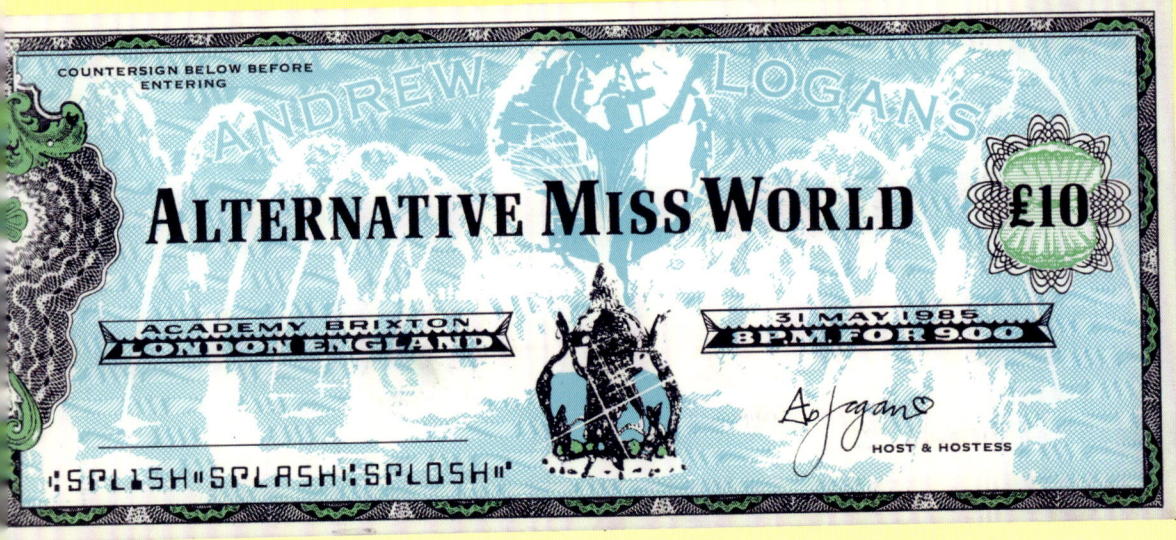

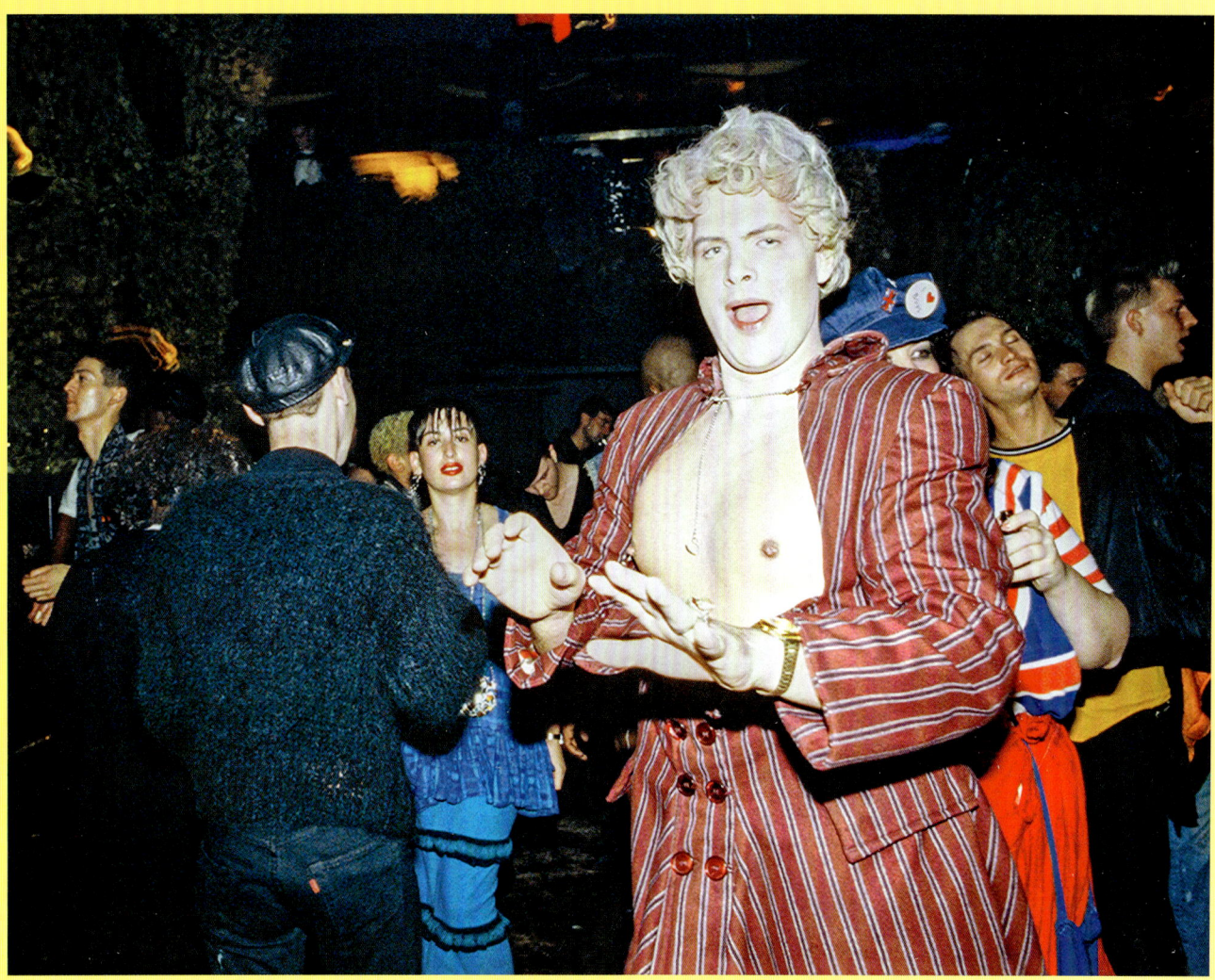

ABOVE
Leigh Bowery at Busby's, 1985

Cannon on the door, a hairdresser at Antenna and *Blitz* magazine cover girl with 'pure white hair shaved at the sides, and earrings which were two chicken's feet. She just sat there and looked bored by everybody arriving.' Spotting Blame 'and Stephen Linard and other really famous club people was just at the beginning of it.' Yvette took Bowery through to the main club: 'This was exactly what I was hoping would happen the day I got off the plane. It took about nine months, but then it did happen. I was so excited. I remember there were mirrors on the side of the dancefloor at Heaven and I kept watching myself and checking out everyone else and trying to copy them.'

WHEN WE GET TO LONDON, WE'RE GOING TO HAVE A SMASHING TIME

The Blitz scene was remarkable because so many of the regulars became successful in their fields; this book celebrates what happened next. In a matter of months, a new influx joined the original Blitz Kids – a little too young for the excitement and anarchy of punk, yet affected by the way it opened up youth culture.

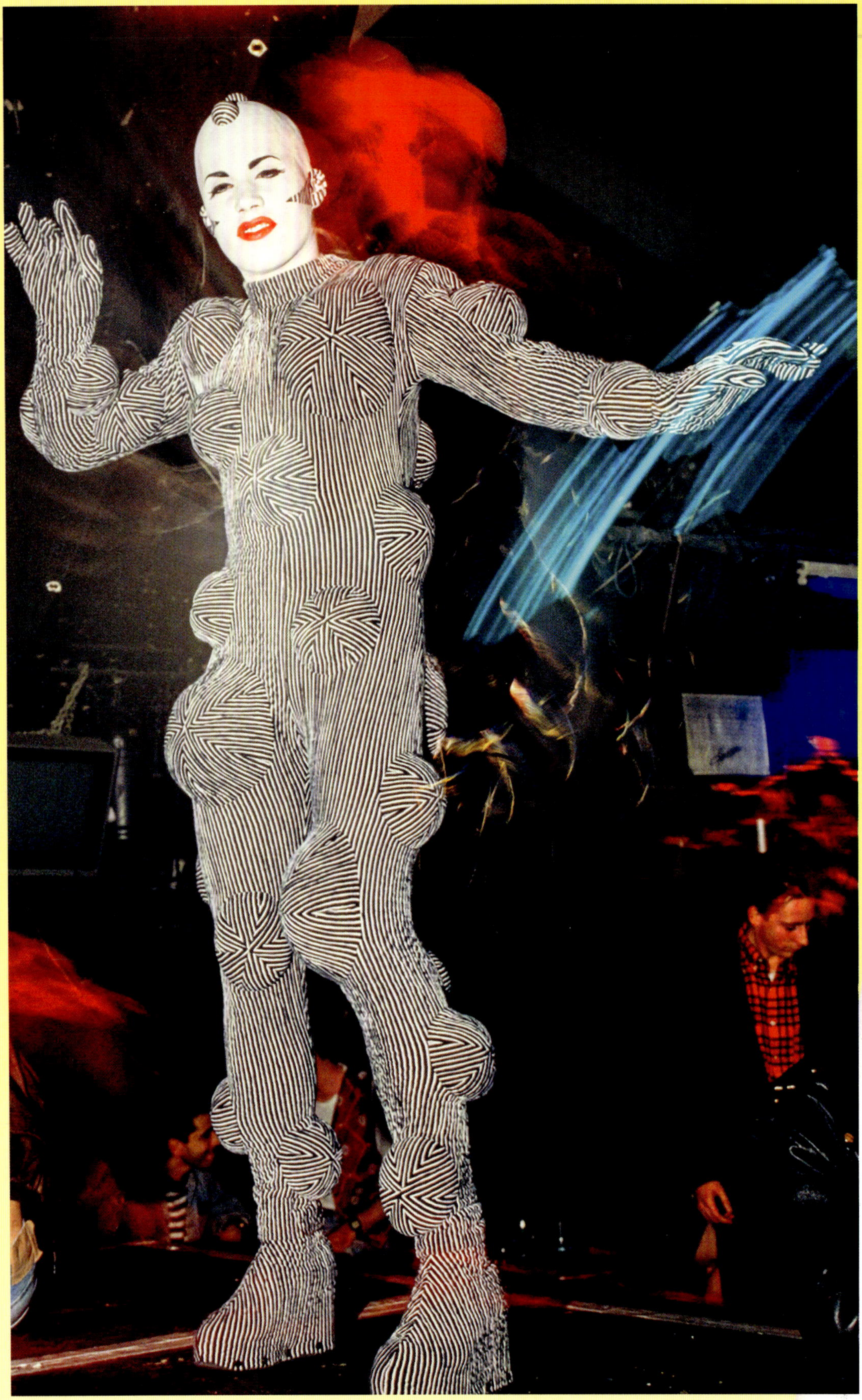

LEFT
David Cabaret at Daisy Chain in 1988

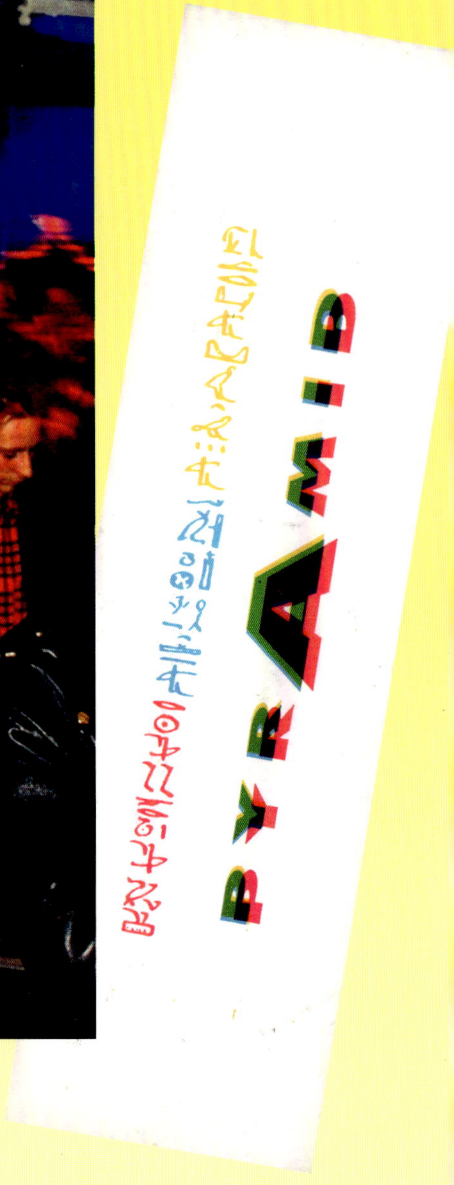

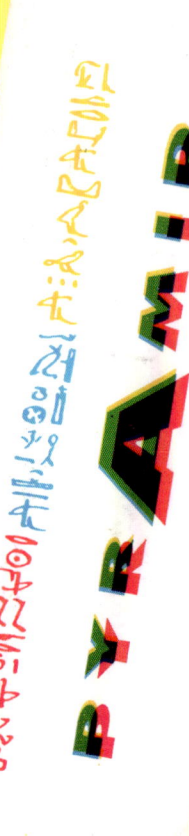

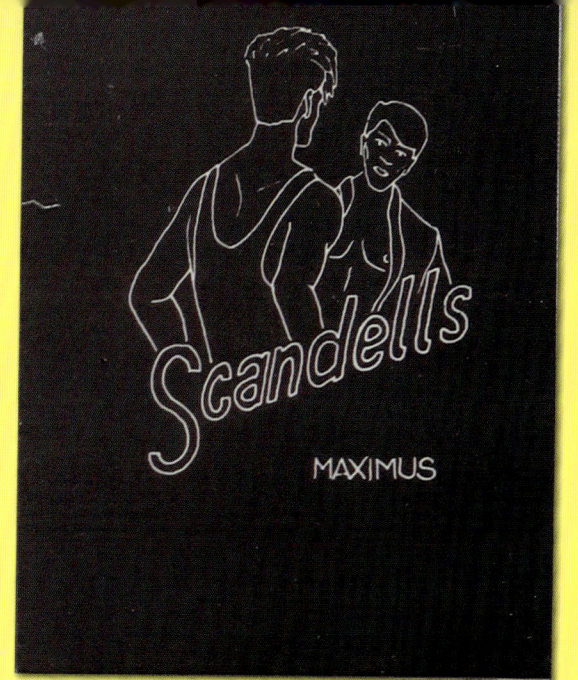
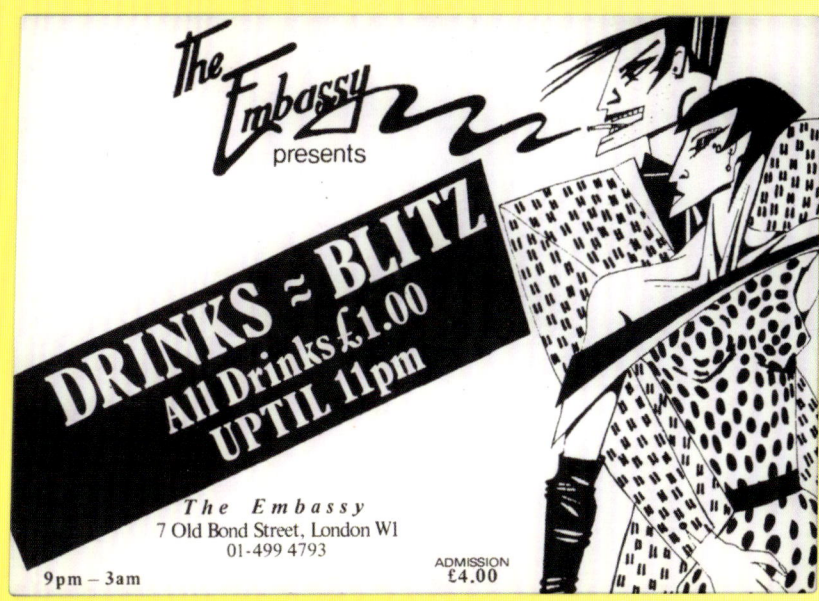

Like Leigh Bowery, they were hanging on the coattails of possibility that the New Romantic crowd forged, and ready for something new. Some of the fashion designers whose pieces are featured in this book and shown in the *Outlaws* exhibition, were, like David Holah and Stevie Stewart of BodyMap, Richard Torry, Judy Blame and Stephen Linard, already established as part of the nightlife scene. Some, such as Elmaz Hüseyin, Mark Lawrence and Dean Bright, came to study fashion and naturally became part of the club crowd. Others, including Paul Bernstock of Bernstock Speirs, Annie La Paz and John Crancher, ran clubs themselves. Students and graduates such as Rachel Auburn, Vaughan & Franks and Joe Casely-Hayford, and unschooled designers such as Wayne and Gerardine Hemingway of Red or Dead and Mark & Syrie, followed the do-it-yourself ingenuity of established scenesters like Martin Degville, Jane Kahn and Patti Bell and set up in markets.

Among the Blitz Kids were the inhabitants of a squat in Warren Street in central London, which was first set up in the late 1970s and became notorious as a grimy breeding ground for creative talent. These included pop stars Boy George and Marilyn, film director John Maybury, make-up artist Lesley Chilkes, DJ Princess Julia, milliner Stephen Jones, stylist Kim Bowen and fashion designers Lee Sheldrick and David Holah. The Warren Street squat afforded its occupants alternative ways of living and working, away from the constraints of the burgeoning capitalist society. Young creatives coming to London in the early 1980s continued to benefit from the broken urban sprawl where properties could be occupied and space adapted. Straitened councils struggling with dereliction often turned a blind eye to squatters or offered peppercorn rents, satisfied that buildings were at least partially maintained. Since 1962, local education

> 'Kensington Market, the Great Gear Market on the King's Road and Camden Market were established centres of 1980s subculture.'

authorities were required to pay the tuition of students attending full-time first-degree courses and provide them with a maintenance grant. The fact that art schools had finally granted fashion courses degree status in the 1970s meant that many of these students were fully funded.

St Martin's School of Art, then on Charing Cross Road, was very much part of the buzz around Soho at the time. Designer Dean Bright remembers from his time there: 'Boy George would come to St Martin's on the first day of term because everyone turned up in a look. So he'd come painted green with Stephen Linard and all of that crew. There was a performance element, and he'd even go into college. The rest of term, you'd go and sign the register then go to the bar or to the Capacetto coffee bar or to the pub.' Patisserie Valerie on Old Compton Street was a daytime meeting place and hangout, and as writer and curator Iain R Webb remembers: 'They used to put cakes on the table and you would see how many you could eat without paying for them. Someone would order some toast so you'd be able to sit there a bit longer. You'd literally survive on a cup of tea and sit in there for half the day.' This was the Soho where the Colony Rooms harboured artists Lucien Freud and Francis Bacon, and jazz musician George Melly mixed with young clubbers at the Soho Brasserie before they left for The Wag, the club on Wardour Street opened by Chris Sullivan, frontman of Blue Rondo à la Turk, and Antenna hairdresser Ollie O'Donnell in 1982. In the 1980s Soho was still a mix of the seamier side of London life and old communities. Old Compton Street was a busy central London thoroughfare choked with diesel fumes from black cabs. The Raymond Revuebar nestled among the sex shops and stairwells of Walker's Court, steps away from the bustling Berwick Street market and round the corner from Lina Stores, the Italian grocers. Cheap after-hours drinking bars like the Cozy on Berwick Street and The Pink Panther on Wardour Street meant

(the rock garden, piazza, covent gdn)

OPPOSITE
Boy George at Taboo

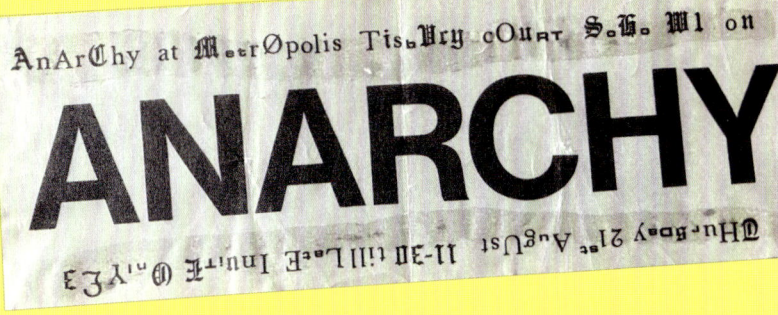

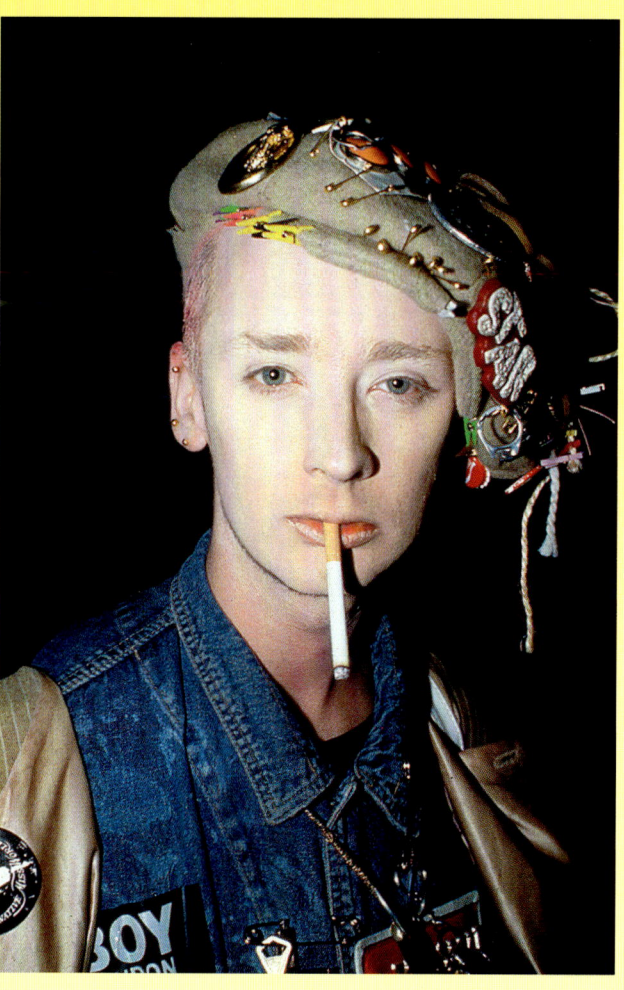

that going home could wait. It was this London, the Soho of Soft Cell's *Non-Stop Erotic Cabaret*, that drew artistic kids from provincial homes to study at St Martin's, to work in avant-garde hair salons, be a make-up artist or stylist, or some other kind of job that didn't exist at home. As well as a place of dreams, London was an unlikely haven. Hairdresser and model Scarlett Cannon put it plainly: 'People were fleeing small towns, villages, places where you weren't accepted. Just because you were gay, really, or because you were different.'

In the 1980s homosexuality was still illegal under the age of 21. Club personality David Cabaret remembers the fear and the thrill: 'If you got caught, you could go to prison. There were alternative gay bars that we were going to, but still there were raids, so you could get into a lot of trouble.' And British schooling was very much indoctrinated with the ideology of conventionality. Flamboyance could attract the wrong kind of attention, and there was much to escape from in the provinces, not least boredom. Small wonder then that 'difference' was a unifying factor in the ambition to come to the capital.

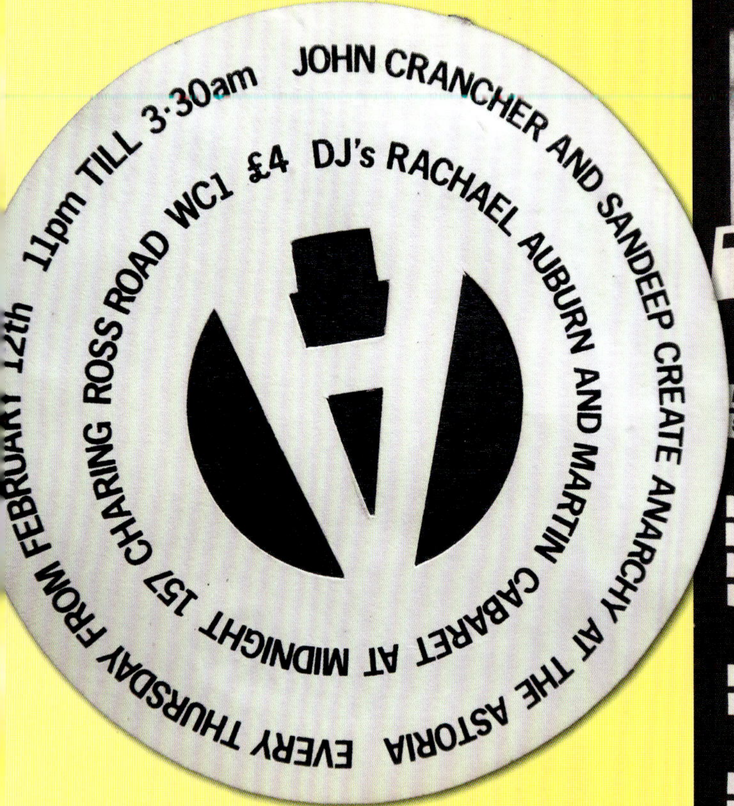

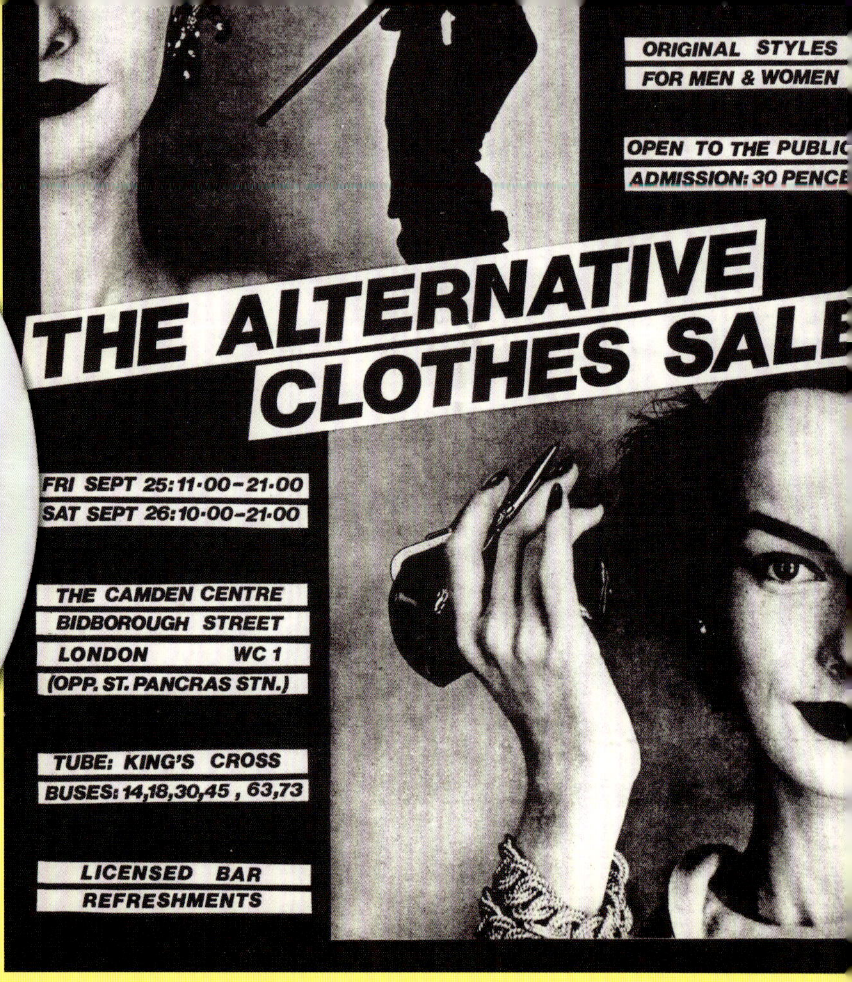

St Martin's was not the only London art school with a reputation for fashion; Rachel Auburn went from foundation in Brighton to Harrow, 'because I'd heard of it, I don't think I knew about St Martin's'. John Richmond graduated from Kingston and met his partner Maria Cornejo, who had studied at Ravensbourne. Middlesex, where the fashion course was based in the old Hornsey School of Art building, produced David Holah and Stevie Stewart from BodyMap, Paul Bernstock, Thelma Speirs and Richard Torry. Annie La Paz met her creative partner Lucy Morahan at Middlesex, where they spent late hours in the print workshops making clothes and decorations for parties. Annie eventually dropped out because the peripatetic warehouse night, Circus, which she ran with Lucy, DJ Jeremy Healy and club promoter Patrick Lilley, created so much interest. They were organising parties for the Chelsea Arts Club, designing clothing and sets for videos as well as devising a Day-Glo painted make-up style. 'I just thought, you've got to jump on your train when it comes. You can't choose when the world's going to notice you,' recalls La Paz.

STALLING OUT

The common thread was the drive for creating their own opportunities. Rachel Auburn had started a stall at Kensington Market, a hub for young creatives and those in search of alternative fashions, with a friend from college, 'but after a

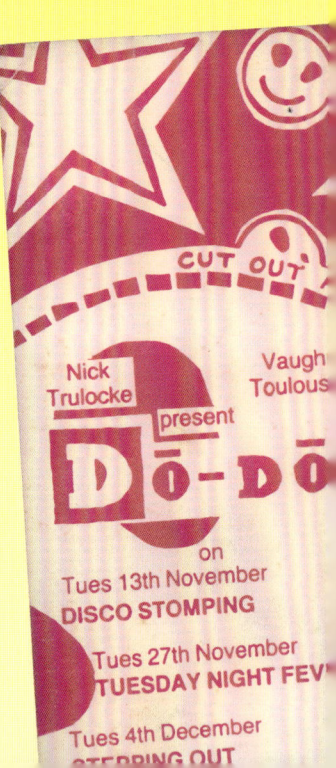

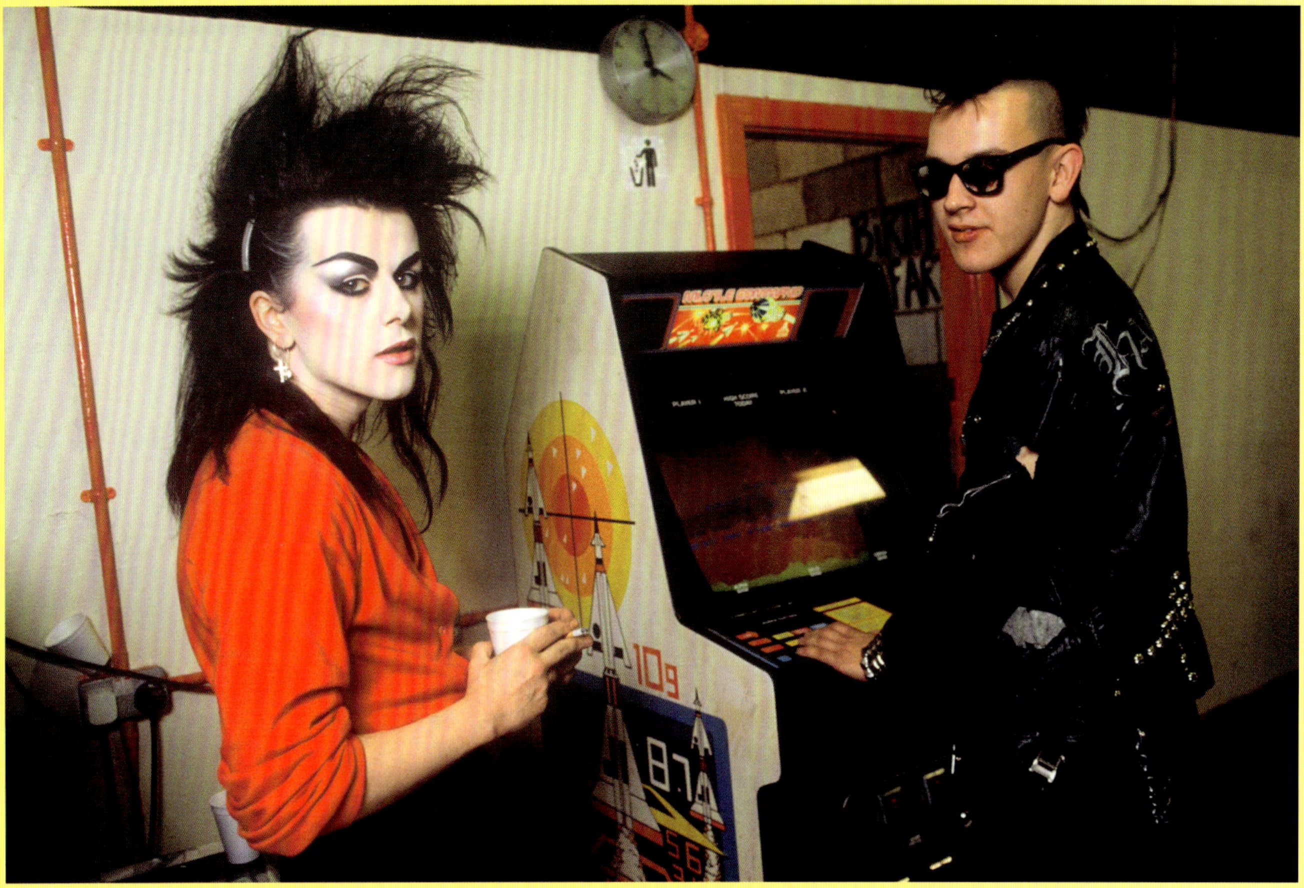

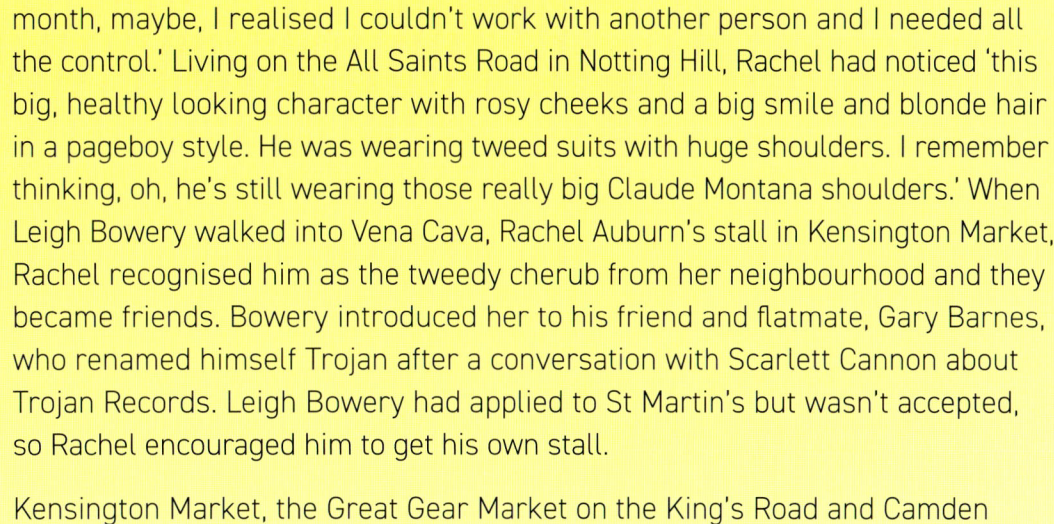

ABOVE
Fashion students at St Martin's School of Art

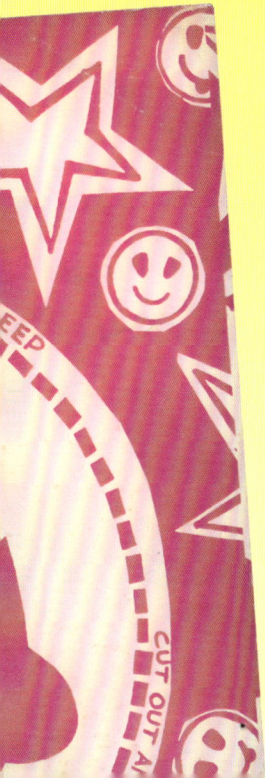

month, maybe, I realised I couldn't work with another person and I needed all the control.' Living on the All Saints Road in Notting Hill, Rachel had noticed 'this big, healthy looking character with rosy cheeks and a big smile and blonde hair in a pageboy style. He was wearing tweed suits with huge shoulders. I remember thinking, oh, he's still wearing those really big Claude Montana shoulders.' When Leigh Bowery walked into Vena Cava, Rachel Auburn's stall in Kensington Market, Rachel recognised him as the tweedy cherub from her neighbourhood and they became friends. Bowery introduced her to his friend and flatmate, Gary Barnes, who renamed himself Trojan after a conversation with Scarlett Cannon about Trojan Records. Leigh Bowery had applied to St Martin's but wasn't accepted, so Rachel encouraged him to get his own stall.

Kensington Market, the Great Gear Market on the King's Road and Camden Market were established centres of subculture that the young 1980s designers had either experienced in their teenage years or heard about on moving to London. They were places to soak up the nightlife atmosphere in the daytime, see where the new styles could be found, exchange news and give out or pick up flyers for the next thing that was happening. Mark Moore remembers hanging out at Rusty Egan's record store, The Cage, in the Great Gear Market as a teenager: 'Tasty Tim ran it and I'd always be there. There's a film called *Posers* made about the King's

INTRODUCTION 21

Road in 1981. It got me buying records, except I didn't have a lot of money in those days, so he gave me money from the till to pretend to pay.' *Posers*, which follows sociologist Ted Polhemus in the subcultural field, closes with a trip to Philip Sallon's club, Planets, in Piccadilly, tracing the day-to-night existence of the youth fashion crowd. It was this seamless way of living and working that fuelled the creative energy of the protagonists of *Outlaws*. When Mark Moore's mother complained, 'You're just going out clubbing all the time. You're not doing anything with your life', the natural solution was to get a job DJing at the Mud Club with Tasty Tim.

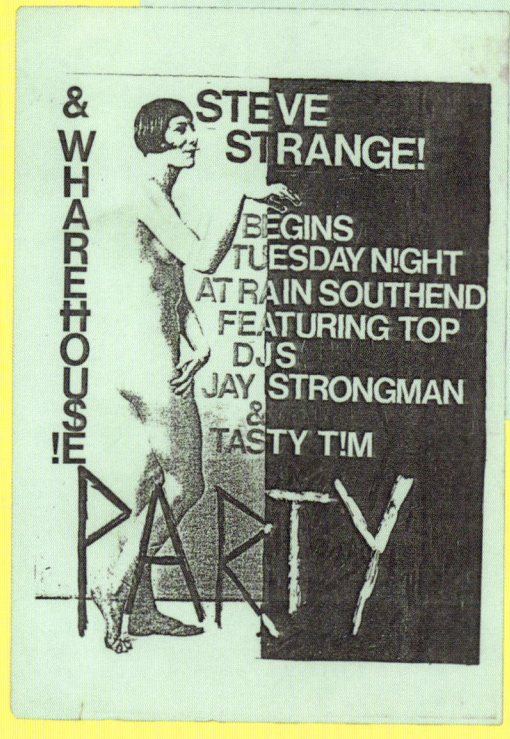

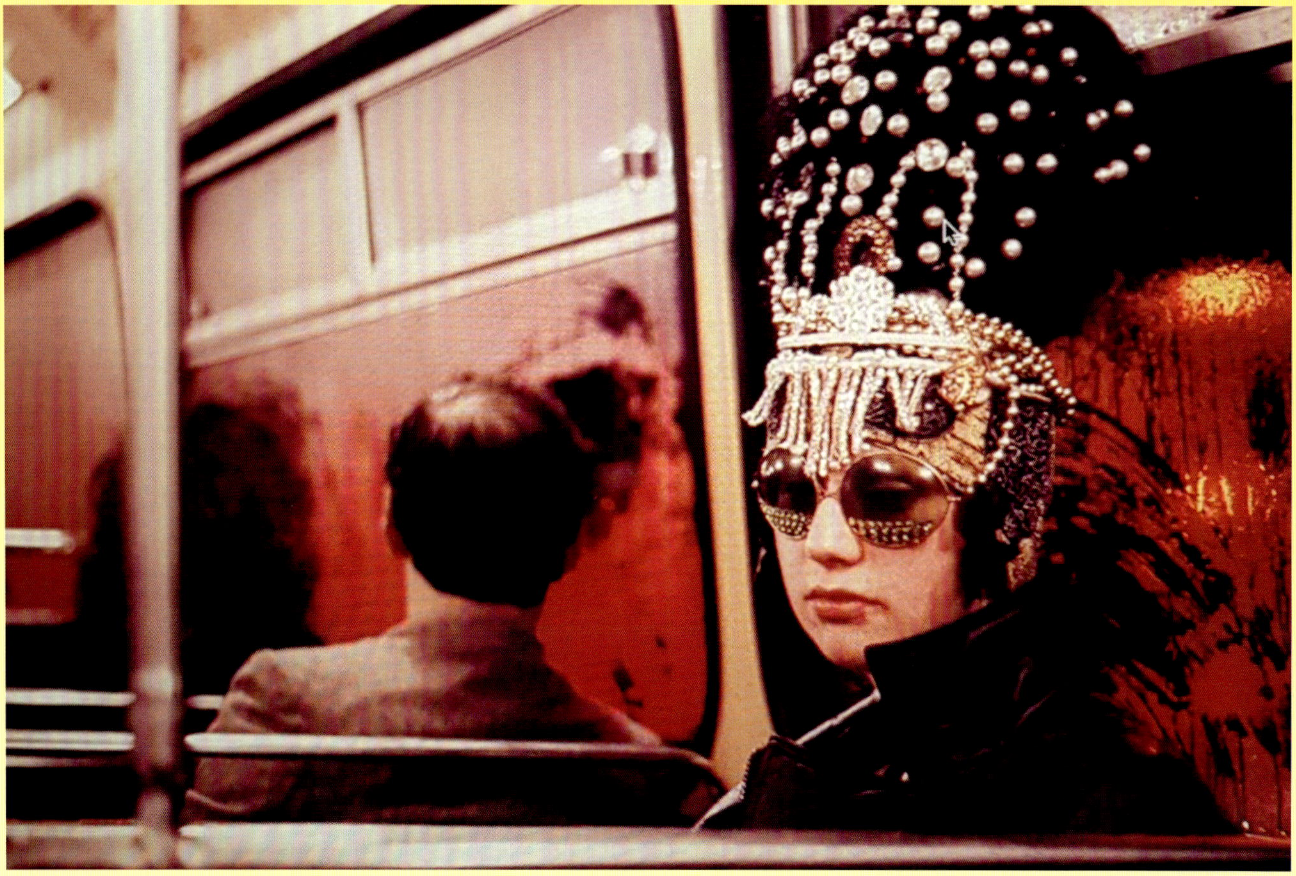

'A bricolage of unexpected components and a provocation that made them laugh permeates the creative output of the Taboo crowd.'

OPPOSITE
Nicola Bateman
on a London bus,
1986

NEW LONDON IN NEW YORK

By 1982 the designs sold from market stalls were beginning to have a certain cachet and recognition, and Susanne Bartsch, an Austrian living in New York, was partly instrumental in fostering a new international interest. Bartsch had decided that what she was missing from her time living in London was 'the ever-changing looks, so I signed up all these kids and gave them a platform in New York'. In 1981 Bartsch opened a store in New York's SoHo designed by Michael Costiff, an old friend from when she had been part of the scene in London in the 1970s. By the early 1980s Michael and Gerlinde Costiff, who were to host the Kinky Gerlinky drag ball nights later in the 1980s, were London nightclub royalty. Gerlinde introduced Bartsch to designer friends, taking her around the stalls in Kensington and Camden markets. Young designers turned up for buying appointments at the Chelsea Arts Club, spreading their handmade wares across Gerlinde's bed, such as Paul Bernstock and Thelma Speirs' hats with netting from Laurence Corner army surplus store. Bartsch devised the New London in New York fashion shows in nightclub settings, for which Rachel Auburn, Leigh Bowery, Stephen Jones, BodyMap, Bernstock Speirs, Nocturne, Richard Torry, Sue Clowes, John Richmond, Annie La Paz, English Eccentrics, Judy Blame and St Martin's alumni Gregory Davis and Elmaz Hüseyin flew over, some of them leaving the UK for the first time. What Bartsch lacked in experience in producing a show, she made up with for with enthusiasm: 'It was total chaos, but it was that chaos that made a huge success, because they'd never seen anything like it.' New York's *Daily News Record* reported the Roxy spectacle as 'more like New London in old and very tired New York', noting the difference between the posturing and dated-looking Manhattan fashion crowd and the exuberance of the London youth. As Rachel Auburn remembers, the British press covered the show in a less supportive way: 'We were on the cover of the *Evening Standard* with a picture of me and Leigh in a dustbin, and there was all this publicity about these rags that

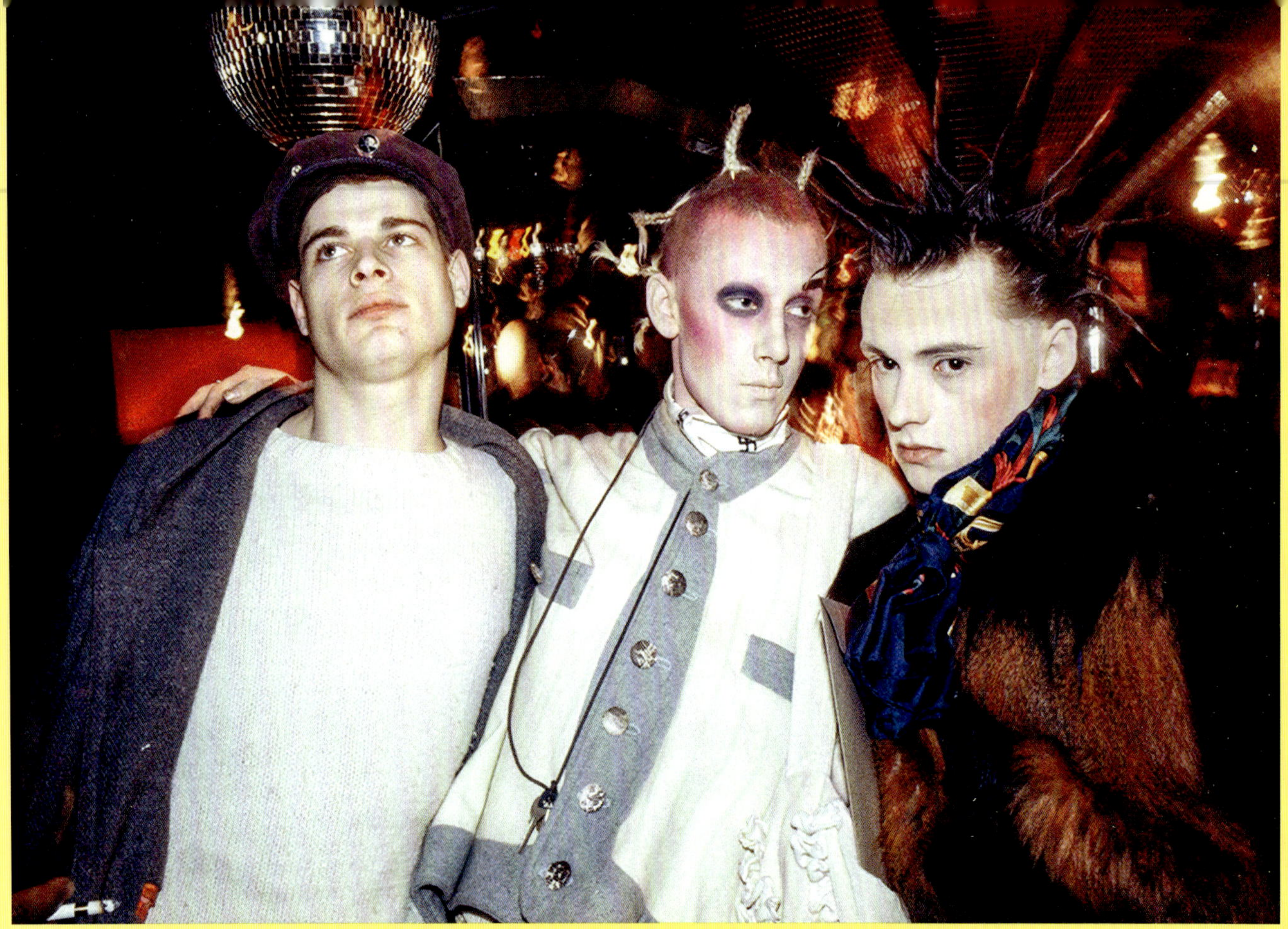

Macy's and Bloomingdale's had ordered.' Sue Tilley, Leigh Bowery's friend who had come to model, remembers Americans following them shouting, 'Boy George! Hey! Boy George!' and Greg Davis being given champagne on the plane because the air hostesses thought he was the pop star Marilyn.

A further trip to Tokyo followed on the invitation of Akira Mori, son of the fashion designer Hanae Mori. This included designers Dean Bright and Dexter Wong as well as some of London's more mainstream fashion offerings, such as Betty Jackson and Crolla, for gravitas. Michael Costiff, who had designed the New York shows, was invited to curate a Trojan art exhibition as part of London Goes to Tokyo. The presentation of the new London scene as underground and alternative had generated excitement in New York, and by the time they got to Japan the designers were treated like stars. Helen David, founder of English Eccentrics, remembers arriving at the airport: 'We walk out of the plane, we see a news flash, and it's us. We're the news. We're seeing ourselves coming off this plane, on the news in Tokyo.' Susanne Bartsch witnessed the impact of her young charges on their Japanese hosts: 'It was just incredible, the appreciation of their creativity. The Japanese prime minister and the English ambassador were sitting in the front row when Rachel Auburn and Leigh Bowery came out in aprons with no underwear. With their butts out, bending over and sticking their arses in the prime minister's face. It was scandalous. It was really wild. So that was a big success as well.'

ABOVE
Mark Batham, Marc Vaultier and Trojan at Taboo, 1986

OPPOSITE
Nicola Bateman and Leigh Bowery at Daisy Chain, 1988

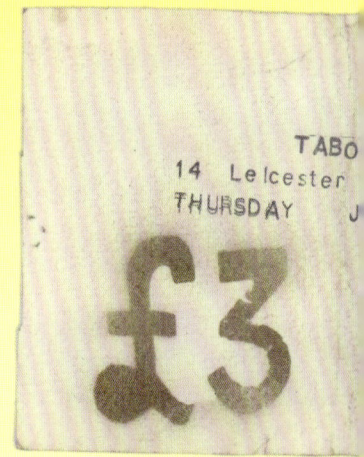

'WOULD YOU LET YOURSELF IN?'
– Marc Vaultier, Taboo doorman

Rachel Auburn identifies the New London in New York and London Goes to Tokyo trips as the point when Leigh Bowery ceased to aspire to a career as a commercial fashion designer. Many young designers struggled with production, making pieces themselves and hiring machinists as factories would not undertake the small runs, and Bowery was no exception. Dean Bright and Vaughan & Franks were among the young designers stocked at Browns who worked long hours to fulfil orders.

While subversive transgression flavoured everything Bowery did, he began to see his looks as his artistic expression, using the dancefloor as his gallery. It was at Paul Bernstock and Dencil Williams' club, White Trash, that Bowery allegedly countered Mick Jagger's sneered 'Fuck off, freak!' with 'Fuck off, fossil!' There was no shortage of possibilities for a fashion-centric disco every night: John Crancher's Anarchy, Stephen Linard's Total Fashion Victims, Annie La Paz and co's Circus... But Taboo, the club that Bowery started with promoter Tony Gordon at the end of January in 1985, was a night where chaos was encouraged and friends were welcome, while 'ordinary' people were kept at bay with a strict door policy upheld by Marc Vaultier wielding a mirror. Mark Moore remembers, 'Sometimes the DJ Jeffrey Hinton would be so

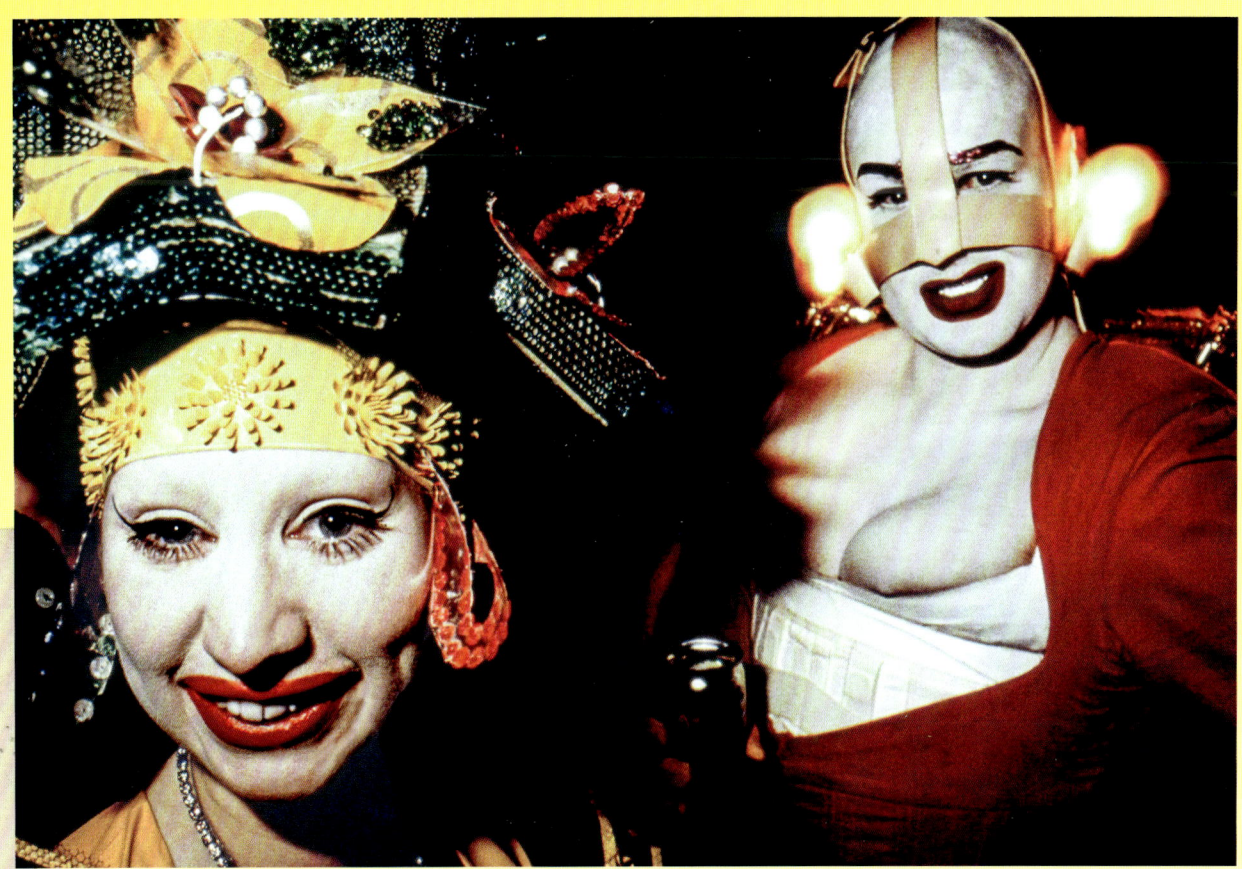

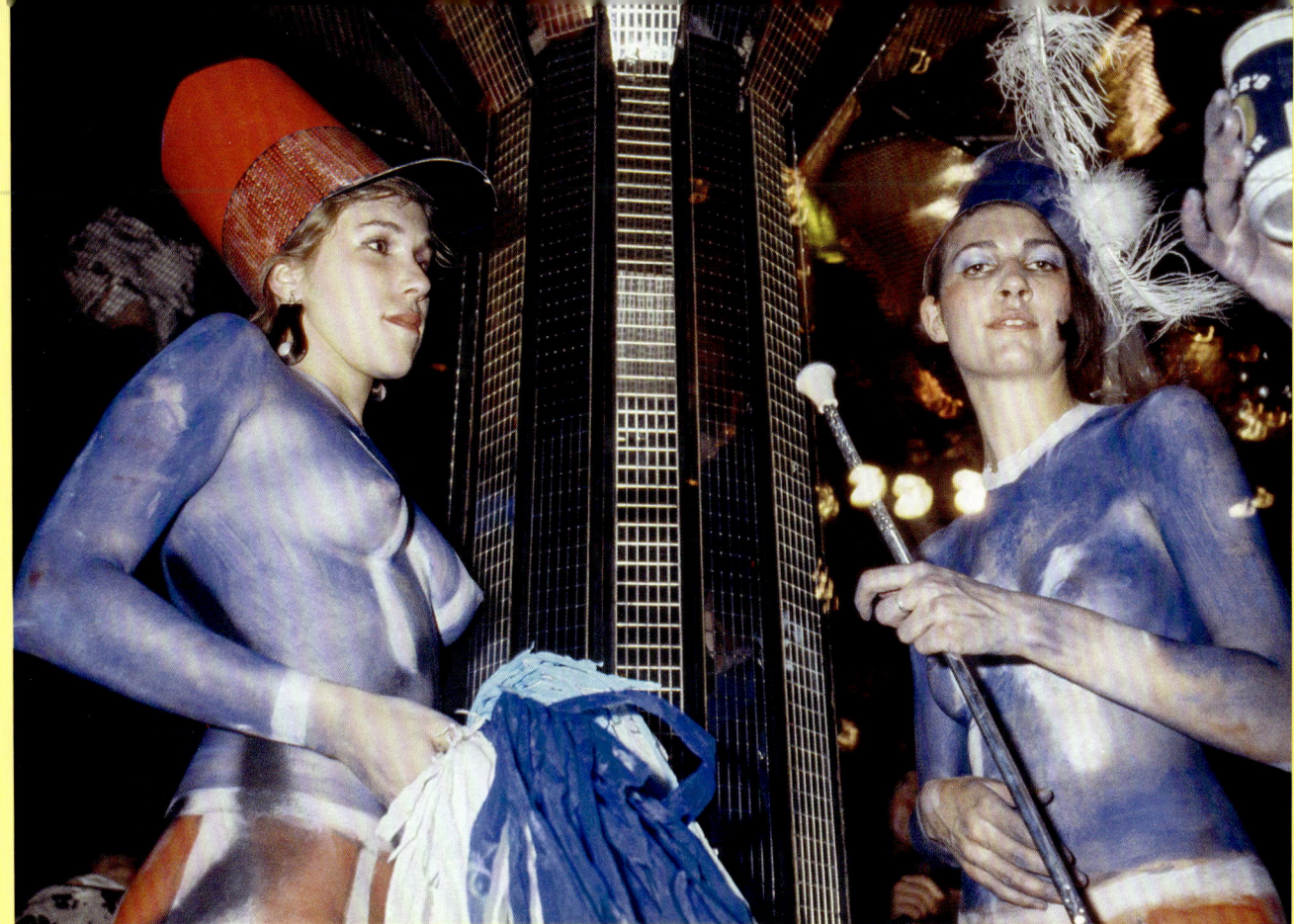

ABOVE
Neo Naturists
at Taboo, 1985

OPPOSITE
Leigh Bowery
at Limelight

off his head, he'd play two records together, literally for two minutes. Ecstasy was coming in. Everyone was just falling on the floor and rolling around; it was definitely a joyous atmosphere. I loved it for the complete bacchanalian mayhem. There was a whole lot of stuff going on all at once, which was extremely creative, and it was to do with the whole fashion thing and people like John Galliano at the club. It was to do with Leigh slowly forging his way to be accepted as a work of art in his own right. Michael Clark was heavily involved with the scene; people hadn't seen ballet presented like his amazing shows ever. People like ABC, Blancmange were there...'

Taboo lasted barely a year, with an article in *The Mail on Sunday* that exposed the drug use at the club provoking its closure. Mark Moore remembers: 'As the months went by it started to get more and more messy, and a bit darker when heroin started creeping in.' In 1986 Trojan died from a heroin overdose, followed a few months later by Taboo doorman Marc Vaultier. Trojan had been by Leigh Bowery's side since his early days on the club scene, and with David Walls they had gone out in Leigh's designs and become known as 'The Three Kings'. Trojan's Picasso-esque make-up and his psychedelic fried-egg sets for Michael Clark's ballets complemented Bowery's costume designs, showing an intuitive shared aesthetic of the surreal, pushing each other to extremes.

A bricolage of unexpected components and a provocation that made them laugh permeates the creative output of the Taboo crowd: a certain camp irreverence, bold flashes of colour, monochrome tailoring cut in experimental ways, reworked found materials, regal opulence and glam pantomimery. The AIDS crisis took many of these creative people early and, after eight years, Leigh Bowery himself, but the garments pictured in this book remain as a record of the way a group of people used the energy of the dancefloor to inspire their work. David Cabaret recorded a sighting of Bowery in a sketchbook in 1986, which encapsulates the spirit of Taboo: 'One of the first times I ever saw Leigh, he was marching up Charing Cross Road, I think from the Hippodrome to the Mud Club, in the crash-helmet look and the green coat and pants with the big sequins on. You could see him a mile off because he was tearing along like the Pied Piper, with this trail of crazy kids all around him, forcing their way through the normal, everyday crowds. And I said to myself, wouldn't it be fabulous if Leigh's army took over the world?'

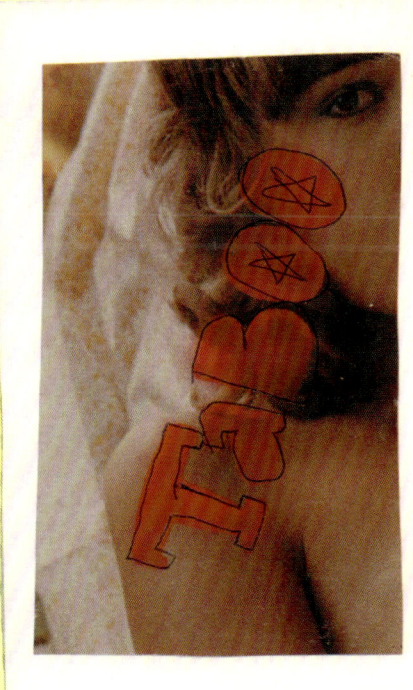

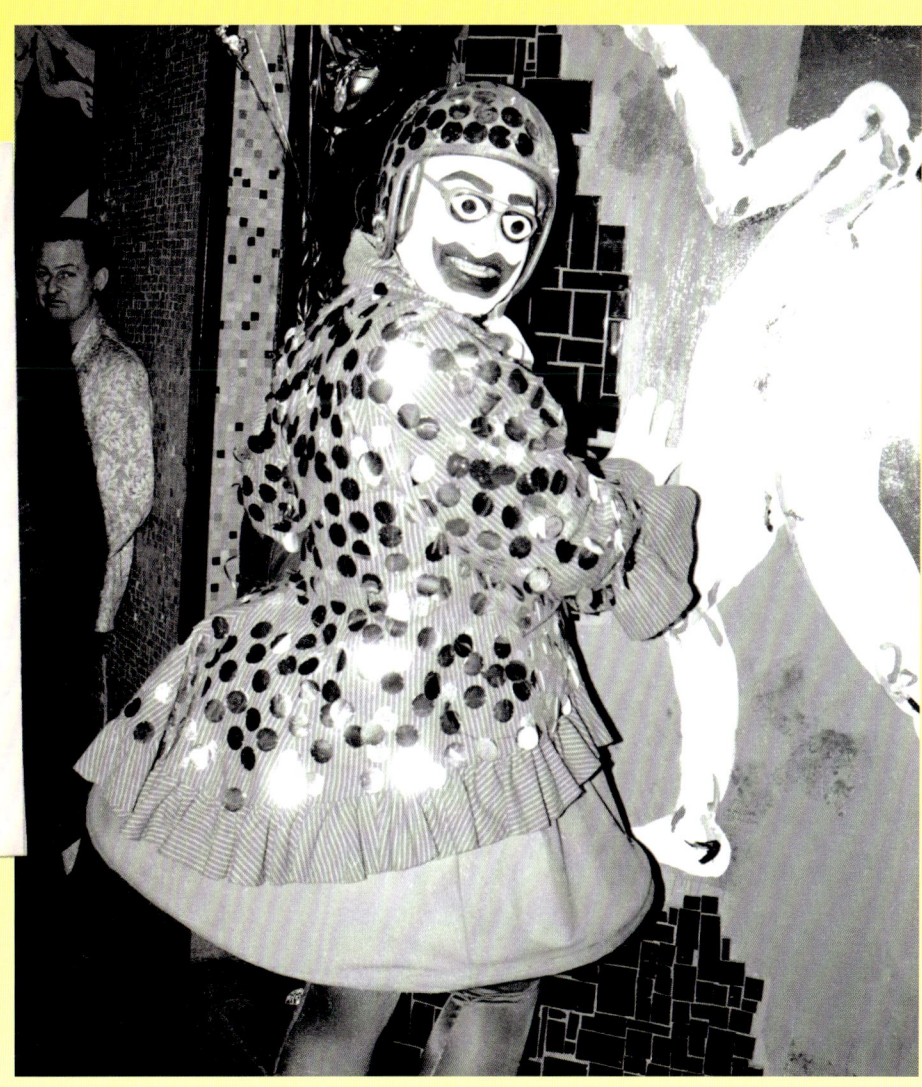

THE DES

IGNERS

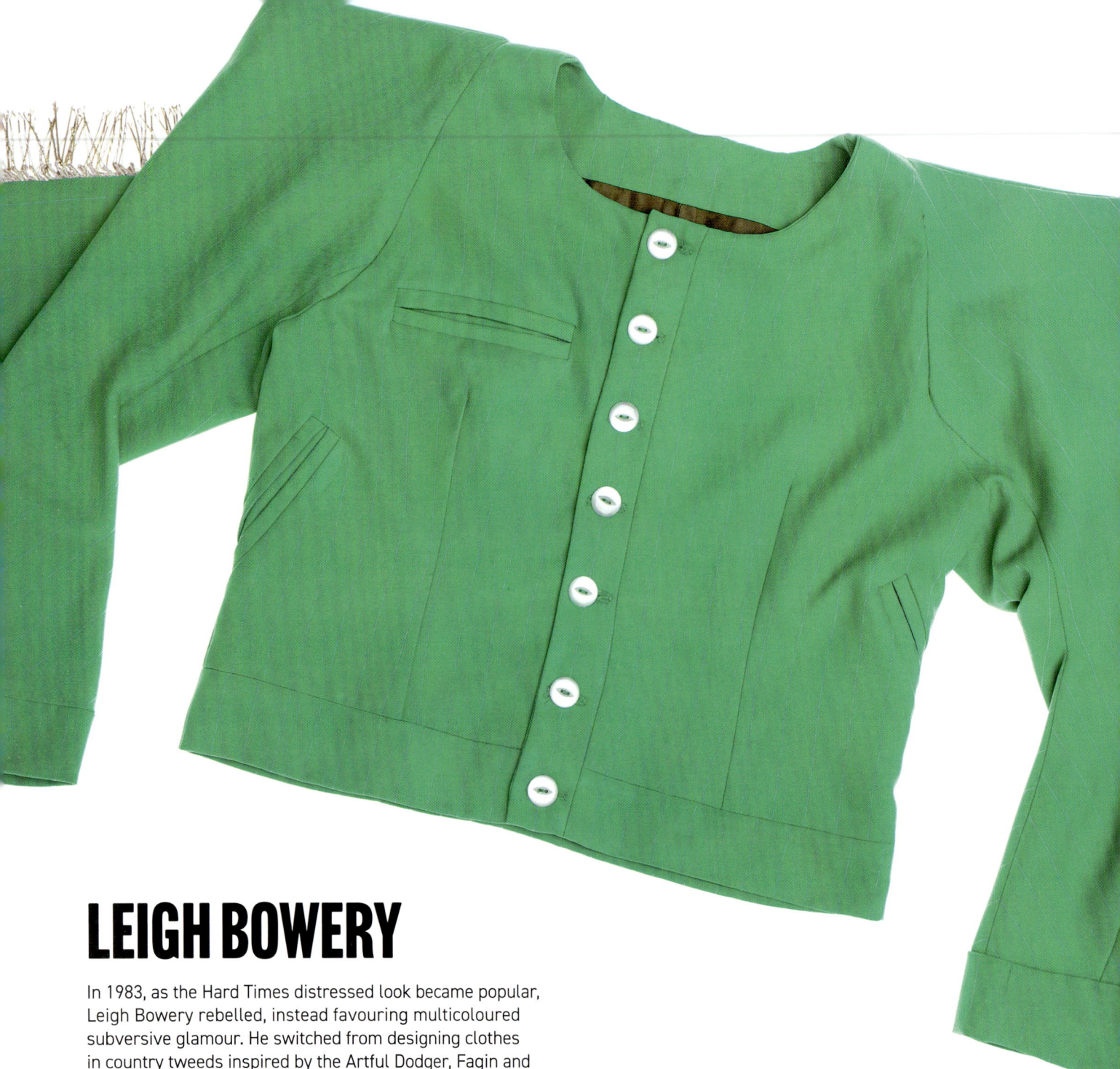

LEIGH BOWERY

In 1983, as the Hard Times distressed look became popular, Leigh Bowery rebelled, instead favouring multicoloured subversive glamour. He switched from designing clothes in country tweeds inspired by the Artful Dodger, Fagin and Rei Kawakubo to using rich velvets, bright Lycra and shiny Indian fabrics.

This New Glitterati direction led to great attention and press coverage, but as his popularity grew, Bowery lost interest in being a commercial designer and closed his stall in Kensington Market.

Although he occasionally sold at Rachel Auburn's Hyper Hyper shop Spend Spend Spend, Bowery concentrated on creating more extravagant clothes for himself and costumes for Michael Clark, Lanah Pellay and Boy George.

In 1985 his club night Taboo opened and Bowery became a counter-cultural star. He died of AIDS in 1994 aged 33.

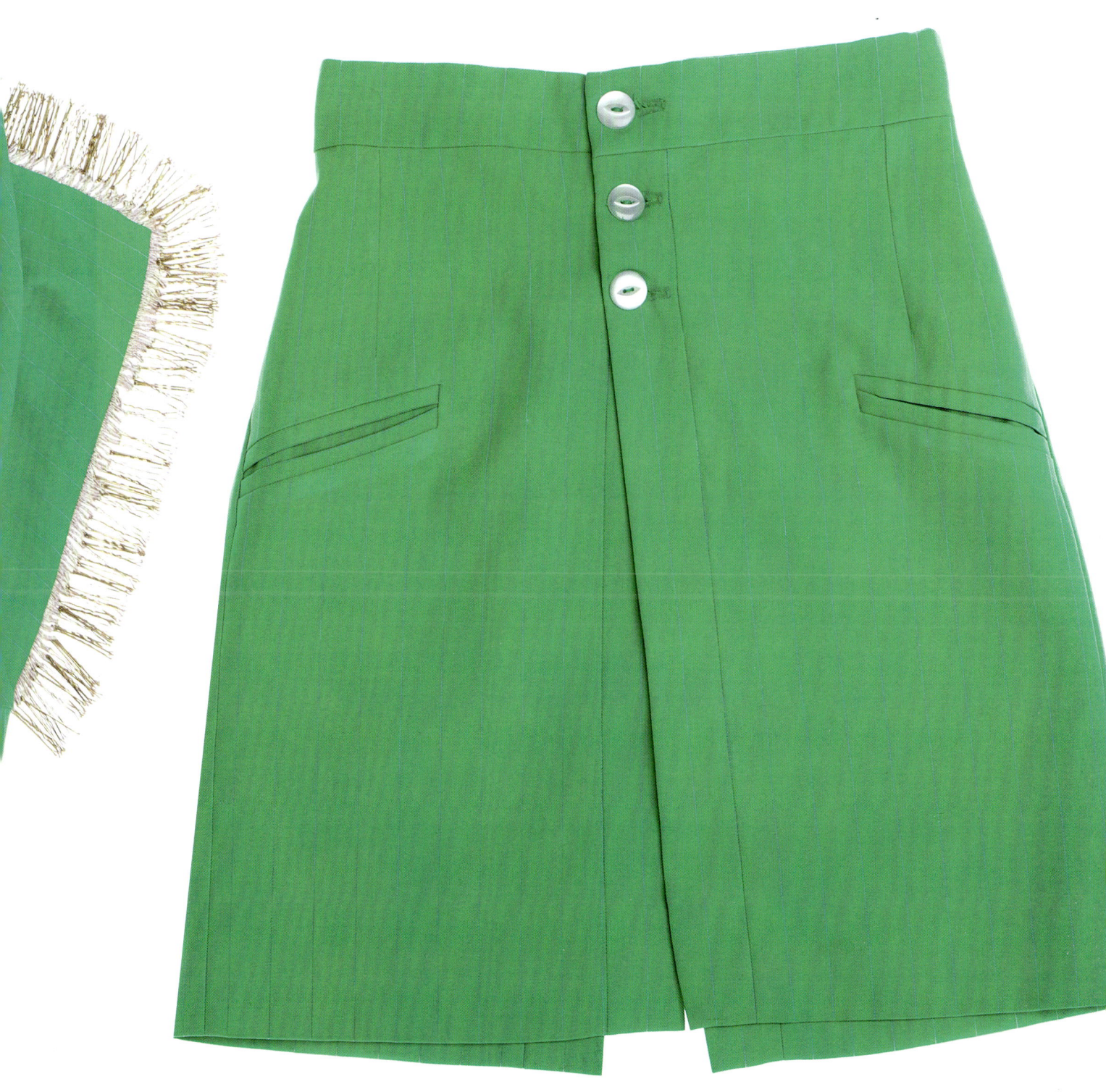

Green ensemble with kirby-grip fringe as worn by singer Lanah Pellay

Tweed hand-painted jacket with red stitching, 1982

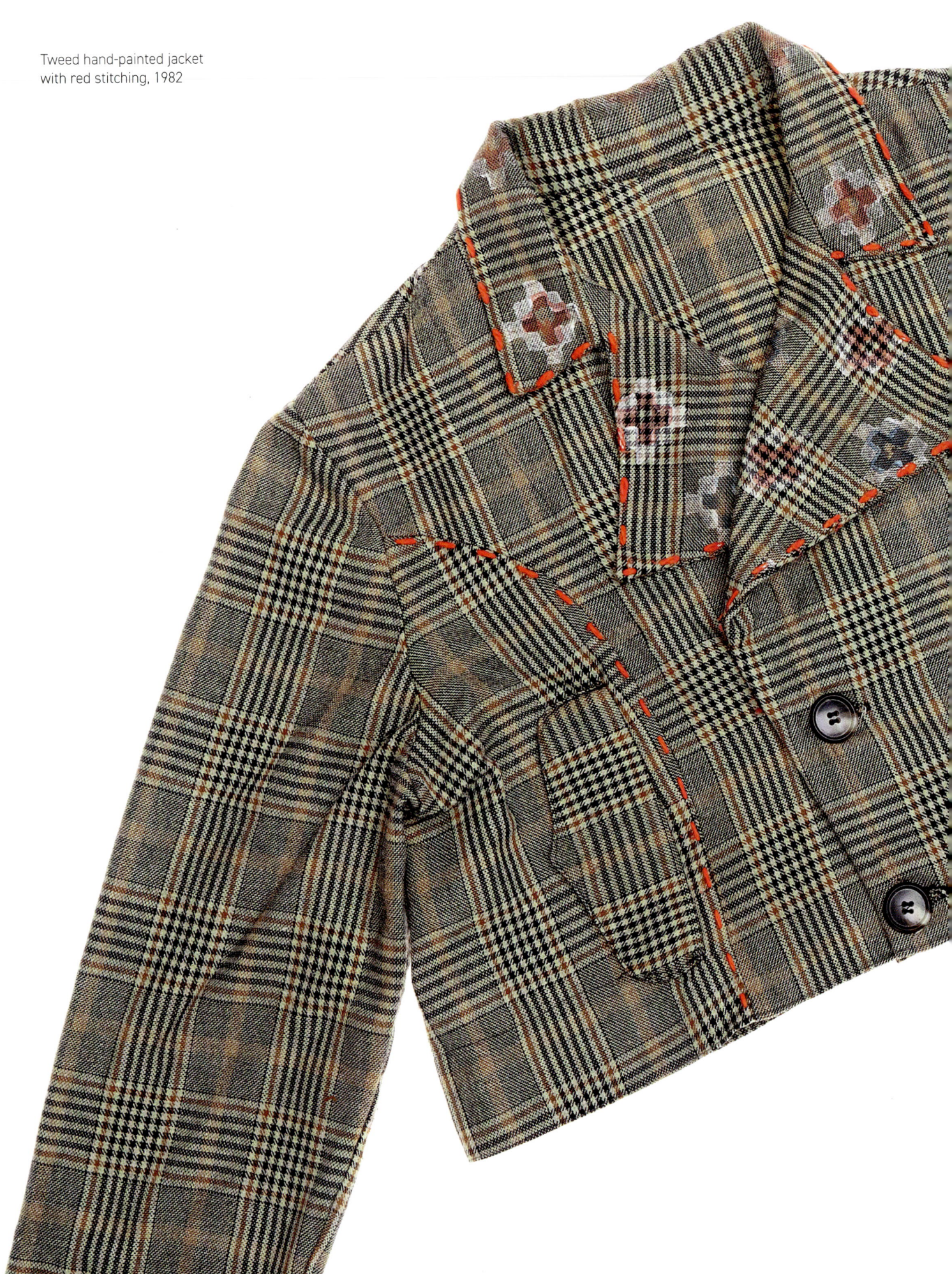

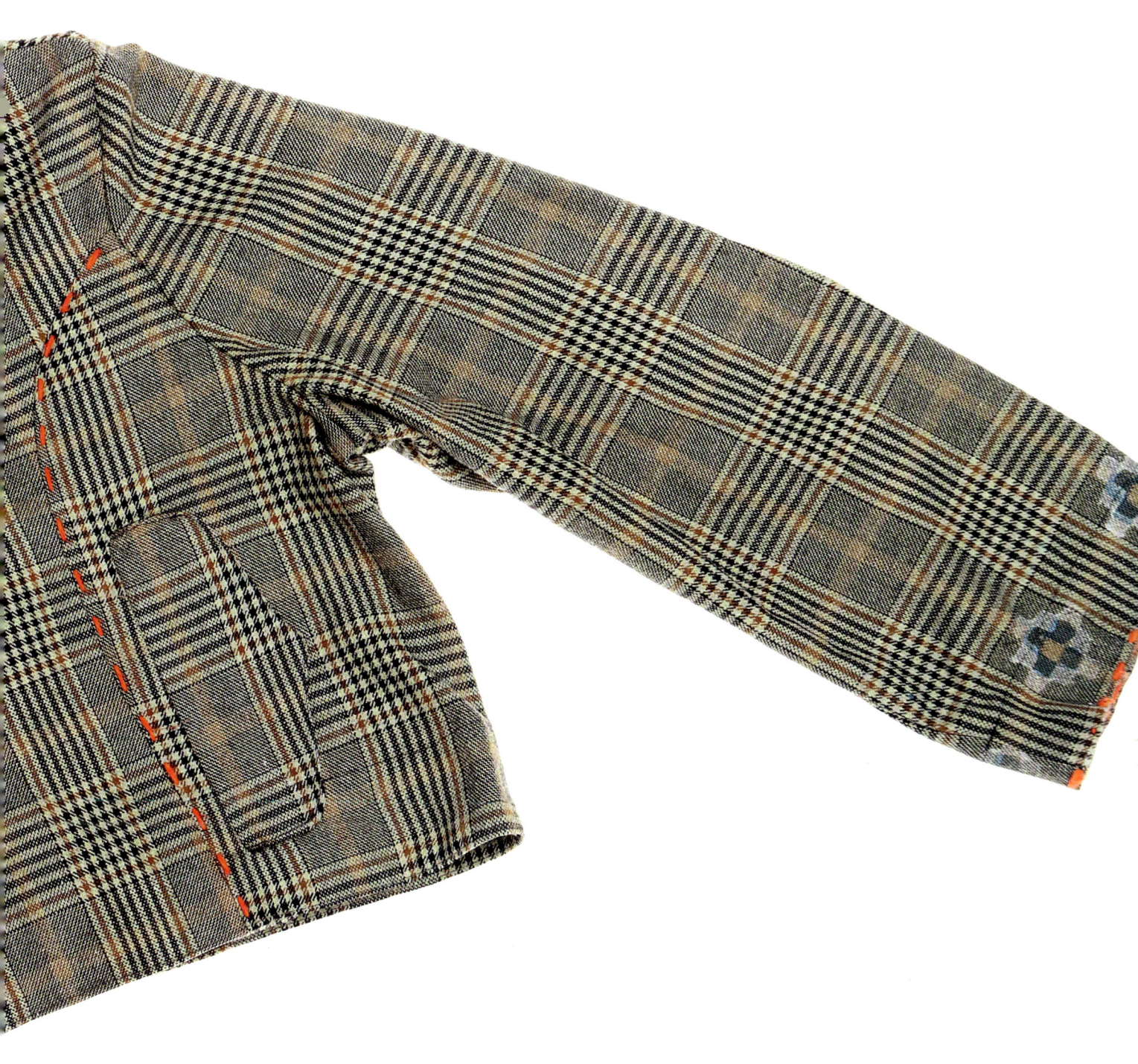

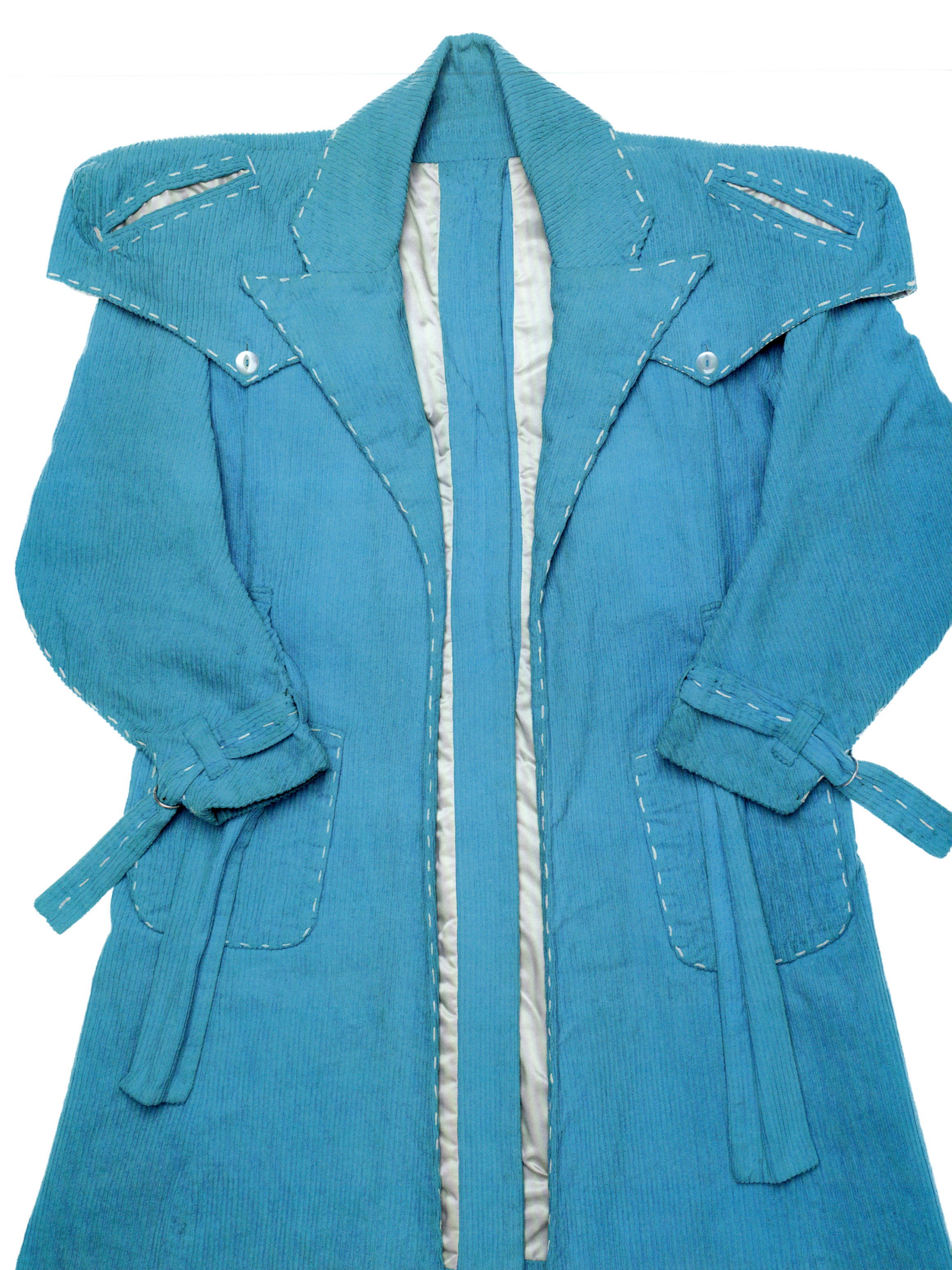

'LEIGH AND MYSELF MADE A MYRIAD TRIPS TO INDIAN AND JEWISH FABRIC SHOPS IN BRICK LANE, WHERE I'D SPEND A TON OF CASH ON MATERIAL, I MEAN £200 A TIME! THAT WAS A FORTUNE IN 1983/84. WE'D STAY UP ALL NIGHT CHATTING, DRINKING VODKA AND PINEAPPLE, EATING CHIPS, CHICKEN OR PIZZA WHILE I WAS BEING FITTED.'

Lanah Pellay, pop star, actress and epicene dream

Left to right Blue corduroy trench coat designed for singer Lanah Pellay, 1986, and featured in ITV's *South of Watford* documentary; Blue pinstripe coat with kirby-grip trim and hand-painted reverse swastika lining, as worn in Michael Clark's *not H.AIR* production in 1985. Also worn by Leigh Bowery in the 1987 film *Hail the New Puritan*

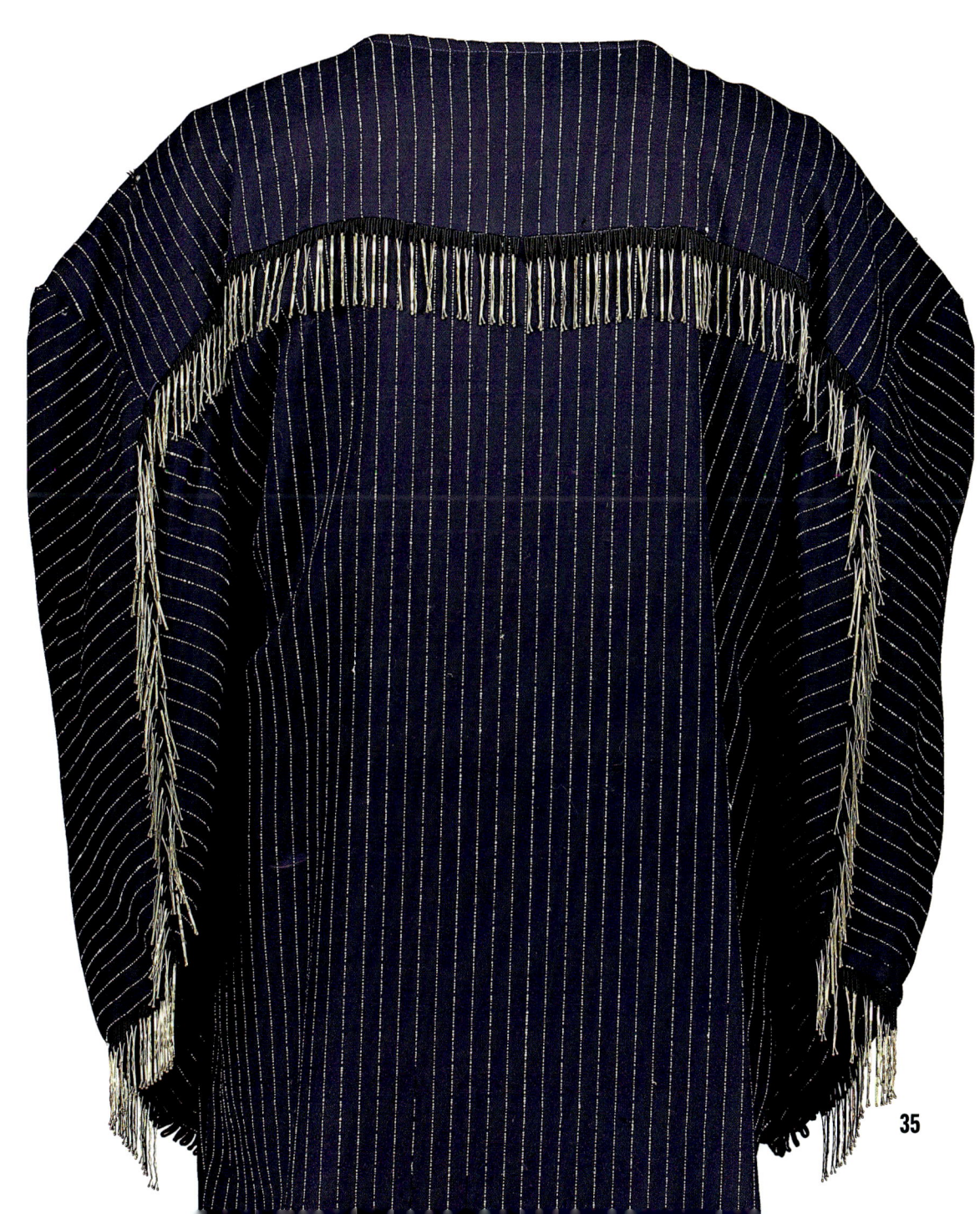

'IN 1996 MY GOOD FRIEND RALPH CADE VISITED A CAR BOOT SALE IN MERTON AND NOTICED A STALL WITH SOME WONDERFUL COSTUMES WHICH LOOKED QUITE FAMILIAR. INTRIGUED, HE CALLED ME TO DESCRIBE THEM, AND I SUGGESTED TO HIM THAT THEY SOUNDED LIKE MICHAEL CLARK COSTUMES. I WENT STRAIGHT ROUND TO HIS HOUSE AND WAS AMAZED TO SEE THAT THEY WERE INDEED COSTUMES BY LEIGH BOWERY AND BODYMAP, MADE FOR CLARK'S SHOWS.'

Sue Smallwood, graphic designer

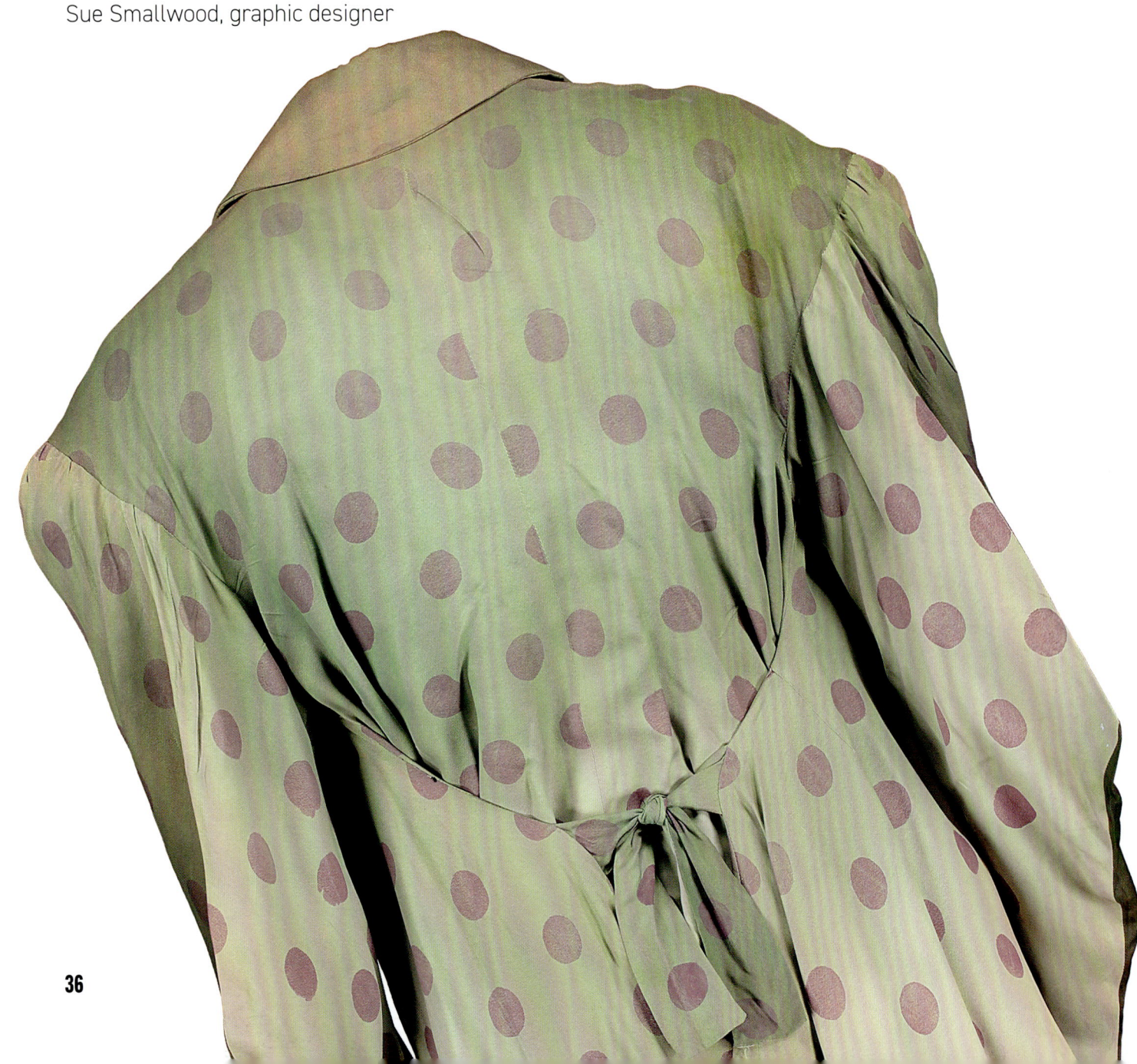

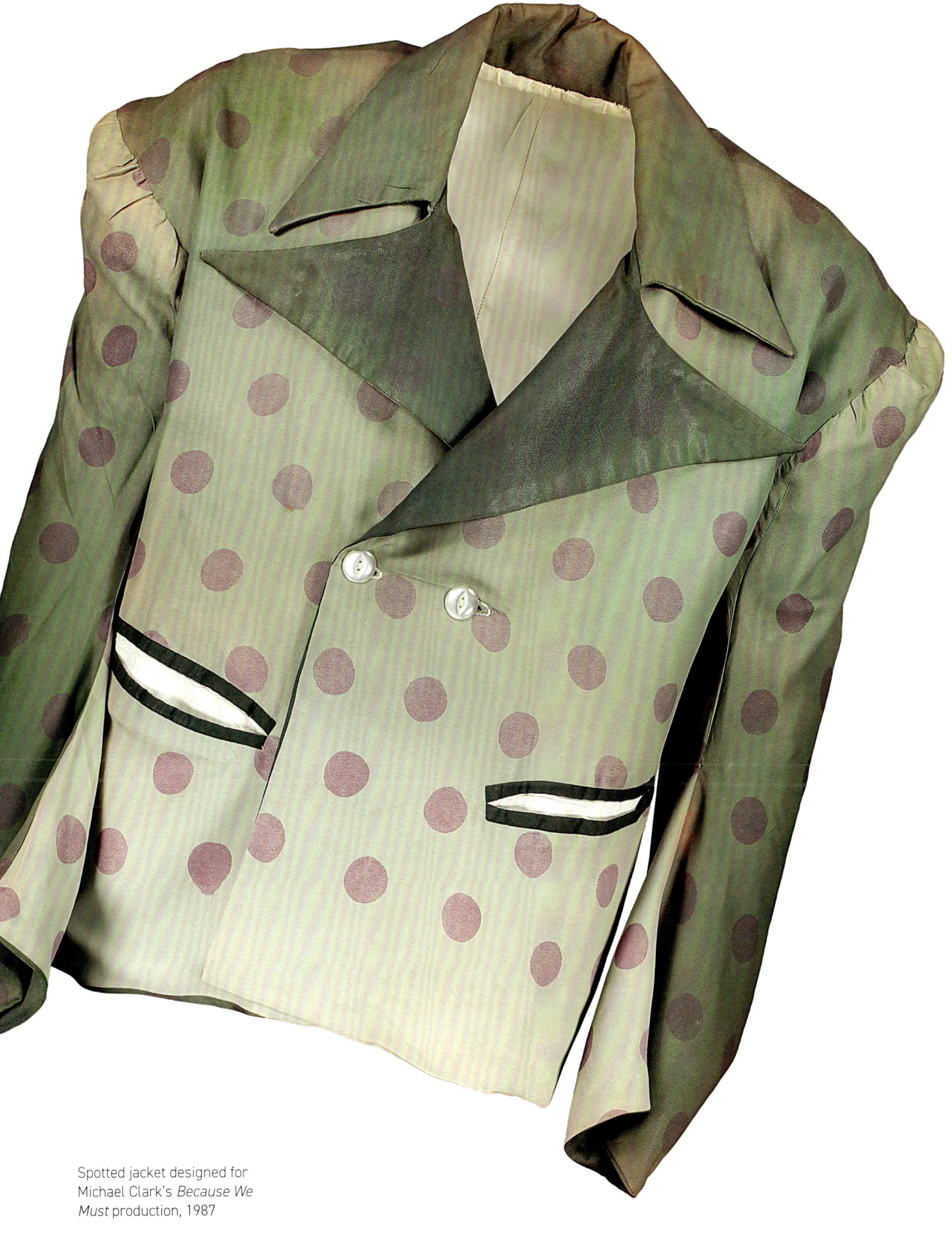

Spotted jacket designed for Michael Clark's *Because We Must* production, 1987

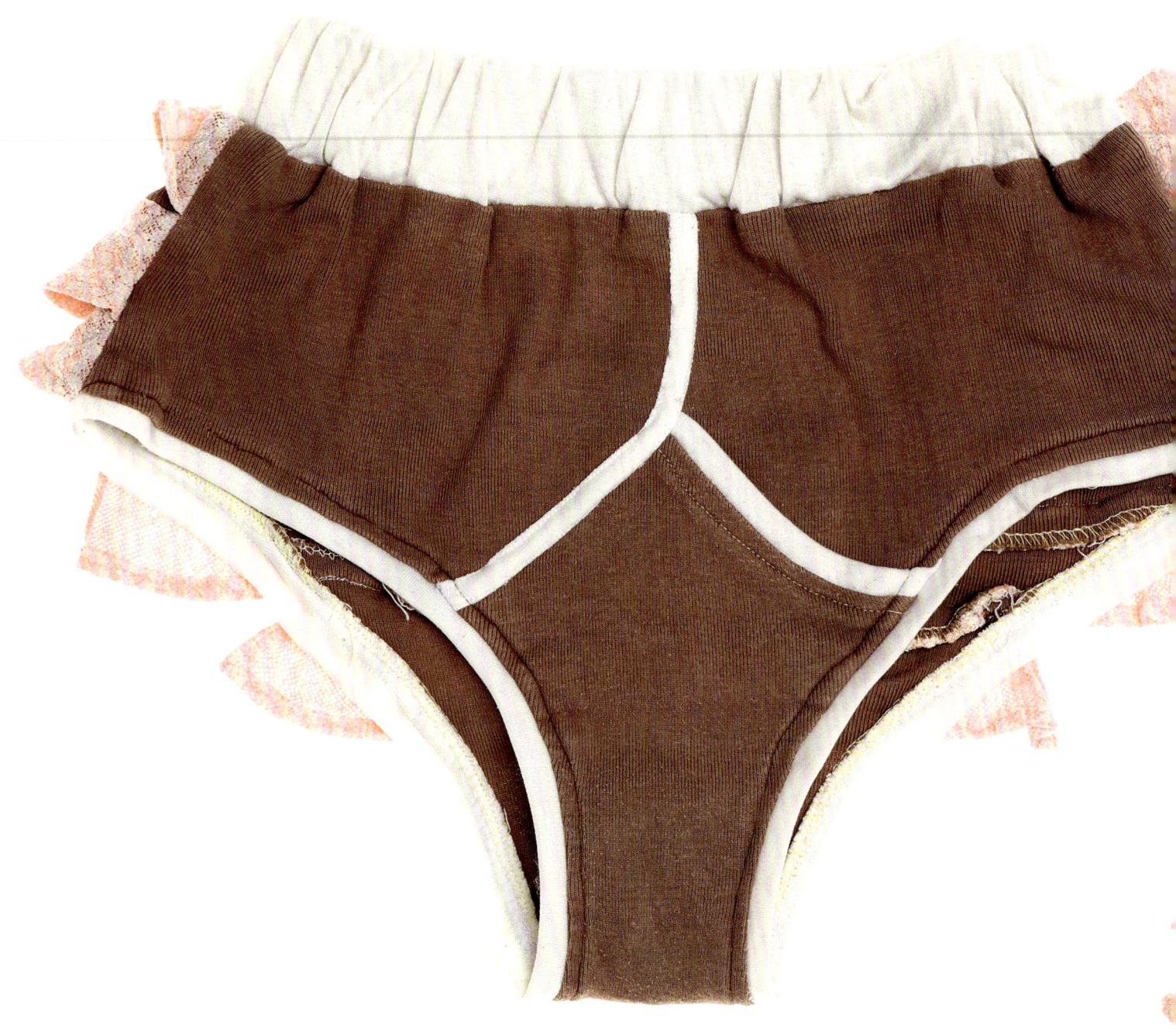

'THE Y-FRONT PANTS I WORE TO KINKY GERLINKY WERE MADE BY LEIGH AND BELONGED TO SPACE PRINCESS, AKA PETER HAMMOND, AS WERE THE TWO JACKETS. EVENTUALLY THEY WERE ALL BEQUEATHED TO PETER ARMSTRONG FOR CARING FOR SPACE IN HIS FINAL YEARS. PETER ALSO NURSED AND CARED FOR JALLE BAKKE IN SWEDEN DURING HIS FINAL MONTHS. HE WAS QUITE AN ANGEL.'

Steven Moore, artist

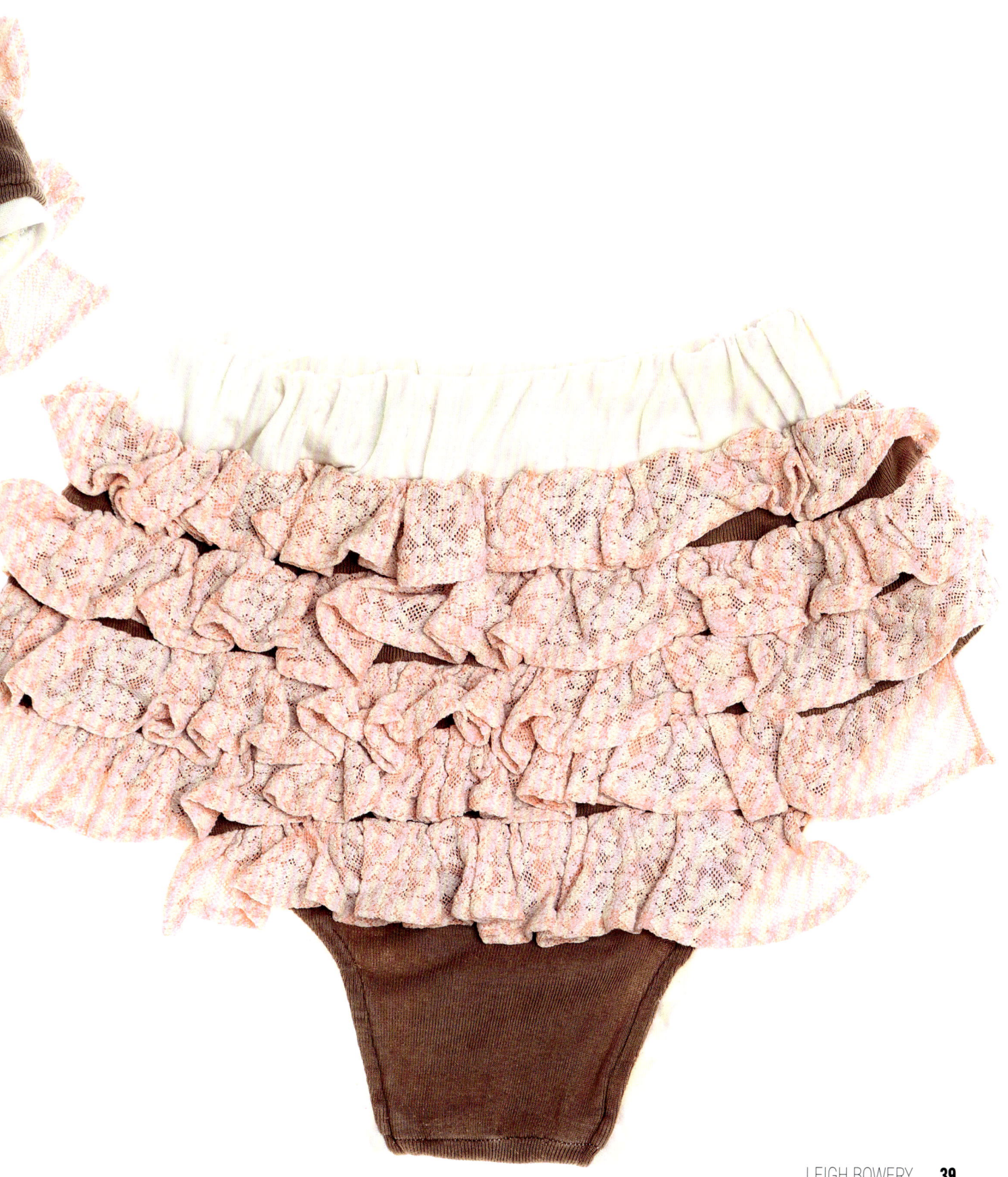

Frilly Y-fronts as worn by the Michael Clark Company, 1985

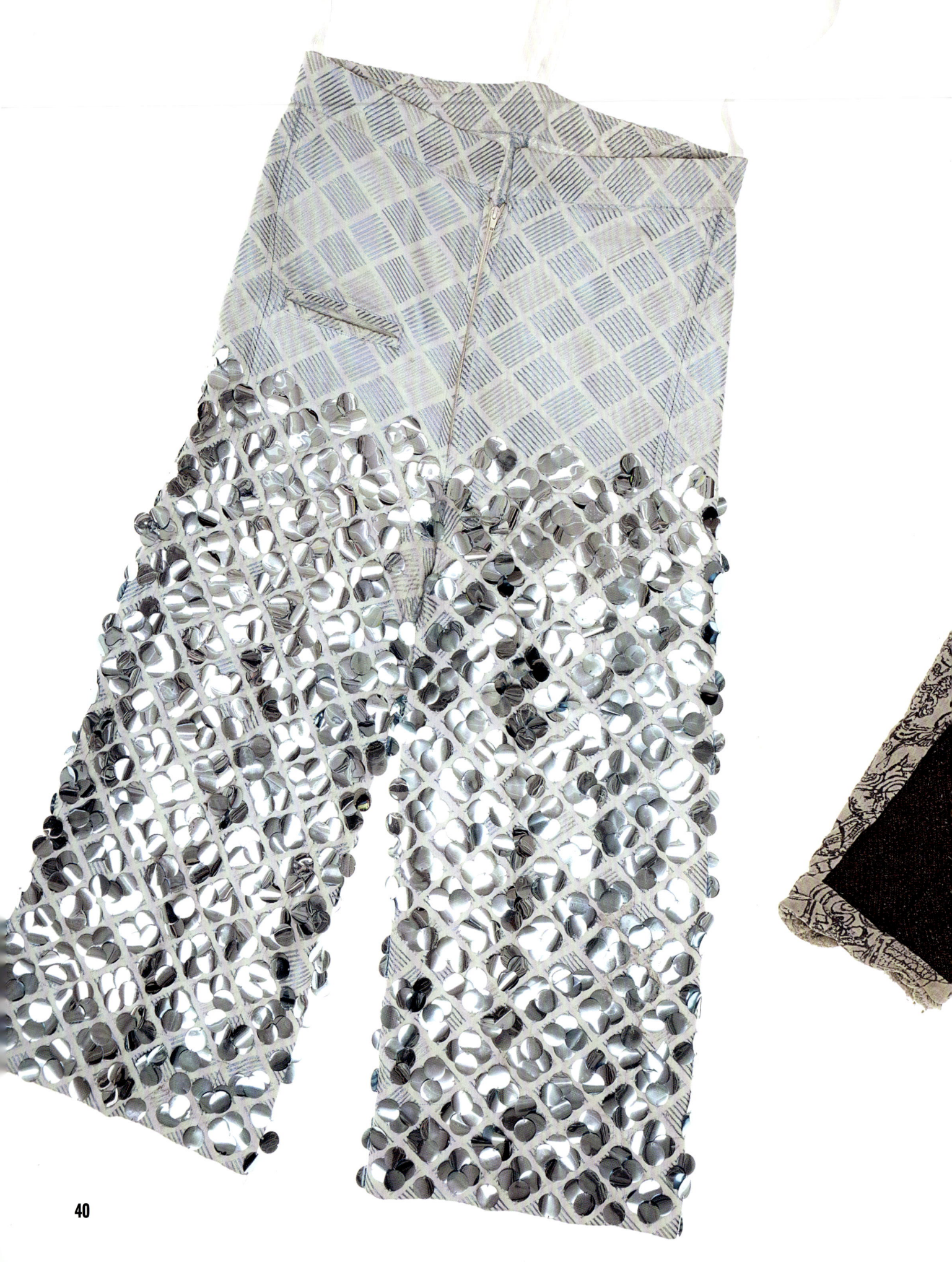

Left to right Sequined trousers, bottom half of two-piece suit, 1988; Chanel-inspired jacket, 1985

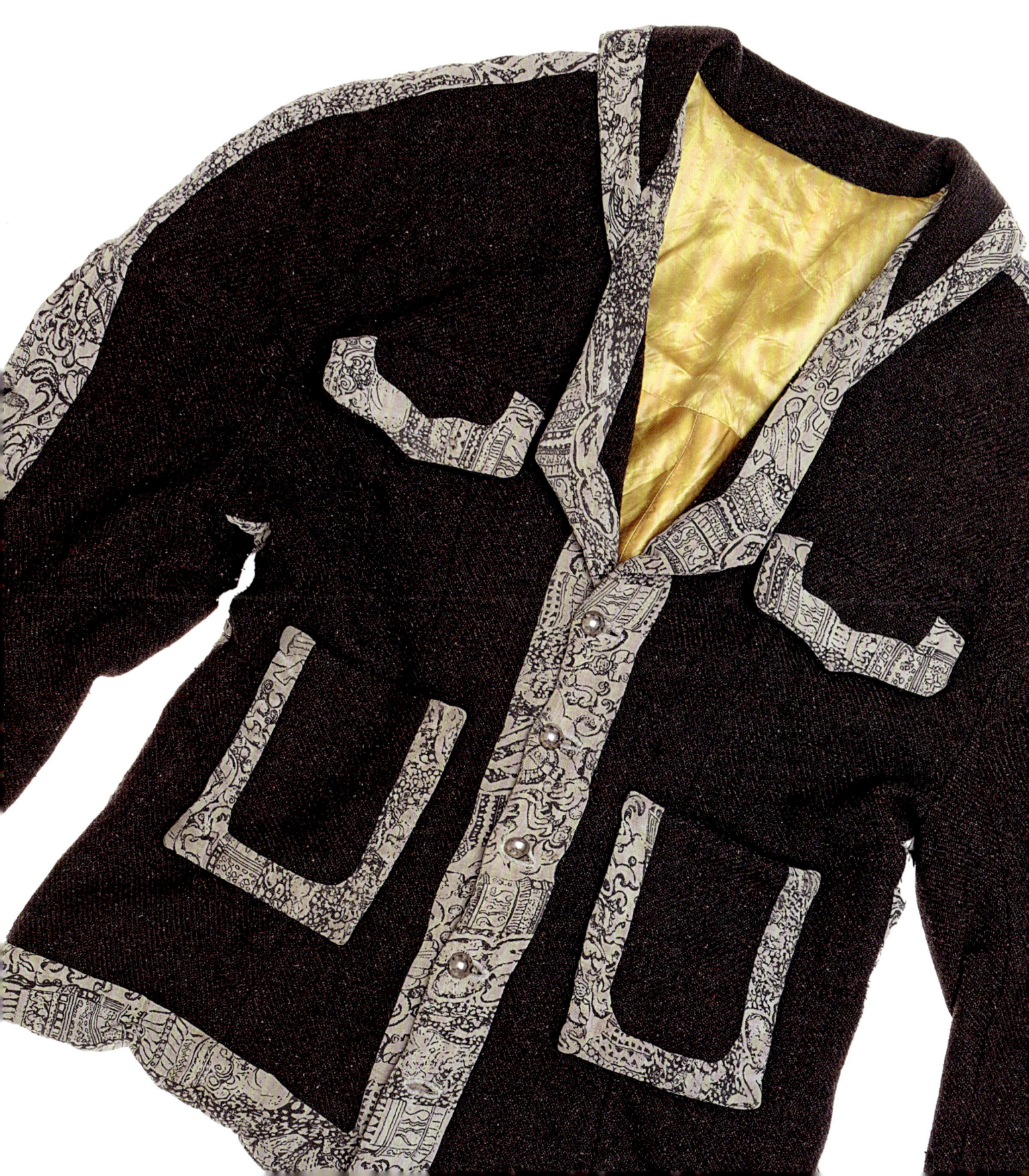

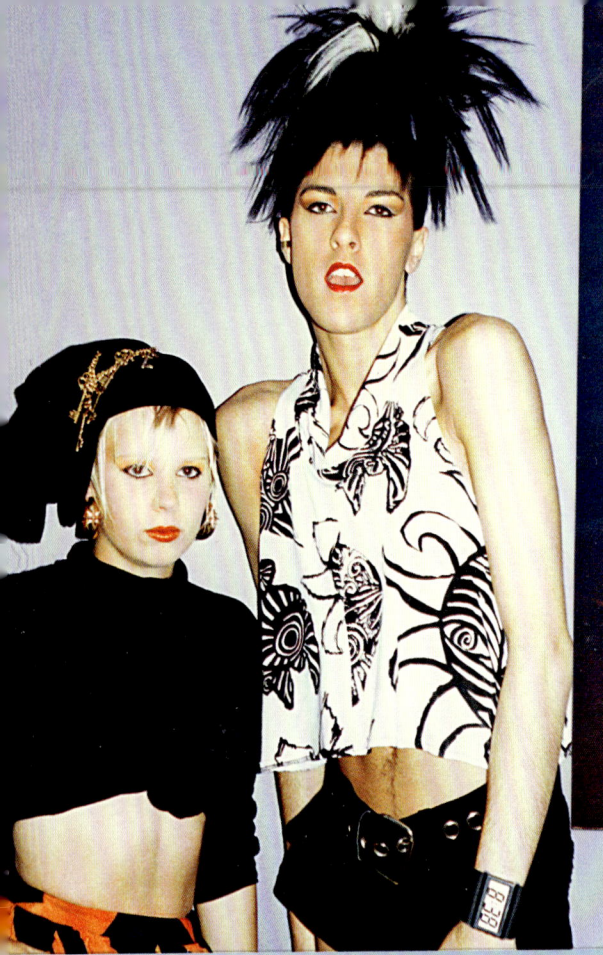
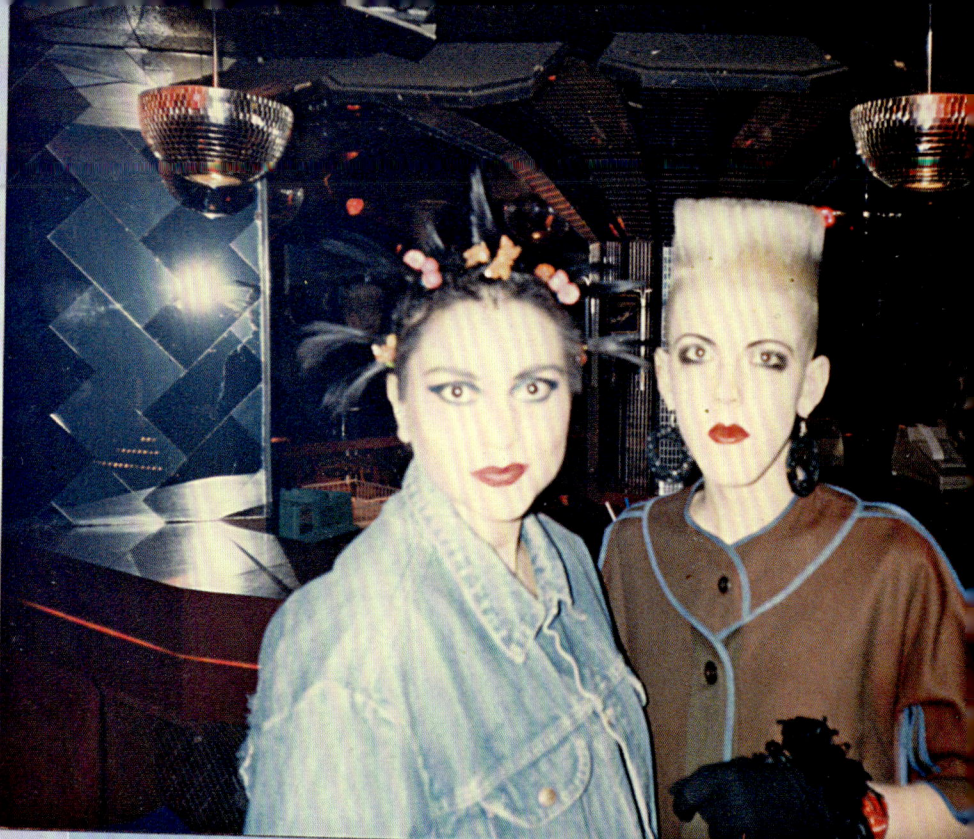

Clockwise from top left Maur Valance (right); Princess Julia (left) with Scarlett Cannon (right); Dean Bright; Mark Lawrence; Lanah Pellay; Holly Johnson; Jeffrey Hinton (centre), Lanah Pellay (in red) and Richard Habberley (right); Molly Parkin.

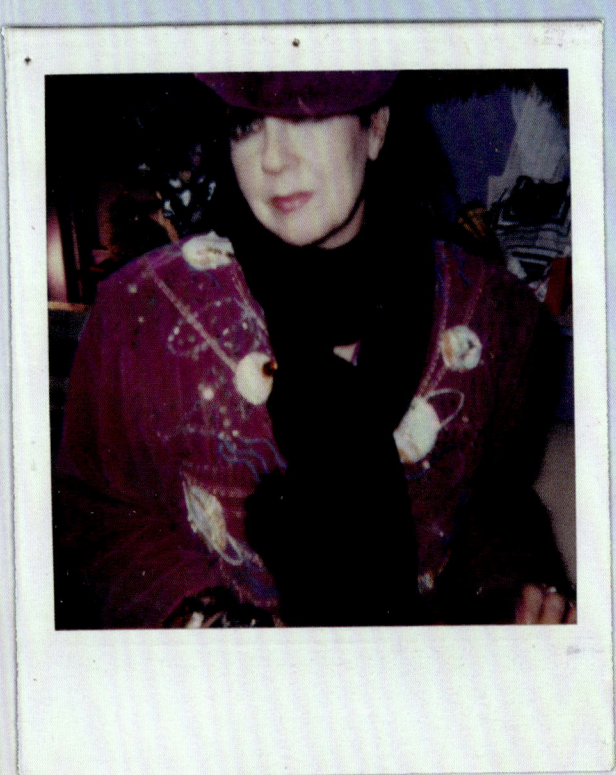
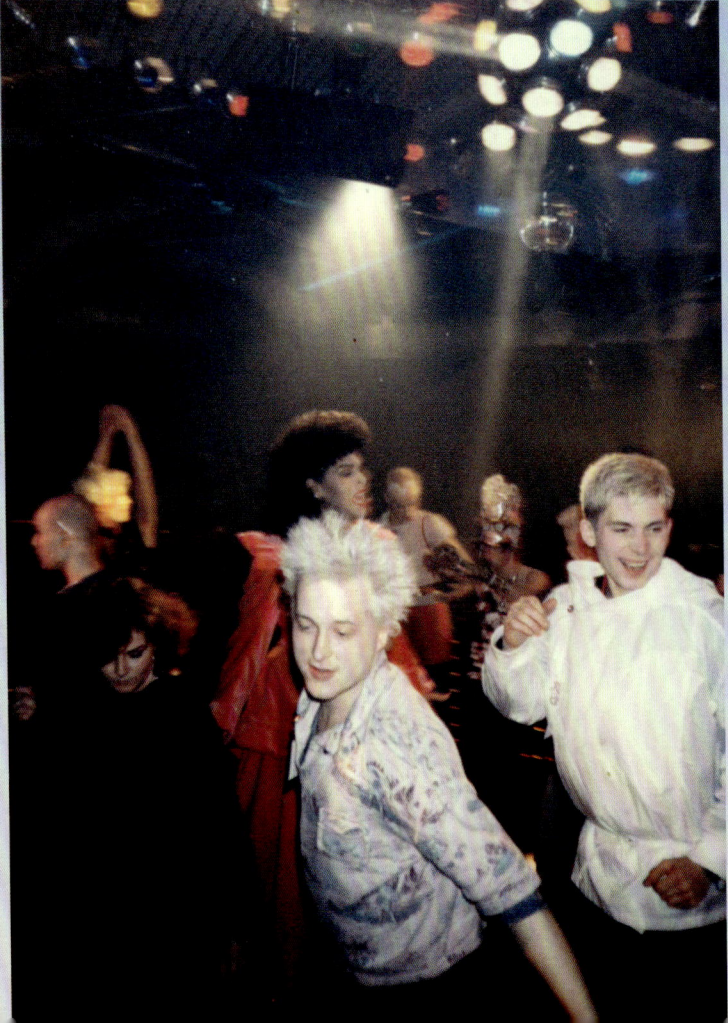

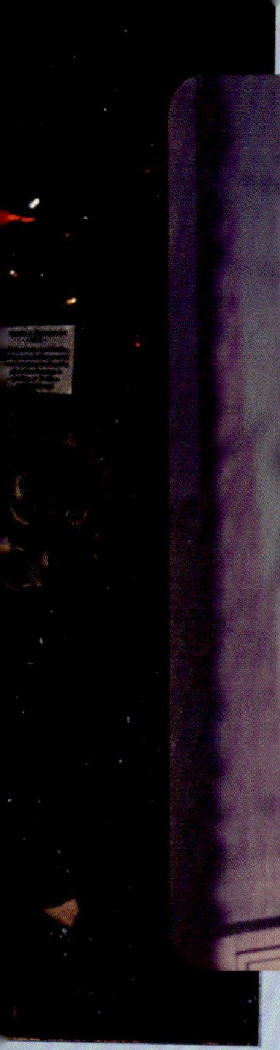

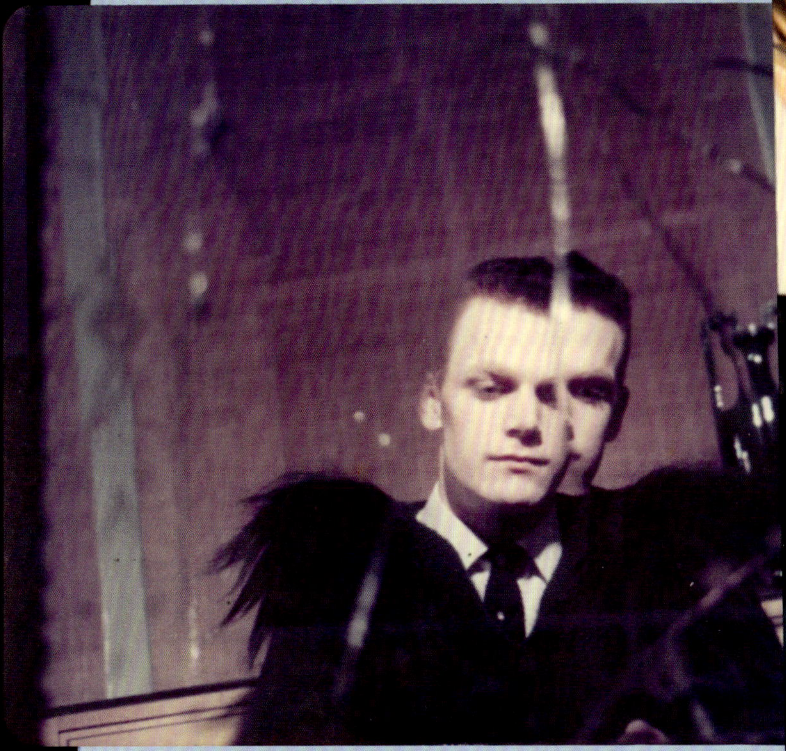

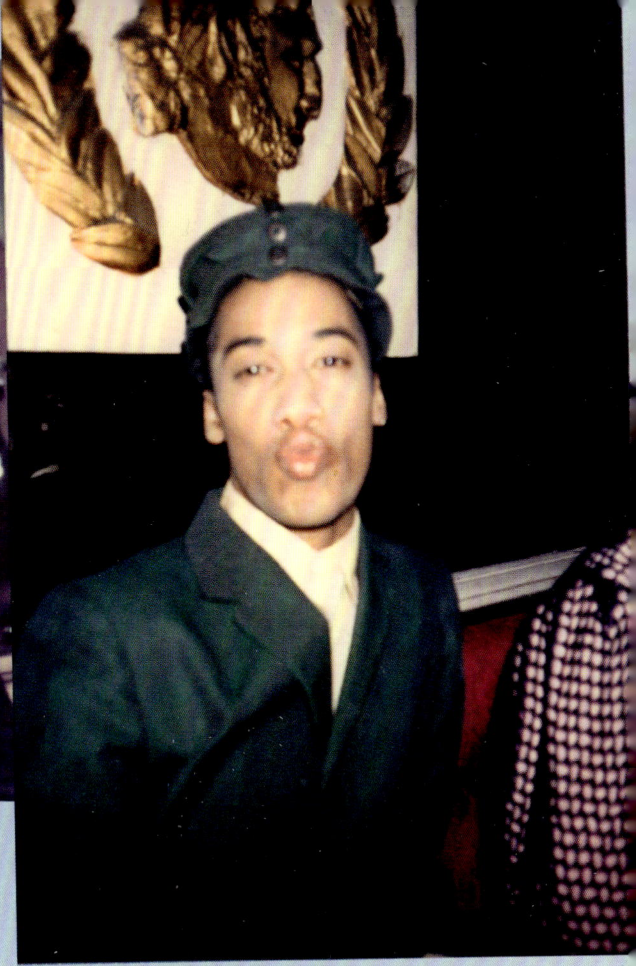

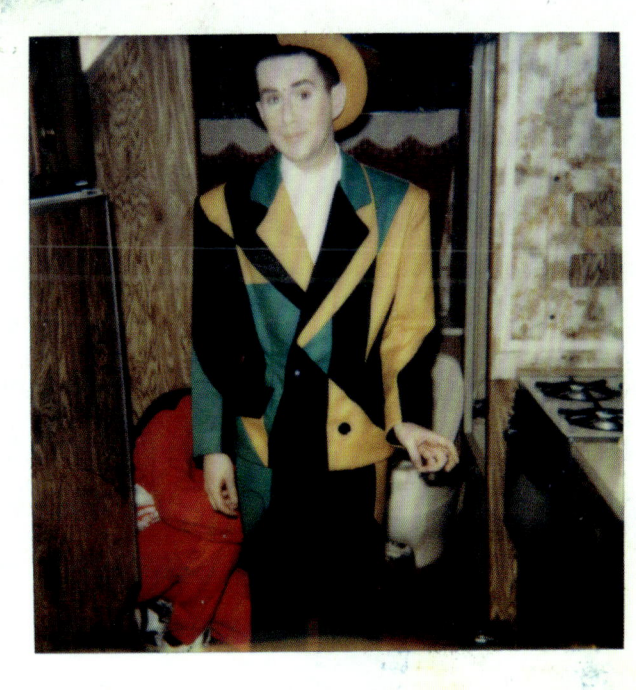
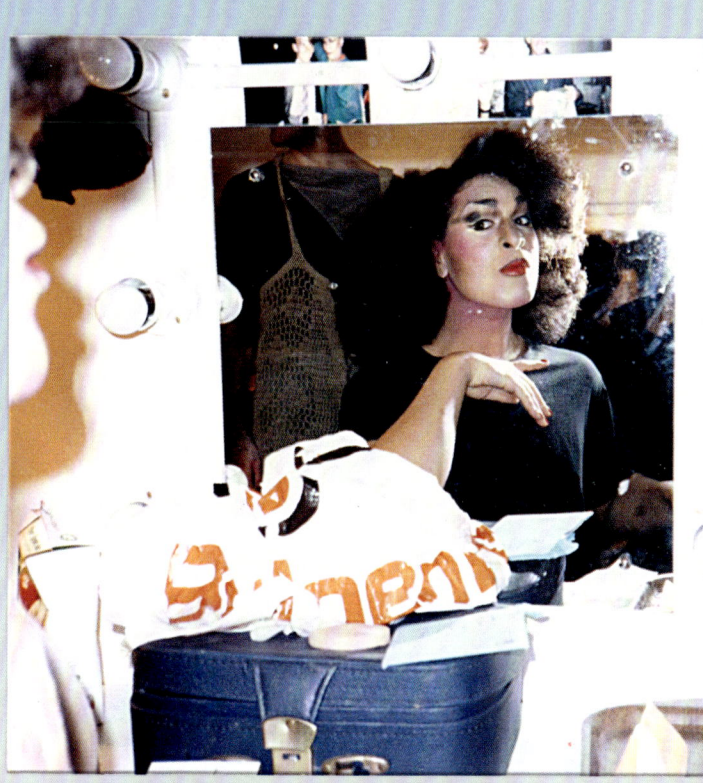

ANNIE LA PAZ

While studying fashion at Middlesex Polytechnic in 1982, Annie La Paz met Lucy Morahan and set up a creative partnership under the name LaPaz. They worked across all media, including production design for live events, styling for bands and setting up Circus, an influential club where Leigh Bowery first met Michael Clark.

At this time La Paz started making herself bright, graphic clothes to go out in. Her creations soon caught the eye of fashion magazines such as *Vogue*, and she was invited to participate in Susanne Bartsch's Young British Designers fashion show in New York. Her showcase collection was produced for retail under the LaPaz label and went on to be stocked by Browns.

LaPaz then moved away from seasonal retail collections and focused on designing bespoke collections for artists such as Kim Wilde. The LaPaz partnership continued during the 1980s, moving into the nascent pop video industry and then the film industry.

La Paz later changed career and retrained as a lawyer.

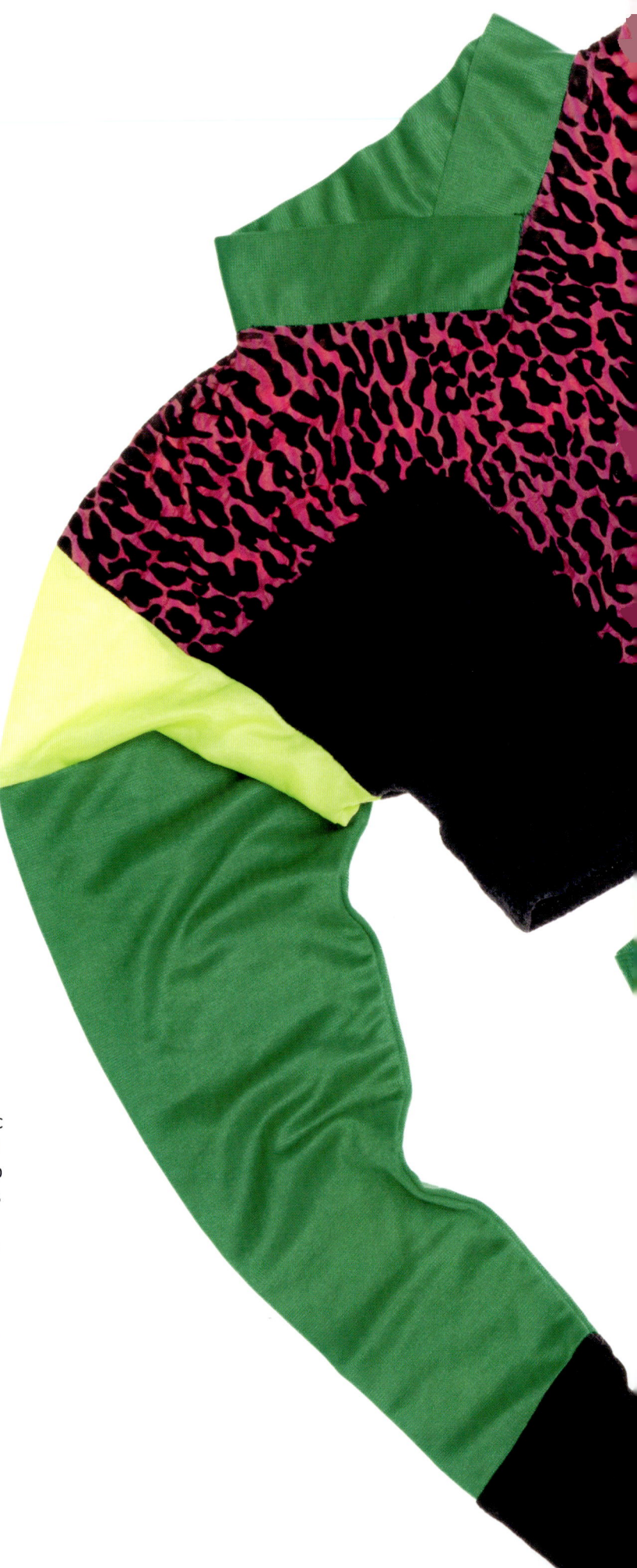

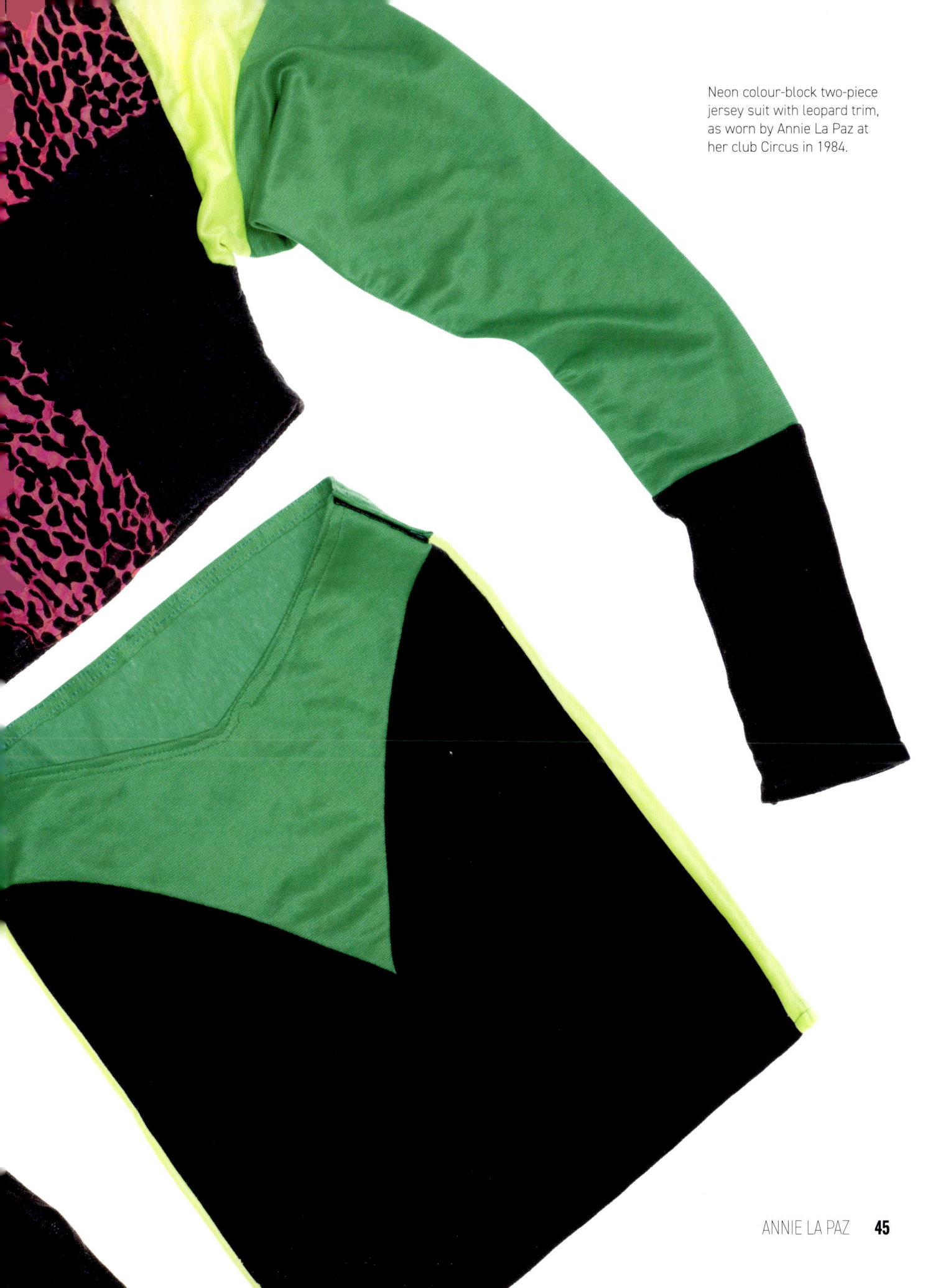

Neon colour-block two-piece jersey suit with leopard trim, as worn by Annie La Paz at her club Circus in 1984.

Annie La Paz design drawings, 1984

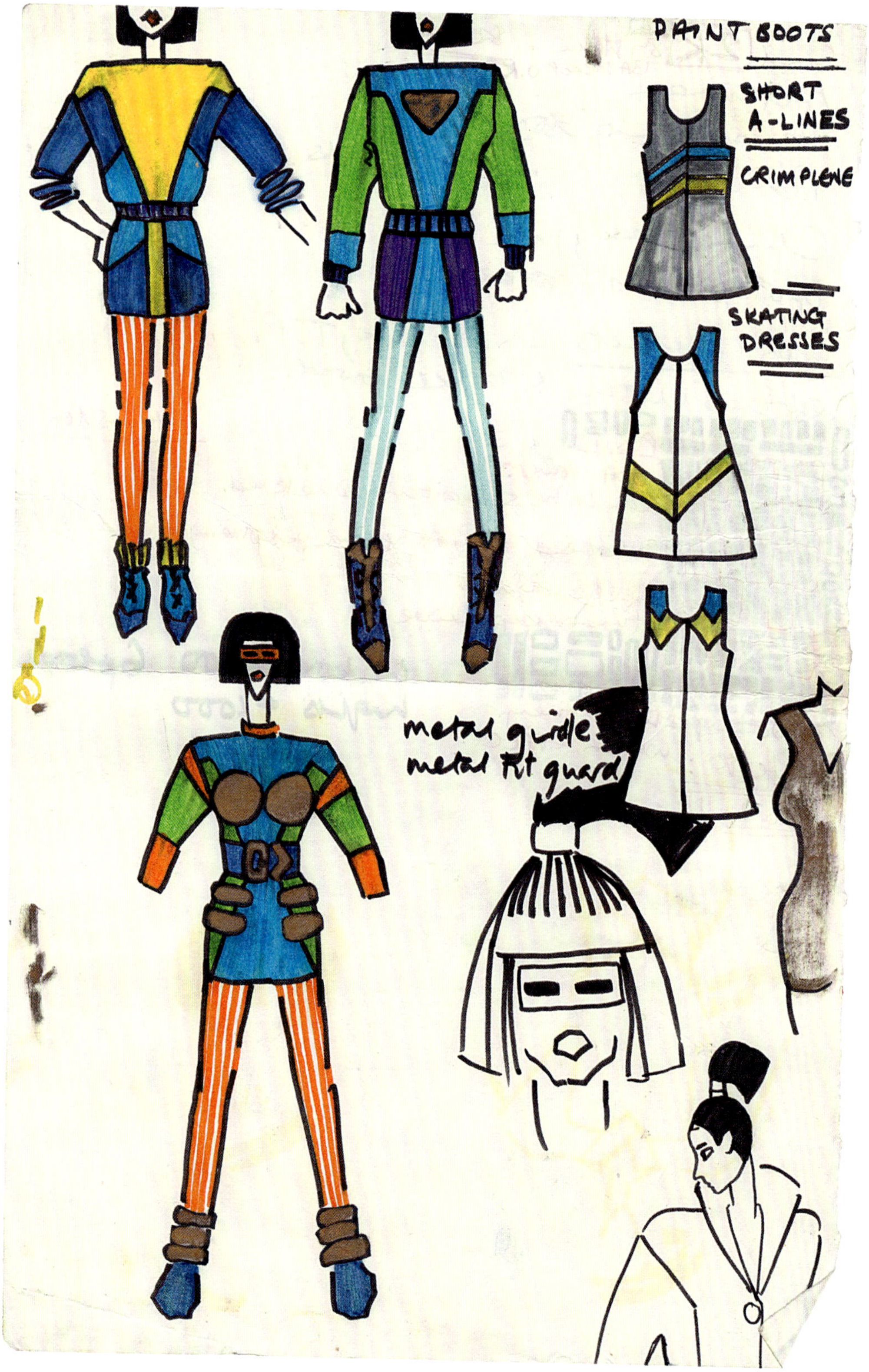

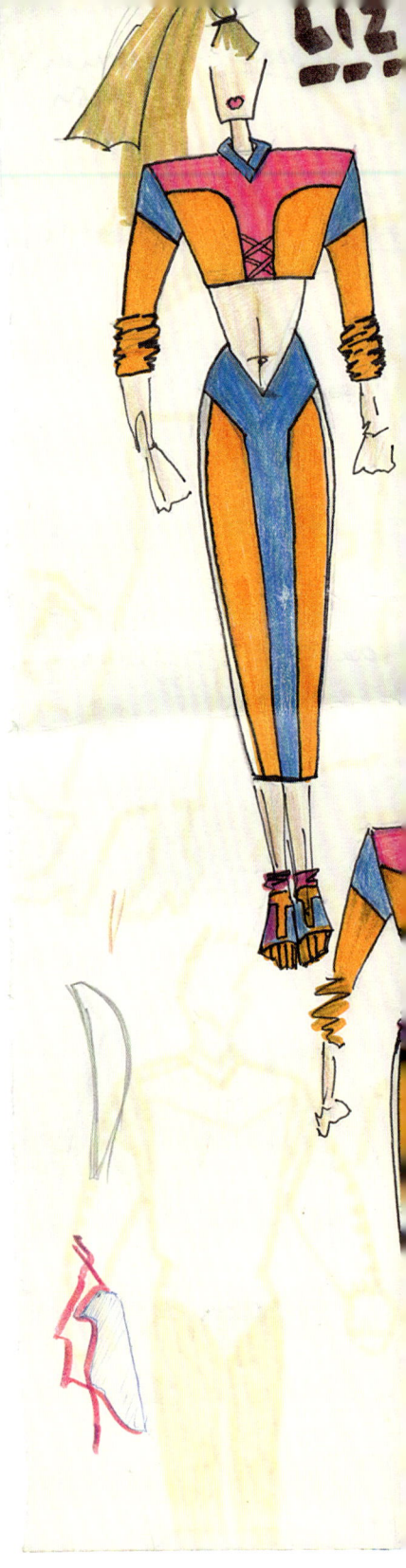

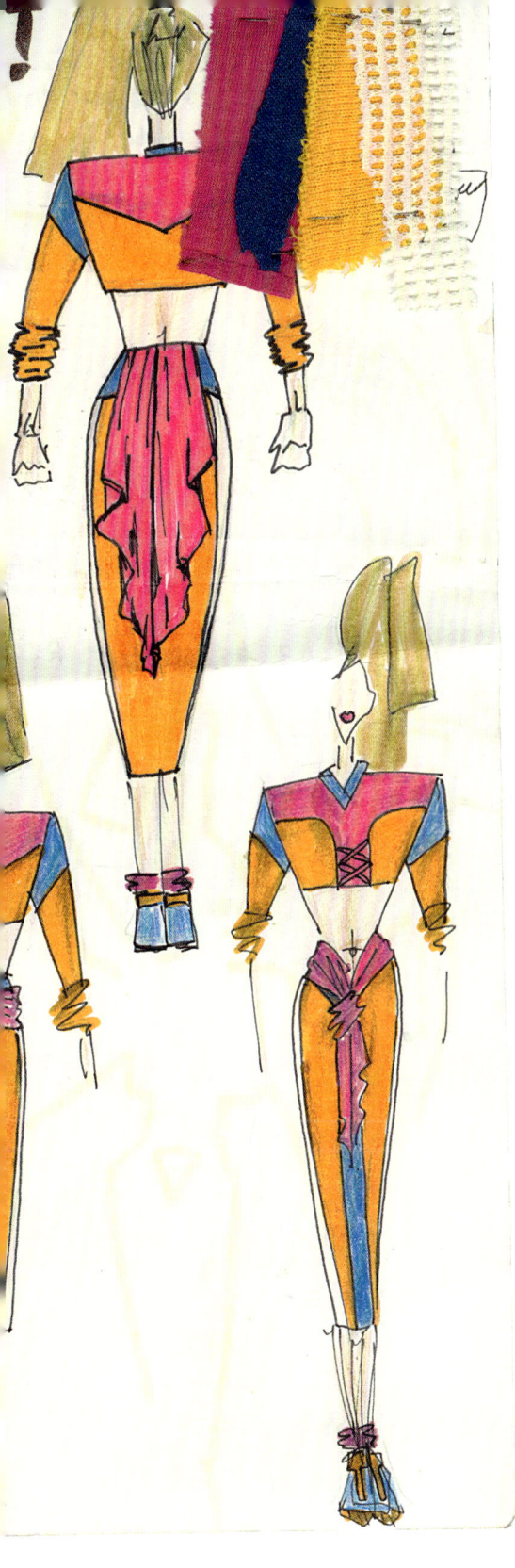

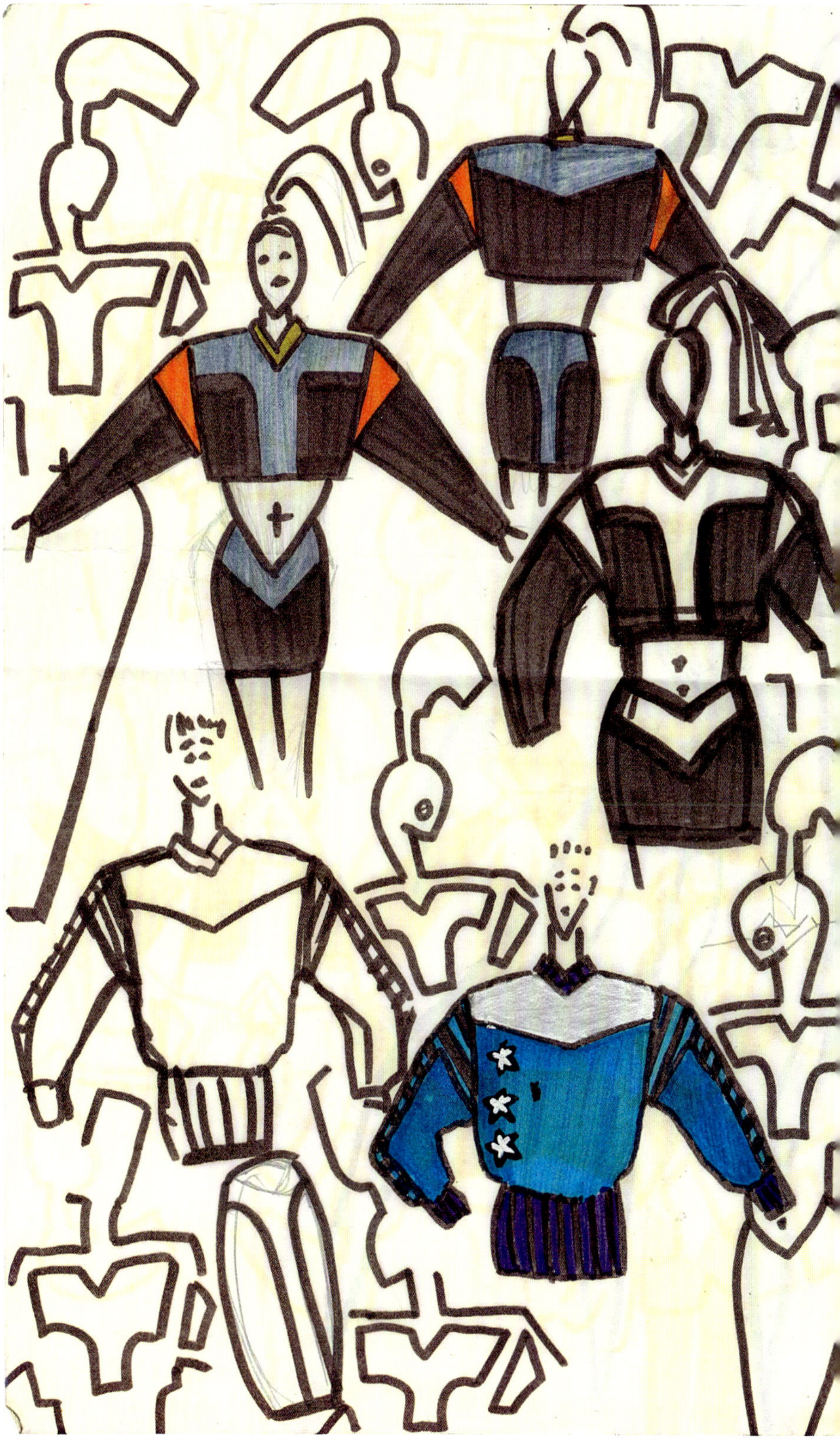

ANNIE LA PAZ 47

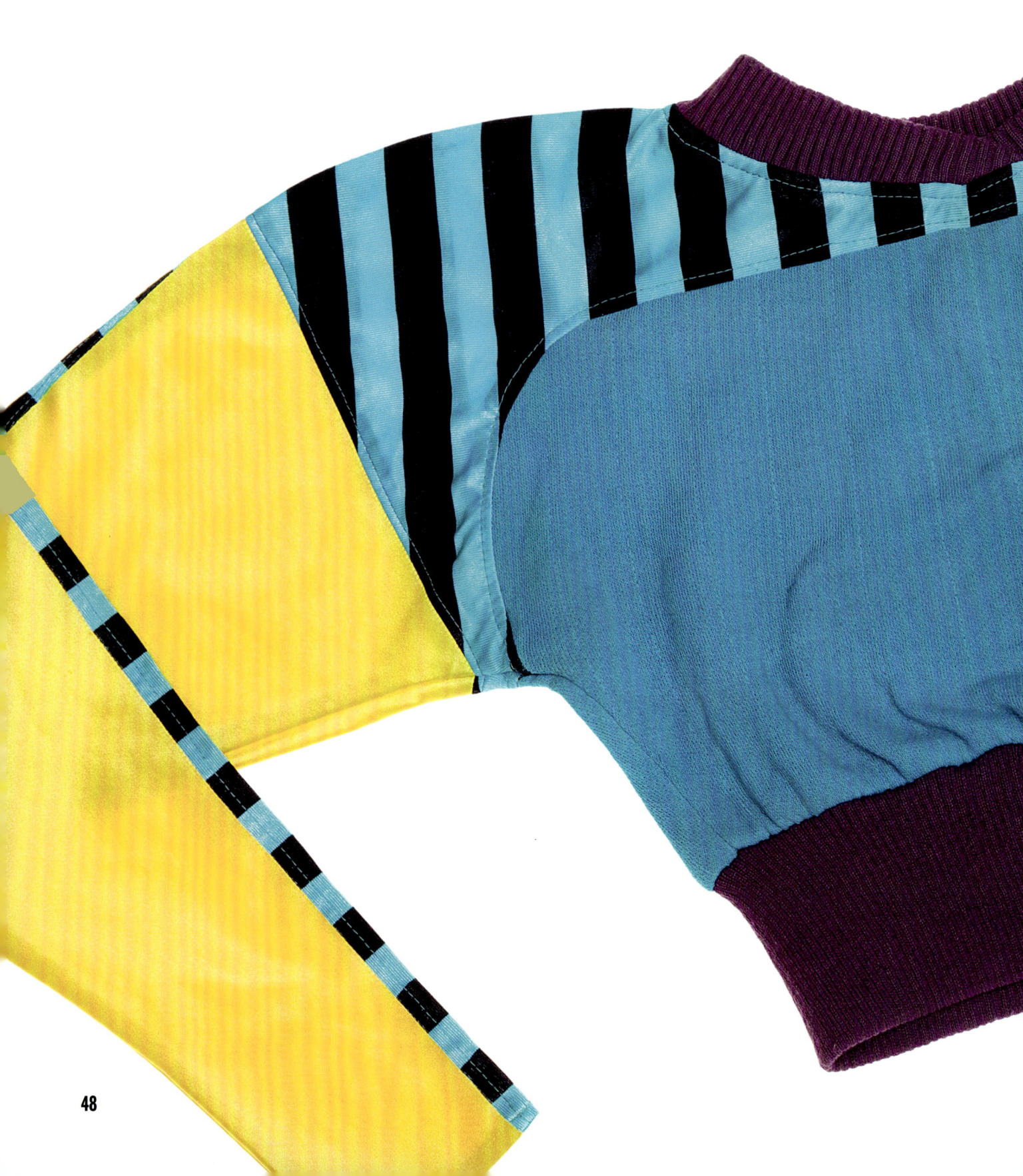

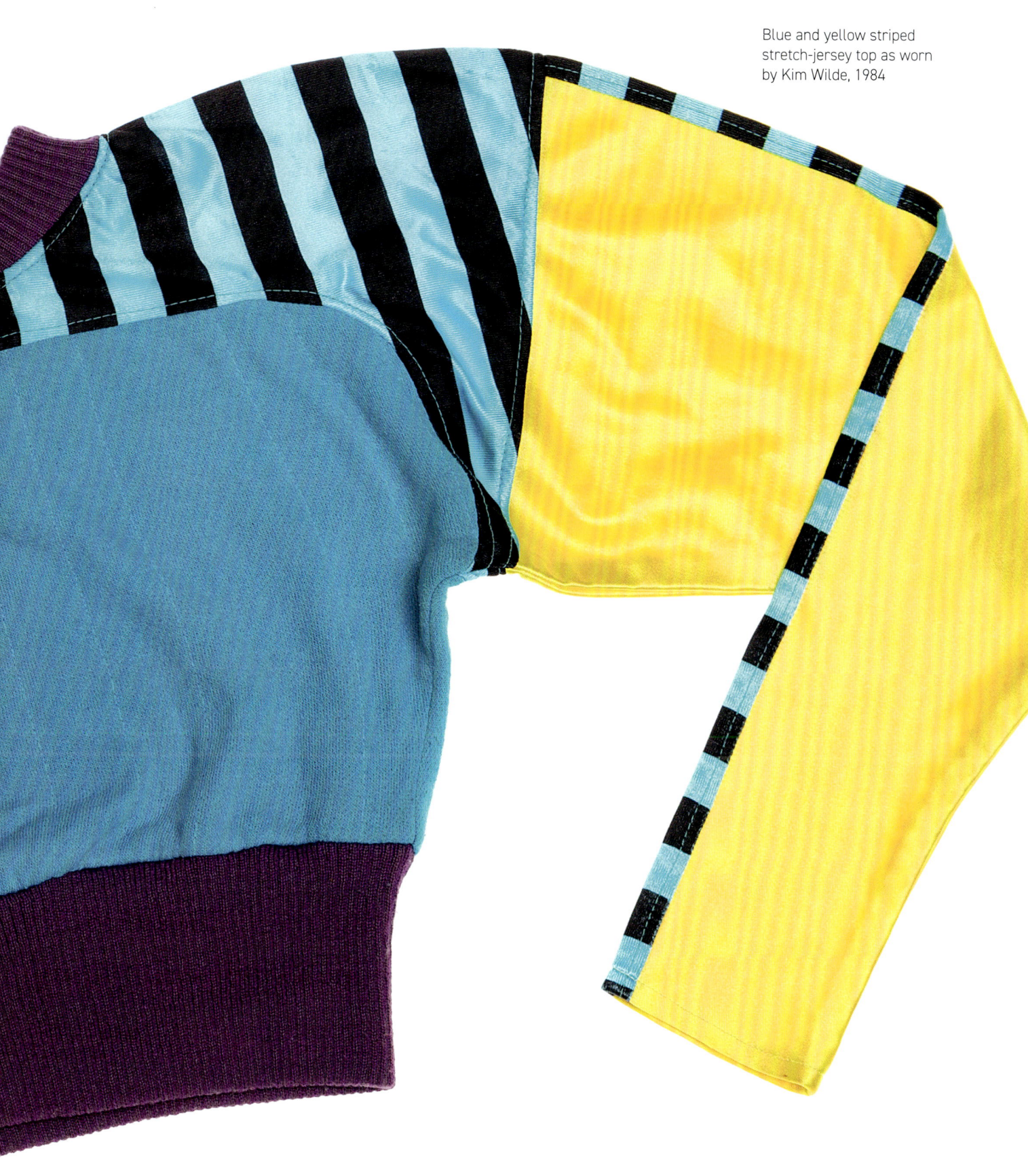

Blue and yellow striped stretch-jersey top as worn by Kim Wilde, 1984

RACHEL AUBURN

While at college Rachel Auburn worked for designer Jean Muir before graduating and setting up her Vena Cava stall at Kensington Market in 1982, where she met Leigh Bowery. He introduced her to Trojan, who soon started working on the stall.

Bowery would sometimes make clothes at Auburn's studio, and they often shared ideas and fabrics. The pair's provocative designs were chosen to represent London's new fashion scene at a series of New York shows organised by Susanne Bartsch.

In 1985 Auburn moved her stall into the newly opened Hyper Hyper and renamed it Spend Spend Spend after the film about scandalous football pools winner Viv Nicholson, who promised to do just that after winning big in 1961. Auburn's new shop assistant was Taboo's doorman Marc Vaultier.

Taboo was also Auburn's first foray into DJing and she played alongside Jeffrey Hinton and Mark Lawrence. This led to a successful parallel career as an international DJ, producer and dance-music artist.

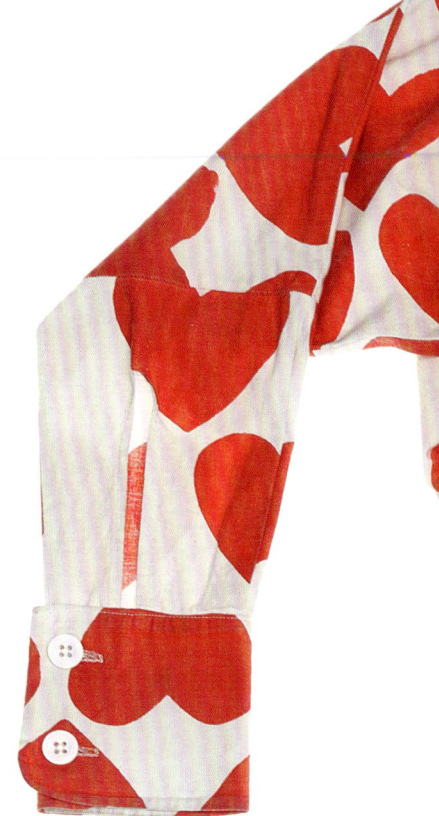

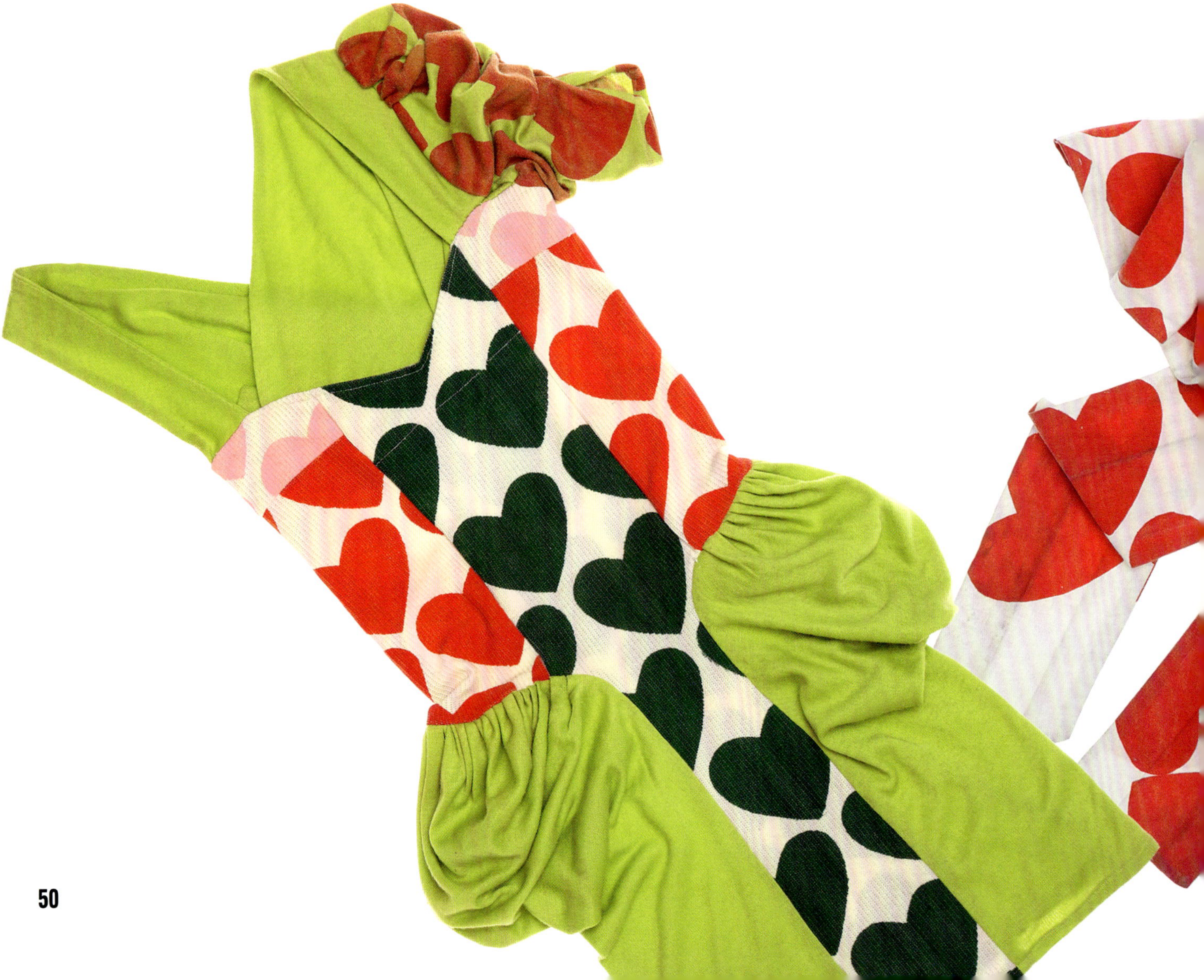

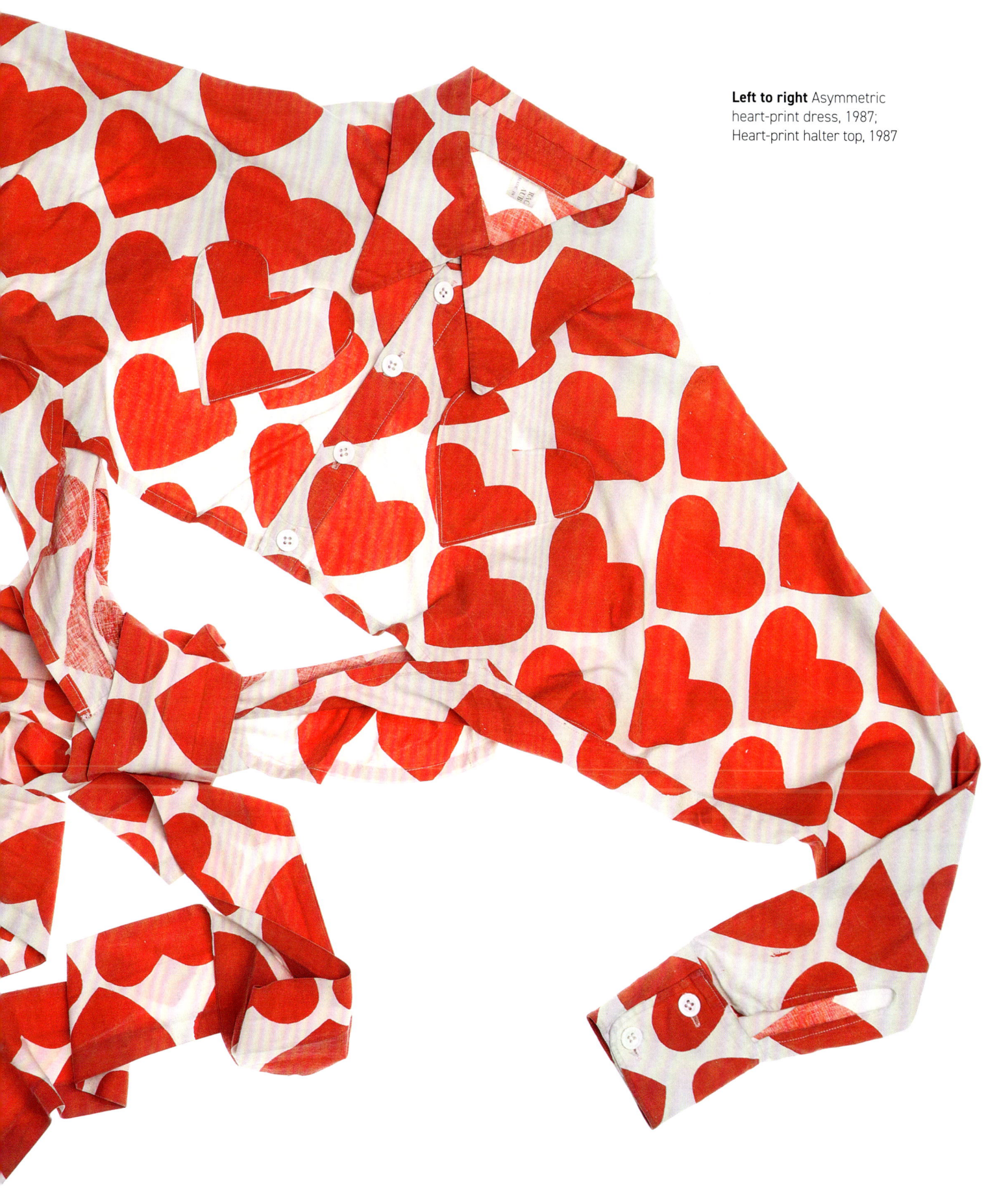

Left to right Asymmetric heart-print dress, 1987; Heart-print halter top, 1987

RACHEL AUBURN

White lace shirt with spotted-fabric pocket flaps, 1985

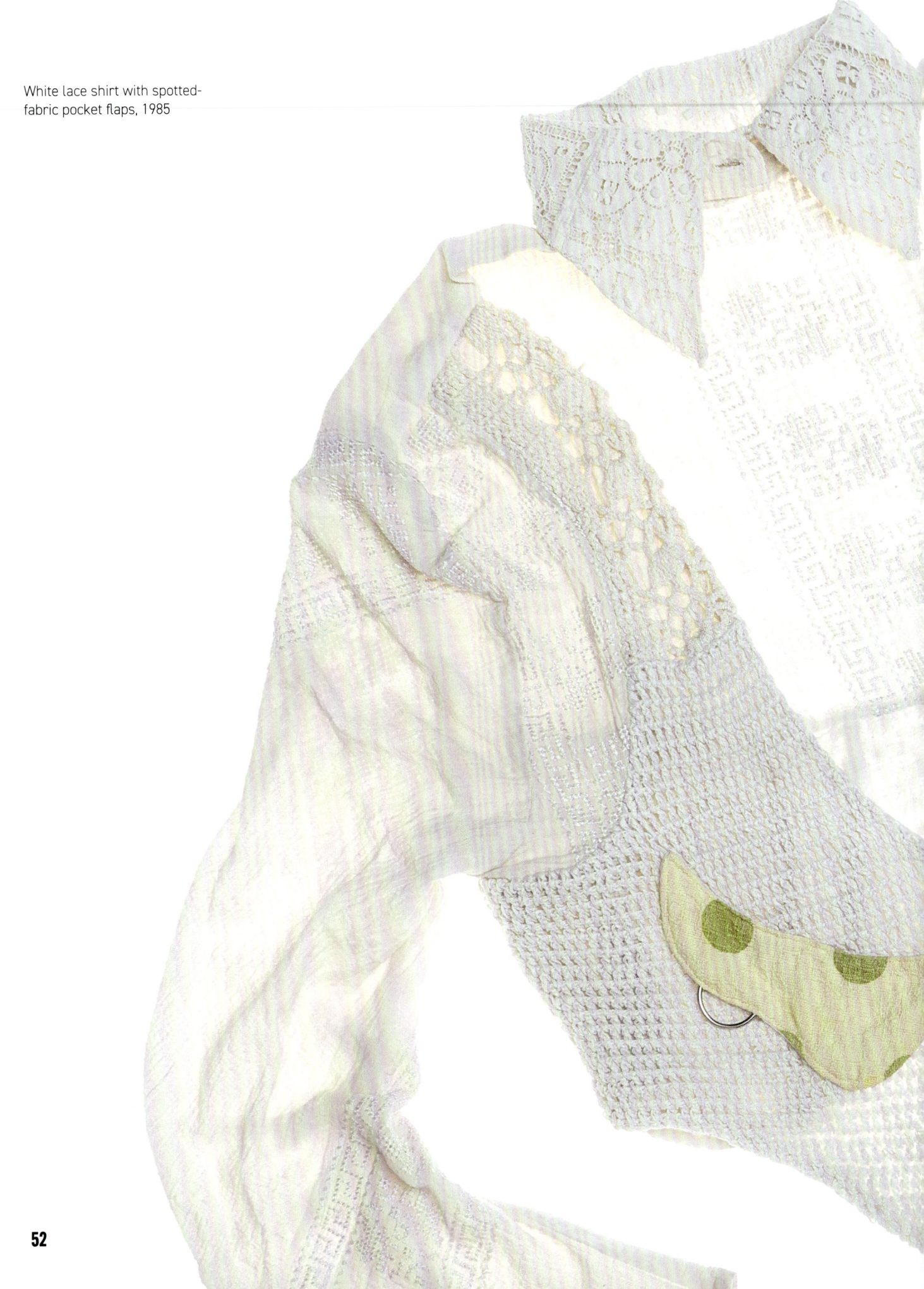

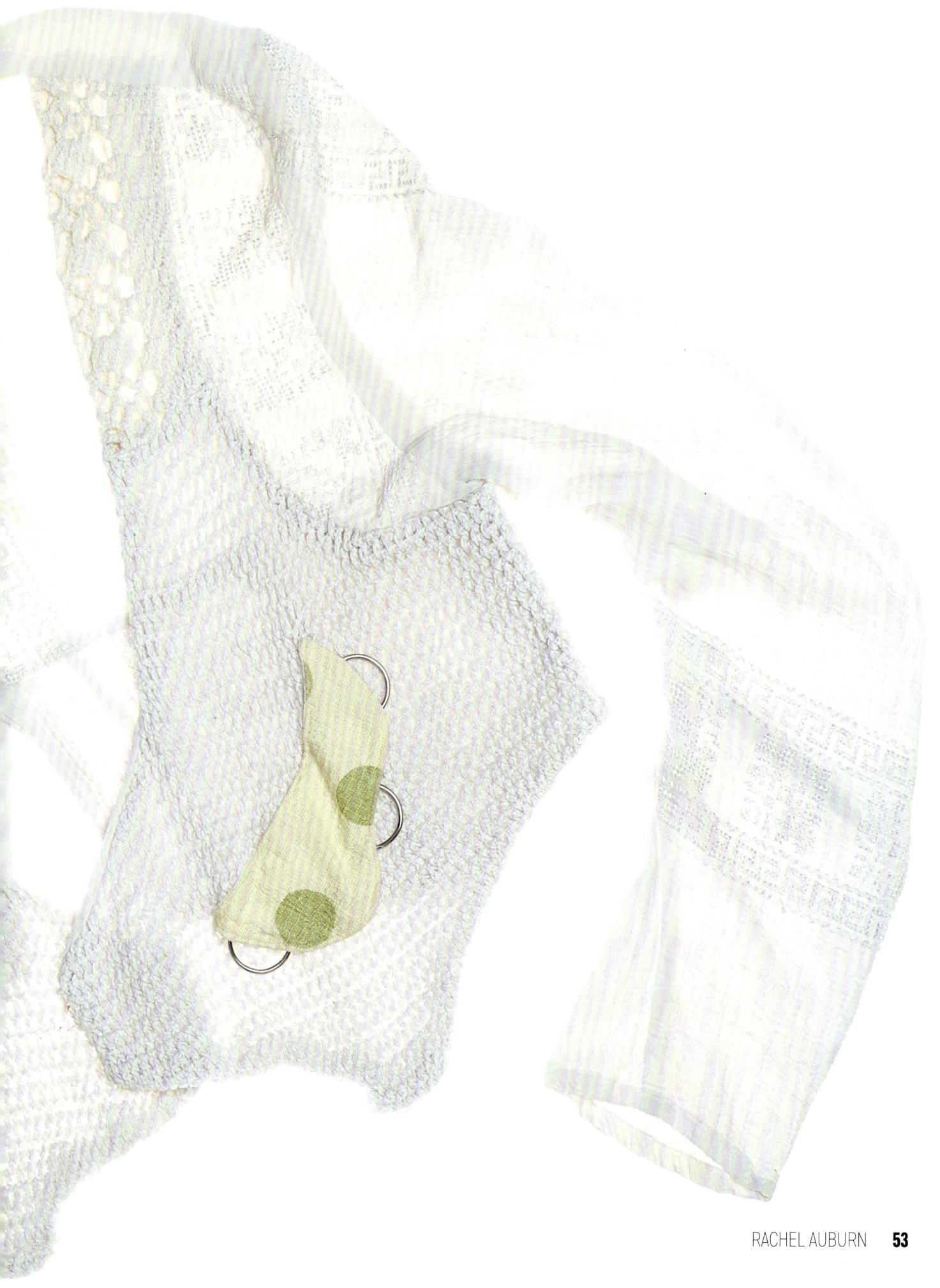

Left to right Pink heart-print skirt, 1987; Blue double-breasted jacket with spotted lining, 1985

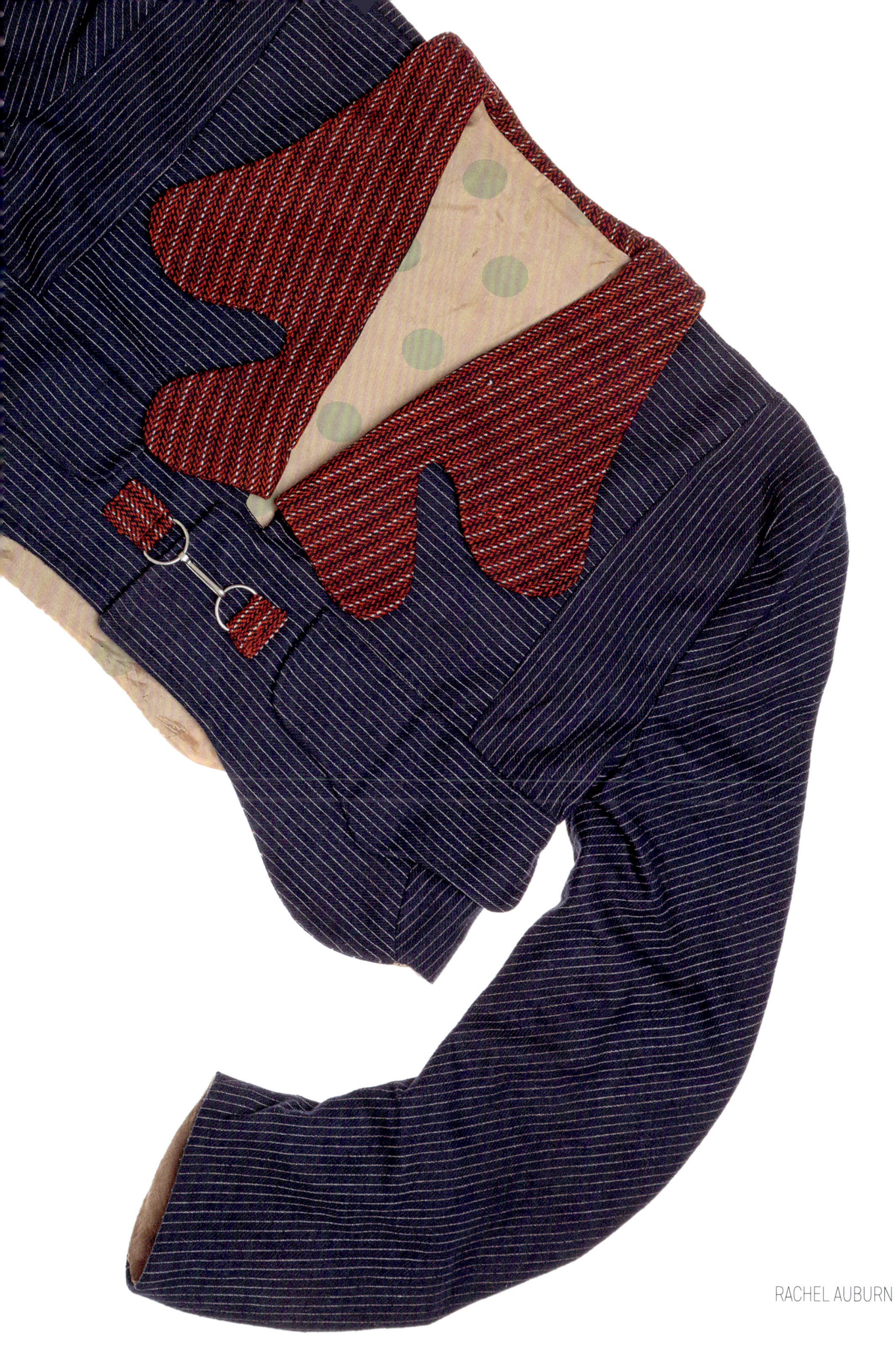

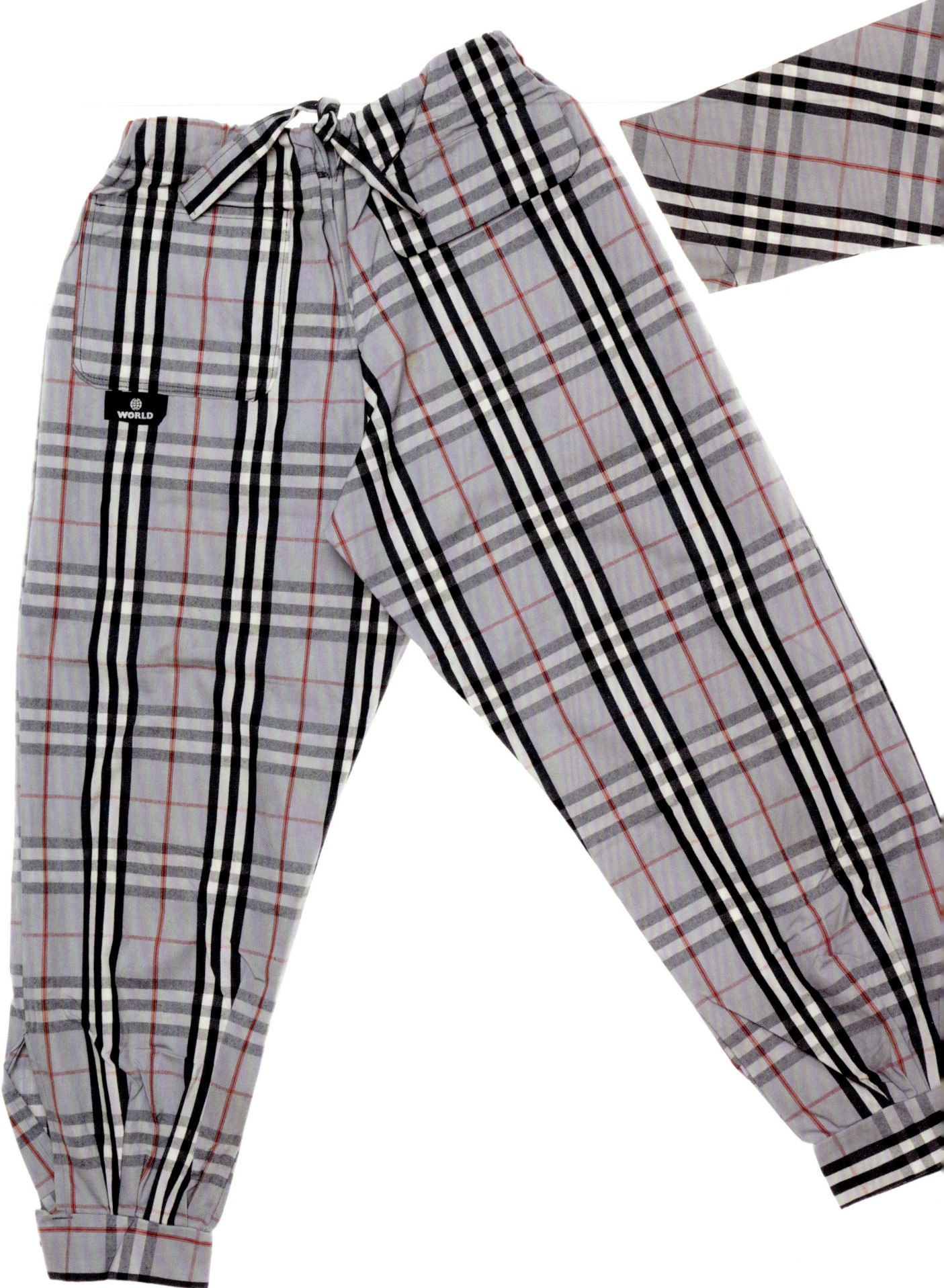

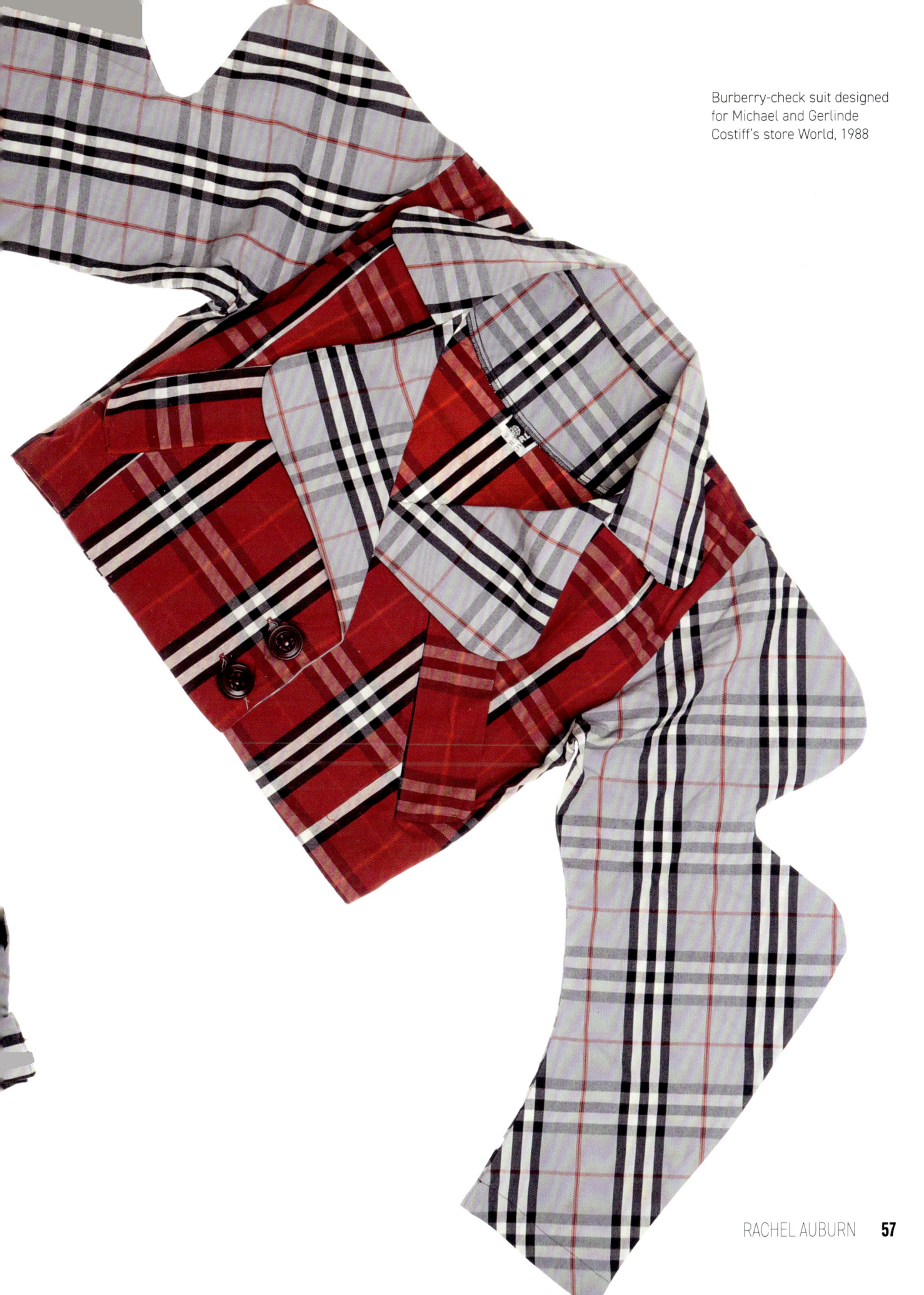

Burberry-check suit designed for Michael and Gerlinde Costiff's store World, 1988

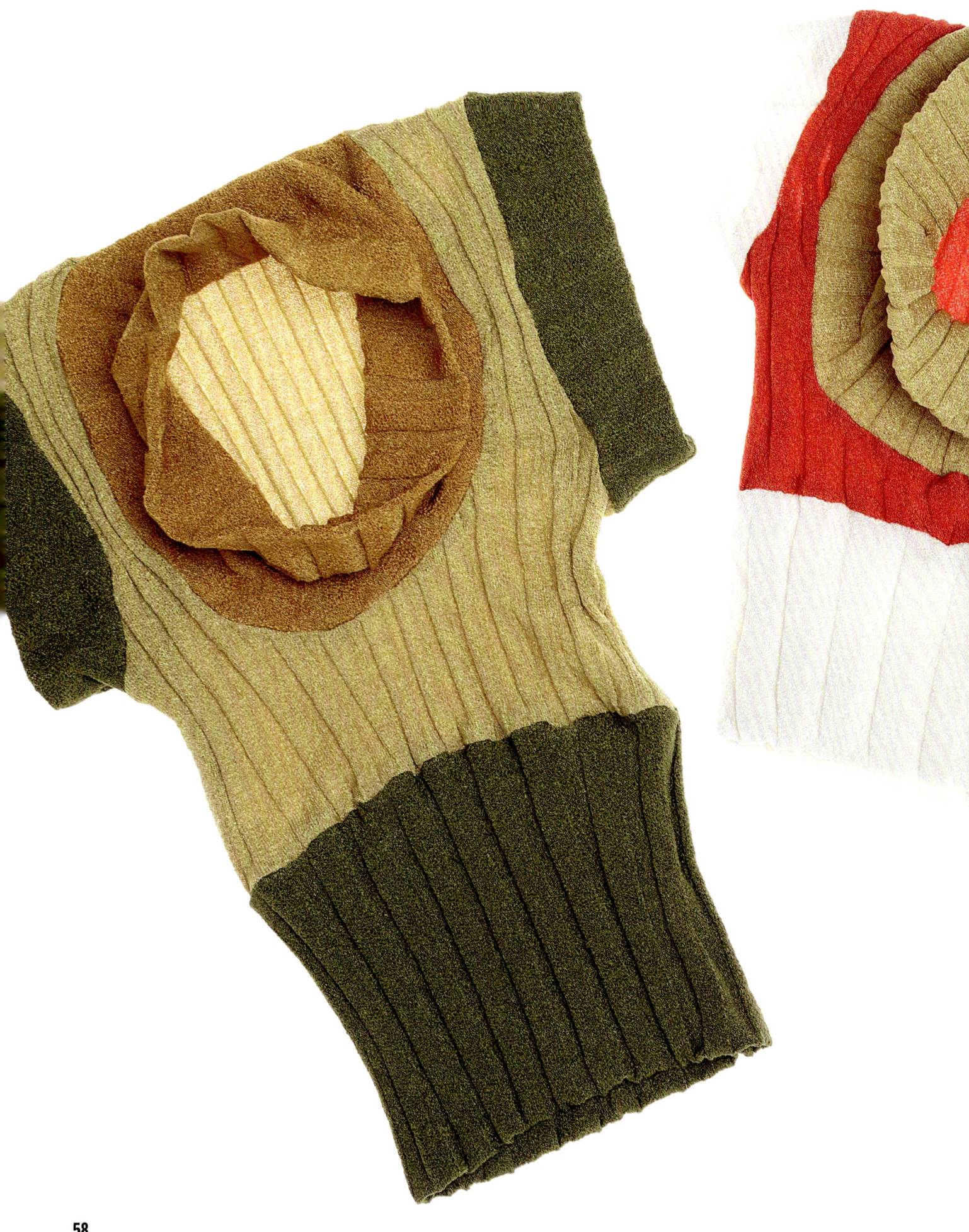

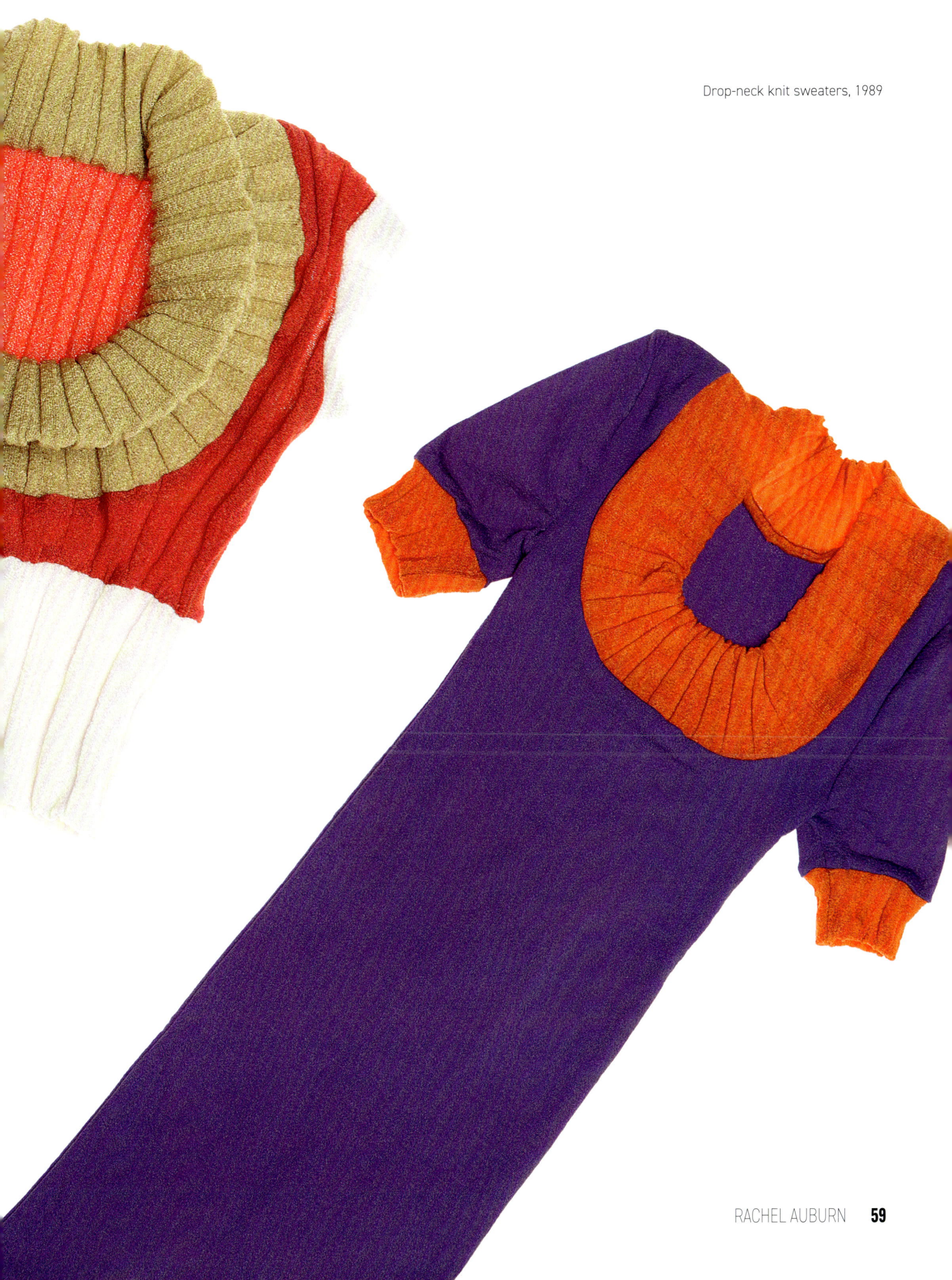

Drop-neck knit sweaters, 1989

NOW EVERYTHING IS NEW*

'I have more effect walking around the Tate Gallery than any of the paintings hanging there,' said Rachel Auburn when I interviewed her for *Blitz* magazine in 1983. 'In New York people thought I was a freak,' she continued, 'but I like to look freaky... I like having an effect on people to kick them out of their complacency.'

While the term 'freak' is intended as derogatory, it was reclaimed and worn as a badge of pride by an alternative creative community who emerged in the late 1970s and early 1980s, having bandied together in a host of one-night-stand nightclubs, which reached a zenith at the notorious Taboo, fronted by Leigh Bowery.

Those nightclubs, which would now be deemed 'safe spaces', were brimming with bright young things (myself included), would-be fashion designers, writers, artists, filmmakers, photographers and the like who were part of a new counter-culture. Club kids lived to dress up, their flamboyance a wonderful V-sign to a New Right government that seemed to be doing everything it could to suppress personal freedom and original thought via social conservatism, the promotion of traditional family values, racial injustice and the introduction of the discriminatory Section 28.

These self-proclaimed 'children of the revolution' were the bastard children of Bolan, Bowie, Malcolm McLaren and Vivienne Westwood, whose own designs were described as 'costumes of provocation'. Having an effect, provoking a reaction, good or bad, became a rallying cry. I once asked Bowery what names his clothes answered to. He simply replied: 'Provocative.'

We lived on the outskirts of society and found strength and sustenance over a snakebite or Pernod and black. We joined forces, encouraging each other and sharing ideas. Because there was little or no money involved, everyone had the same aim: to create something not yet imagined. We had nothing, so we had nothing to lose. In the face of recession and rising unemployment, the AIDS crisis and even the threat of conscription, uncertainty shaped the landscape but, ironically, fostered an atmosphere of unbridled freedom. Experimentation and the desire to push boundaries, question the status quo and challenge social constructs became our *raison d'etre*. In 1980 a trio of magazines – *Blitz, The Face* and *i-D* – emerged, shining a spotlight on this new army of dreamers, allowing us to be seen and to explore our radical concepts.

In 1986 the *Herald Tribune* profiled this threesome, describing the new approach as 'blissfully liberated with a lot of fun-poking at the Establishment'. The writer noted how the magazines promoted the idea that 'fashion is a happening' and 'no longer for those that can afford it'. She also observed that the styled fashion shoots made *Vogue* look like 'a string quartet next to a punk band'. In 2018, in *System* magazine, milliner Stephen Jones told writer Tim Blanks, 'those magazines... helped hundreds of thousands of 16- and 17- and 18-year-olds to grow up with a completely different sense of fashion'.

As fashion editor of *Blitz*, I wanted to inspire the readers to experiment with fashion rather than go shopping. Punk's DIY ethos was ingrained. Nobody wanted to be labelled by their clothes. The overarching desire was to be seen as an individual; the emphasis on personal style and what you wore being more likely influenced by an old movie or new lover than a picture in a fashion magazine or a model on a catwalk. We cobbled together looks from a variety of sources (charity shops, jumble sales, a few designer threads knocked up by designer friends and the odd jacket from a boyfriend's bedroom floor) into a post-modern collage of wide-ranging references.

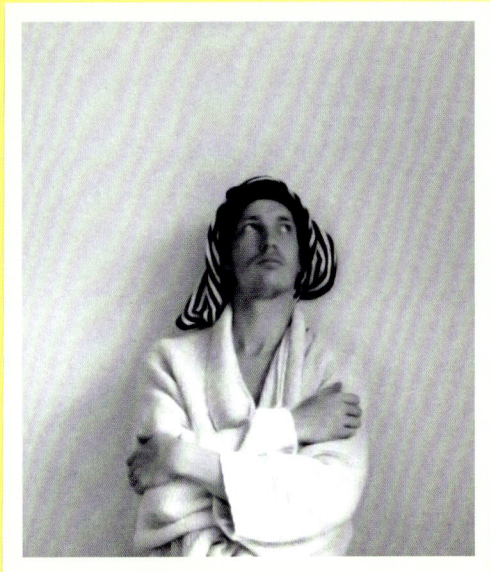

Fashion was nothing like the industry it is today – these young art-school-meets-club-kid designers often started out selling on market stalls in Camden, Kensington and on the King's Road. Hyper Hyper in Kensington High Street gave the concept a smart makeover, over two decades before Dover Street Market. The nightclubs were our catwalk and red carpet combined.

My pages in *Blitz* chronicled these characters and so, while Princess Julia, Kate Garner, Mark Moore and Mark Lawrence modelled, fashion stories were filled with clothes by Pam Hogg, Mark & Syrie, John Crancher, BodyMap, Bernstock Speirs, Richmond Cornejo, Judy Blame, Auburn and Bowery. I also gained them wider visibility in the mainstream: readers of *YOU, The Mail on Sunday* colour supplement, were treated to the glamazon sportswear-inspired silhouettes of Annie La Paz, photographed by a jejune Mario Testino, who had just arrived from Brazil and was living in a squat in an abandoned ambulance station in Covent Garden, and the 'Comic Cuts' of Elmaz Hüseyin, modelled by Bruno and Denis, handsome French boys my friend and I had picked up in Club Sept in Paris. For another feature on Hüseyin in *Blitz*, the designer and her best friend Isaac Julien (now CBE and an internationally lauded artist and filmmaker) hand-painted the backdrop. The model was Baillie Walsh, who later masterminded ABBA Voyage. My first fashion page for the *Evening Standard* featured Blame.

I was excited to promote my designer and artist friends on an international level in publications such as *Mademoiselle* in the US and *L'Uomo Vogue* and *Weststuff* in Italy.

In 1985, when Luisaviaroma hosted a party for London creatives in Florence, I curated the accompanying brochure that featured the fashion pack alongside artists including Trojan, Peter Doig, Holly Warburton and John Maybury. 'Those were such great times and all on a shoestring,' remembers Doig, who moonlighted from painting with a series of in-your-face-sperm print T-shirts. 'The shirts were a form of self-advertisement,' says Doig. 'More people can see your work when someone is wearing it than in a gallery.'

* from 'Lay All Your Love on Me' by ABBA

IAIN R WEBB

WRITER, CURATOR, ACADEMIC

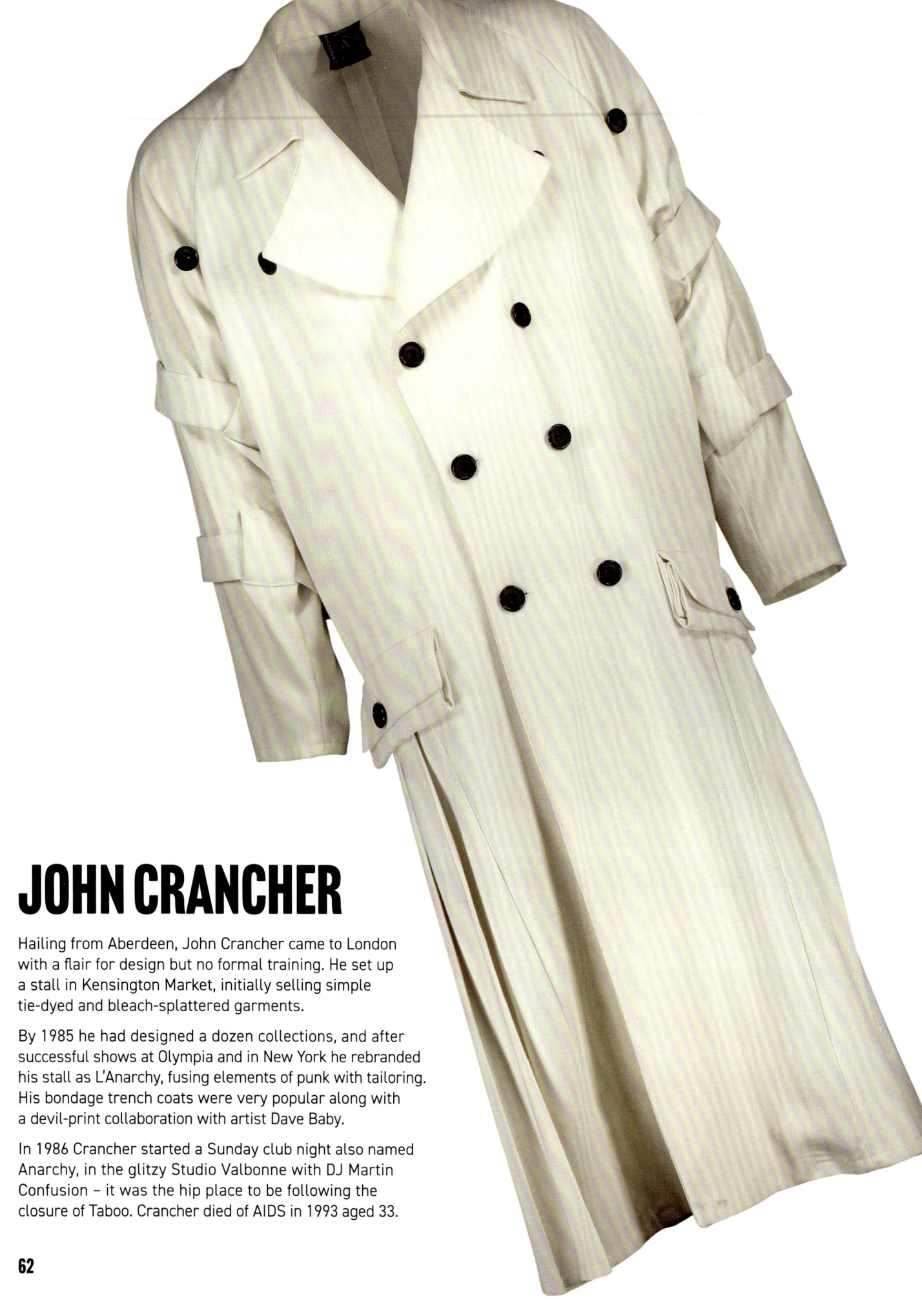

JOHN CRANCHER

Hailing from Aberdeen, John Crancher came to London with a flair for design but no formal training. He set up a stall in Kensington Market, initially selling simple tie-dyed and bleach-splattered garments.

By 1985 he had designed a dozen collections, and after successful shows at Olympia and in New York he rebranded his stall as L'Anarchy, fusing elements of punk with tailoring. His bondage trench coats were very popular along with a devil-print collaboration with artist Dave Baby.

In 1986 Crancher started a Sunday club night also named Anarchy, in the glitzy Studio Valbonne with DJ Martin Confusion – it was the hip place to be following the closure of Taboo. Crancher died of AIDS in 1993 aged 33.

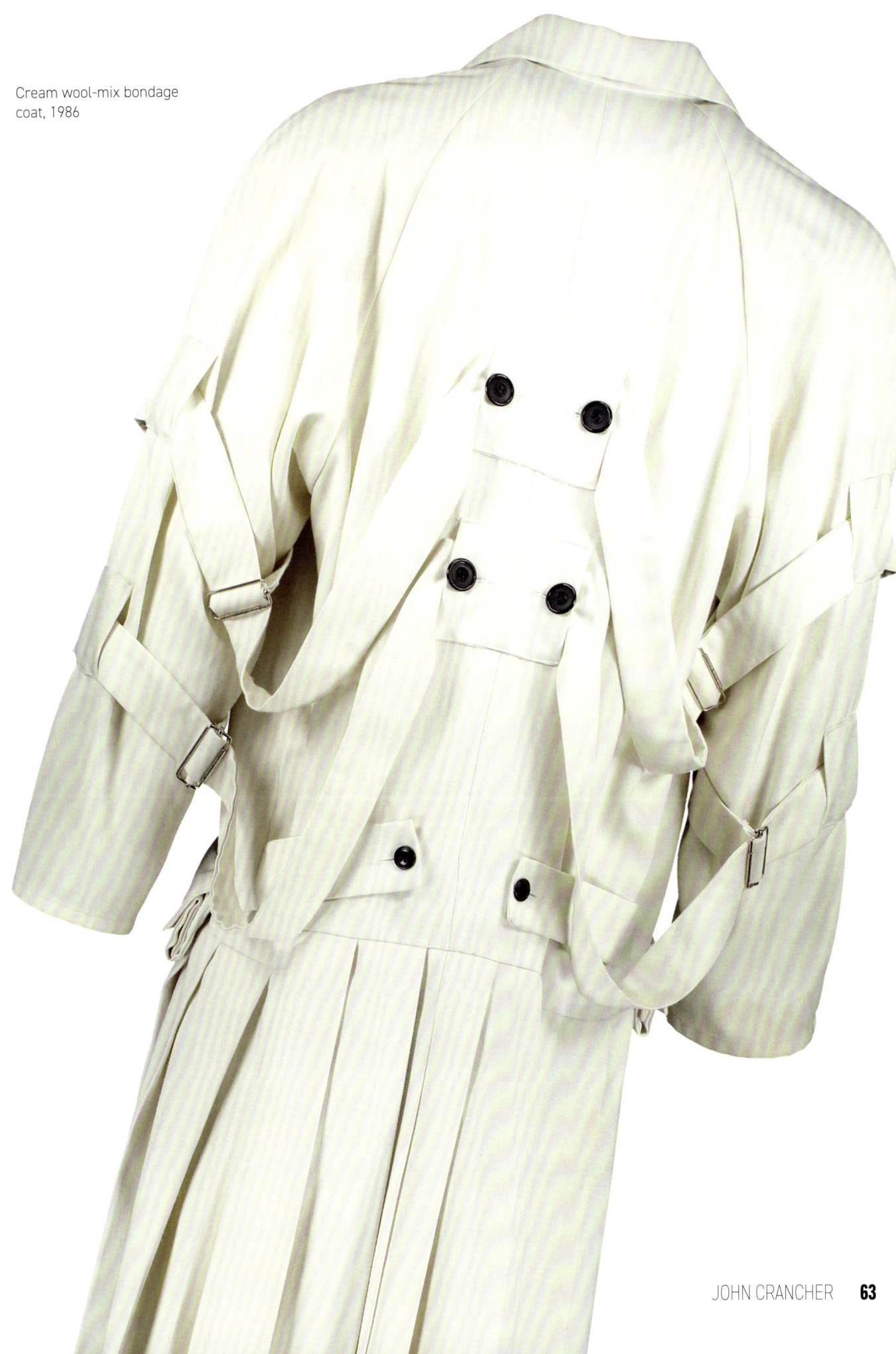

Cream wool-mix bondage coat, 1986

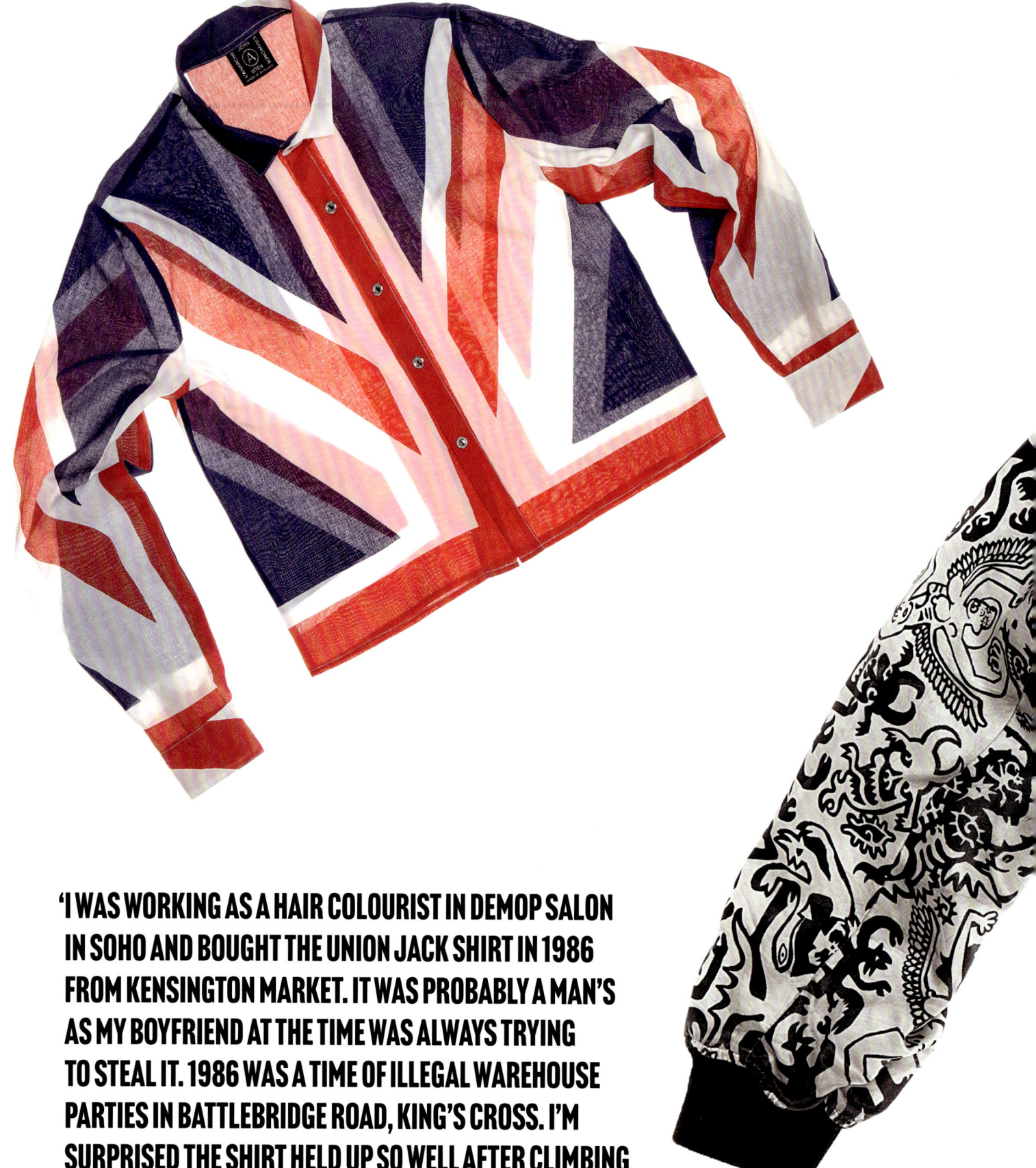

'I WAS WORKING AS A HAIR COLOURIST IN DEMOP SALON IN SOHO AND BOUGHT THE UNION JACK SHIRT IN 1986 FROM KENSINGTON MARKET. IT WAS PROBABLY A MAN'S AS MY BOYFRIEND AT THE TIME WAS ALWAYS TRYING TO STEAL IT. 1986 WAS A TIME OF ILLEGAL WAREHOUSE PARTIES IN BATTLEBRIDGE ROAD, KING'S CROSS. I'M SURPRISED THE SHIRT HELD UP SO WELL AFTER CLIMBING IN AND OUT OF DISUSED WAREHOUSE WINDOWS.'

Steph Avery, artist and educator

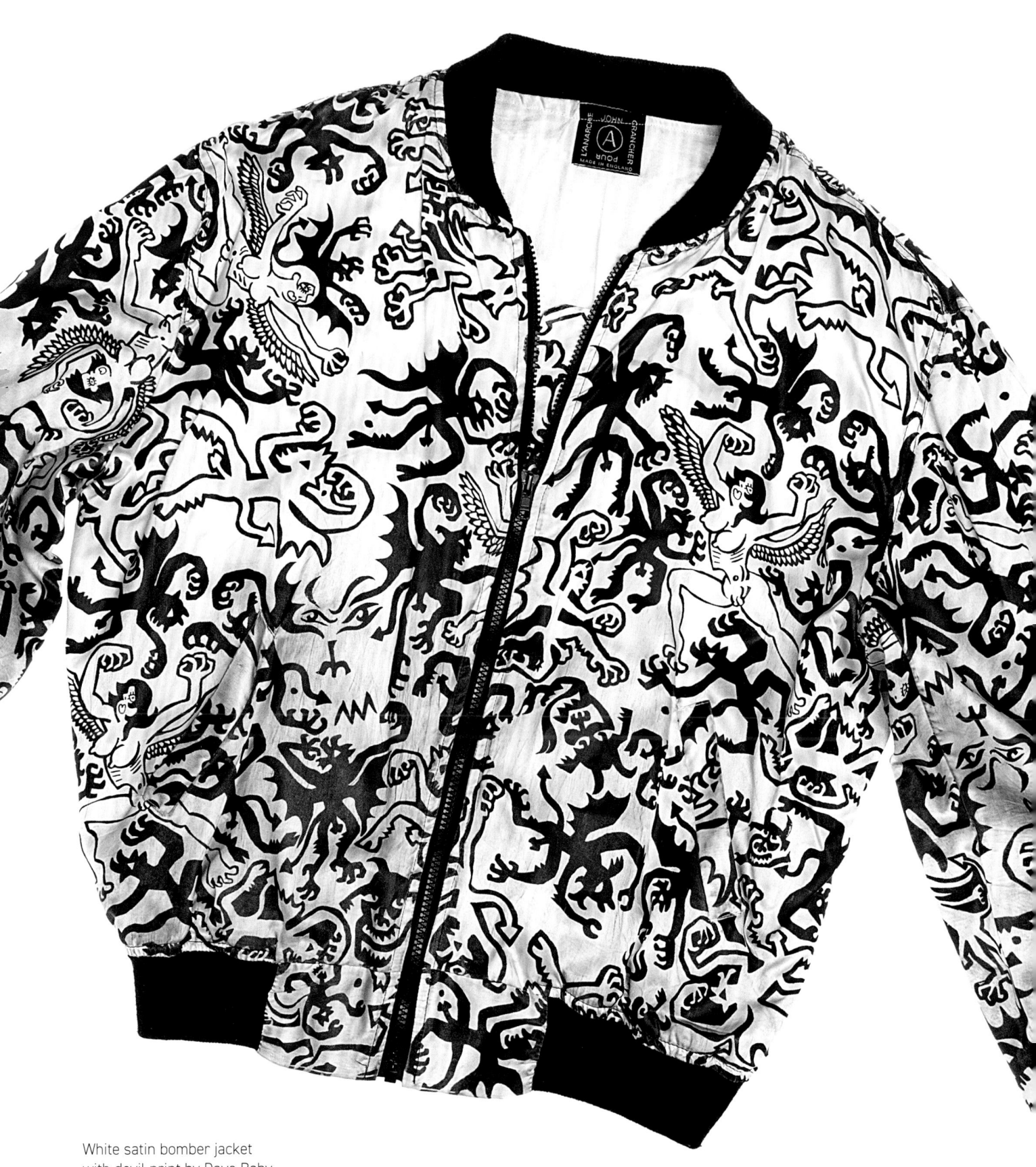

White satin bomber jacket with devil print by Dave Baby, 1986, worn by DJ Mark Moore

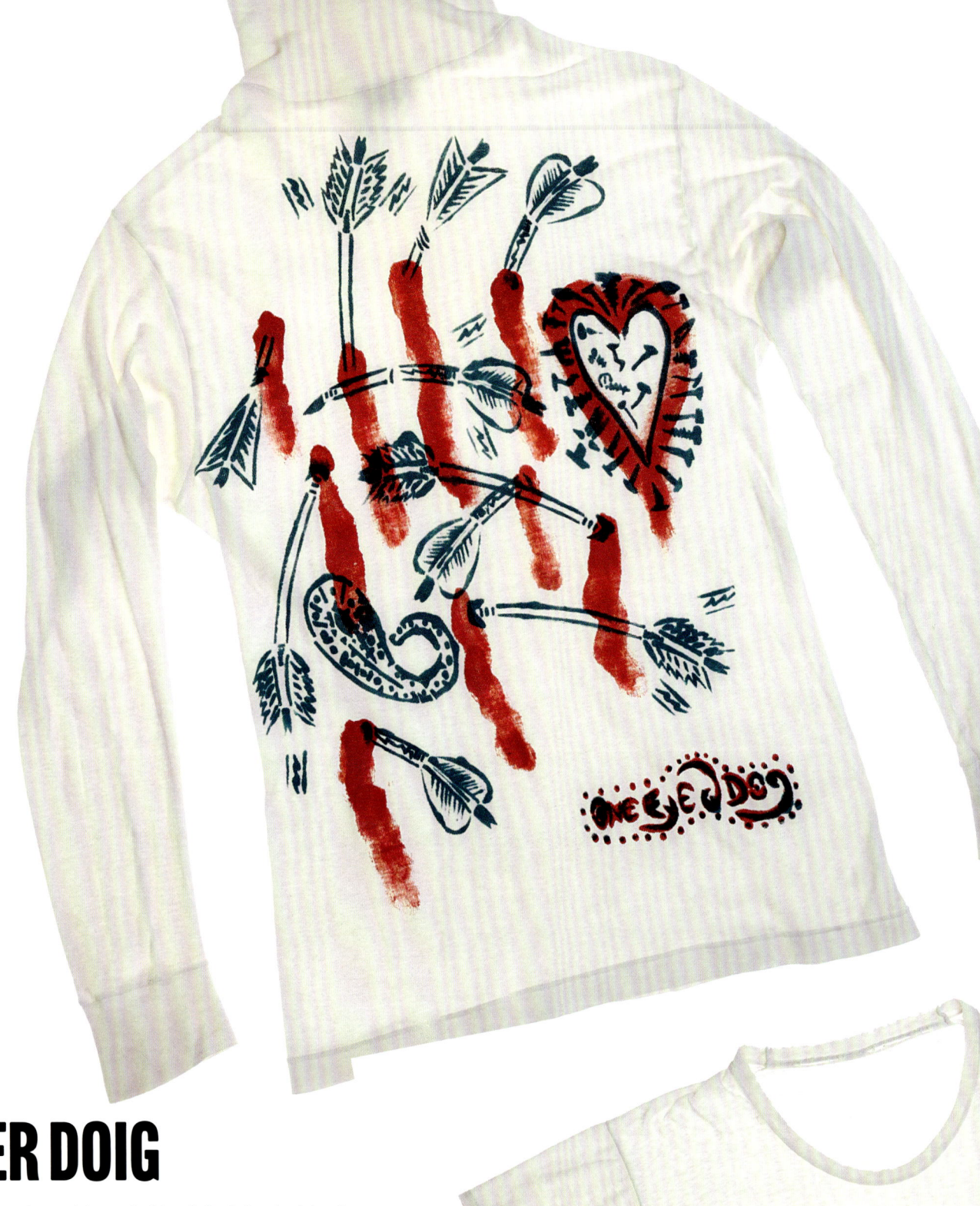

PETER DOIG

Peter Doig graduated from St Martin's School of Art in 1983 having studied alongside John Galliano, Stephen Jones and Stephen Linard. After graduating Doig worked part-time as a dresser at the English National Opera.

In 1991 he exhibited at Whitechapel Gallery and his reputation grew throughout the 1990s, culminating in a solo show at Tate Britain in 2002.

Doig's continual success has earned him the accolade as one of the UK's greatest living painters.

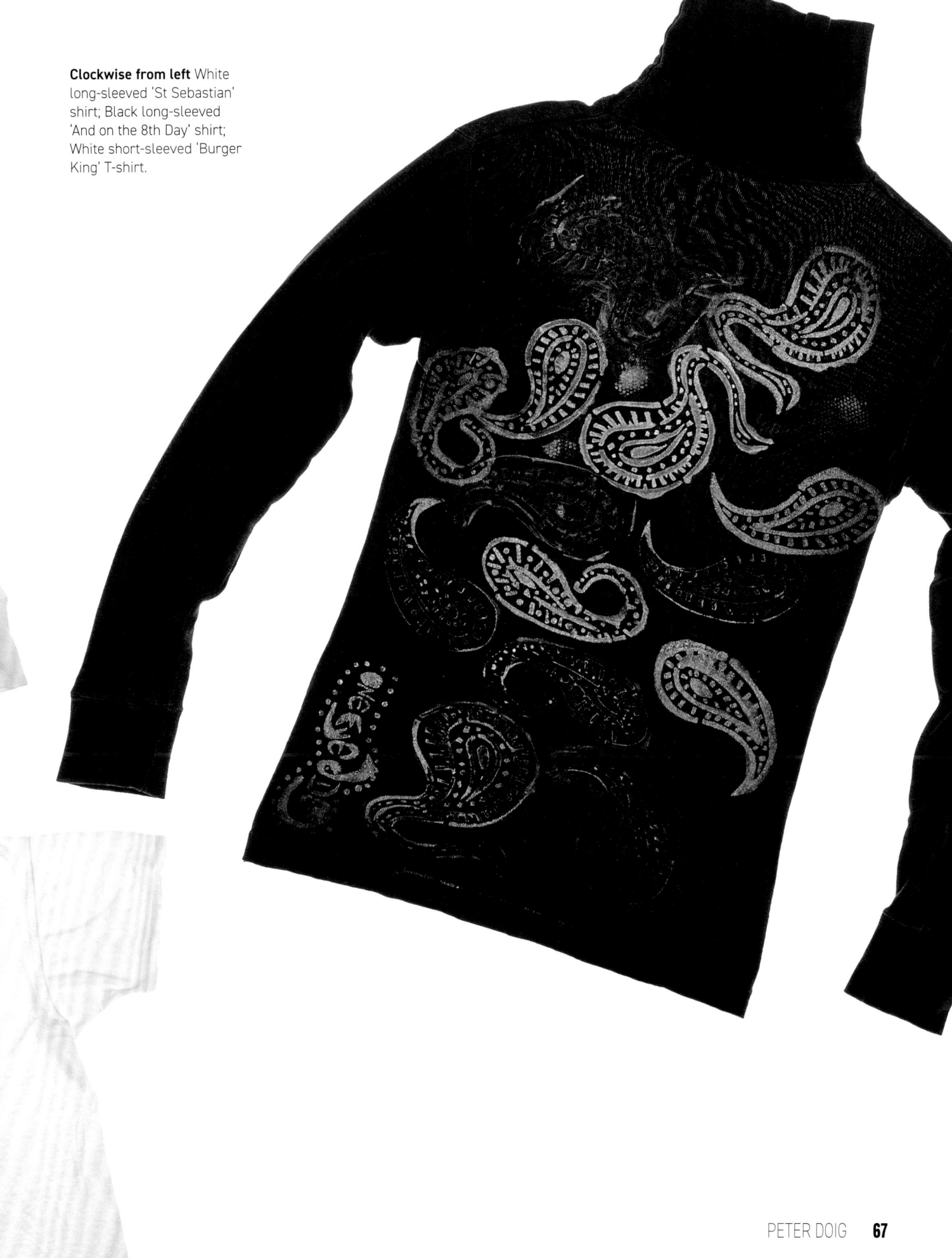

Clockwise from left White long-sleeved 'St Sebastian' shirt; Black long-sleeved 'And on the 8th Day' shirt; White short-sleeved 'Burger King' T-shirt.

PETER DOIG

IN CONVERSATION WITH
PETER DOIG

One of the UK's most renowned and successful living artists.

Interview by Martin Green

MG: **You were at St Martin's School of Art with some extraordinary talents. What was the experience like and how much cross-creativity was there between the design and art courses?**

PD: There was certainly a lot of mixing between the courses, the painters and the fashion department. There was an attraction between the students in many ways. Of course there was Soho, and that's where all the clubs we all went to were, and that was a connection. That all came back into the studios. John Galliano, who was studying fashion, was very close friends with artist David Harrison, who was almost like a mentor to him, being a little bit older and a bit more experienced. So John Galliano was often in the painting studios, as was Elmaz Hüseyin, who was often being painted. That's how work was inspired. There was also the Alternative Fashion Show, where anyone in the college could put in a collection. David Harrison always made a collection, which was often quite sensational. Wilma Johnson, a painter involved with the Neo Naturists, did a collection as well. The gel was social interest in clothes, going out, music and being very excited about being in London.

MG: **When were you first aware of Leigh Bowery and his scene?**

PD: Just after I left St Martin's in July 1983. I remember going to a party in a warehouse in Wapping. Elmaz and Sue Came shared a studio, and we went to an opening party and, all of a sudden, this gang arrived wearing clothes made out of carpets, and they were all on acid. They looked extraordinary. The next time I saw Leigh he was with Trojan at Circus dressed almost in a T. Rex kind of way, with big hats with stars. This was all pre-Taboo, pre him working with Michael Clark. He definitely stood out in an arena where a lot of people stood out.

MG: **What was your experience of Taboo and did you have any favourite clubs?**

PD: There were many favourites. There wasn't a night of the week where there wasn't a club on or a bar or a pub you could go to. The scene was very open and welcoming, if you knew the right people, and being at St Martin's was a ticket for entry. Right behind St Martin's was Le Beat Route, Steve Mahoney and Ollie O'Donnell's club, where everyone would go to after college. We would go to The Cambridge, and upstairs was a jukebox where people would gather, not just from St Martin's but those from other fashion colleges like Middlesex. Chris Sullivan opened The Wag Club and prior to that there was 21 Club on Oxford Street. I just missed Blitz by the time I moved to London. Of course, when Taboo opened it was one of those places where you did not want to miss a night.

> 'I remember my very first day at St Martin's. I walked into the canteen and there was Stephen Linard dressed in full Culloden shock with a white face and a kilt. He looked like he'd been scraped off the battlefield.'

MG: **That period saw the merging of fashion and art. How did your T-shirt designs come about and what was the inspiration?**

PD: I always made T-shirts. When I was at St Martin's I used a lot of stencilling in my paintings, and so, often I would use the same stencils on a T-shirt and just give them to friends. My girlfriend was working for BodyMap right from the beginning and they were making all their prints, and Hilde Smith was a print designer – I would make T-shirts to give to them. I probably only made about 30 in total and just gave them away. At one point I actually made a label and sold a few, but they were really just for friends.

MG: **How did a St Martin's education combined with the 1980s club, fashion and art scene affect your creative practice?**

PD: I think a lot of creative individuals are very determined. A case in point was Trojan: I'm astonished at the output considering he seemed to live a life going out and spending all night taking all sorts of this and that. He was only 21 when he died, but he still managed to produce a large body of work of great quality, humour and pathos. A lot of people were similarly productive and were driven because there wasn't much else. No one was going to hand anything to you on a plate. I think back to the early decades of working on my own throughout that whole time when I was by no means a successful artist and no one had ever seen my work. They knew I was a painter and they used to call me Peter the Painter, but I wasn't a successful painter at all. Everyone had their day jobs. Everyone scuttled off in the mornings to do whatever they did. I don't think anyone expected success in the way that they do now. It was more the fact that we were doing things, and it was a given that you had something to do. I felt sorry for those who didn't, and they're the ones that I think fell by the wayside, Trojan obviously the exception.

I keep thinking about people from those days. There was a guy at St Martin's called Duggie who was an unlikely fashion student. He came from some sort of West London gangster family somehow connected to the Christine Keeler world. When he was at St Martin's he tried to rob a bank and was arrested for armed robbery. Duggie disappeared for a year and when he came back he made this collection based on the female form of Venus of Willendorf and the materiality of Victorian diving helmets.

There were also the better-known students like Stephen Linard. I remember my very first day at St Martin's – I was quite nervous. I'd done the foundation and gone to clubs, so I knew the scene from the periphery, but on my first day, I walked into the canteen and there was Stephen Linard dressed in full Culloden shock with a white face and a kilt. He looked like he'd been scraped off the battlefield, a Culloden dandy.

Then there was Darla Jane Gilroy, Fiona Dealey and Richard Ostell at 10 a.m. dressed up like they had just stepped out of the Blitz and I thought: 'Oh my god! This is the canteen!' It was an exciting place and at that point I would imagine there were only 100 people in the world who would dress that way. It hadn't gone global yet; this was 1980 and that look was very much part of the London scene.

GALLAGHER WALLS

David Walls and George Gallagher were childhood friends from South London and part of the Taboo family. Walls was a former flatmate of Bowery and Trojan and one of the original 'Three Kings' who caused a commotion in clubland, while Gallagher studied at Ravensbourne College of Art and modelled for all of Bowery's UK fashion collections.

Between 1984 and 1988 the duo designed and made clothes mixing dandy and utility, a style that became popular among the underground fashion set who commissioned pieces. They also sold capsule collections at Kensington Market, Soho fashion shop Site, Michael and Gerlinde Costiff's shop World and in New York and Tokyo.

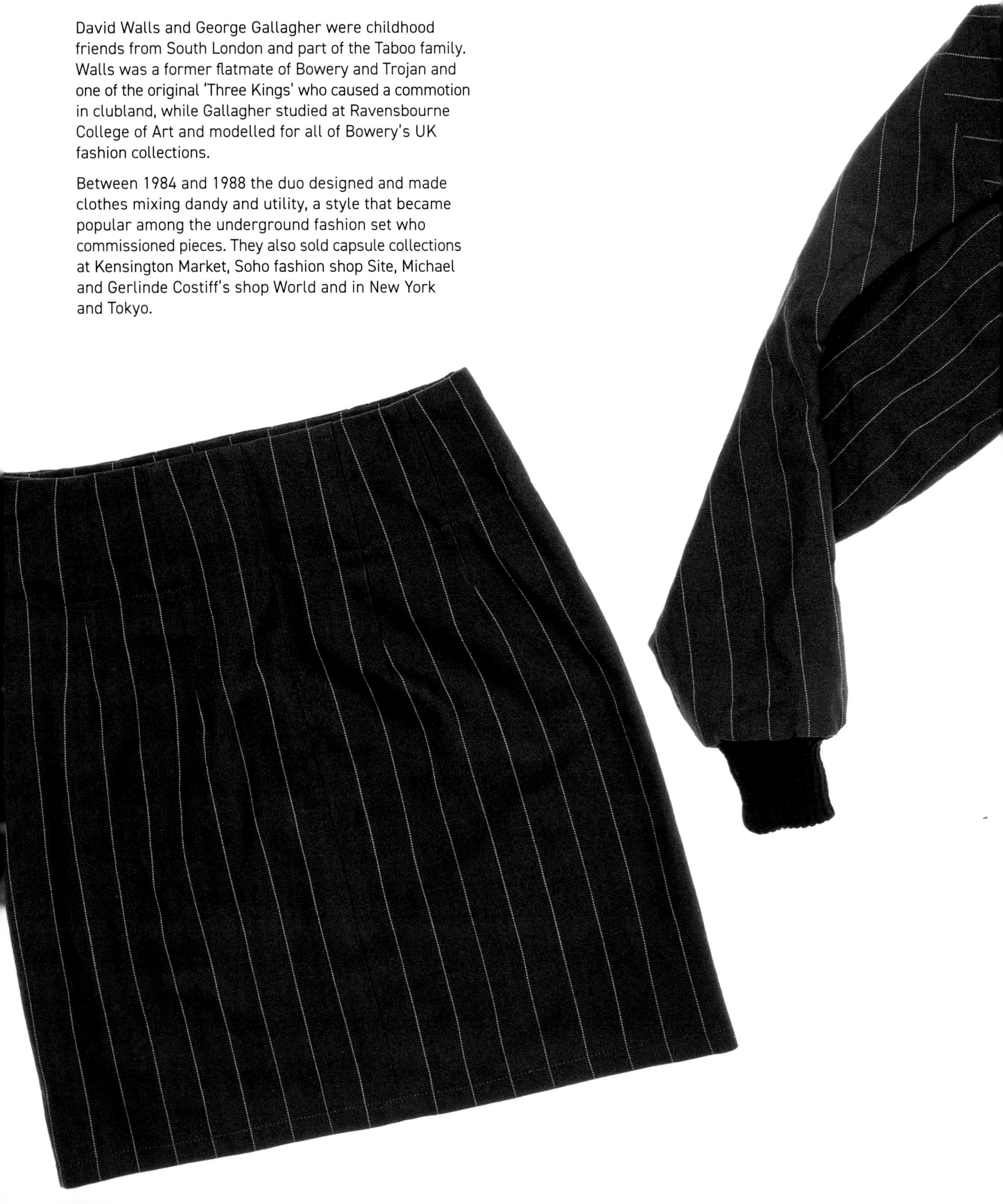

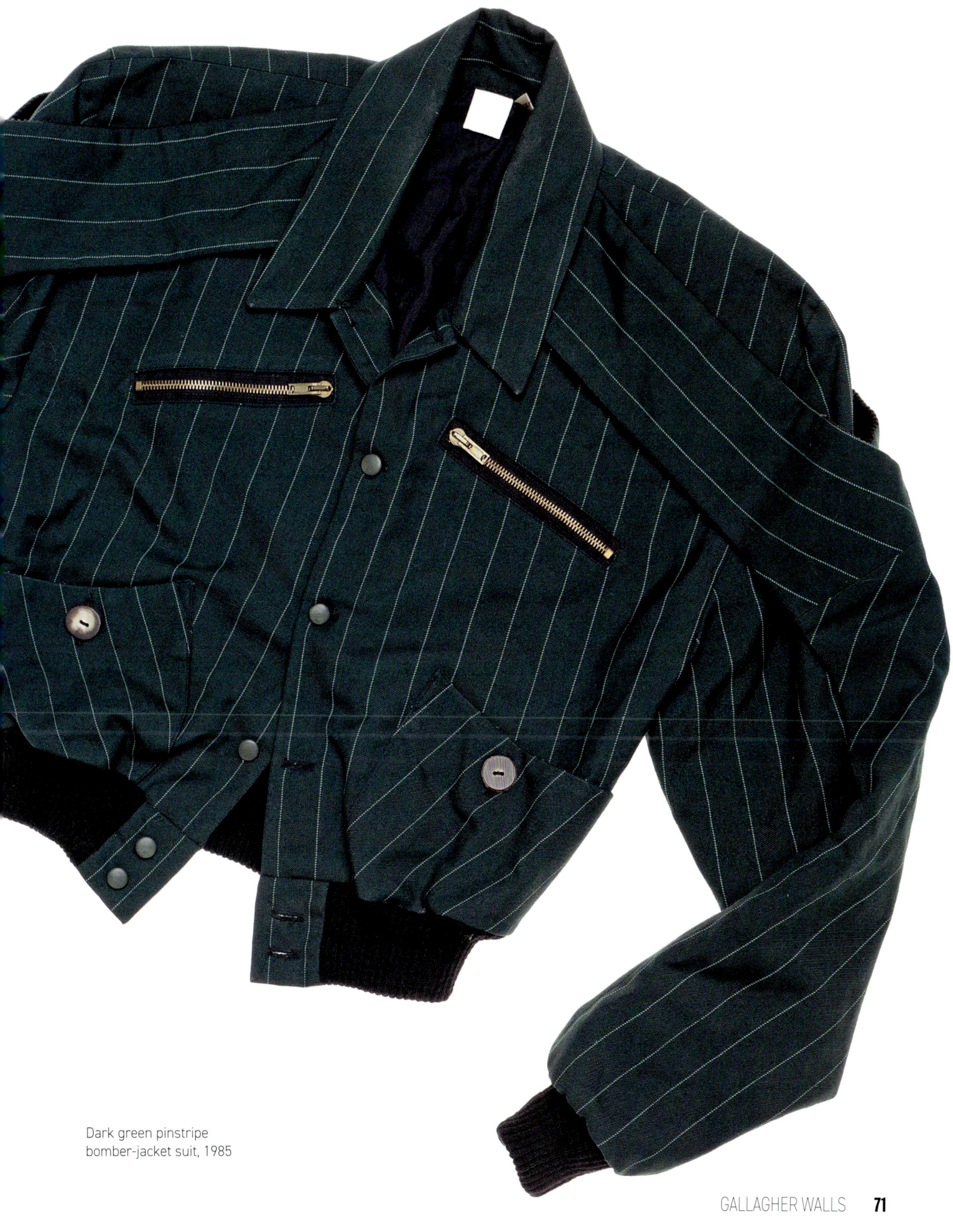

Dark green pinstripe bomber-jacket suit, 1985

JOHN FLETT

John Flett became a part of the high-fashion scene in 1985 when he exhibited at London Fashion Week shortly after graduation from St Martin's School of Art.

He was a highly regarded inspirational designer, and according to *The Guardian*, 'along with his friend John Galliano, Flett pioneered a new type of bias-cutting technique which imbued garments with a special fluidity and grace.' By 1988 his designs were available in 70 stores worldwide.

Flett died of a heart attack in 1991 while working in Florence. He was 27.

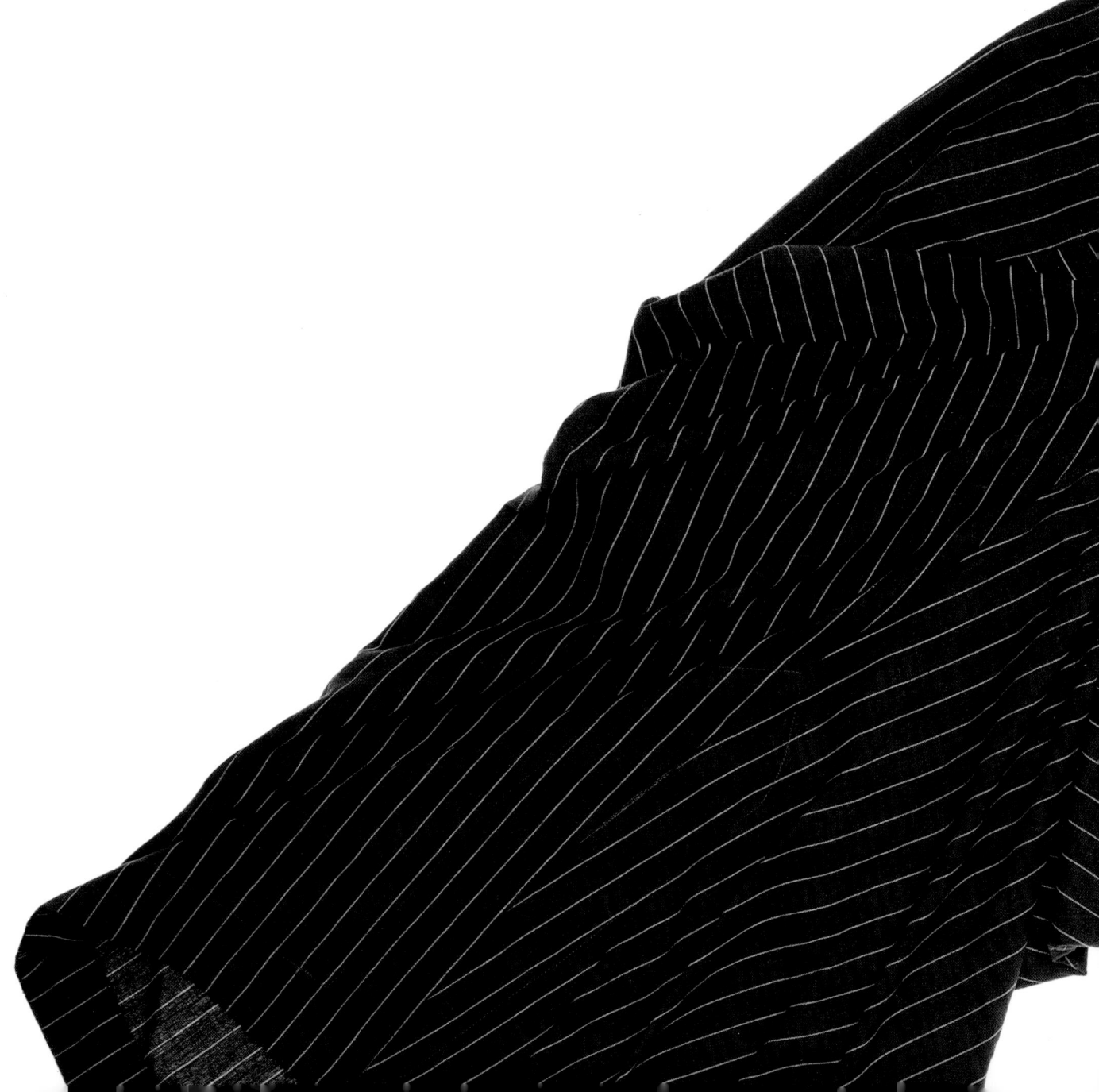

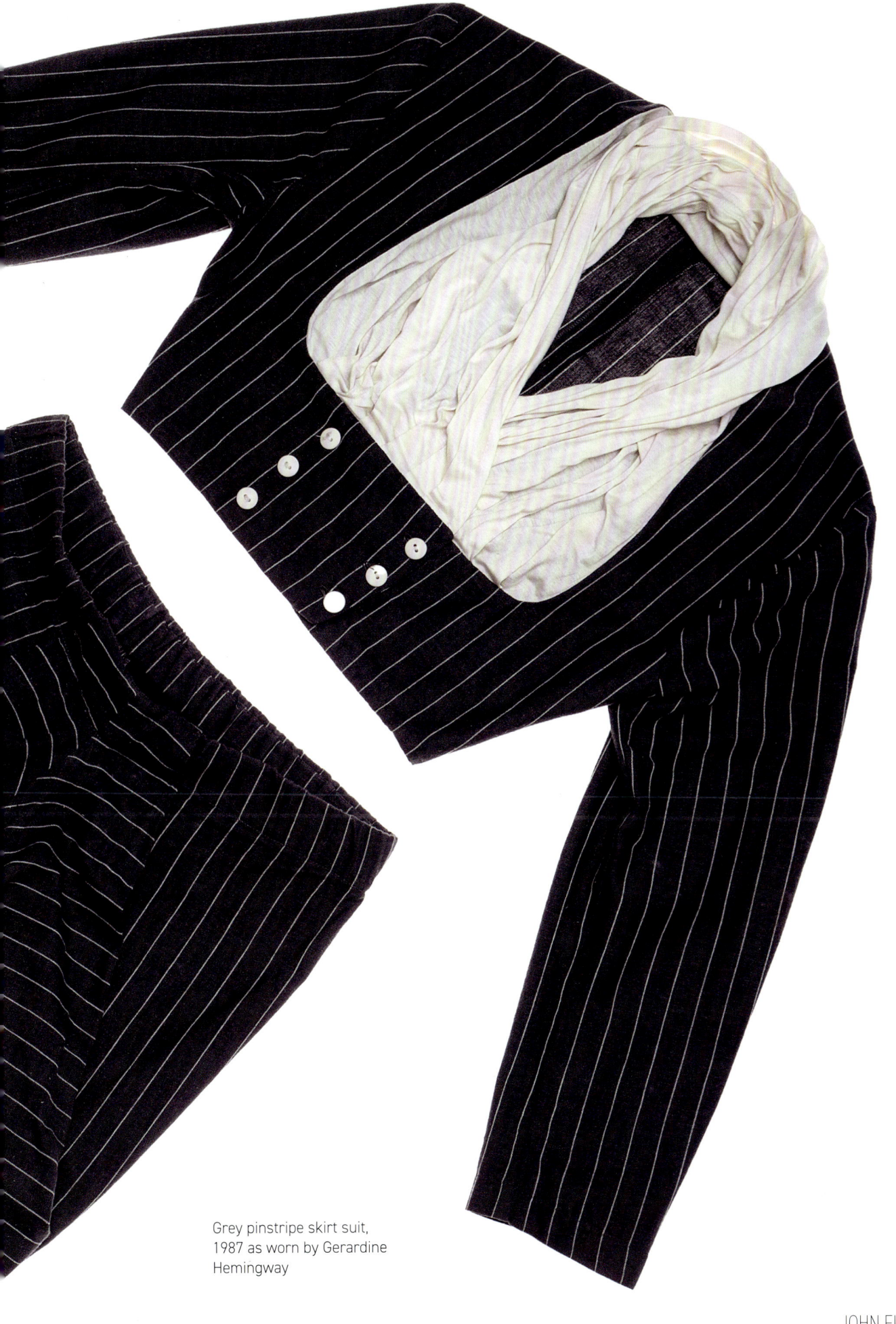

Grey pinstripe skirt suit, 1987 as worn by Gerardine Hemingway

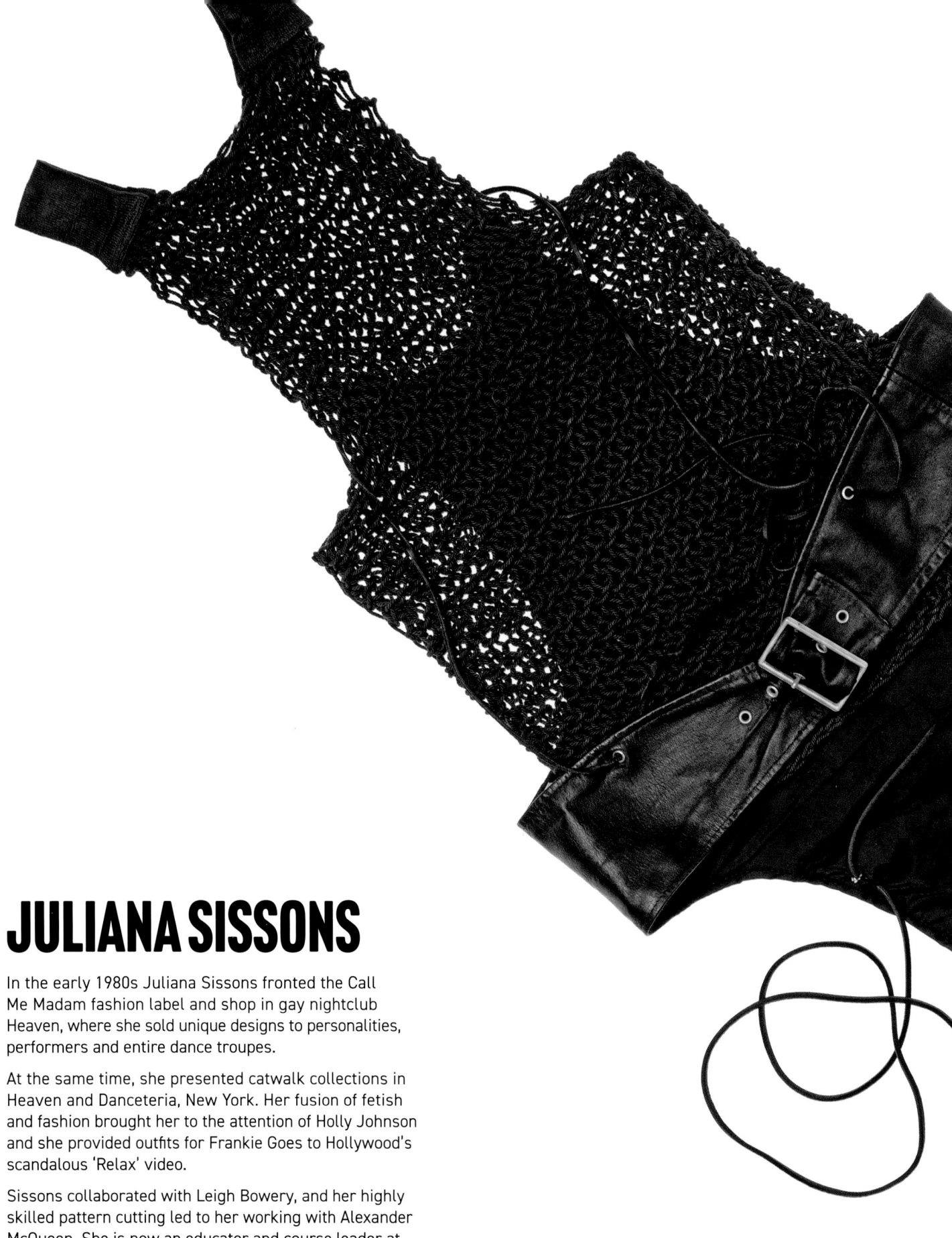

JULIANA SISSONS

In the early 1980s Juliana Sissons fronted the Call Me Madam fashion label and shop in gay nightclub Heaven, where she sold unique designs to personalities, performers and entire dance troupes.

At the same time, she presented catwalk collections in Heaven and Danceteria, New York. Her fusion of fetish and fashion brought her to the attention of Holly Johnson and she provided outfits for Frankie Goes to Hollywood's scandalous 'Relax' video.

Sissons collaborated with Leigh Bowery, and her highly skilled pattern cutting led to her working with Alexander McQueen. She is now an educator and course leader at Nottingham Trent University.

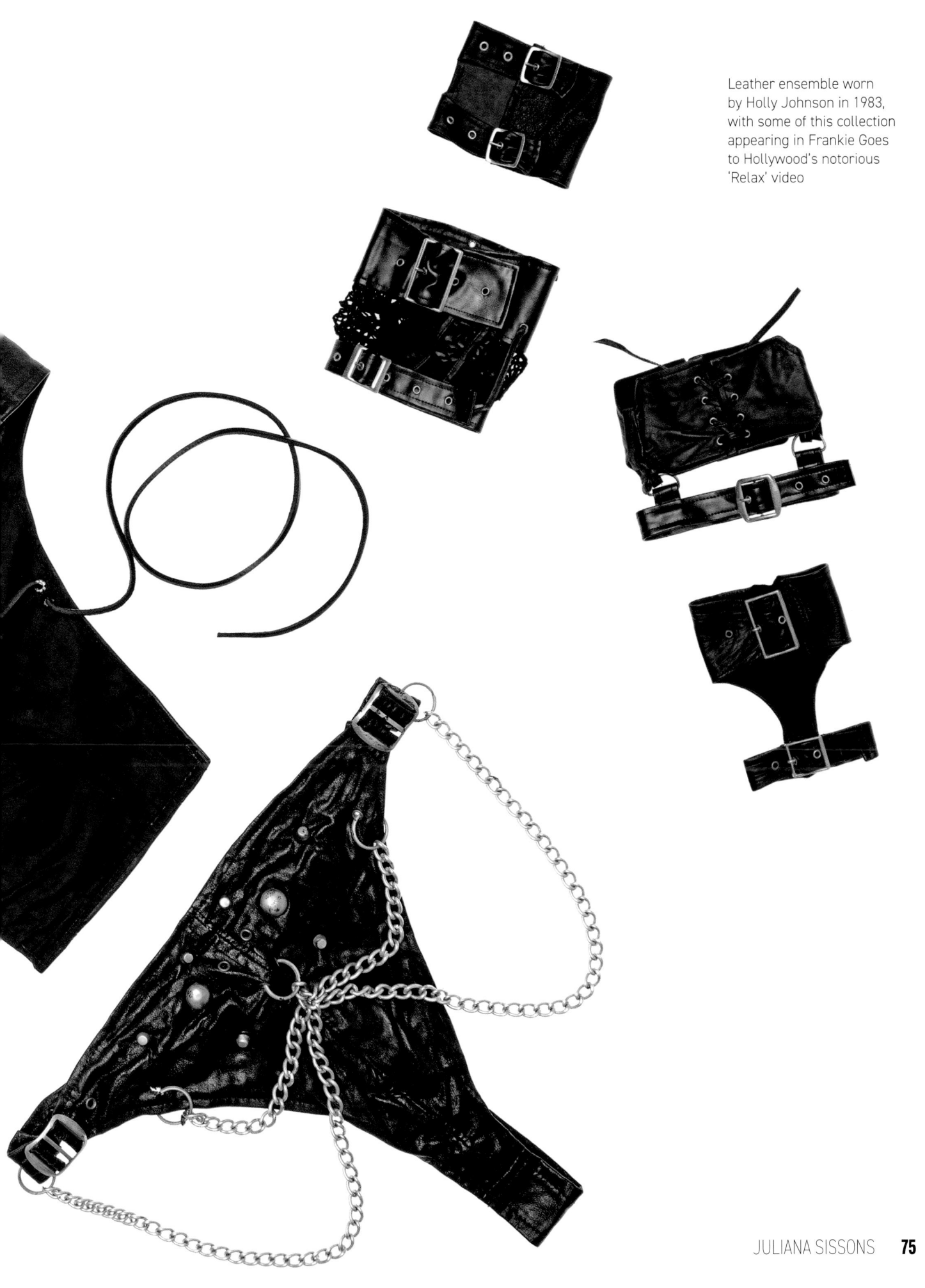

Leather ensemble worn by Holly Johnson in 1983, with some of this collection appearing in Frankie Goes to Hollywood's notorious 'Relax' video

IN CONVERSATION WITH

HOLLY JOHNSON

Singer, songwriter, artist and former frontman of 1980s supergroup Frankie Goes to Hollywood. Pioneer of LGBTQ+ fashion and culture.

Interview by Martin Green and James Lawler

MG: **How did your distinctive look develop and when did you discover the power of appearance?**

HJ: I think I always dressed differently from a very young age, certainly from about 14 when I started hanging around with my mate Peter May. We were fans of T. Rex and David Bowie – they were the benchmarks. Marc Bolan's androgyny and David Bowie's bird of paradise Ziggy Stardust creation were huge influences – it was a very theatrical look and that's what we aspired to as teenagers. We didn't want to look like everyone else, we wanted to look fabulous!

MG: **How did the collaboration between you and Leigh Bowery come about?**

HJ: I knew about Leigh because I'd met him in Heaven and he said to me, 'D'you wanna come for a daaance?' and he explained his look to me. He said, 'I made some of the masks for the first "Relax" video that people wore, up on the balcony.' And that's how I met him.

When I wanted to do the Terrence Higgins Trust benefit show in 1988, the director Baillie Walsh recommended I got Leigh to make me something for the show, so I did and he made me a version of the hairpin jacket. He'd come round to the house in his daytime looks, which were stranger than his clubwear.

MG: **What were your favourite clubs?**

HJ: Heaven was my clubbing heyday. There was Heaven and there was Cha Cha, where Frankie

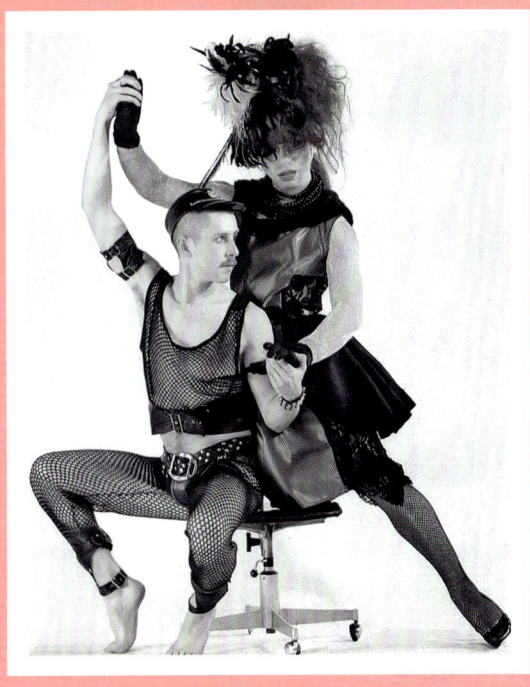

'Marc Bolan's androgyny and David Bowie's bird of paradise Ziggy Stardust creation were huge influences – it was a very theatrical look and that's what we aspired to as teenagers. We didn't want to look like everyone else, we wanted to look fabulous!'

Goes to Hollywood performed in our leather look, leather knickers, shin pads and all kinds! Heaven really symbolised everything that was modern about a clubbing experience; it had the most fabulous lights and was men only on a Saturday night. I'd come down from Liverpool just to go there with friends. Heaven under David Inches and owned by Virgin was an amazing place. It was very cosmopolitan and you felt you were somewhere!

MG: **Tell us about the Juliana Sissons leather pieces?**
HJ: I came across Juliana when I was visiting London and staying with Mark Tyme, a dancer from Hot Gossip. He started dragging-up one day and said: 'We're doing a photo session, d'you wanna come along?' So I went along and ended up modelling leather bits, string vests dyed black and made into leggings and a string vest top, things like that. And that's how I met Juliana.

MG: **How did you end up working with Judy Blame and Dean Bright?**
HJ: Judy Blame did the styling for the 'Atomic City' video, and I told Judy I really liked this Italian Futurist suit I had a picture of in a book. Judy went to Dean and said 'Will you make this for Holly?', and they did, in a slightly different colourway to the original. They also supplied the Bernstock Speirs hat to go with the suit, but it was an Italian Futurist design originally.

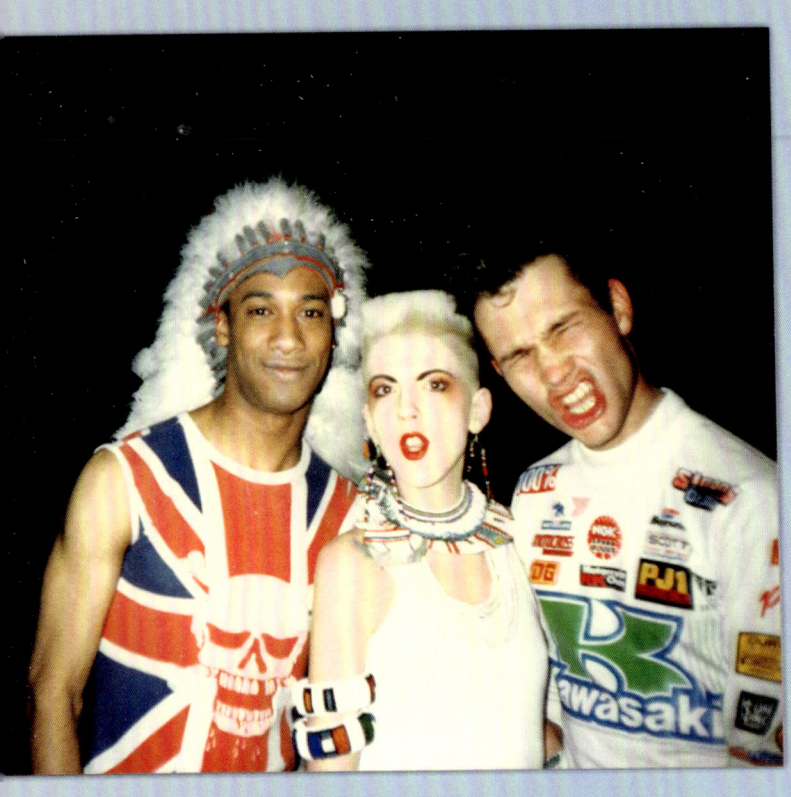
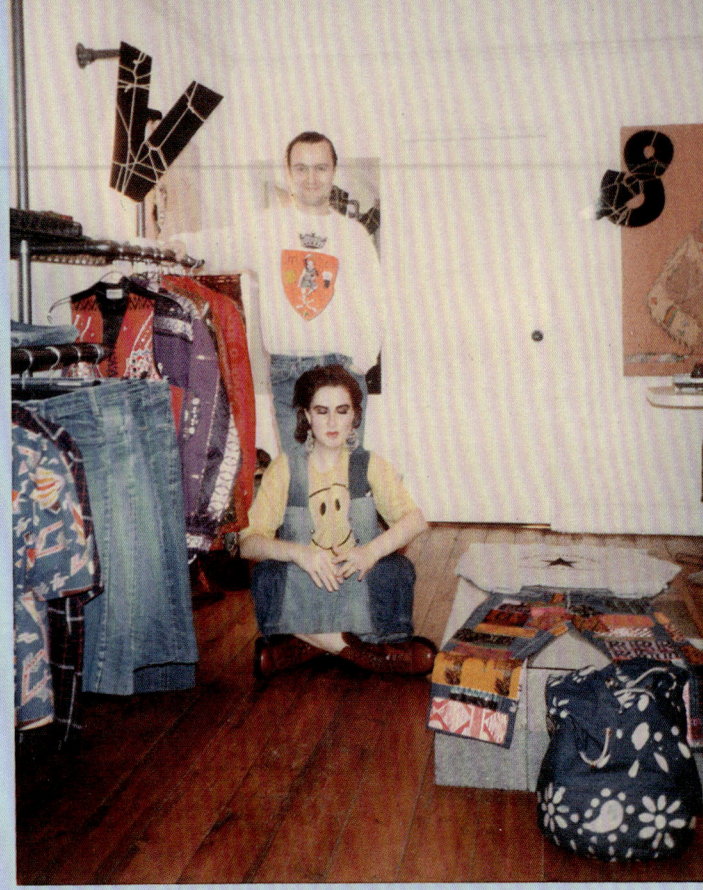

Clockwise from top left Mark Lawrence (left), Scarlett Cannon (centre), John Maybury (right); Vaughan & Franks; Maia Norman wearing Rachel Auburn; Nicola Bateman; Leigh Bowery (right) in Tokyo; Marc Vaultier wearing Leigh Bowery; Mike Nichols (left) and Matthew Hawkins (right).

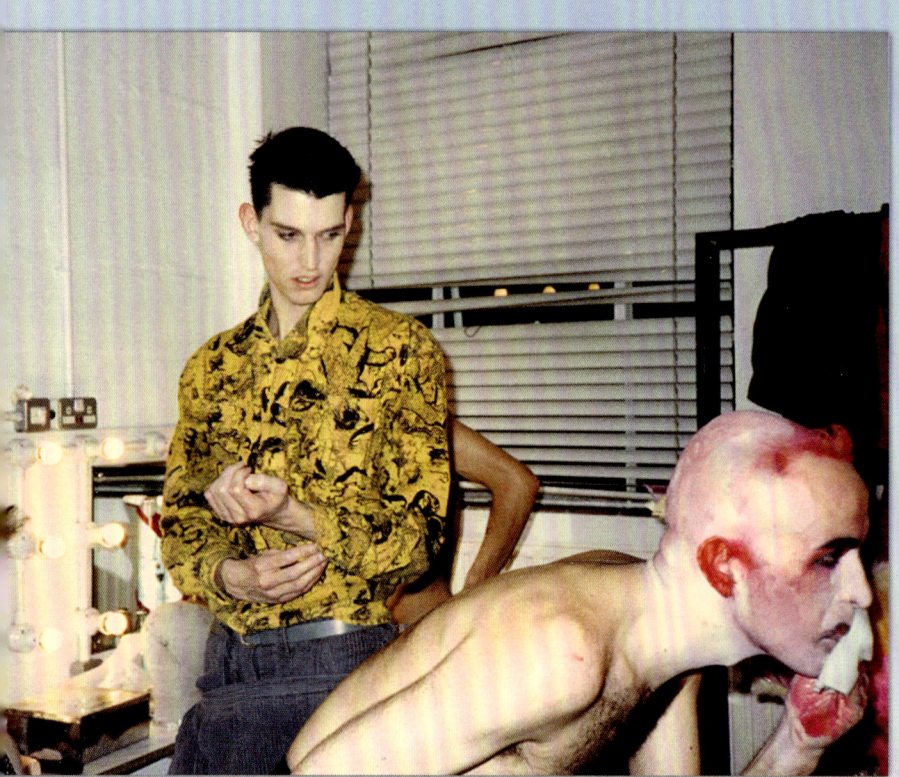
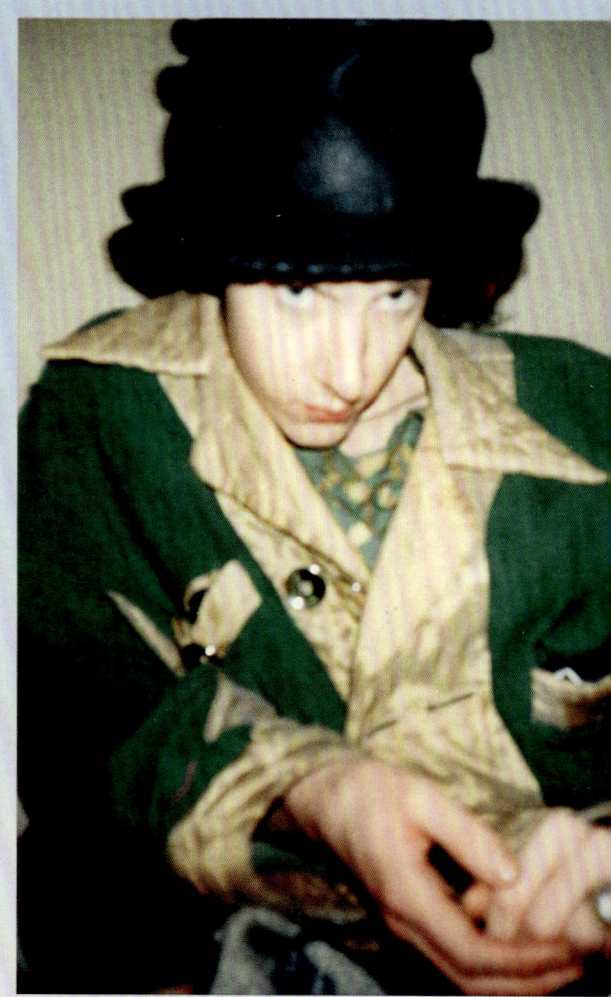

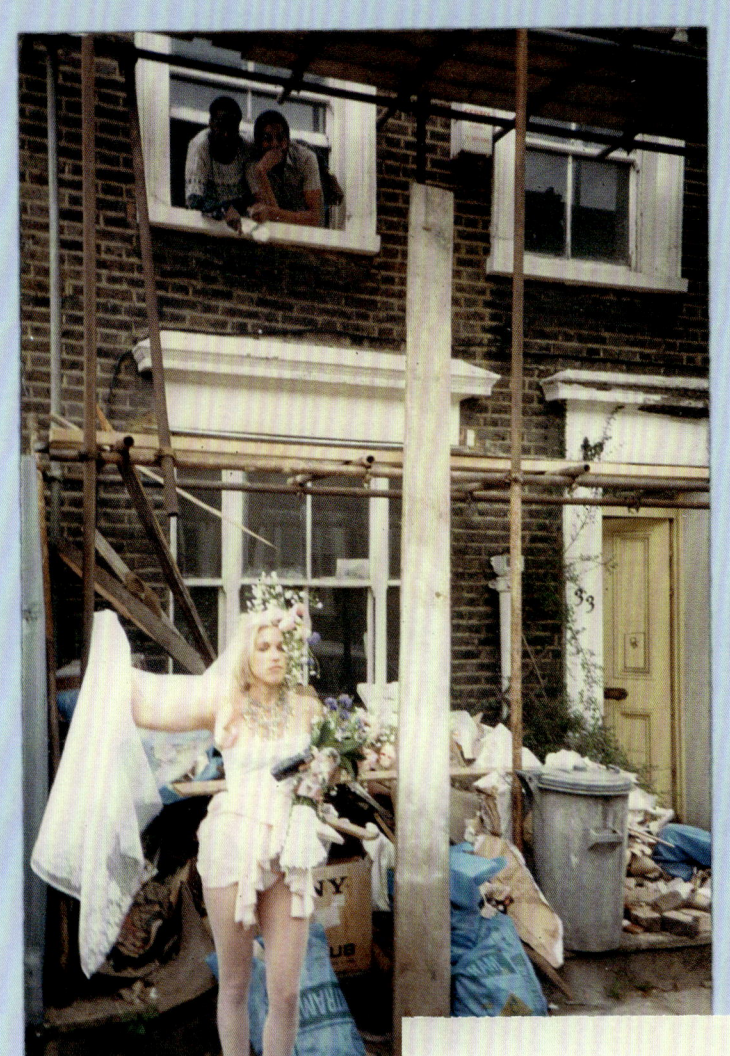
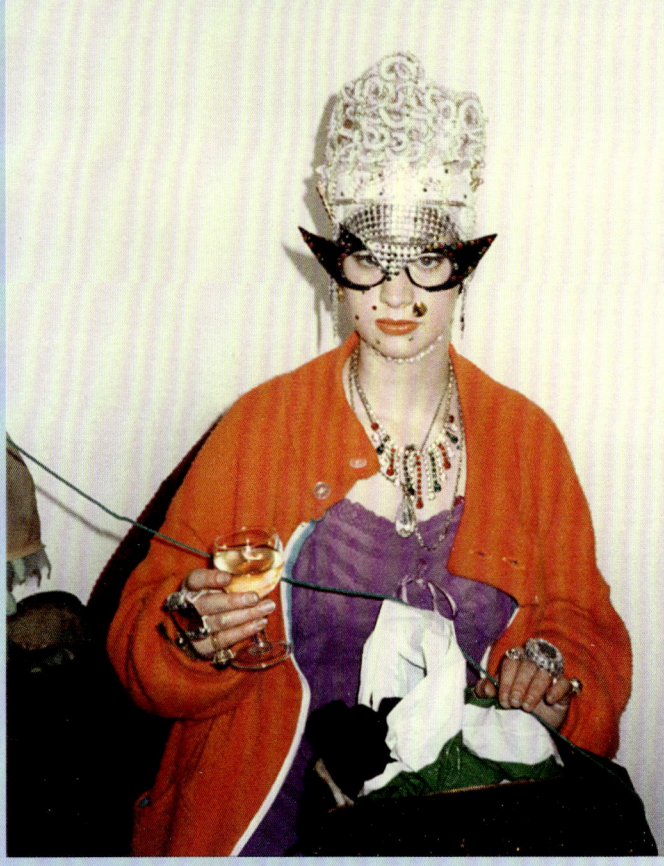
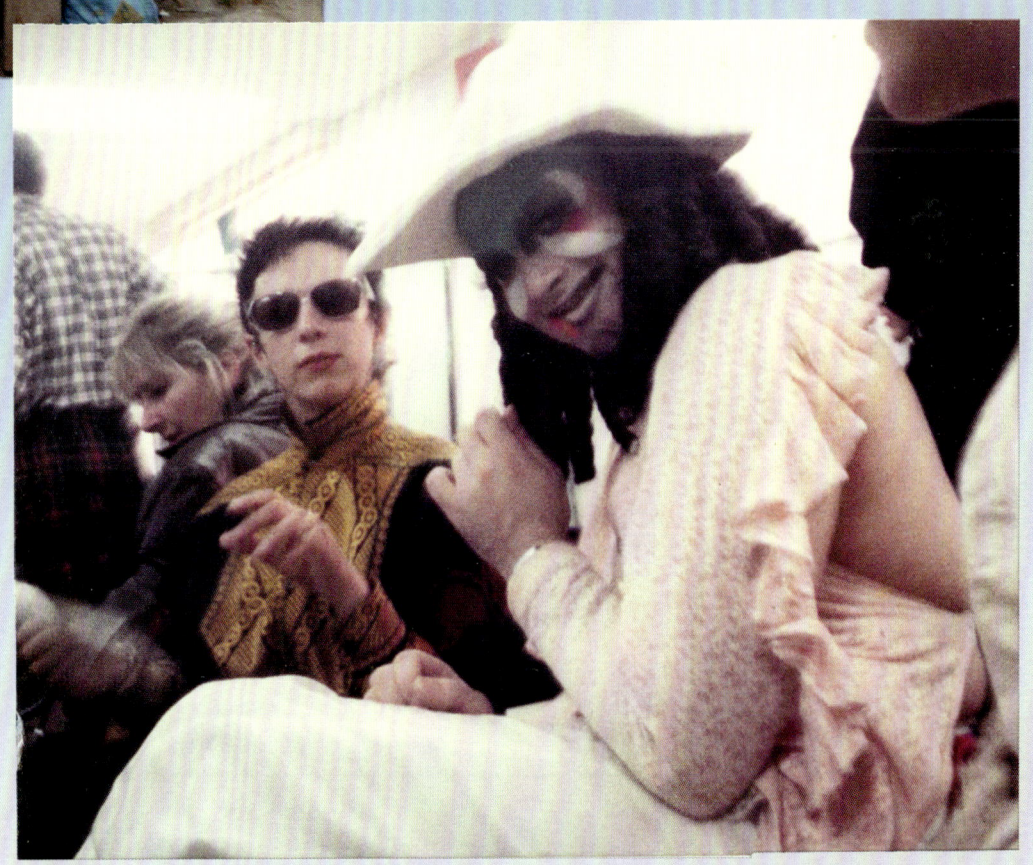

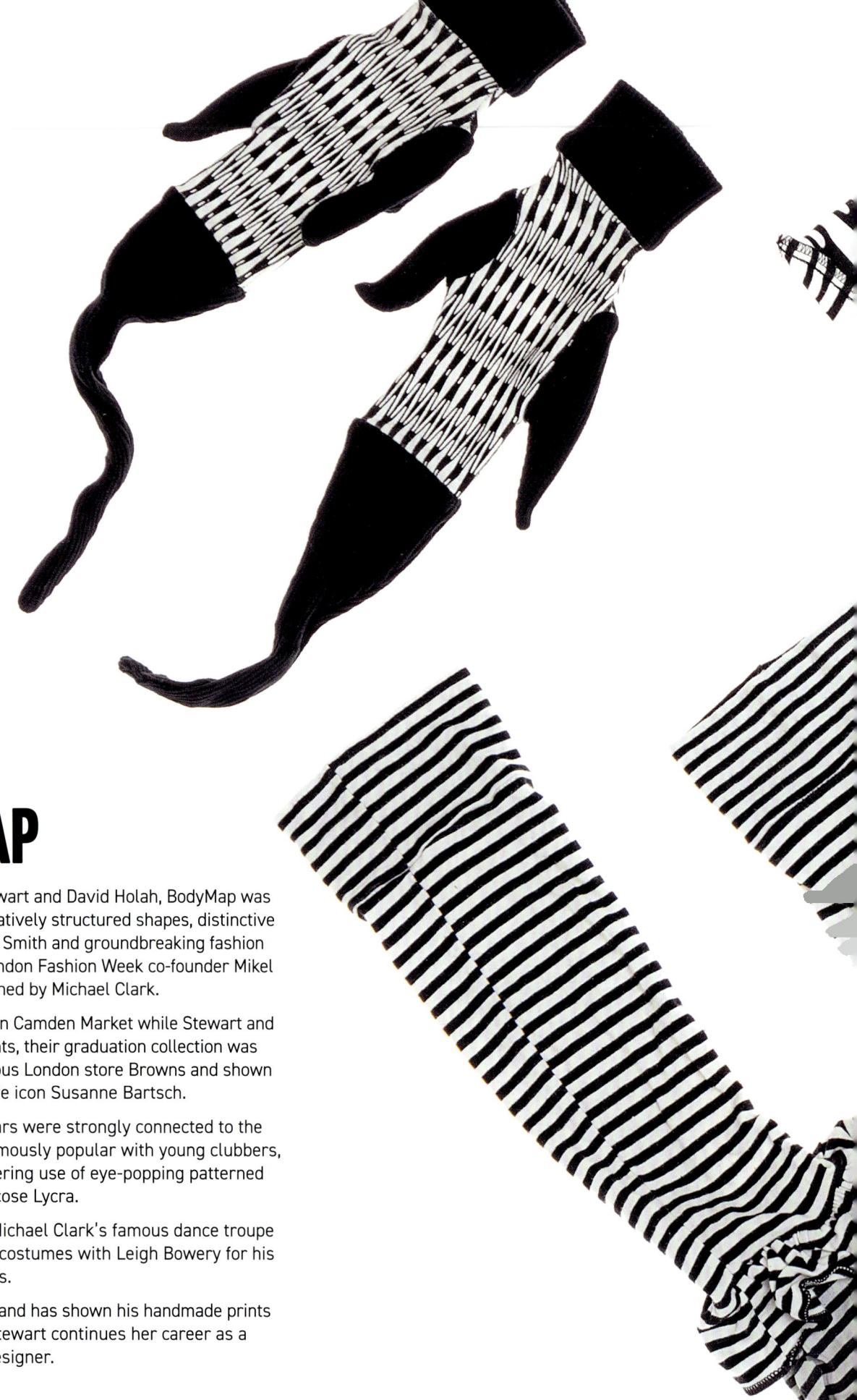

BODYMAP

Founded by Stevie Stewart and David Holah, BodyMap was renowned for its innovatively structured shapes, distinctive graphic prints by Hilde Smith and groundbreaking fashion shows produced by London Fashion Week co-founder Mikel Rosen and choreographed by Michael Clark.

Launched from a stall in Camden Market while Stewart and Holah were still students, their graduation collection was bought by the prestigious London store Browns and shown in New York by nightlife icon Susanne Bartsch.

The instant fashion stars were strongly connected to the Taboo scene and enormously popular with young clubbers, who loved their pioneering use of eye-popping patterned stretch jersey and viscose Lycra.

In 1987 Holah joined Michael Clark's famous dance troupe and BodyMap created costumes with Leigh Bowery for his groundbreaking ballets.

Holah now creates art and has shown his handmade prints in many exhibitions. Stewart continues her career as a successful costume designer.

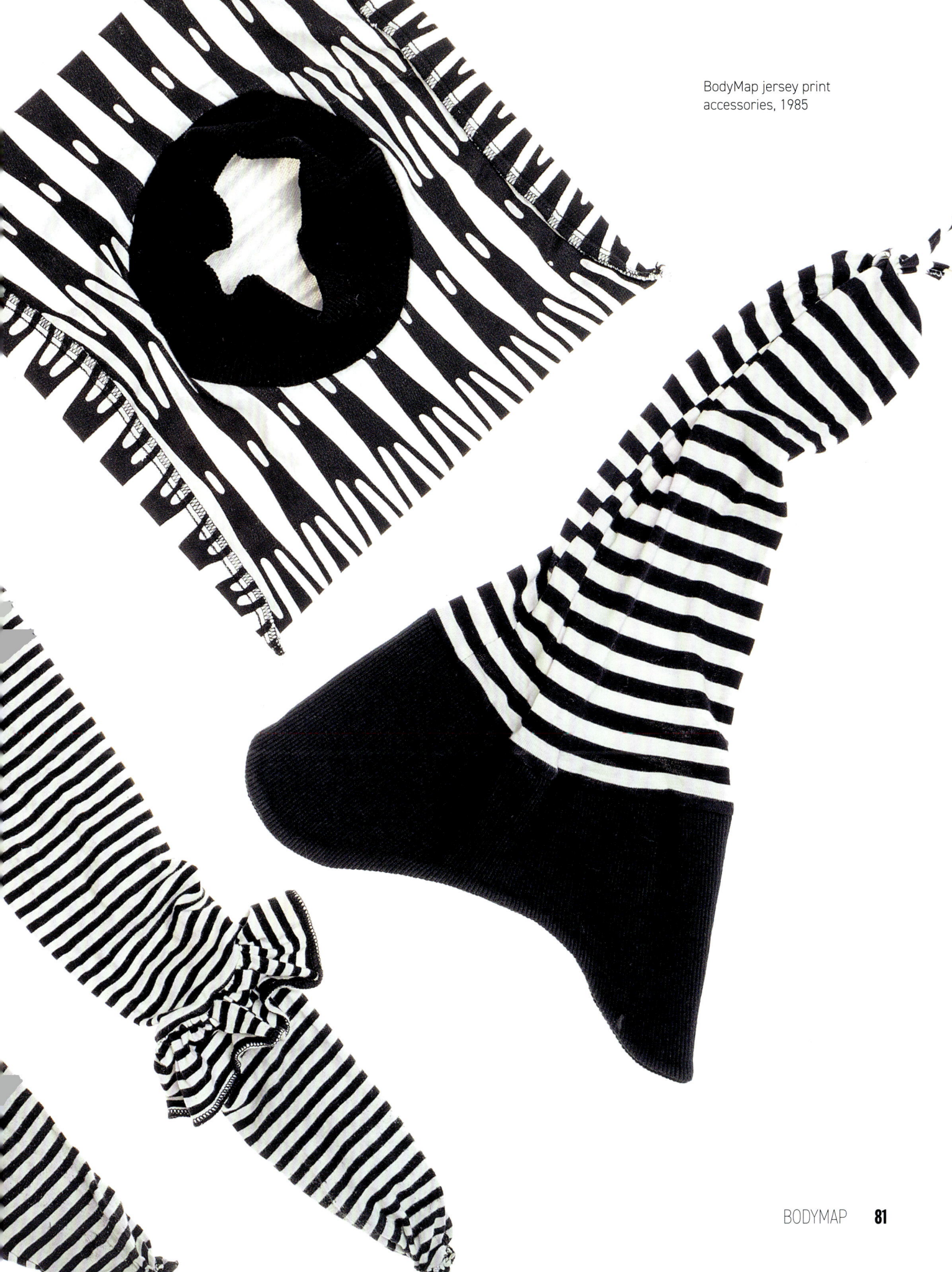

BodyMap jersey print accessories, 1985

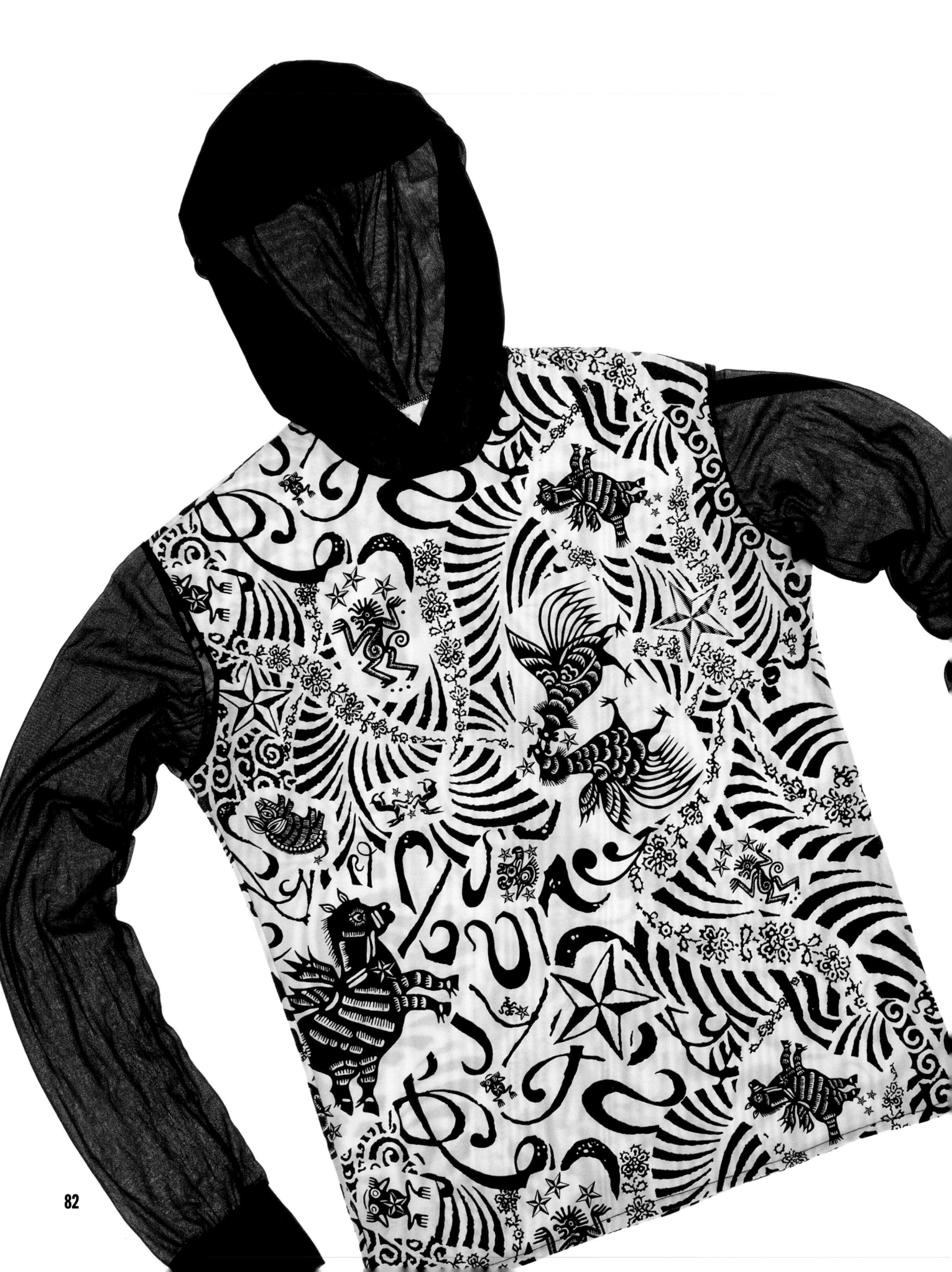

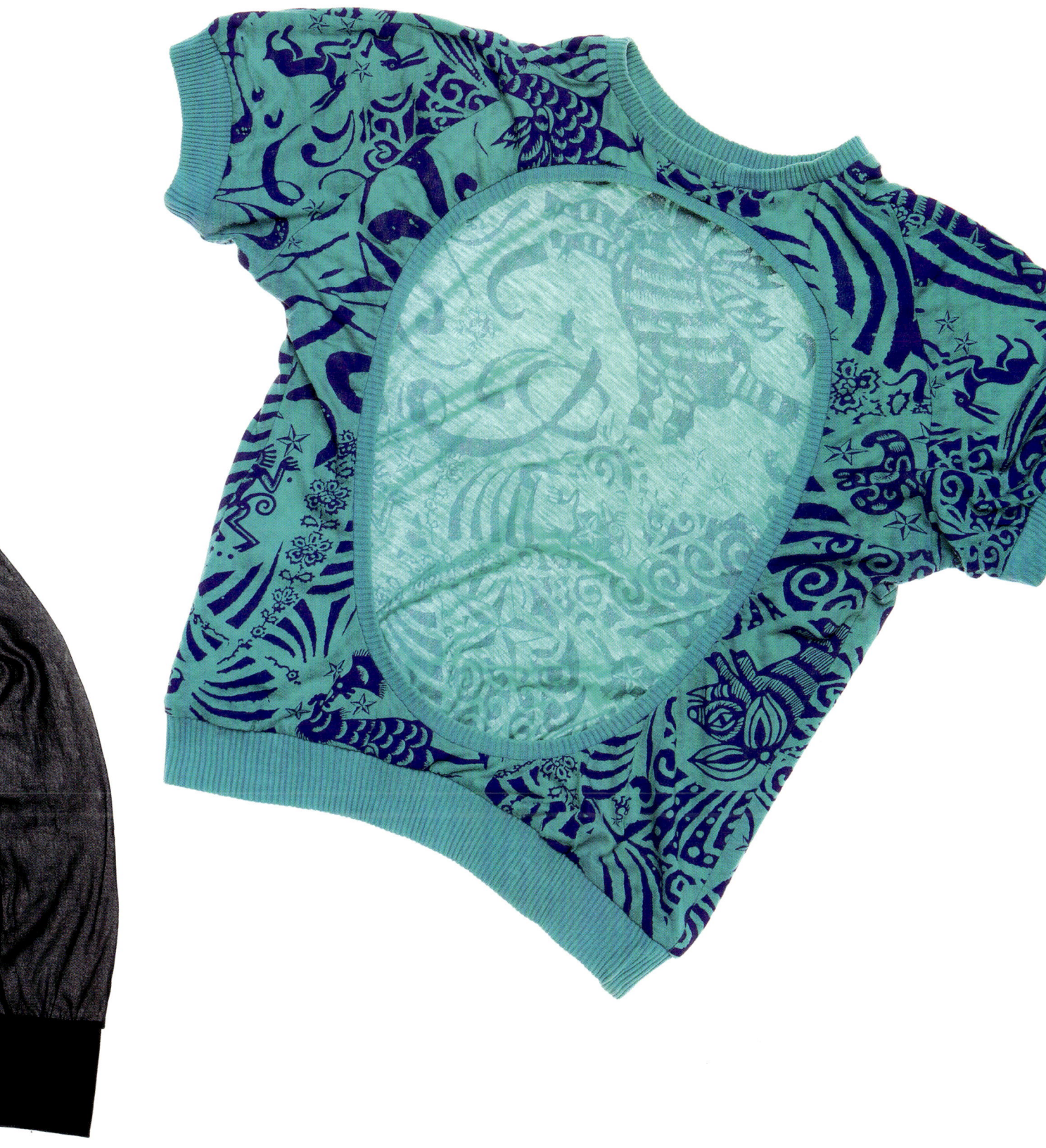

Left to right Black and white hooded sweatshirt, 1985; Turquoise open-back stretch-jersey top, 1985

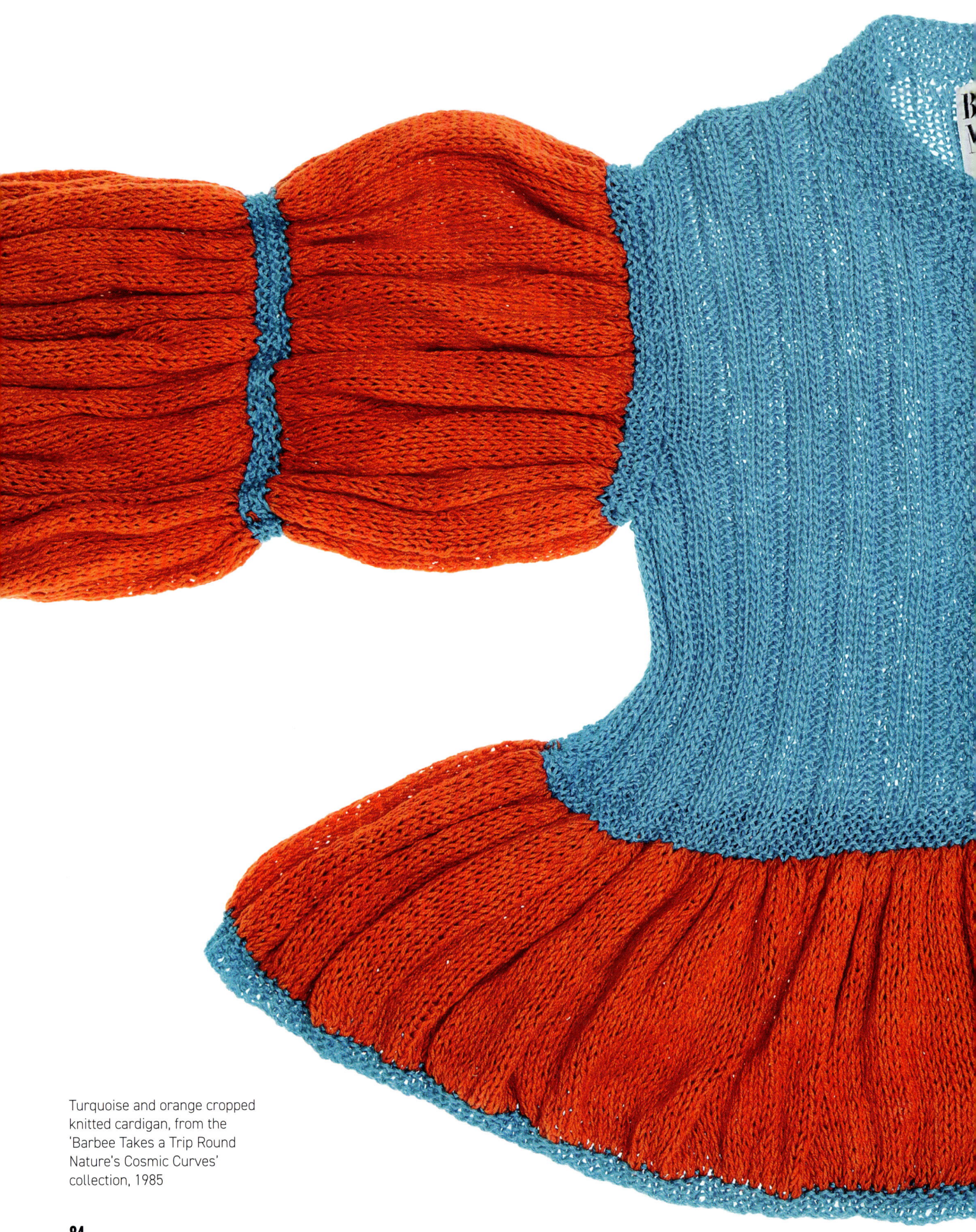

Turquoise and orange cropped knitted cardigan, from the 'Barbee Takes a Trip Round Nature's Cosmic Curves' collection, 1985

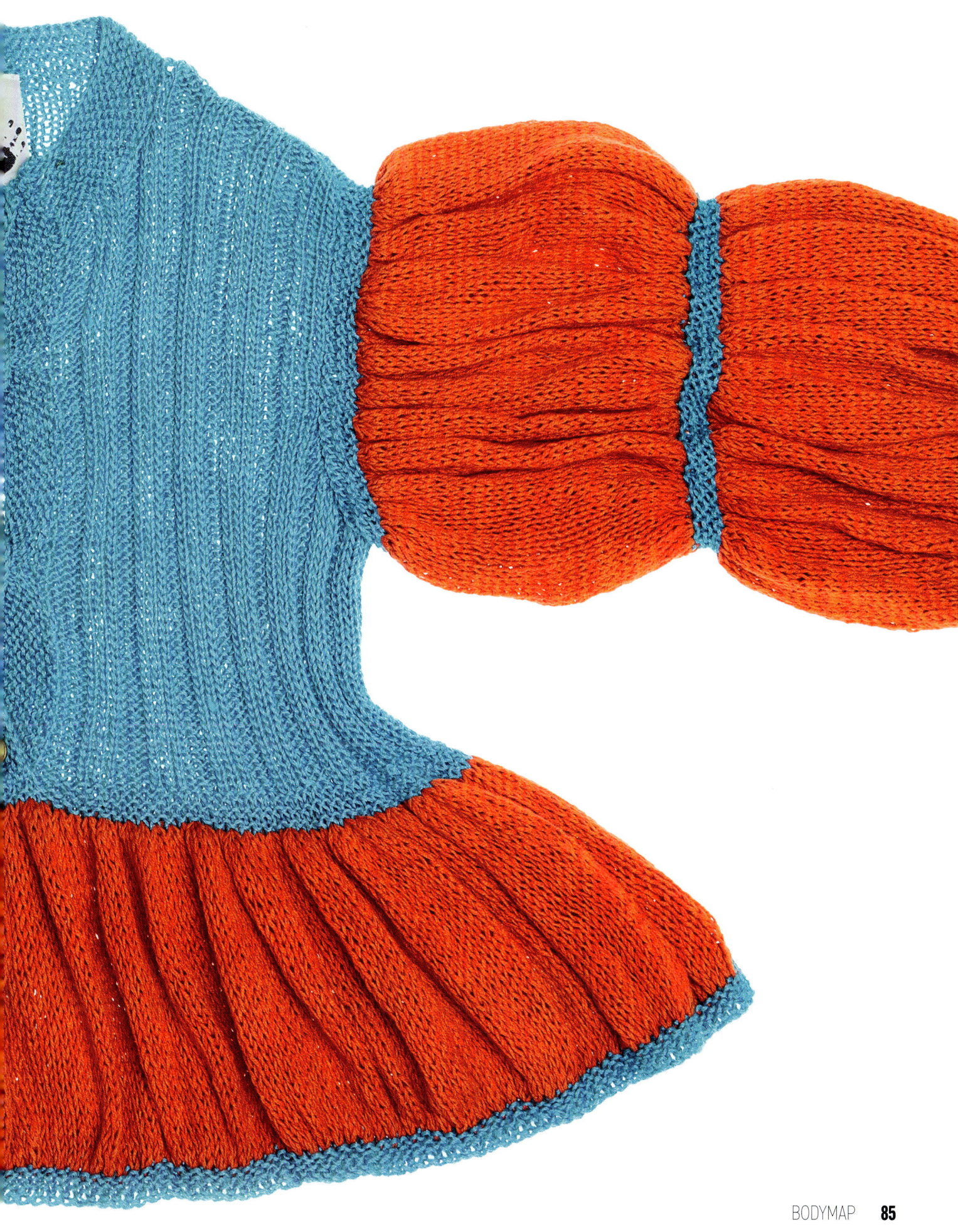

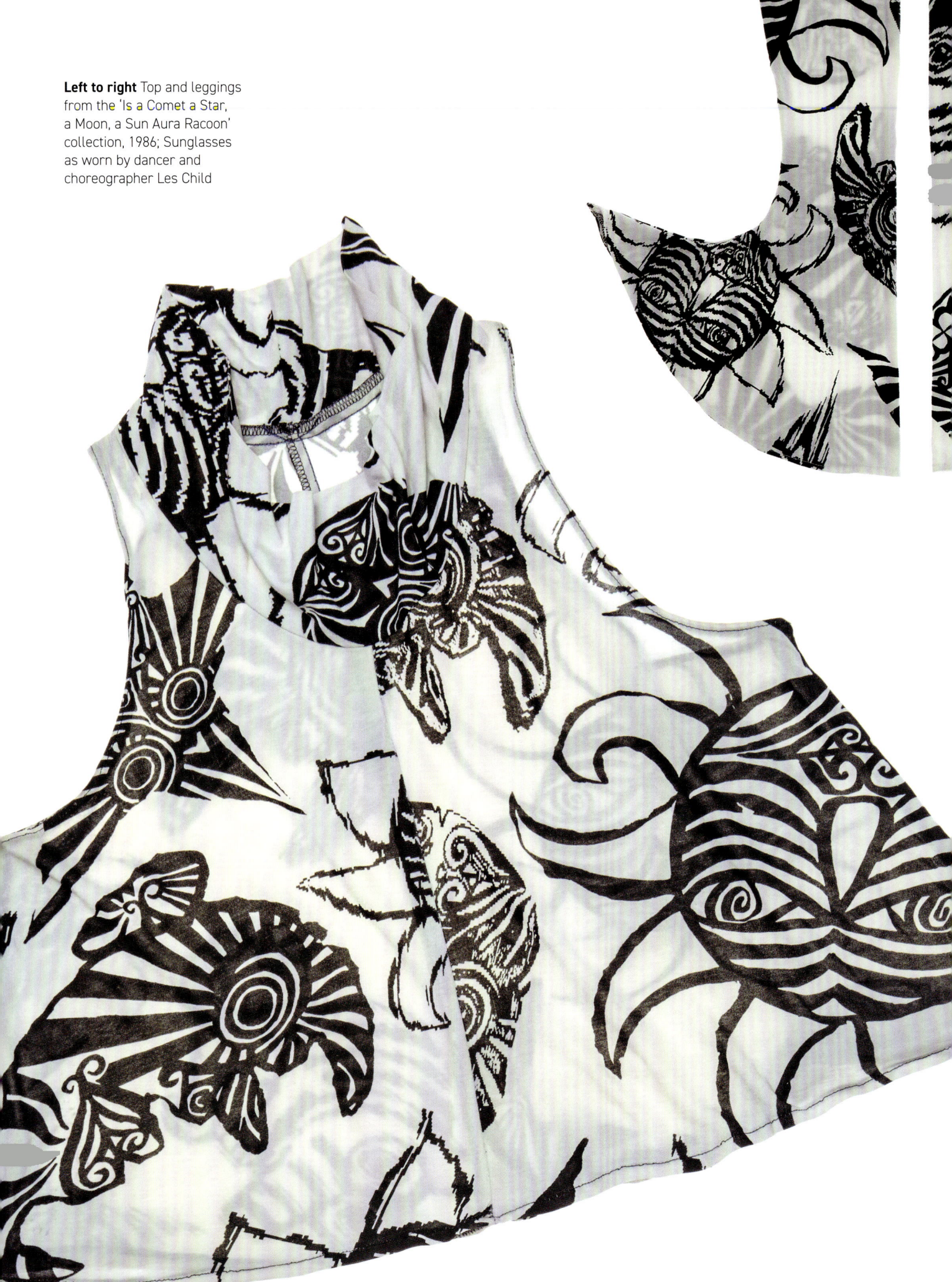

Left to right Top and leggings from the 'Is a Comet a Star, a Moon, a Sun Aura Racoon' collection, 1986; Sunglasses as worn by dancer and choreographer Les Child

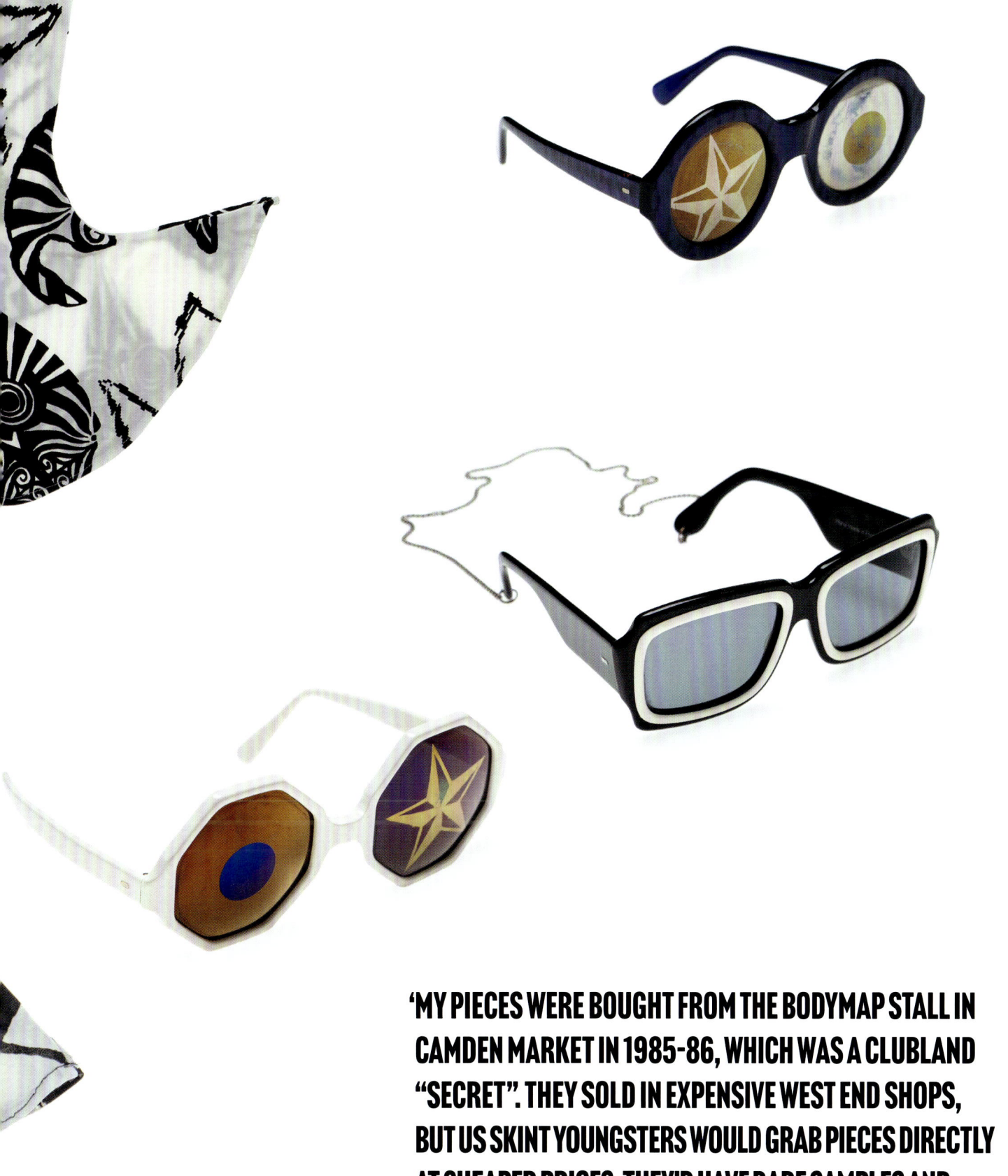

'MY PIECES WERE BOUGHT FROM THE BODYMAP STALL IN CAMDEN MARKET IN 1985-86, WHICH WAS A CLUBLAND "SECRET". THEY SOLD IN EXPENSIVE WEST END SHOPS, BUT US SKINT YOUNGSTERS WOULD GRAB PIECES DIRECTLY AT CHEAPER PRICES. THEY'D HAVE RARE SAMPLES AND ONE- OFFS. YOU NEVER KNEW WHAT YOU'D FIND.'

Maur Valance, nightclub perennial and north London landlady

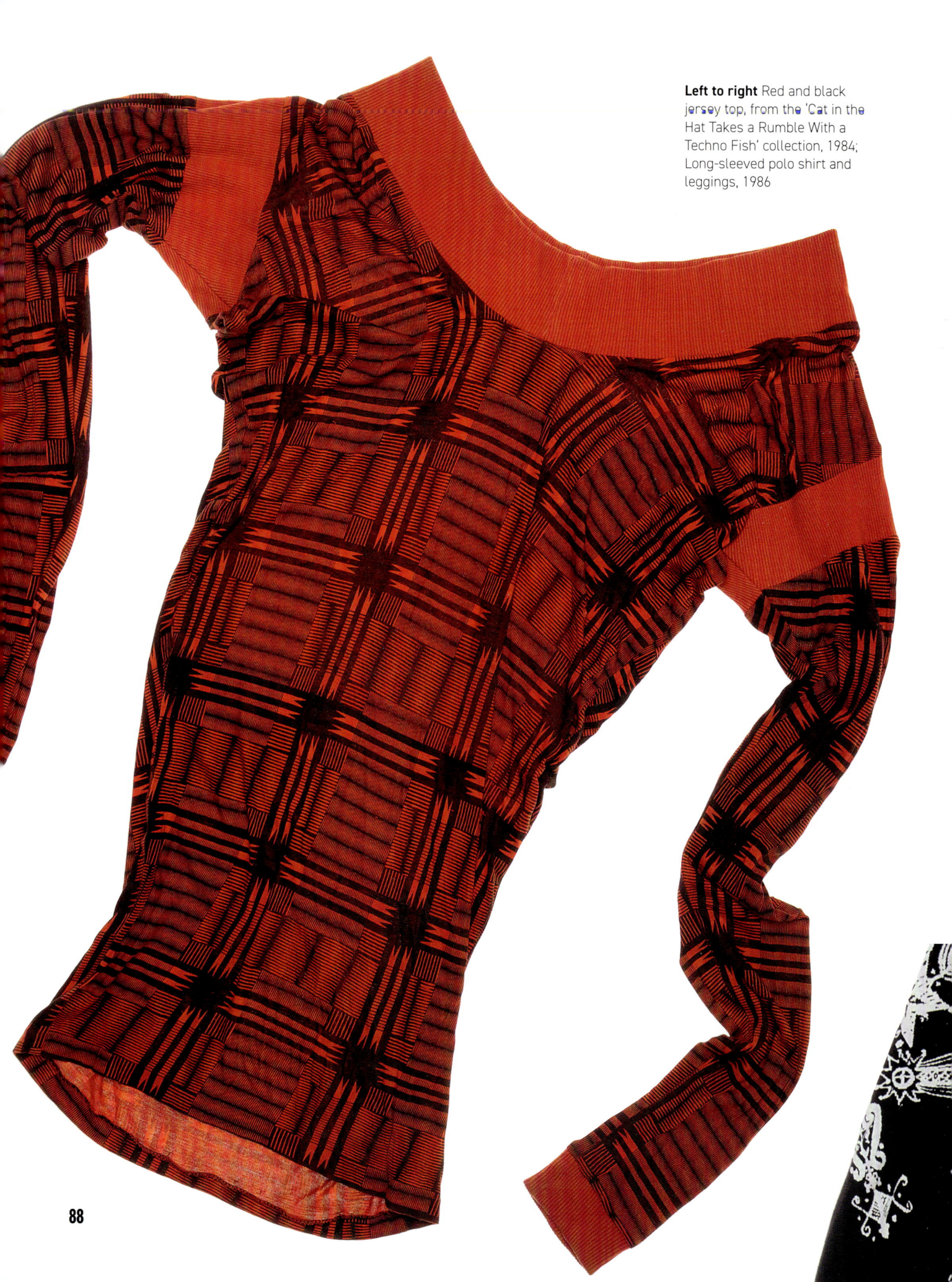

Left to right Red and black jersey top, from the 'Cat in the Hat Takes a Rumble With a Techno Fish' collection, 1984; Long-sleeved polo shirt and leggings, 1986

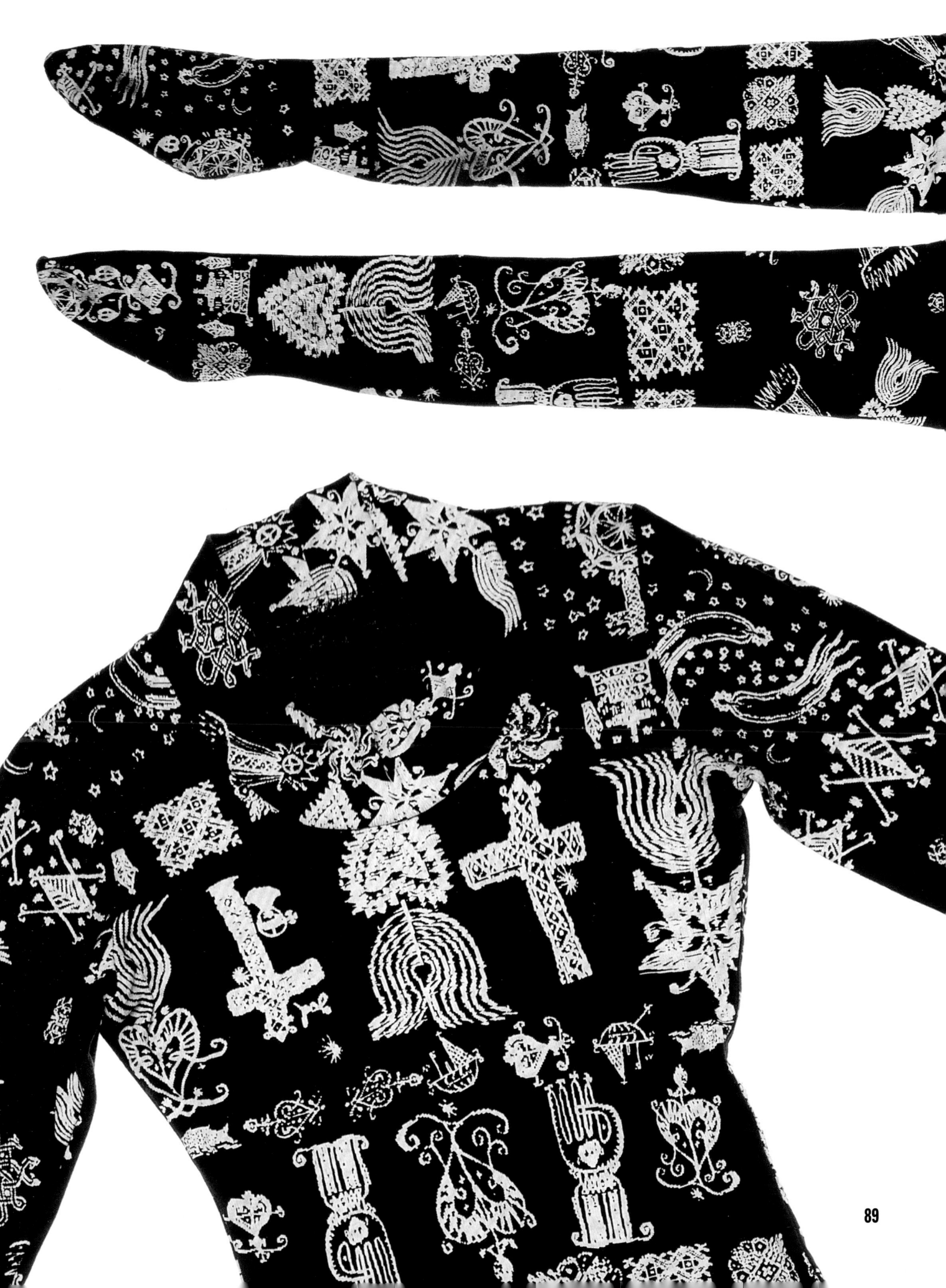

89

Embroidered long velvet coat and hat made for fashion editor Molly Parkin, 1985

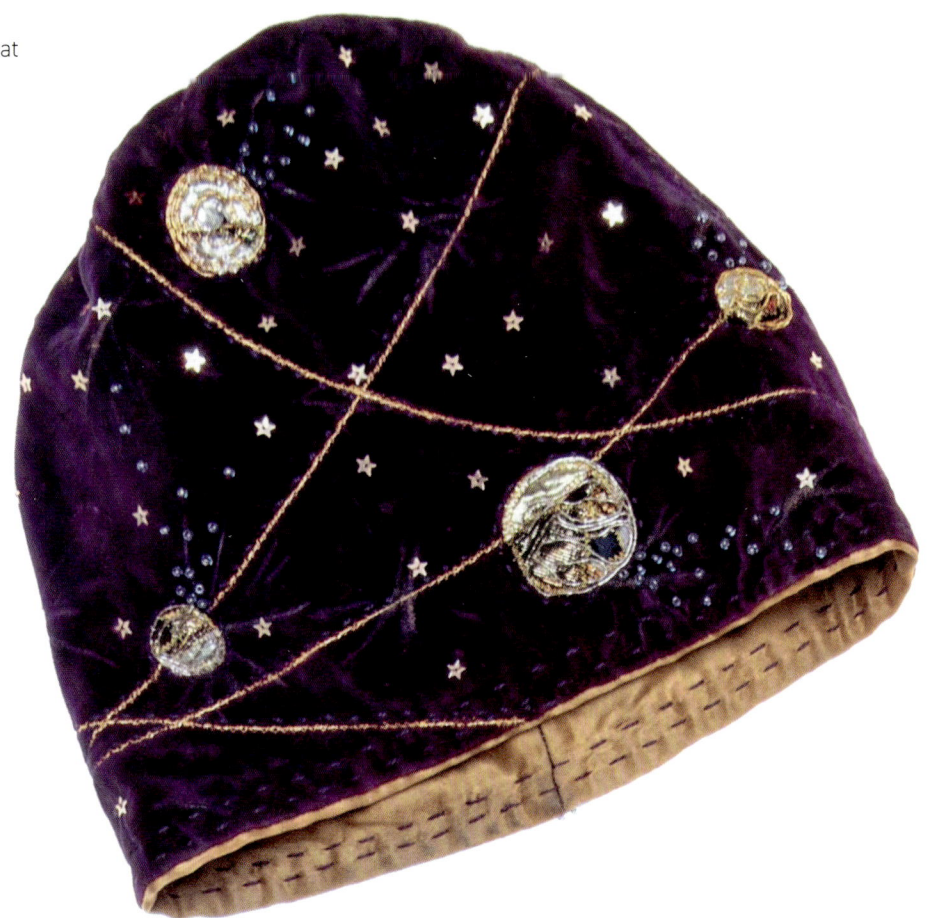

DEAN BRIGHT

In 1984 Dean Bright's St Martin's School of Art graduation collection of rich velvet and lush satin menswear caused much excitement when first exhibited in the window of Browns on South Molton Street.

These luxurious clothes were immediately sought after by pop stars such as Visage frontman Steve Strange, David Bowie and Dead or Alive's Pete Burns. Burns wore Bright's purple coat on the cover of Dead or Alive's *Youthquake* album and in the video for its massive hit single 'You Spin Me Round'.

Between 1984 and 1987 Bright sold his designs to high-end shops across the world, before becoming more focused on selling directly to artists for videos and live performances. He went on to create outfits for Holly Johnson, Boy George and The Thompson Twins as well as Andy Bell and Erasure.

Bright still designs and creates special commissions for private clients.

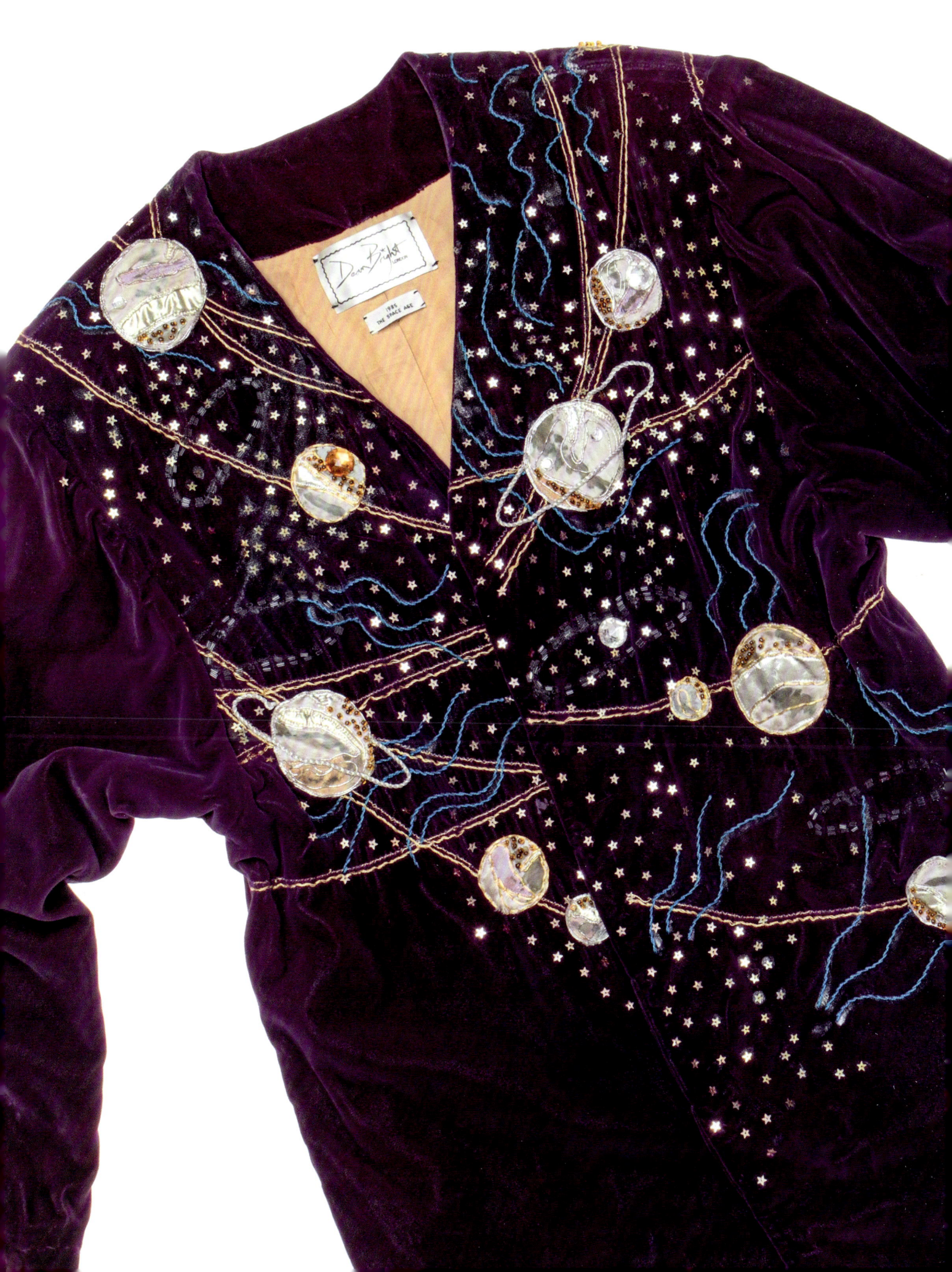

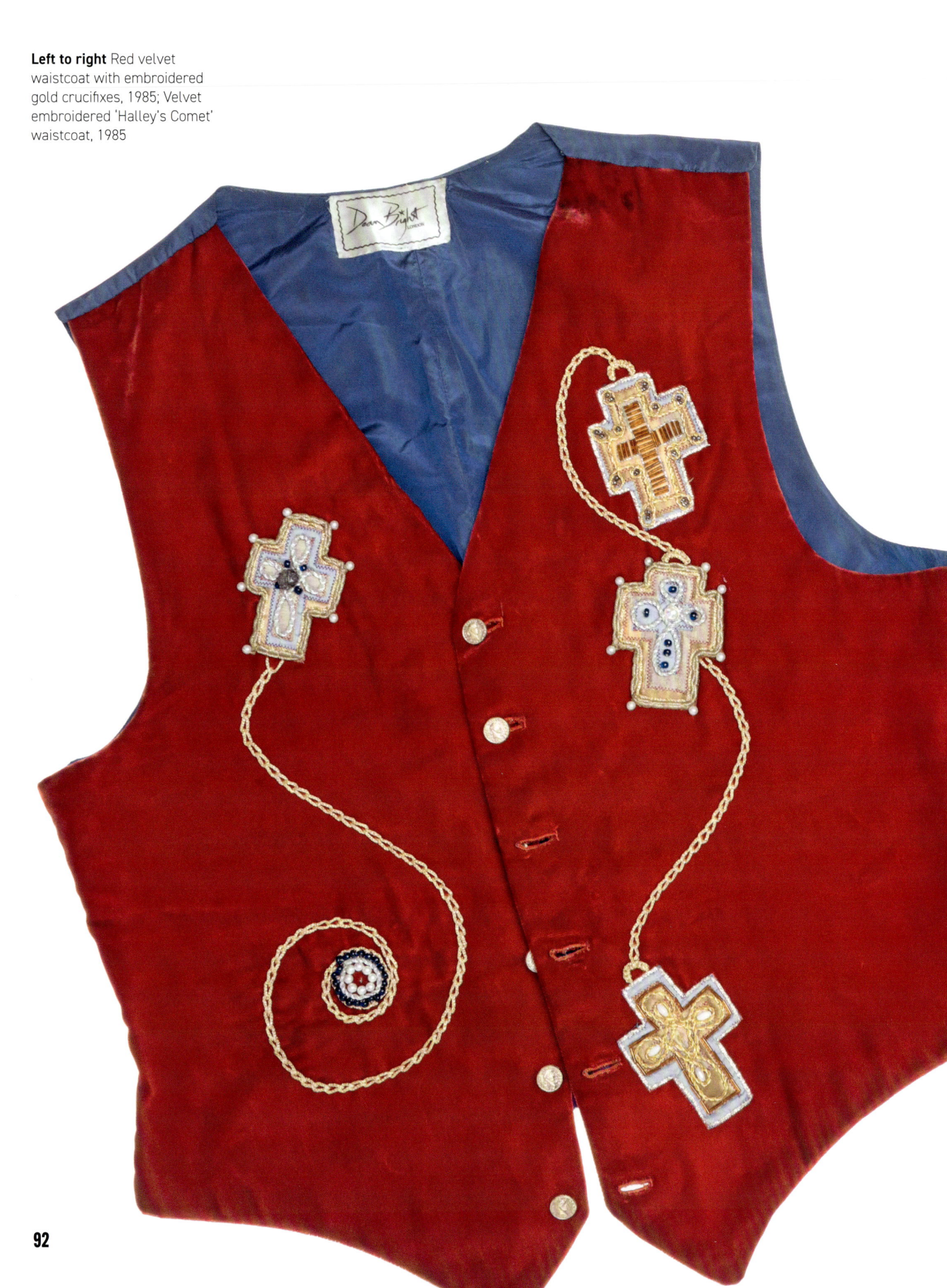

Left to right Red velvet waistcoat with embroidered gold crucifixes, 1985; Velvet embroidered 'Halley's Comet' waistcoat, 1985

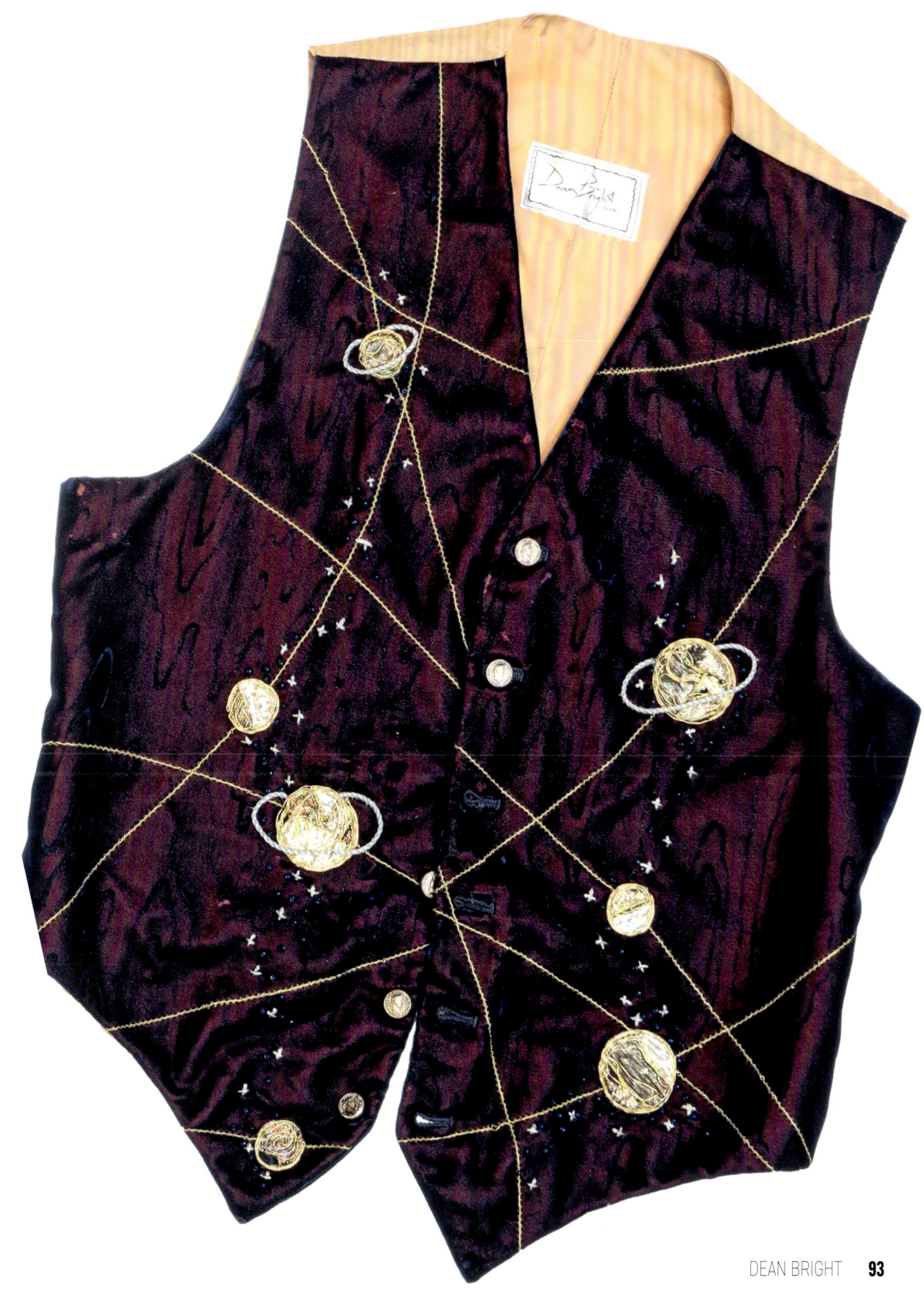

DEAN BRIGHT

Velvet top, 1984 graduate collection, as worn by Steve Coy from Dead or Alive in the 'You Spin Me Round' video. Singer Pete Burns wore a coat from the same collection on the cover of the band's *Youthquake* album

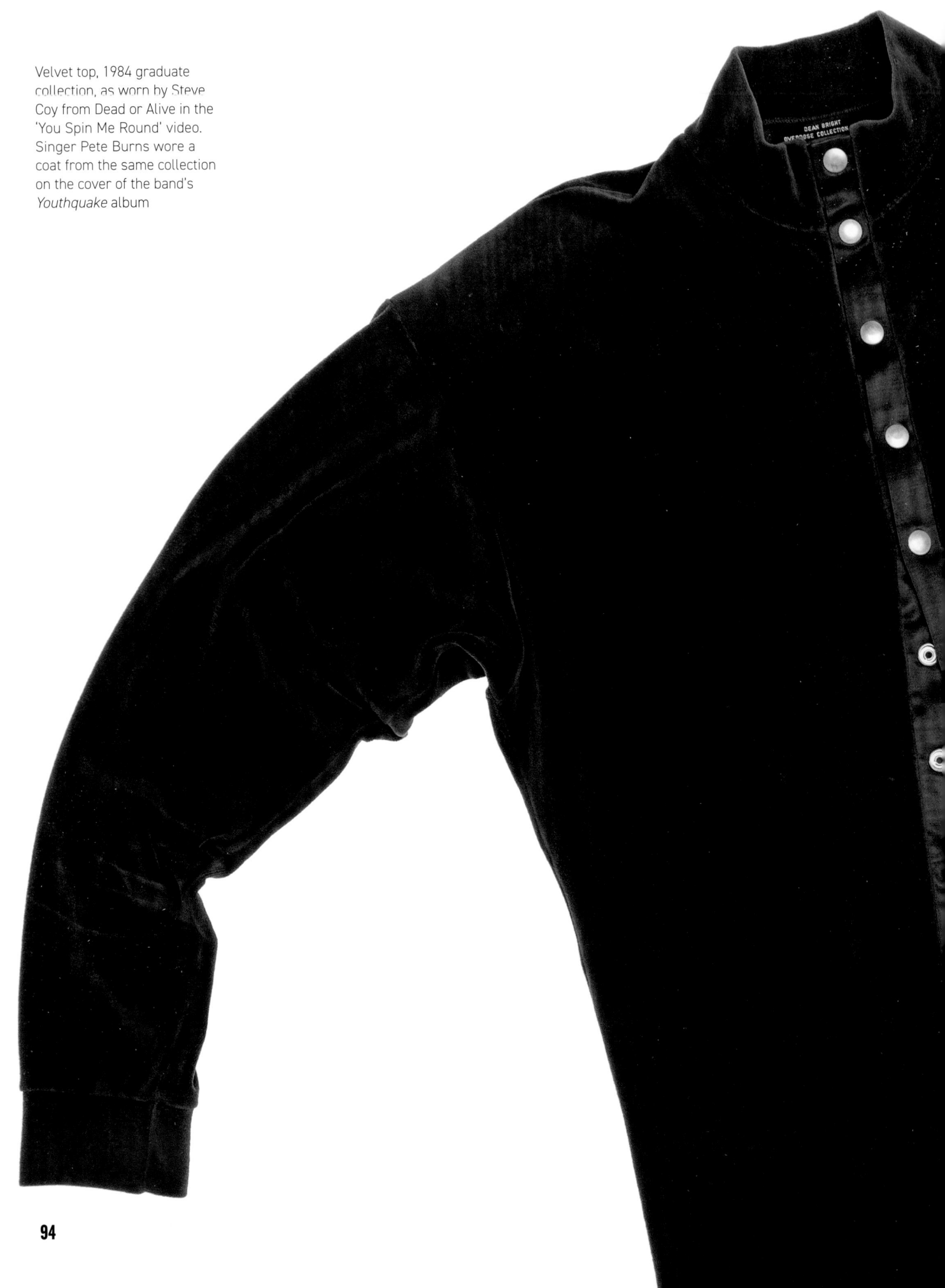

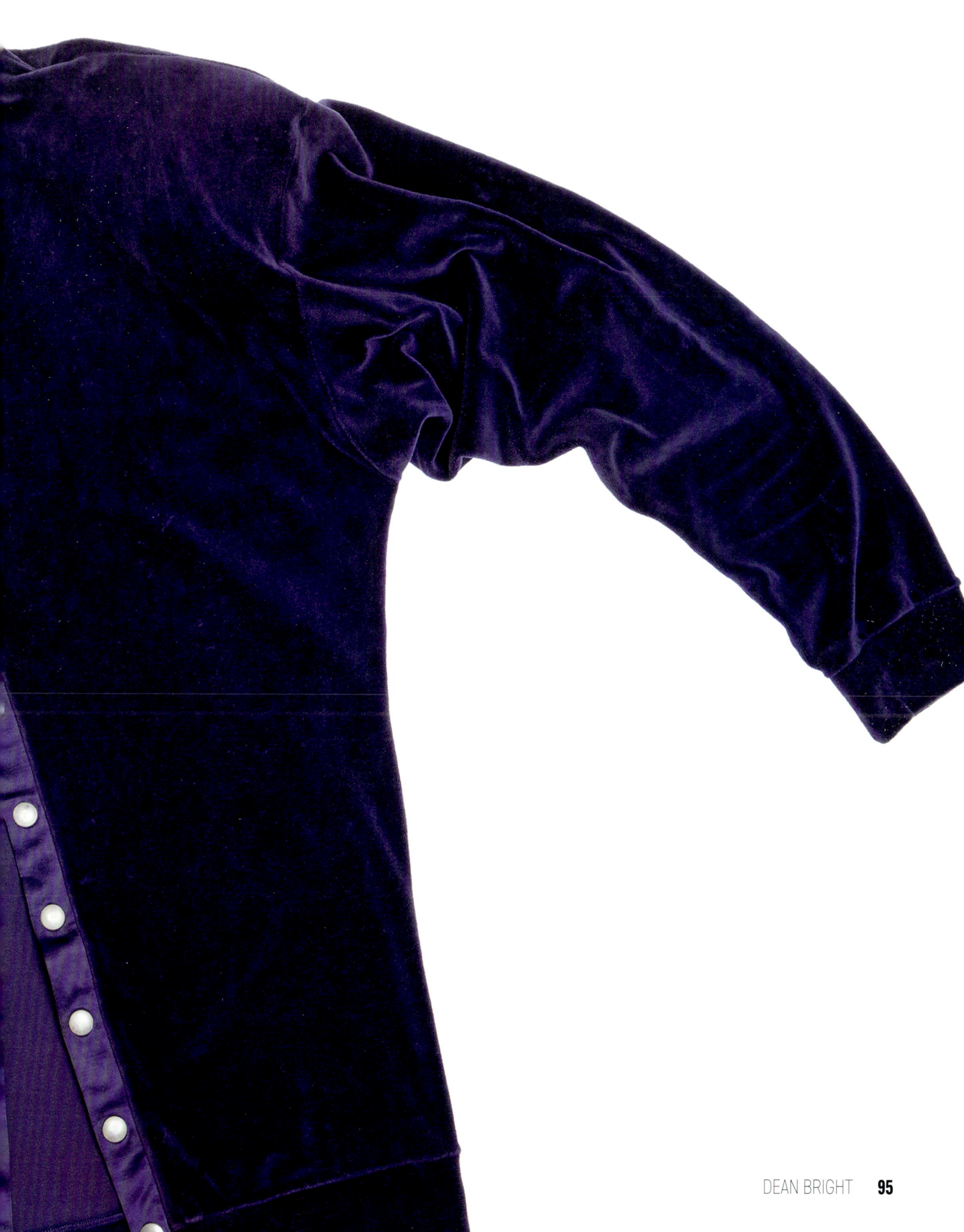

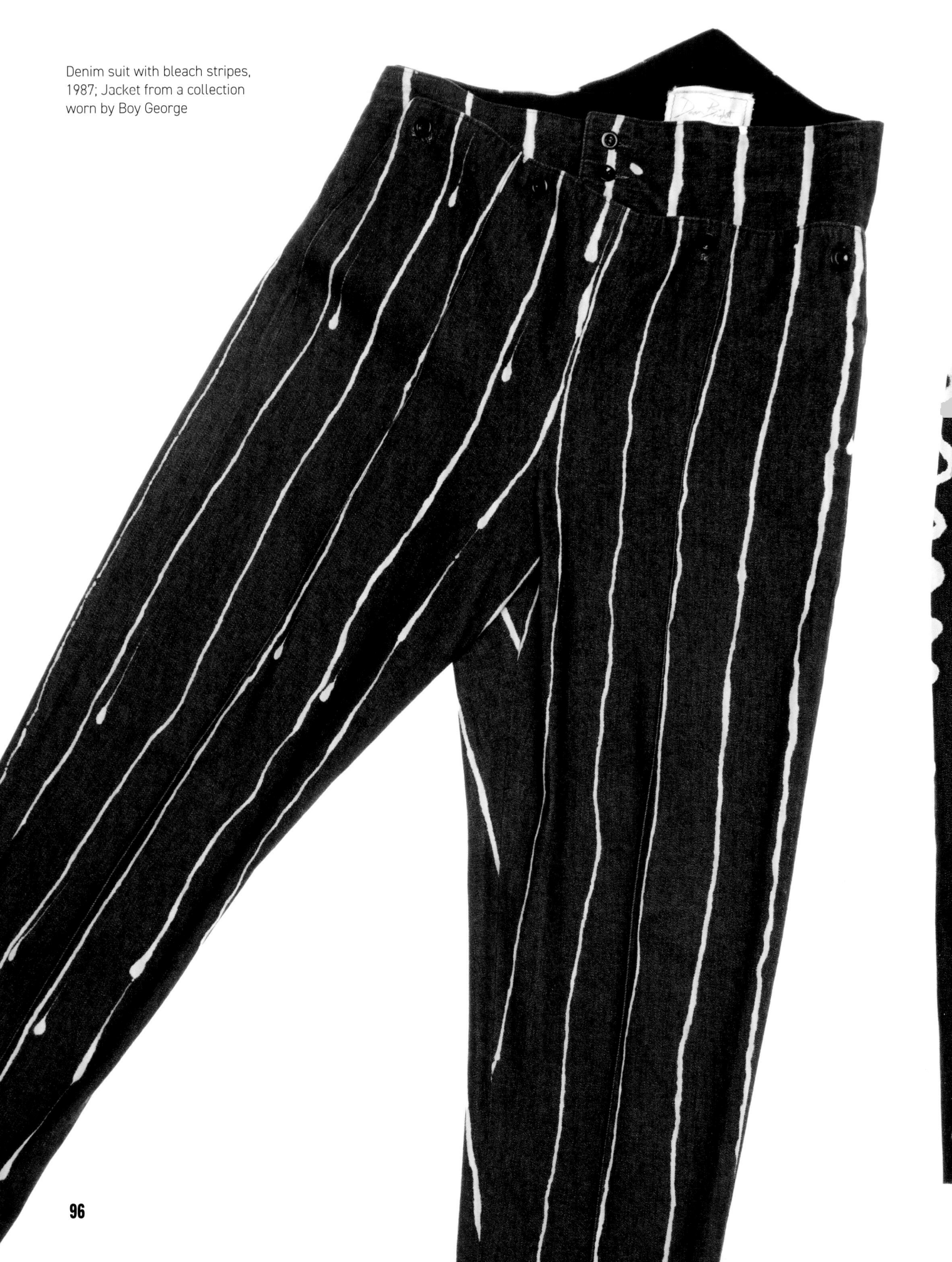

Denim suit with bleach stripes, 1987; Jacket from a collection worn by Boy George

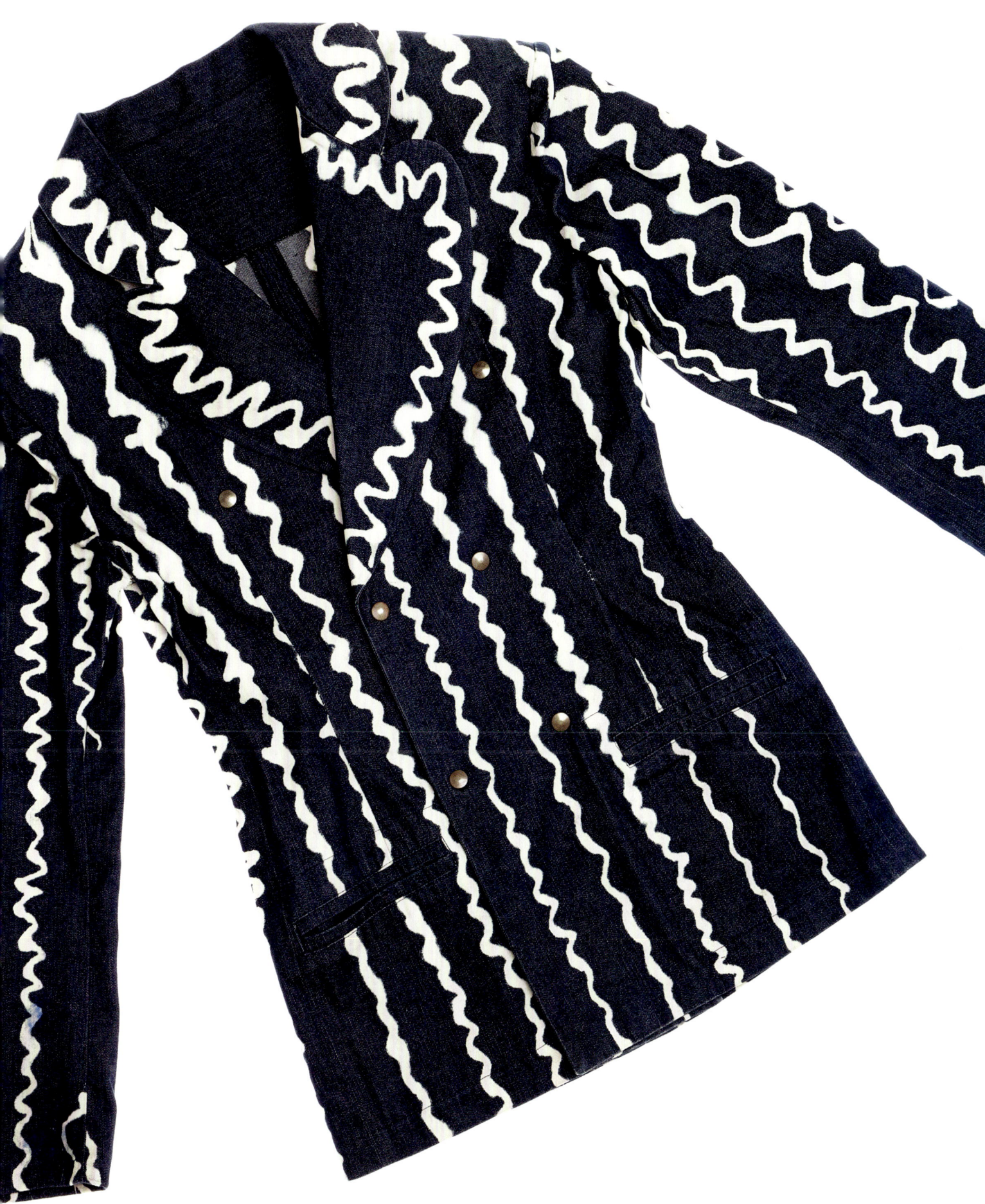

A YEAR IN FASHION

The prolific make-up artist and hairdresser Jalle Bakke moved to London from Karlstad, Sweden, and swiftly established himself due to his immense talent.

He was always in high demand and regularly worked with pop stars, designers and photographers such as Nick Knight, Monica Curtin and Sheila Rock.

Bakke was an intrinsic and much-loved part of London's clubland and can be seen looking very cool with bleached blonde hair, a cropped fringe and sunglasses during the party scene in the 1987 film *Hail the New Puritan*, a fictionalised day in the life of the Scottish dancer and choreographer Michael Clark.

Bakke died of AIDS in 1996 at just 35, leaving his diaries as a record of the era.

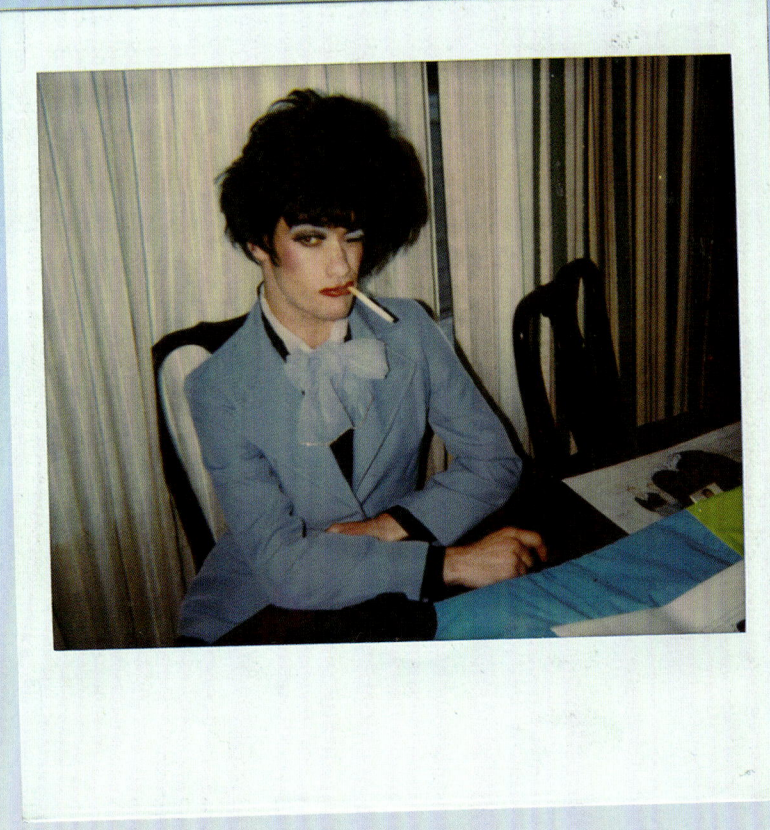

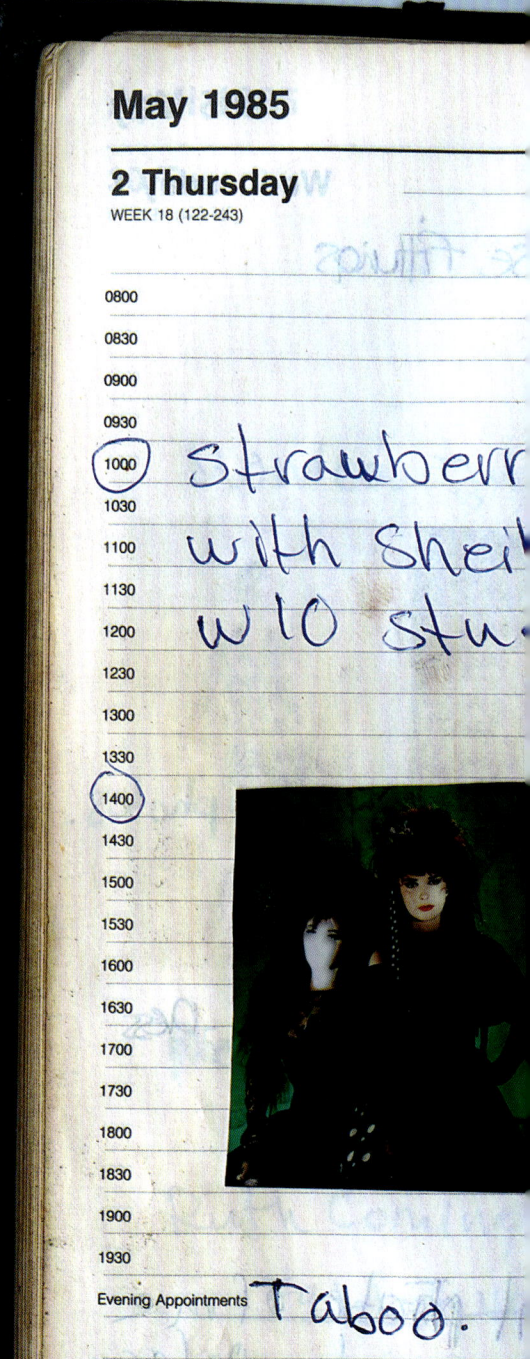

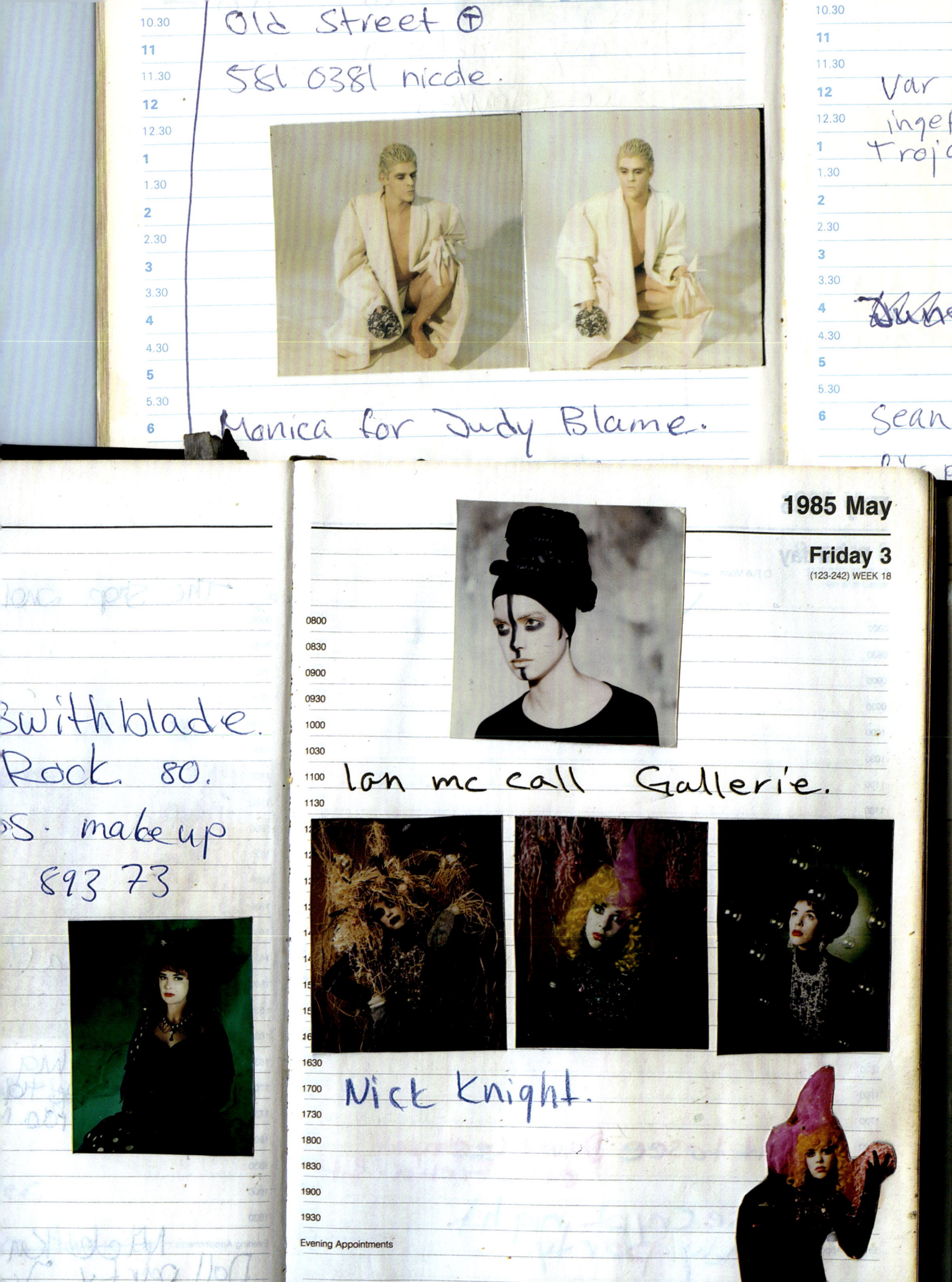

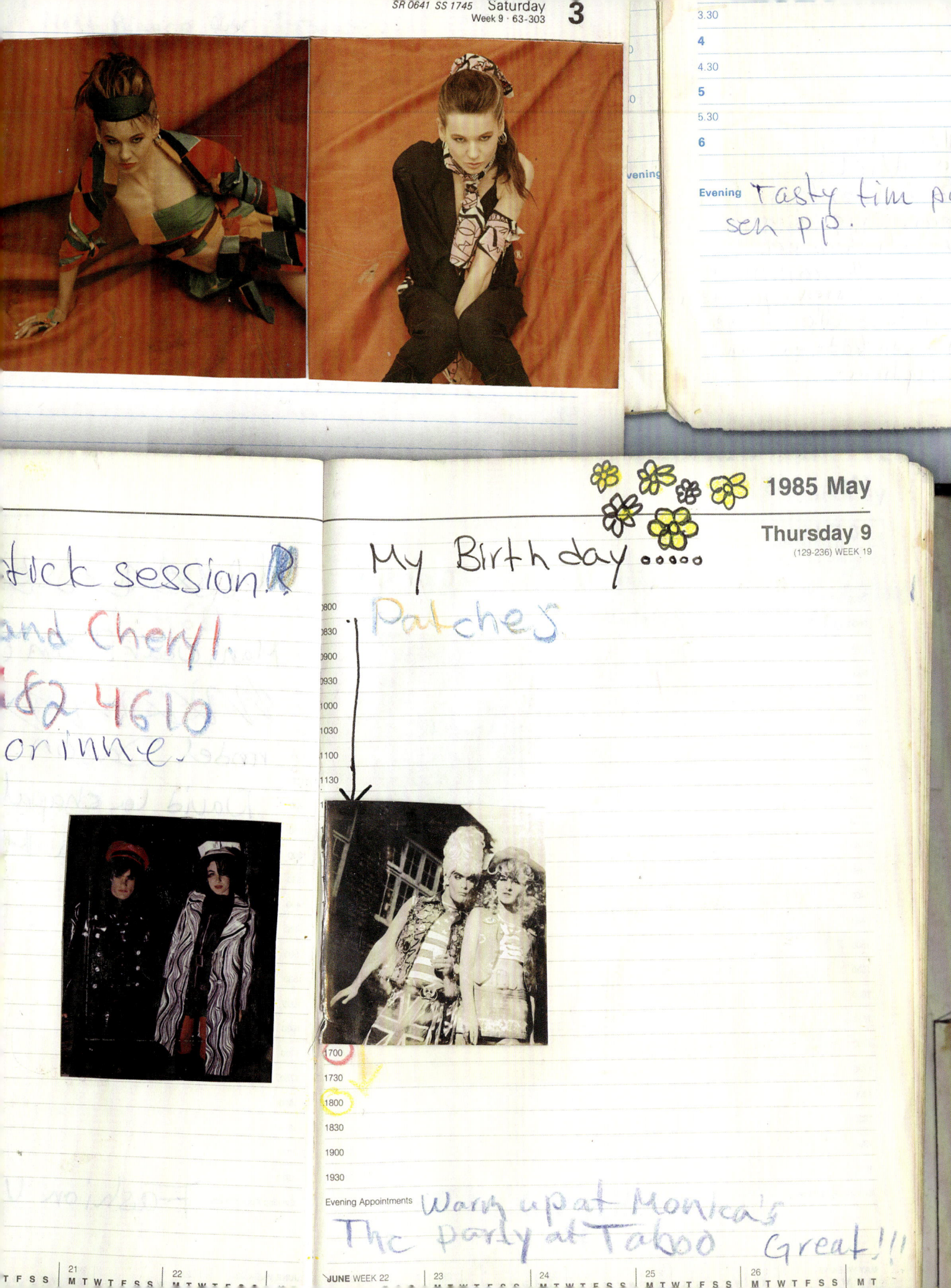

Saturday 3
Week 9 · 63-303

Evening tasty tim pa
sch p.p.

1985 May
Thursday 9
(129-236) WEEK 19

My Birthday.....

Patches

...tick session.
and Cheryl.
...82 4610
...orinne.

Evening Appointments Warm up at Monica's
The party at Taboo Great!!!

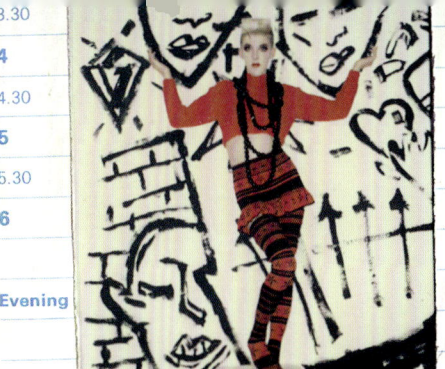
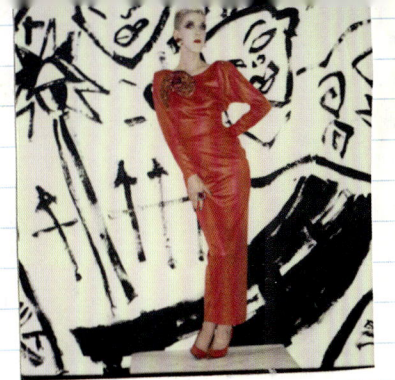

på white trash

Kina restaurang
med Monica o Crispin.

JULY	AUGUST	SEPTEMBER	OCTOBER
M 2 9 16 23 30	M 6 13 20 27	M 3 10 17 24	M 1 8 15 22 29
T 3 10 17 24 31	T 7 14 21 28	T 4 11 18 25	T 2 9 16 23 30
W 4 11 18 25	W 1 8 15 22 29	W 5 12 19 26	W 3 10 17 24 31
T 5 12 19 26	T 2 9 16 23 30	T 6 13 20 27	T 4 11 18 25
F 6 13 20 27	F 3 10 17 24 31	F 7 14 21 28	F 5 12 19 26
S 7 14 21 28	S 4 11 18 25	S 1 8 15 22 29	S 6 13 20 27
S 1 8 15 22 29	S 5 12 19 26	S 2 9 16 23 30	S 7 14 21 28

1985 April
Tuesday 9

ABC
960 8377. Sheila Roe
West 10 studios
10 Conland st. W10.
near Harrow rd.
Bernadette Coyle
phonogram press office
50 New bond st. W1.

coming around.

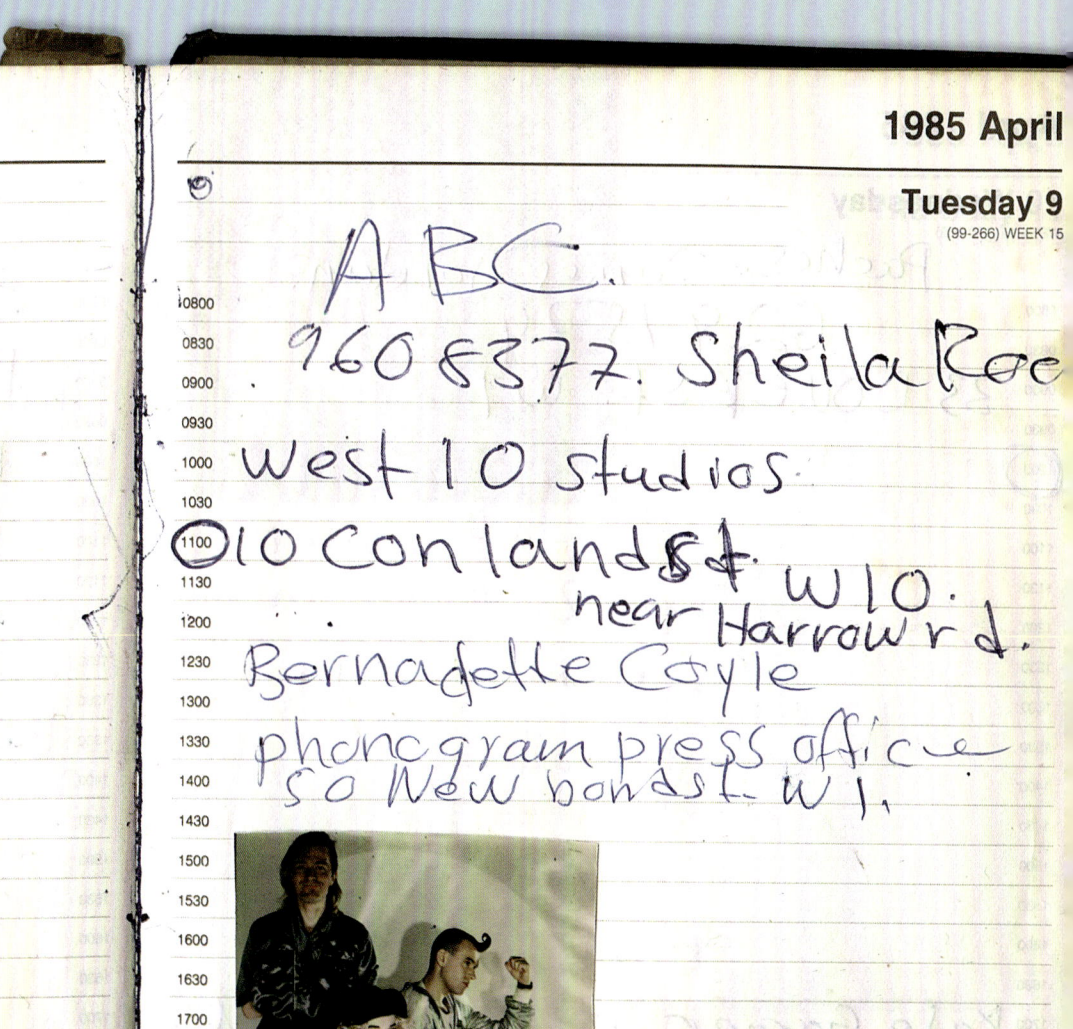

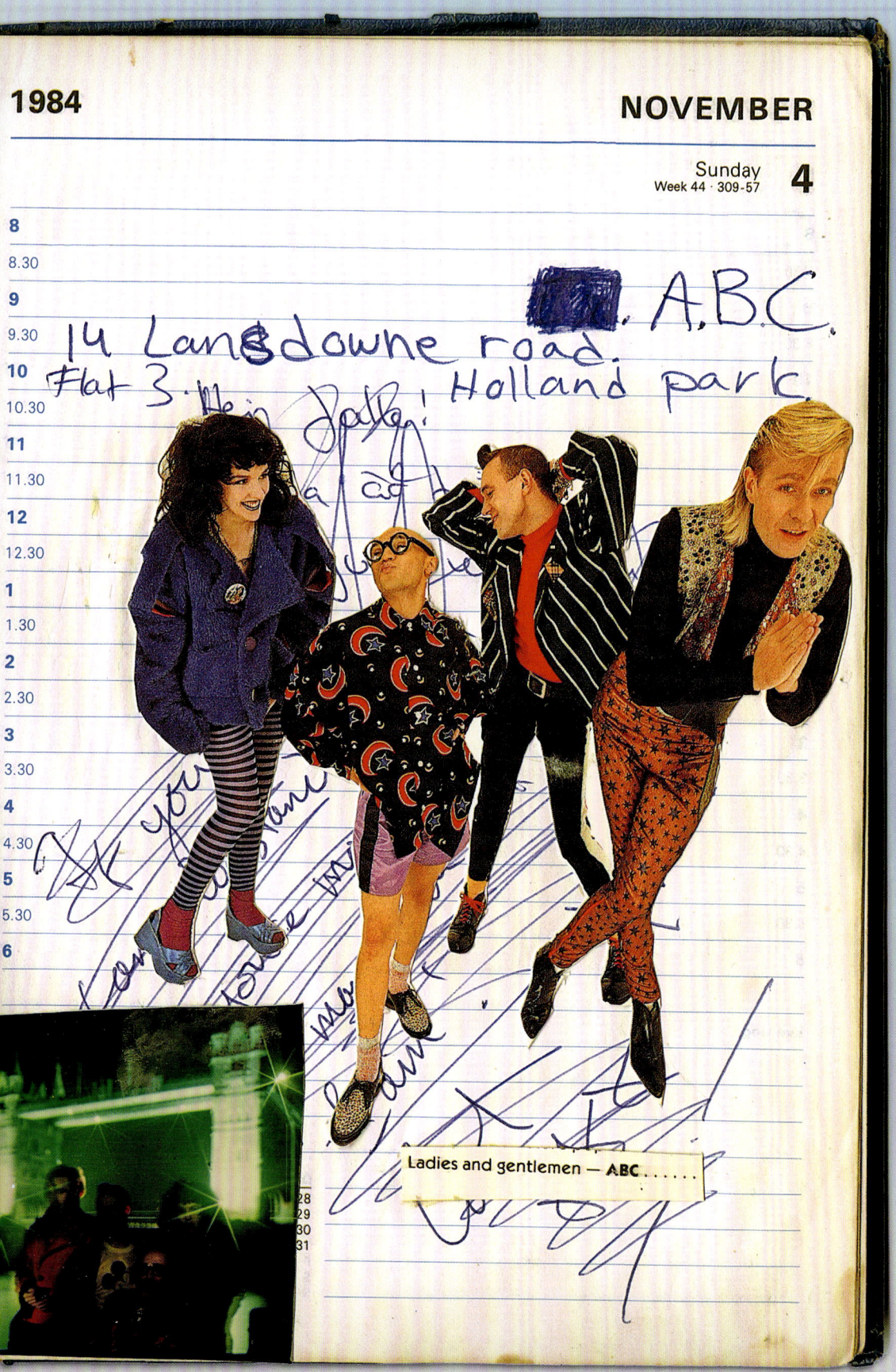

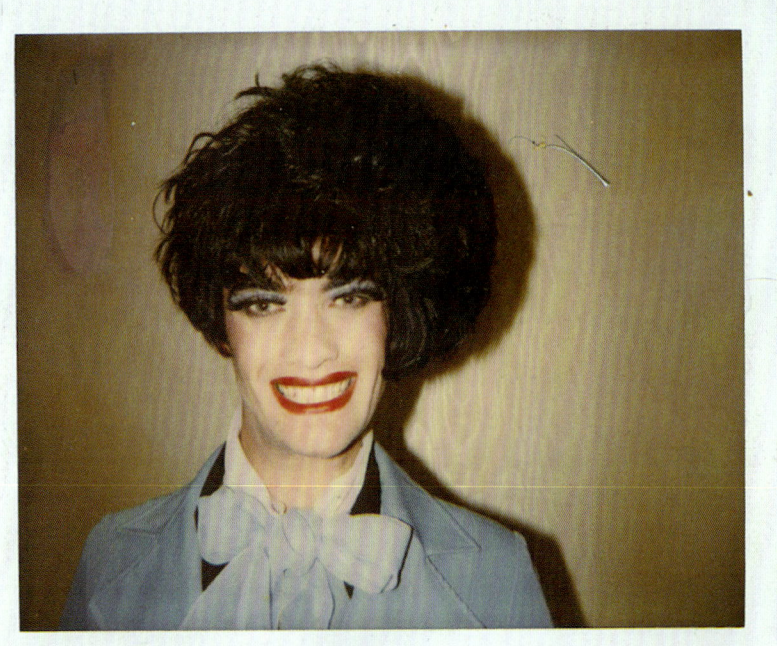
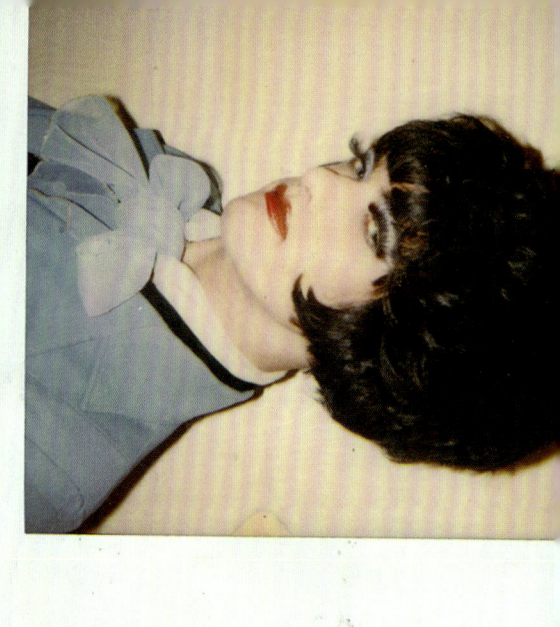

1985

Thurs
(157-20

0800
0830
0900
0930
1000   Jason.
1030   8 Colville Terrace.
1100   Grou
1130
1200
1230
1300
1330
1400
1430
1500   Kate taking my pictur
1530
1600
1630
1700
1730
1800
1830
1900
1930

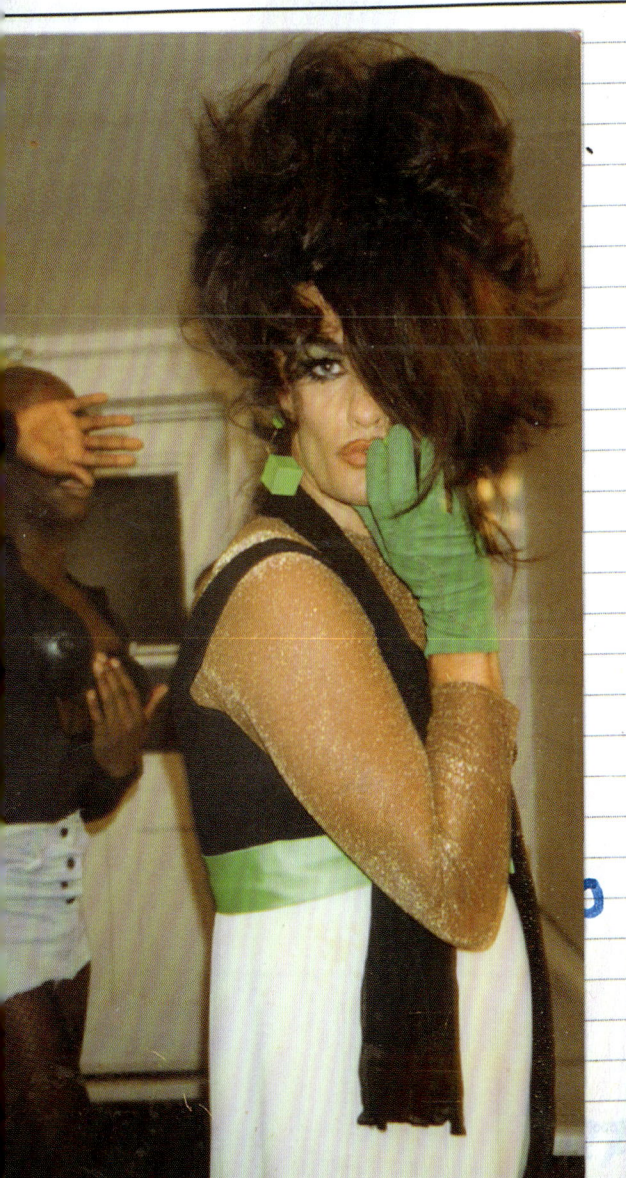
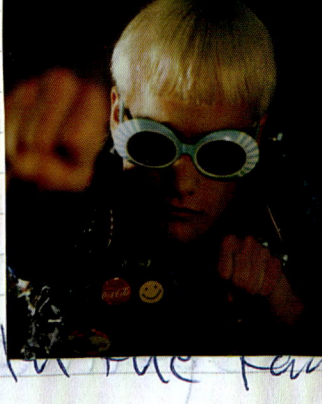

BOYS WONDER

Founded by twins Ben and Scott Addison in 1985, the band's dynamic fusion of mod, punk, glam rock and contemporary fashion paved the way for Britpop. Both modelled for Pam Hogg and Ben designed the band's look with Claire Tranter and Rebecca Pond. His blue PVC suit is emblazoned with writing from the Moloko Korova milk bar in *A Clockwork Orange* and the £5-note suit was inspired by Mark & Syrie. Boys Wonder split in 1990 and Ben and Scott went on to form the band Corduroy.

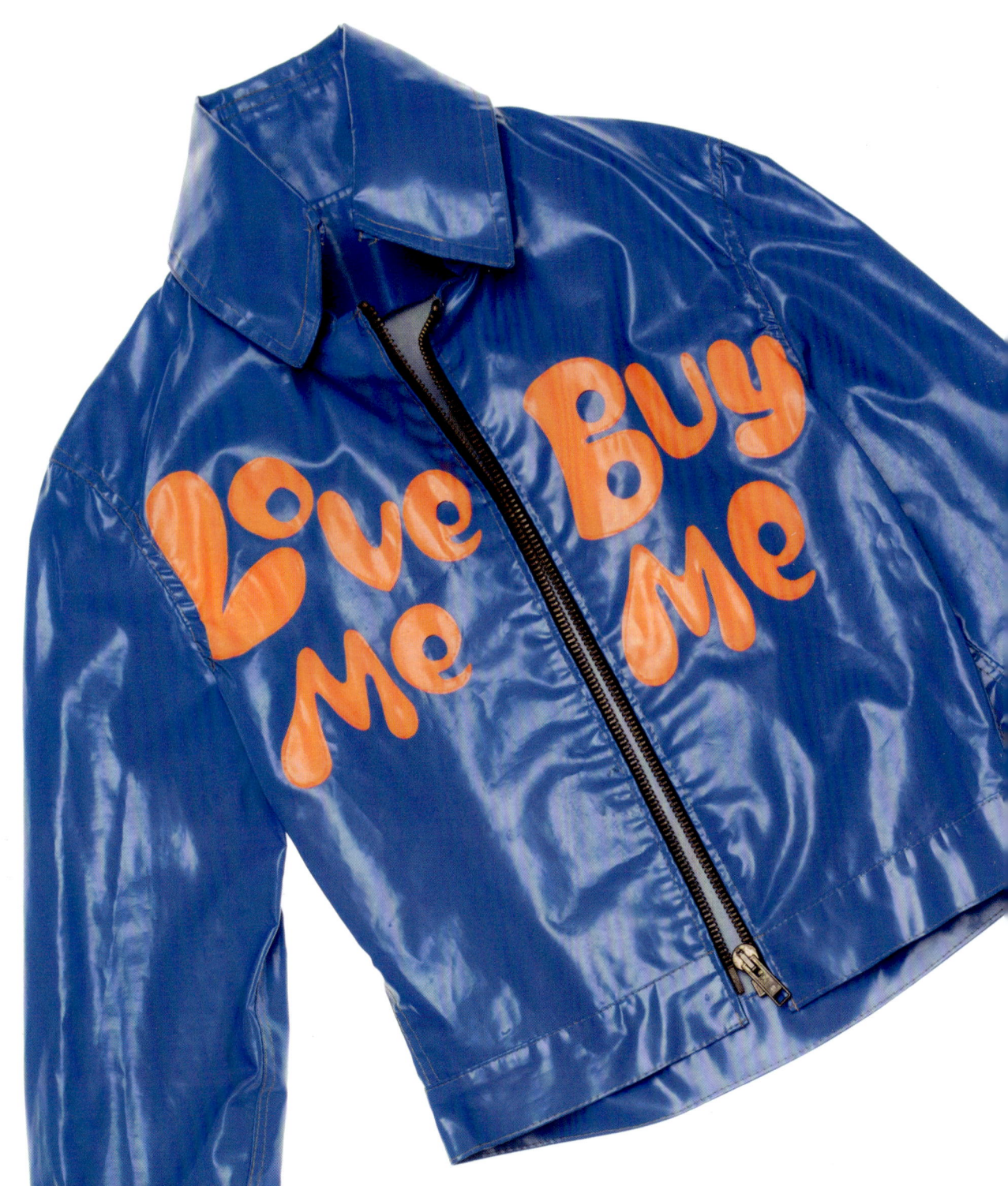

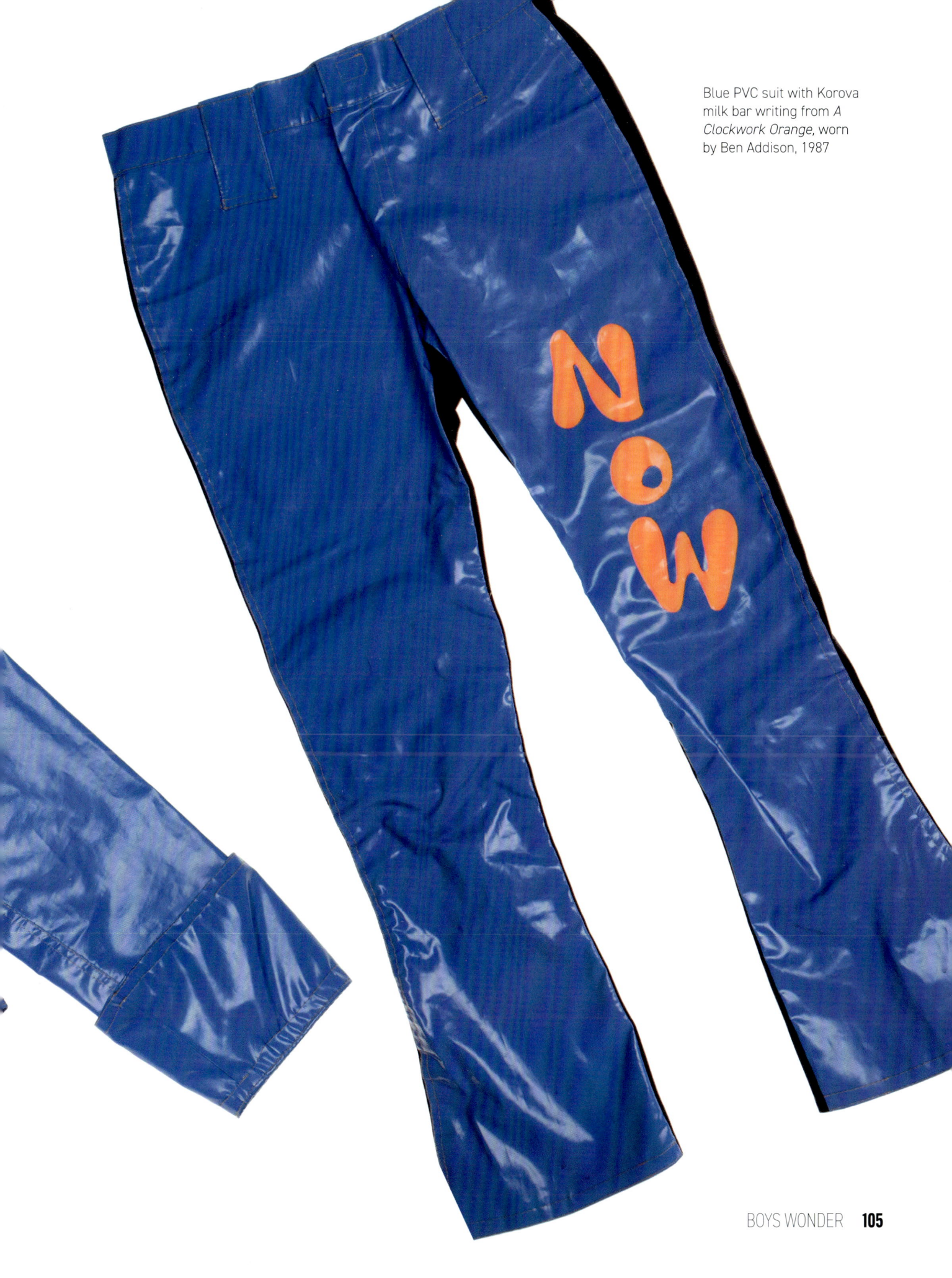

Blue PVC suit with Korova milk bar writing from *A Clockwork Orange*, worn by Ben Addison, 1987

BOYS WONDER

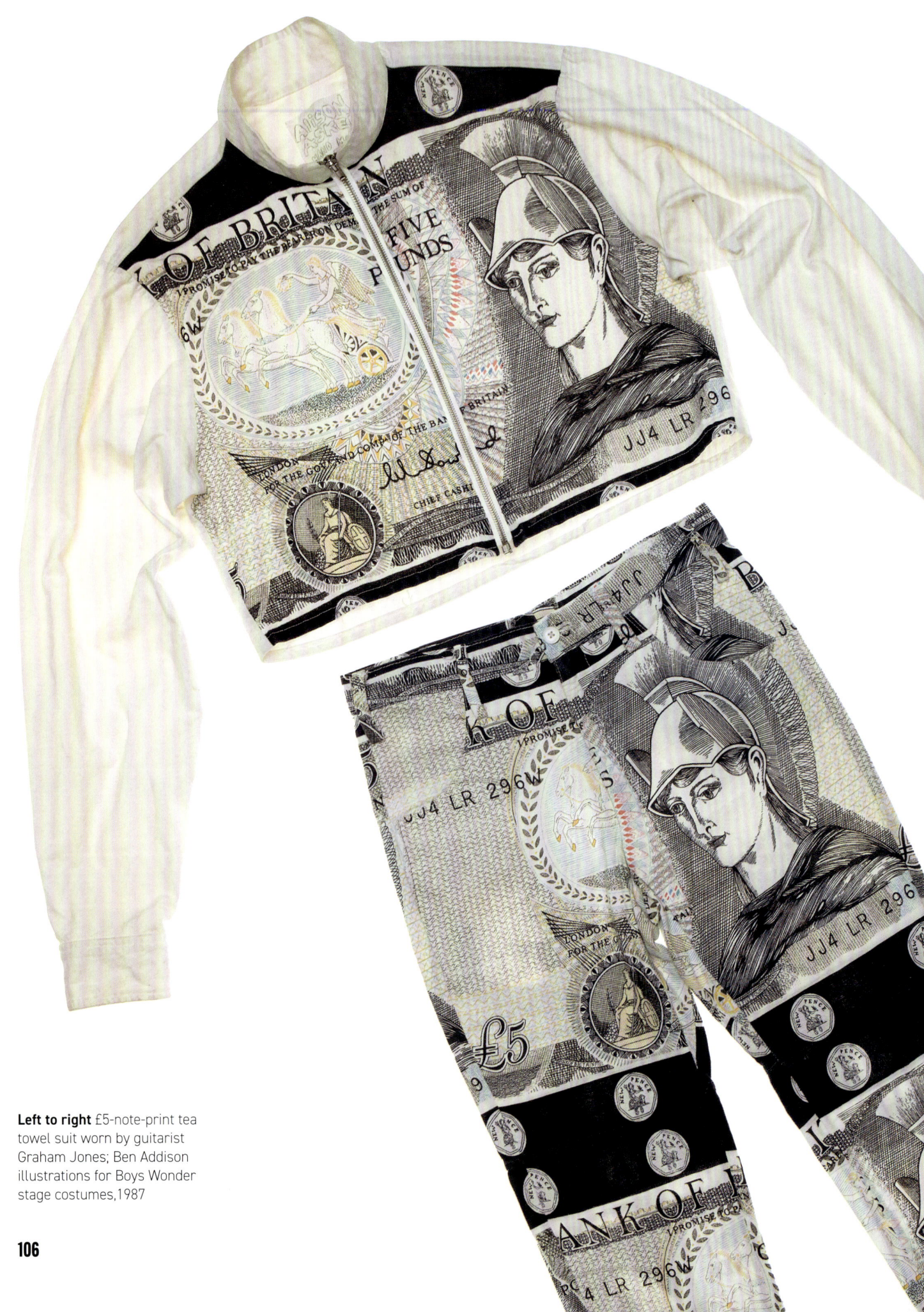

Left to right £5-note-print tea towel suit worn by guitarist Graham Jones; Ben Addison illustrations for Boys Wonder stage costumes, 1987

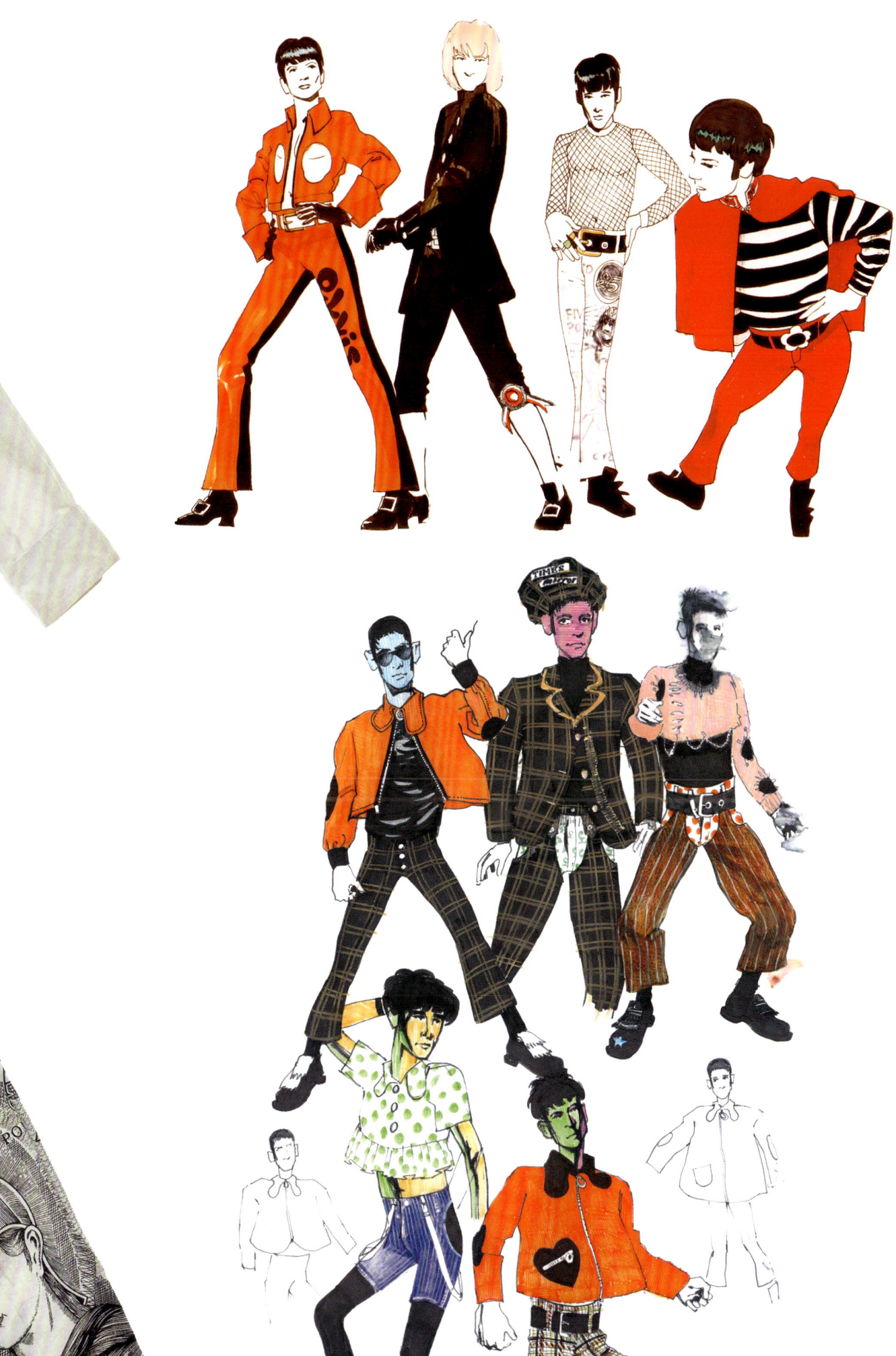

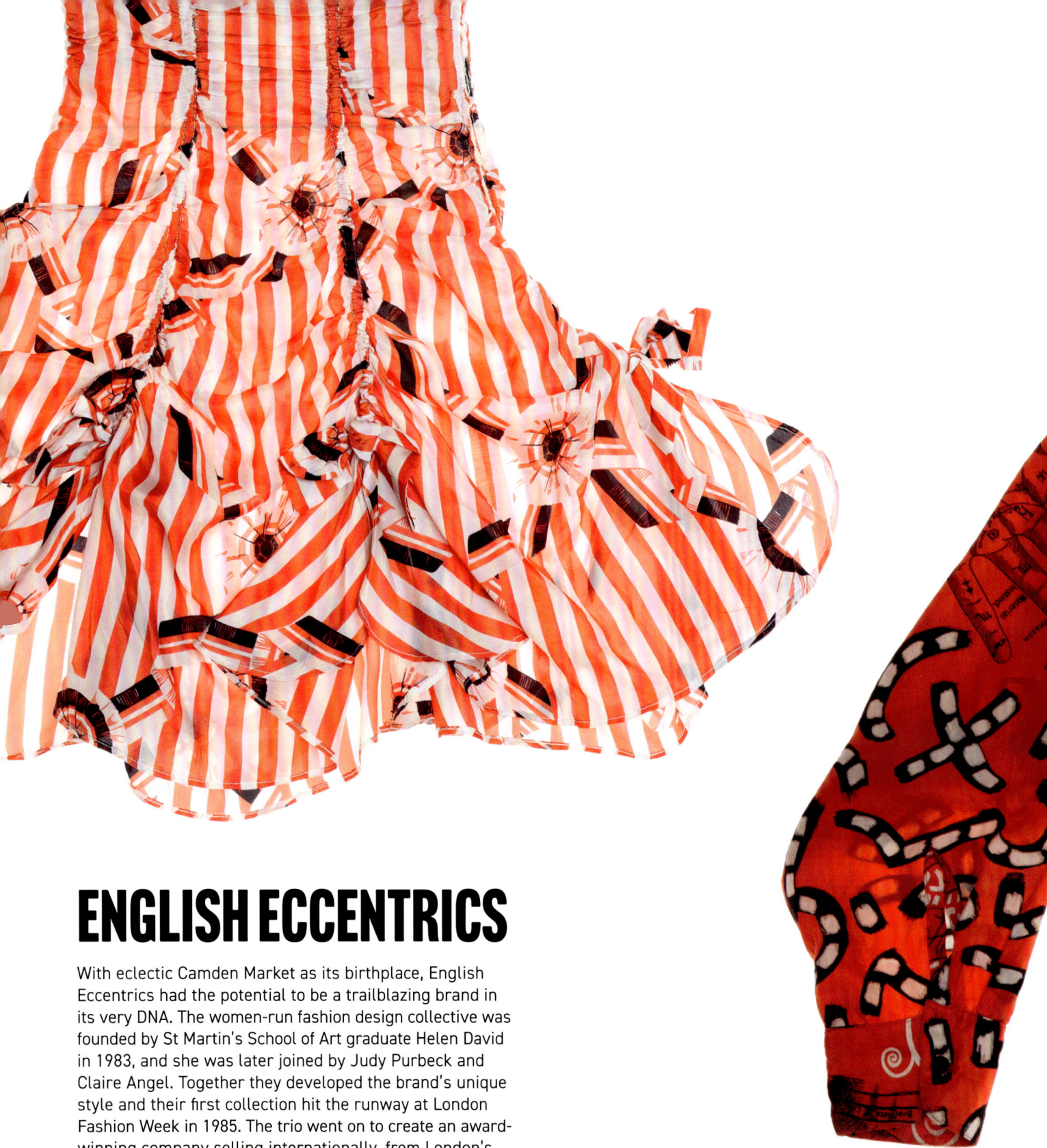

ENGLISH ECCENTRICS

With eclectic Camden Market as its birthplace, English Eccentrics had the potential to be a trailblazing brand in its very DNA. The women-run fashion design collective was founded by St Martin's School of Art graduate Helen David in 1983, and she was later joined by Judy Purbeck and Claire Angel. Together they developed the brand's unique style and their first collection hit the runway at London Fashion Week in 1985. The trio went on to create an award-winning company selling internationally, from London's Liberty to Bergdorfs in New York, with their own store opening on Fulham Road in 1987.

English Eccentrics has dressed A-list celebrities including Prince, Mick Jagger, Helen Mirren, Paul McCartney, Duran Duran and Helena Bonham Carter, and won the British Fashion Award for Evening Wear in 1999.

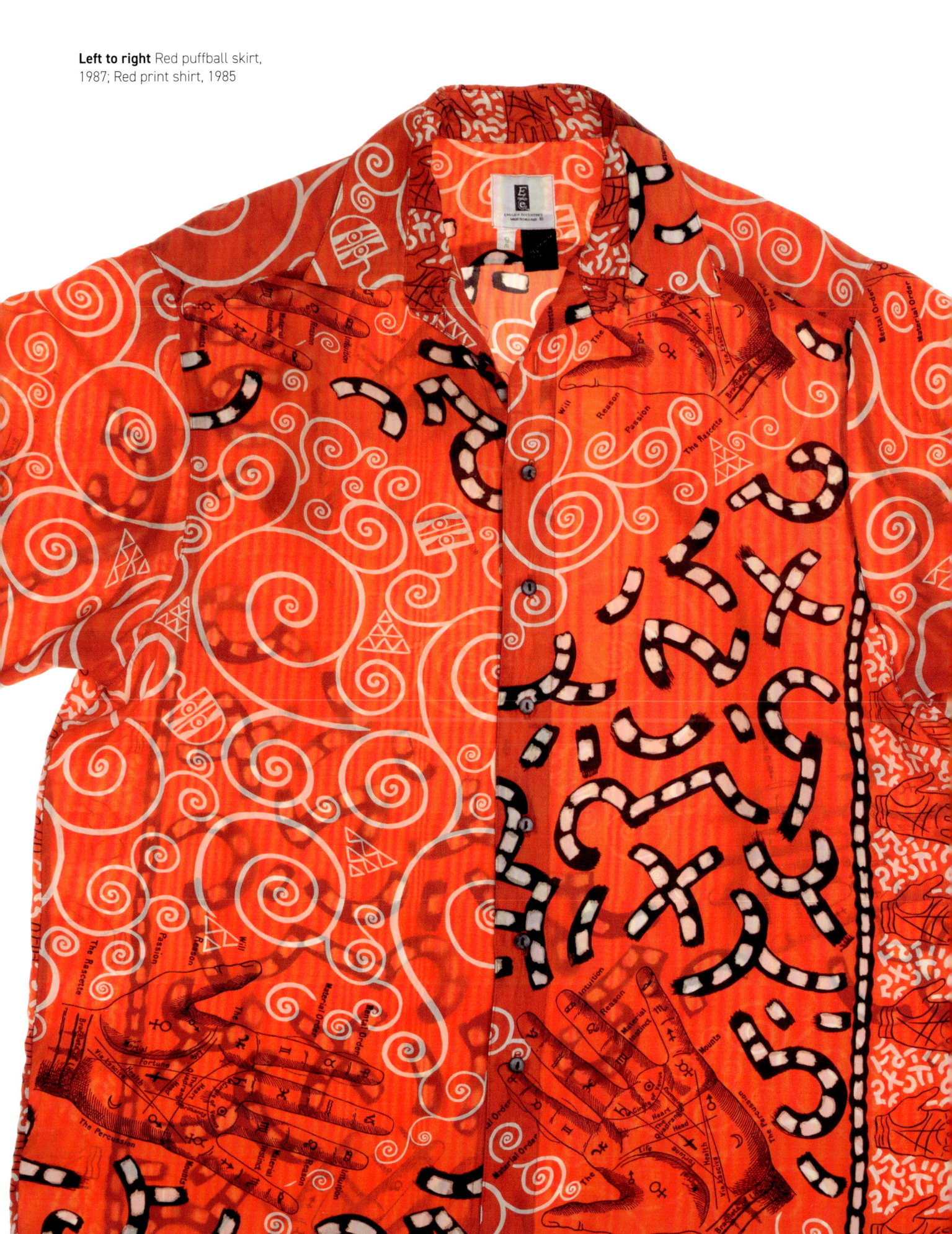

Left to right Red puffball skirt, 1987; Red print shirt, 1985

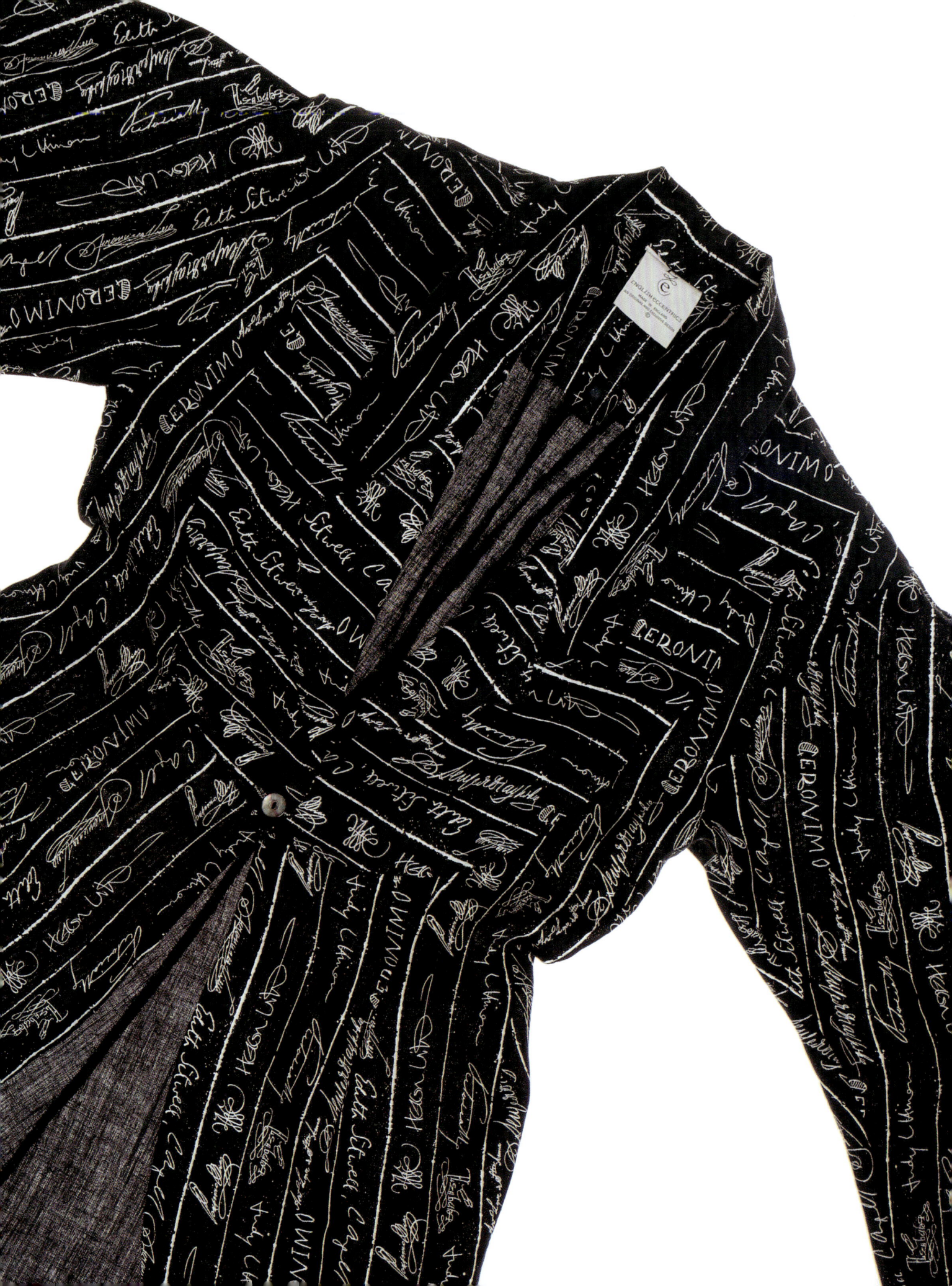

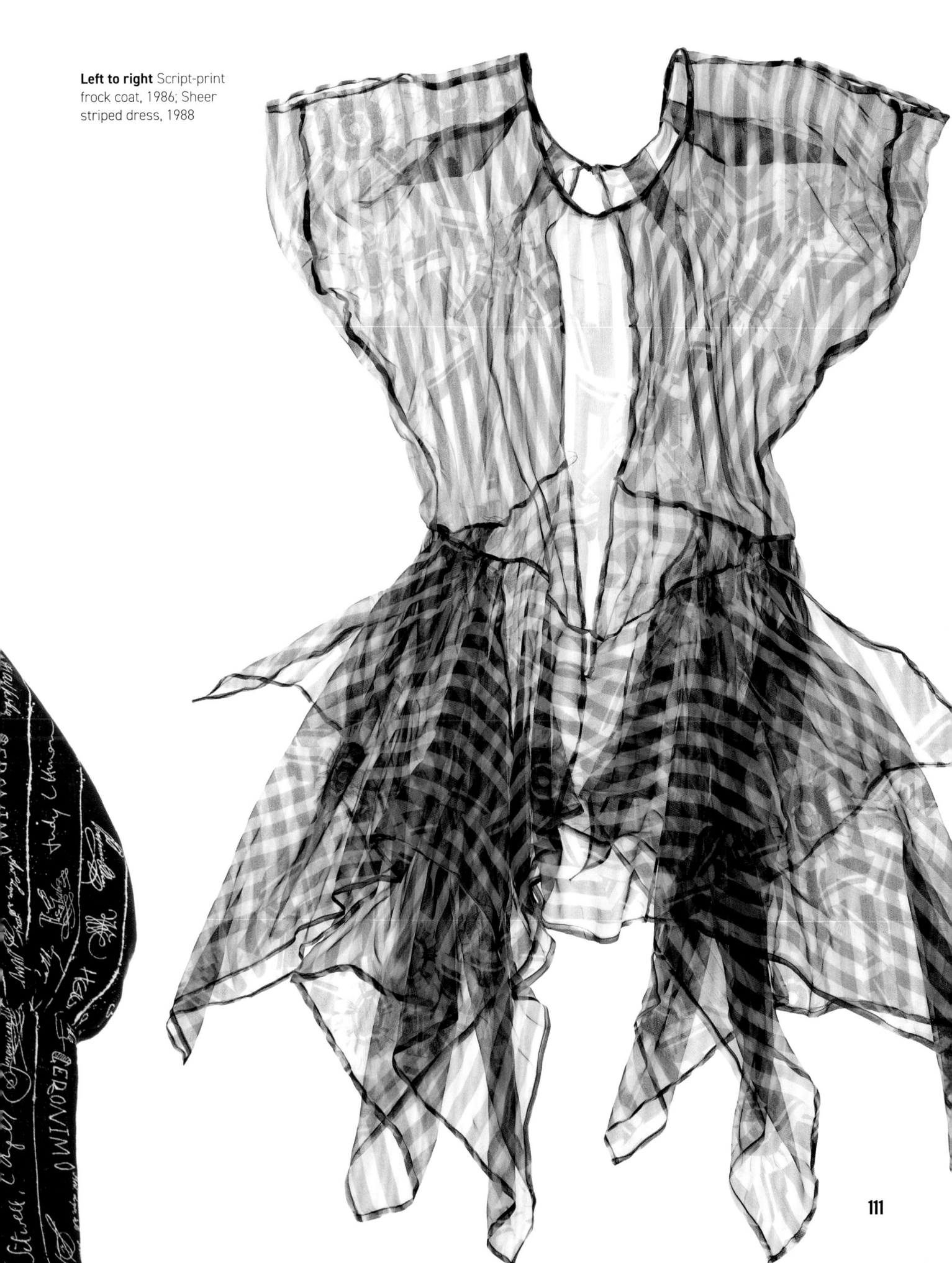

Left to right Script-print frock coat, 1986; Sheer striped dress, 1988

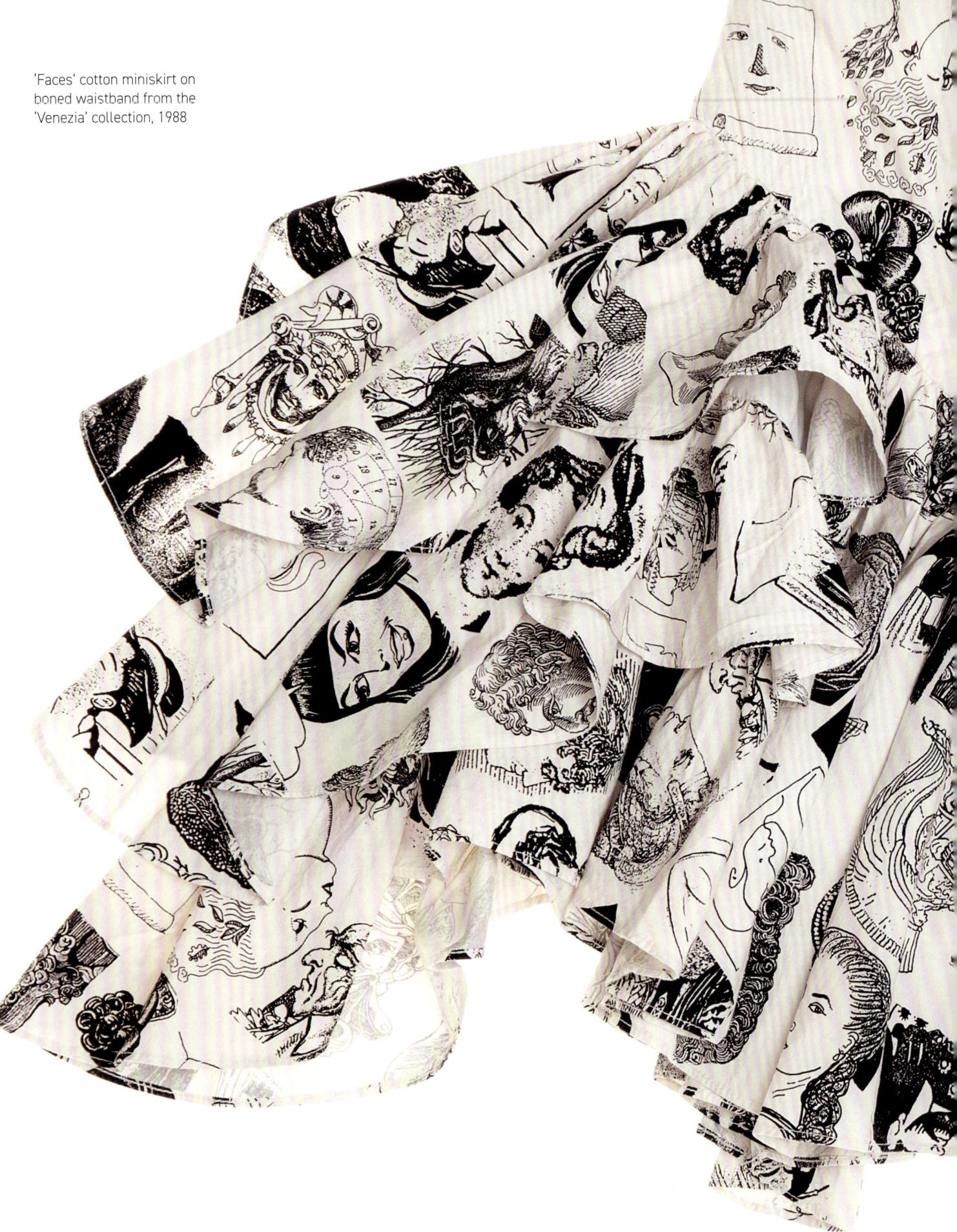

'Faces' cotton miniskirt on boned waistband from the 'Venezia' collection, 1988

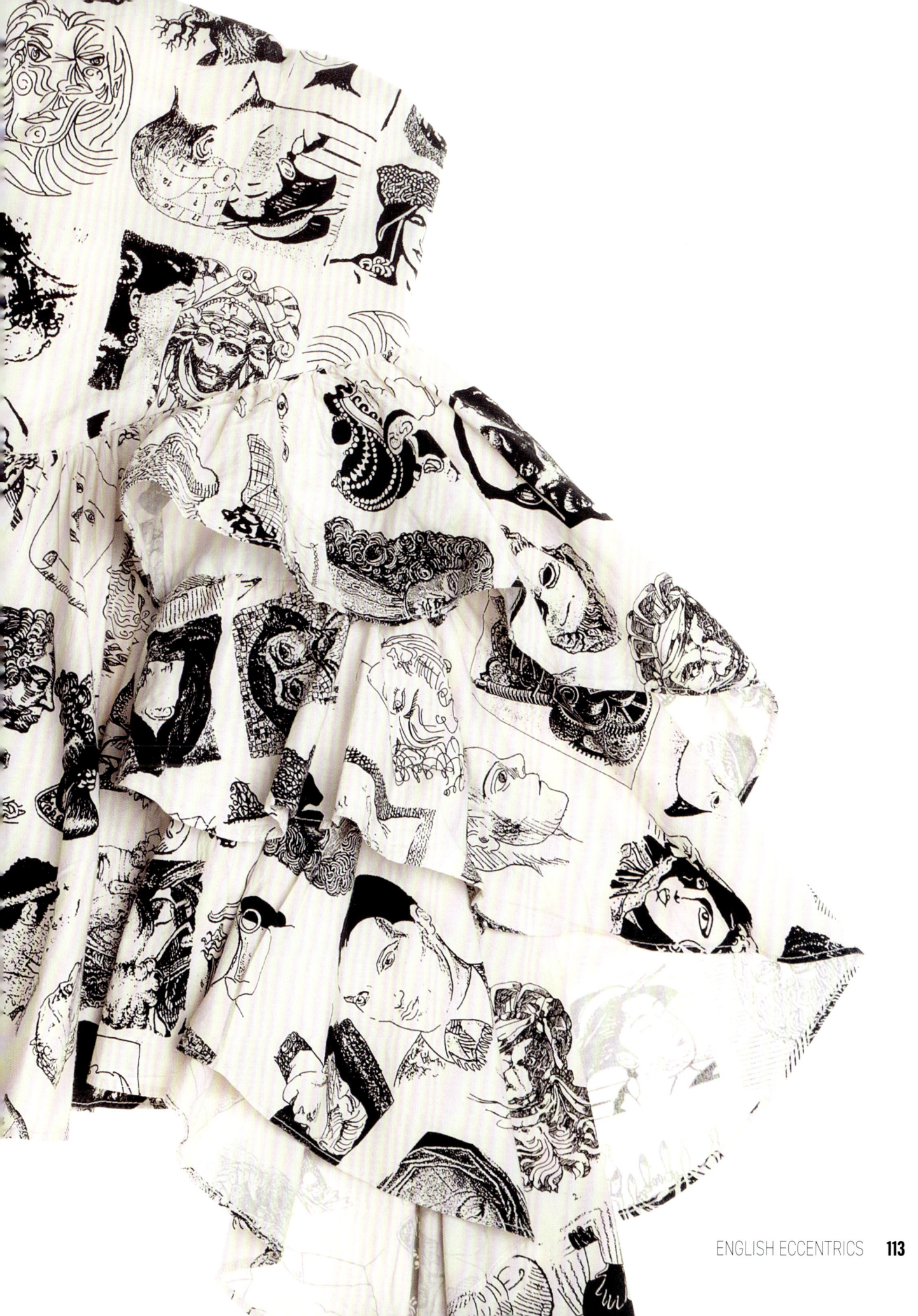

ENGLISH ECCENTRICS

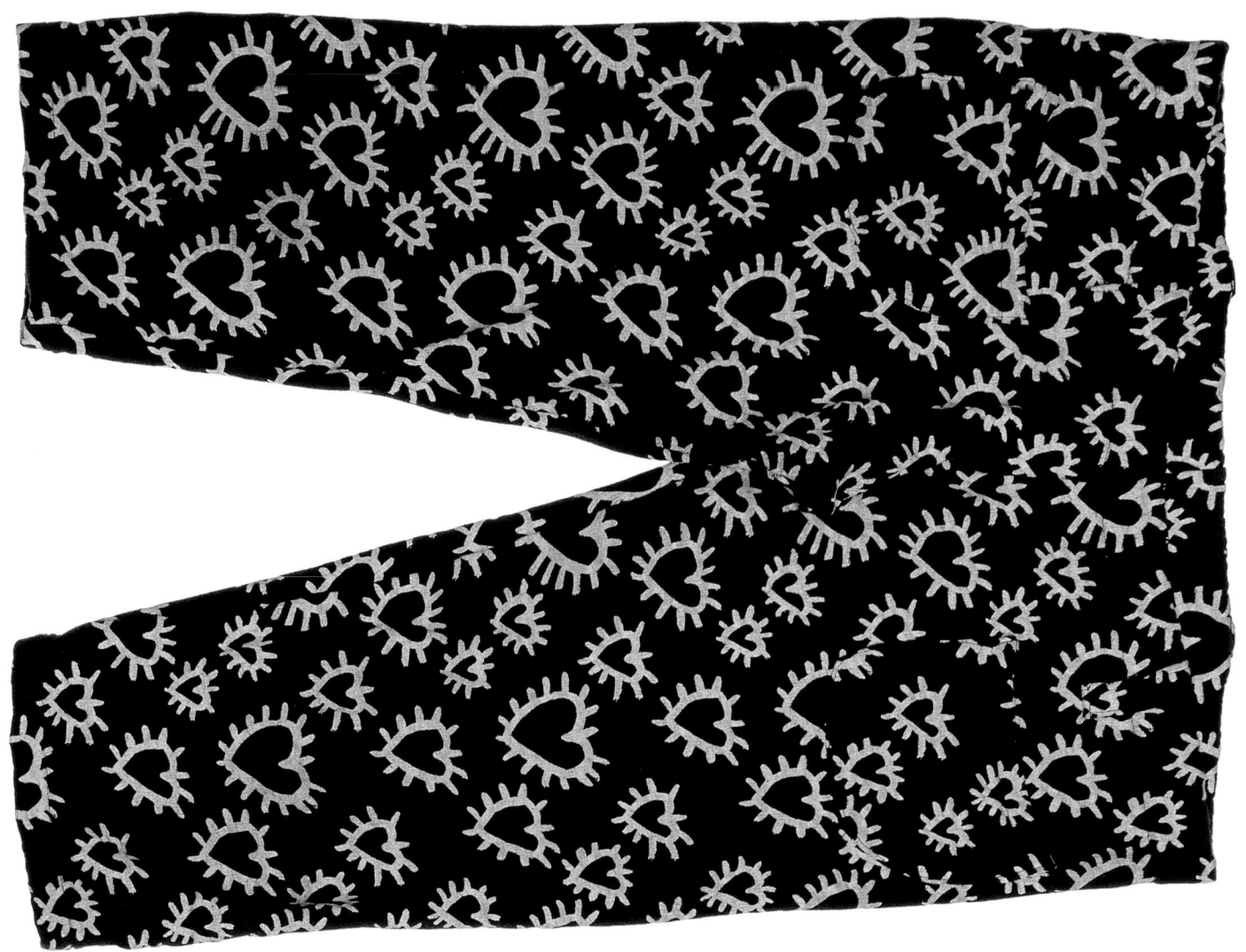

PX

Helen Robinson and business partner Steph Rayner opened their boutique PX in 1978, selling military-inspired clothing with nightclub promoter and Visage frontman Steve Strange and DJ Princess Julia as shop assistants. The interior was designed by stylist Roger Burton, who repurposed hi-tech fittings from MI5 when their building was being demolished.

A year later PX moved to Endell Street in Covent Garden and became a hub for the Blitz club regulars, who came to be known as the Blitz Kids, with milliner Stephen Jones setting up a salon in the basement.

In 1984 Robinson produced a collection featuring her distinctive loveheart print, as worn by Morrissey on the cover of The Smiths' album *The Queen is Dead*.

'I BOUGHT MY "SPIKEY HEART" PIECES IN 1985 AS I LOVED THE POSITIVE/NEGATIVE MONOCHROME EFFECT. IN THE SHOP I WAS SERVED BY SINGER KEANAN DUFFTY, WHO HAD A RECORD OUT CALLED "WATER SPORT". I'D SEEN HIM IN MAGAZINES AND WAS JEALOUS OF HIS THICK, FLAME-RED HAIR. PX HAD ENTHRALLED ME AS A YOUNG TEENAGER AND GOING THERE WAS LIKE THE HOLY GRAIL.'

Maur Valance, nightclub perennial and north London landlady

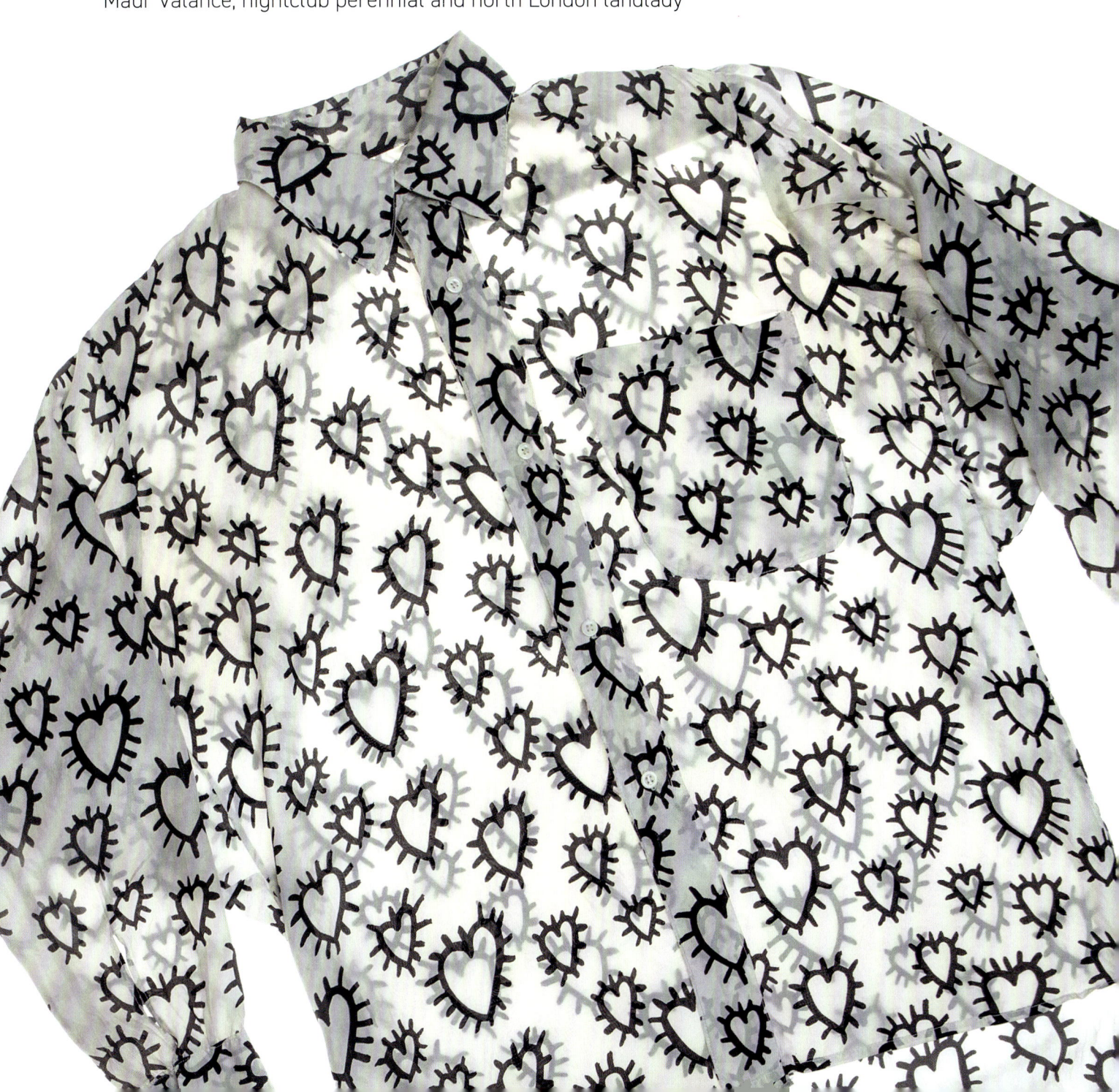

JUDY BLAME

Legendary stylist and accessory designer Judy Blame embraced a DIY punk aesthetic that proved to be highly influential.

During the mid-1980s Blame was part of The House of Beauty and Culture design collective, along with John Moore, Dave Baby and Christopher Nemeth, located in the then-rundown area of Dalston, north-east London.

Blame's creations deployed a wide range of scrap metal, buttons, badges and found objects to create highly distinctive statement pieces. He also worked as a stylist for *The Face*, *i-D* and *Blitz* magazines as well as for Neneh Cherry, Björk, Boy George and Kylie Minogue.

In 2016, while collaborating with Kim Jones, Blame was feted with a major retrospective at the Institute of Contemporary Arts. He passed away two years later.

Beret with buttons as worn by TV producer Andrew Newman, famously photographed by Dave Swindells at Shoom as the face of acid house, 1988

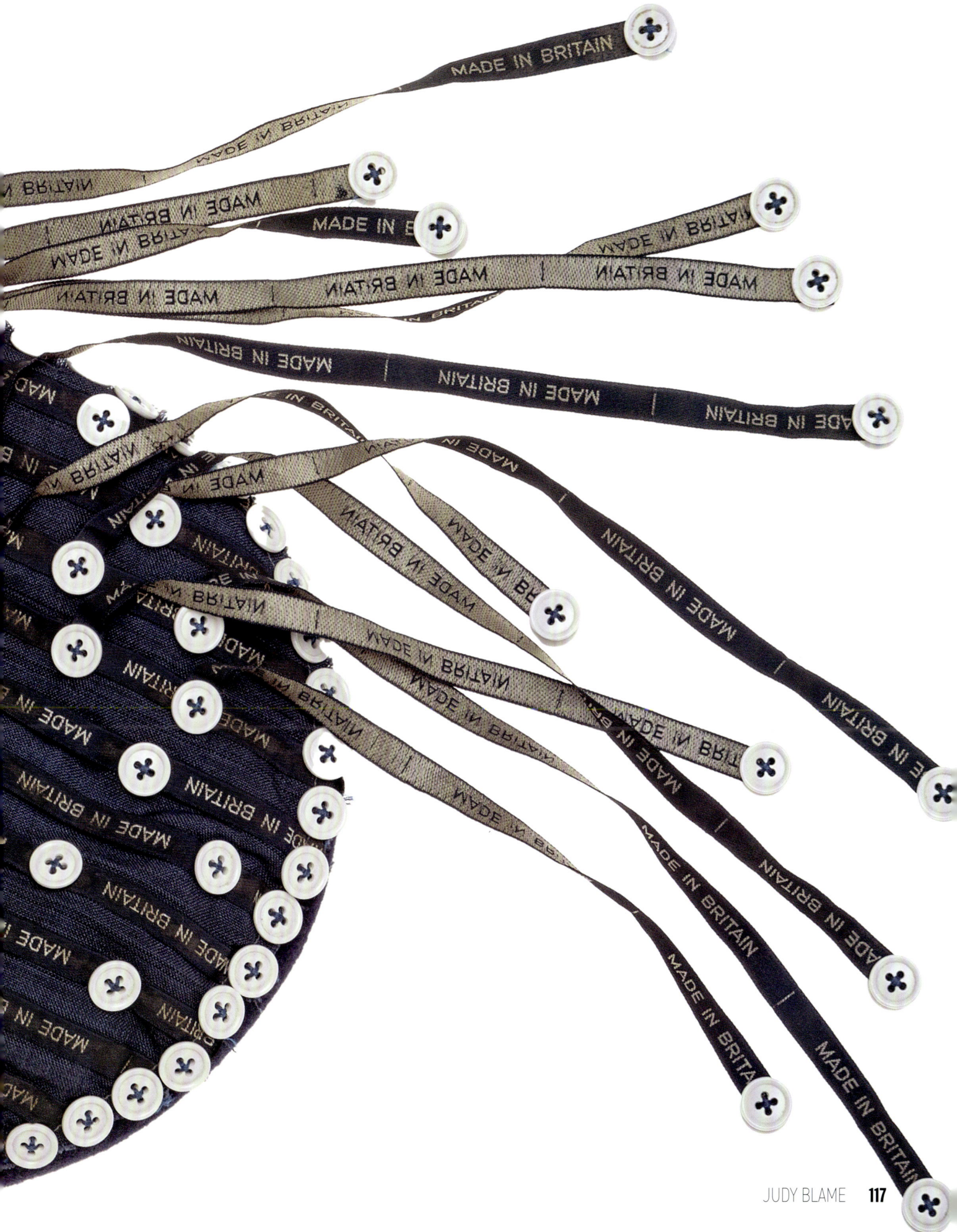

'I WORKED FOR JUDY AS AN ASSISTANT IN THE VERY EARLY 1990S FOR THREE YEARS. HAVING BEEN A HUGE ADMIRER OF HIS WORK AS A SUFFOLK TEENAGER, THIS WAS A DREAM COME TRUE FOR THE COUNTRY GIRL THAT COVETED ALL HER COPIES OF "THE FACE" AND "I-D". THIS BRA WAS HANGING IN HIS FLAT IN ELGIN AVENUE AND HAD BEEN MADE FOR NENEH CHERRY. I ADMIRED IT AND JUDY, IN HIS TYPICALLY GENEROUS STYLE, IMMEDIATELY GAVE IT TO ME. I DEFINITELY GOT TO PARTY IN IT A FEW TIMES, DESPITE ME AND NENEH BEING DIFFERENT SIZES. IT'S AN OLD WONDERBRA AND ONE OF MY MOST TREASURED POSSESSIONS.'

Emma Day, make-up artist

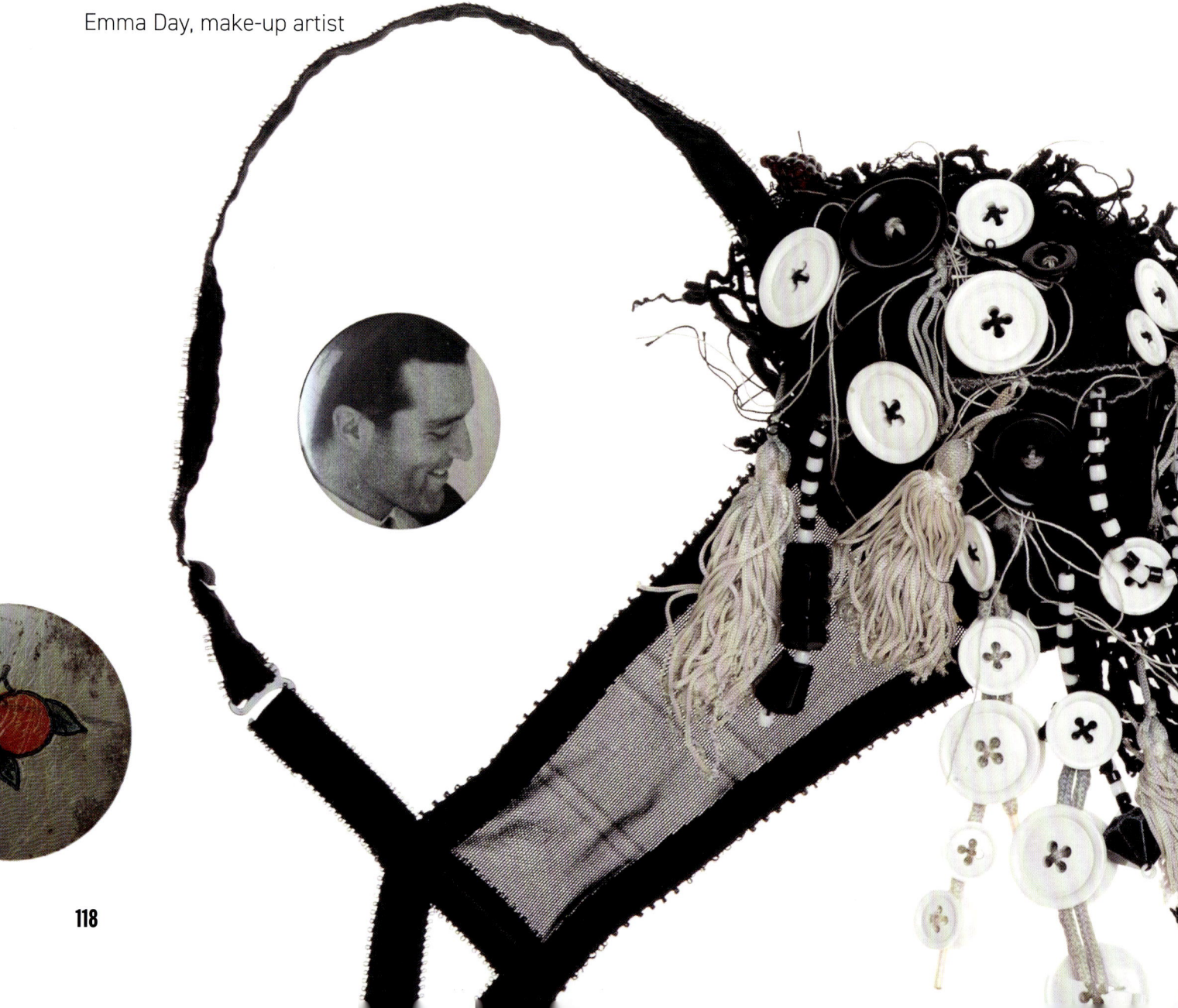

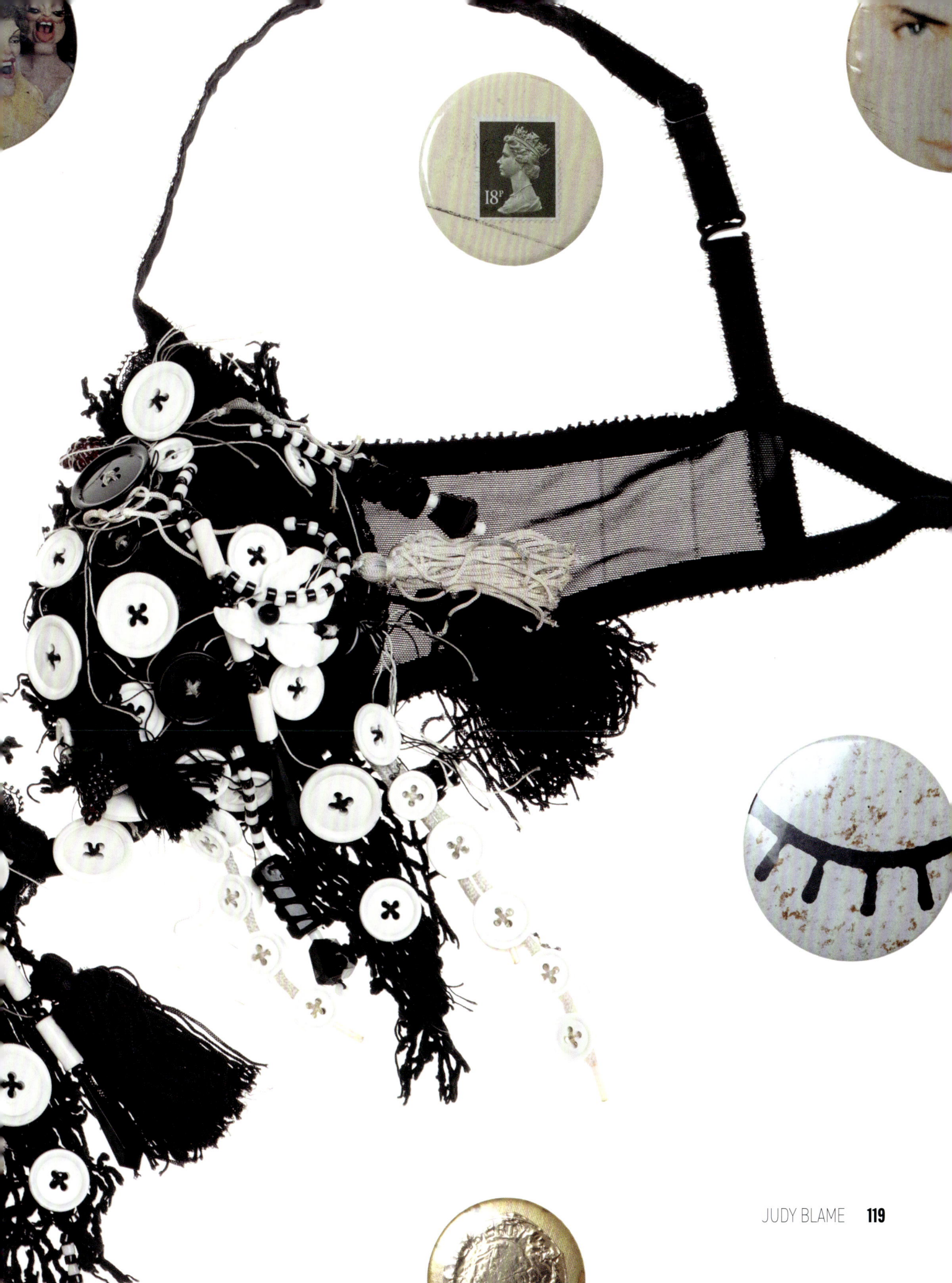

JOHN GALLIANO

Arguably the most famous and influential designer of his generation, John Galliano graduated in 1984 from St Martin's School of Art with a first-class honours degree.

His graduation collection was inspired by the French Revolution and entitled 'Les Incroyables'. It received rave reviews and was famously bought in its entirety for resale in the London high-end fashion boutique Browns. Galliano was just 24.

In 1989 Galliano left London and moved to Paris, eventually becoming creative director of Givenchy, Dior and now Maison Margiela.

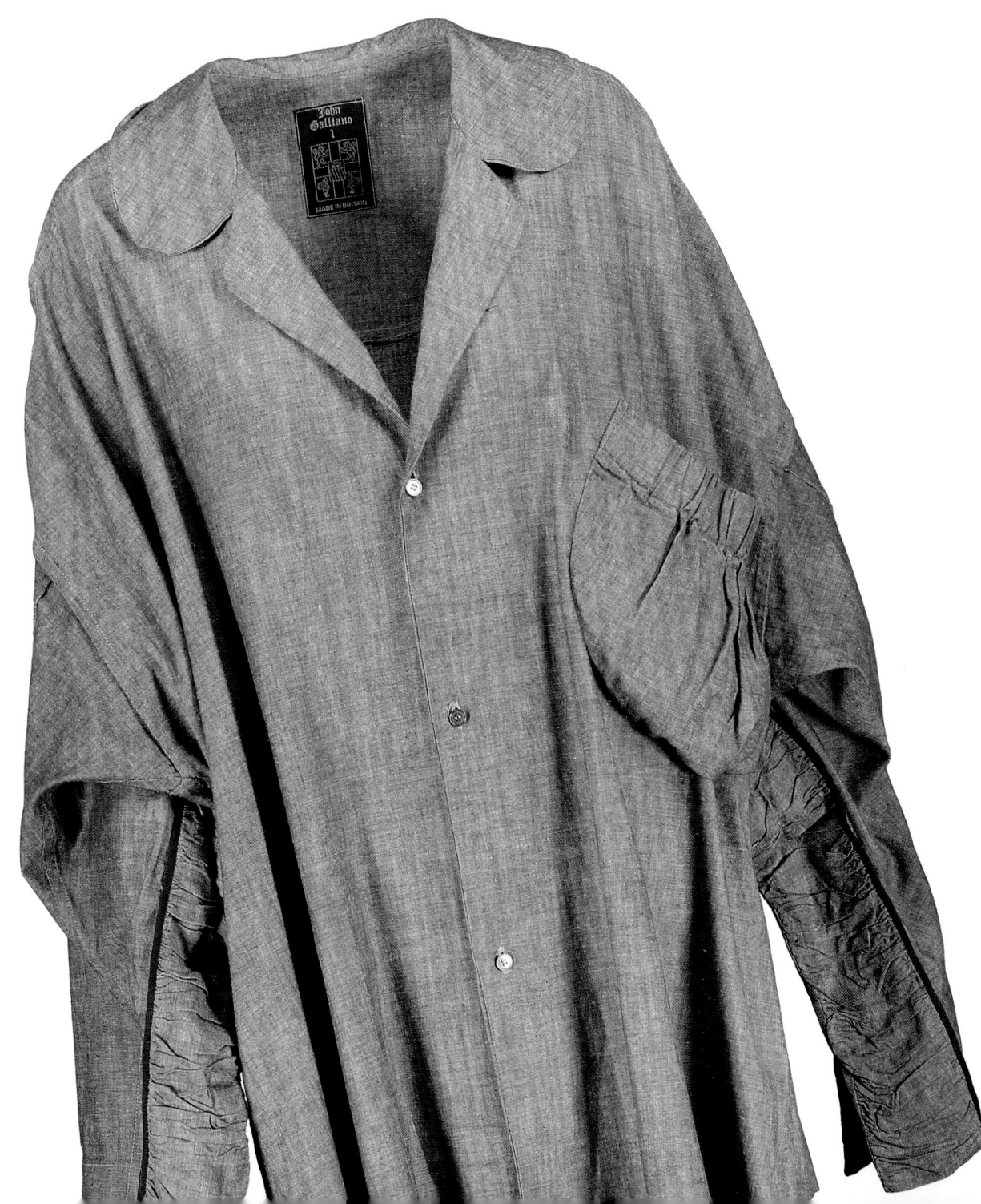

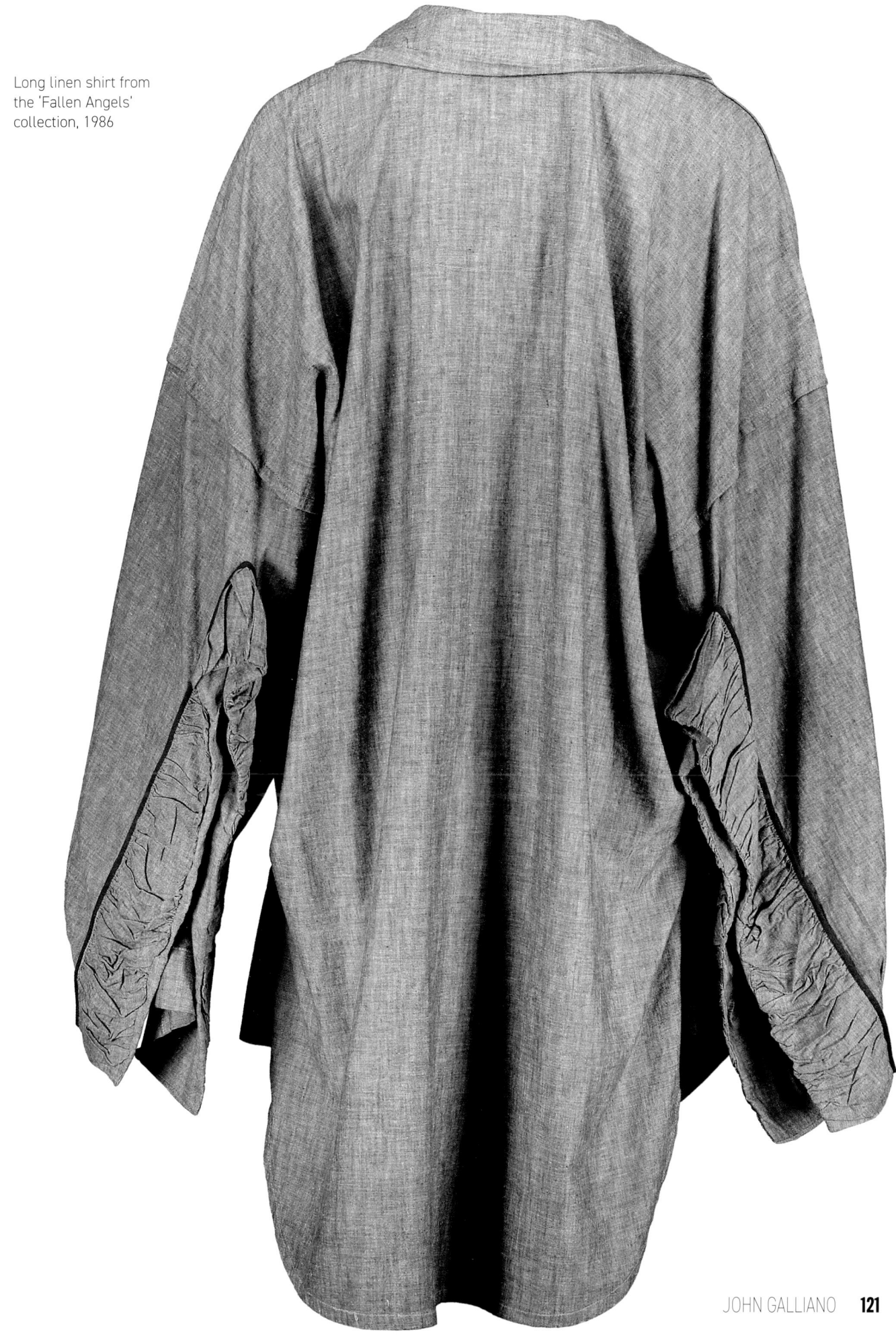

Long linen shirt from the 'Fallen Angels' collection, 1986

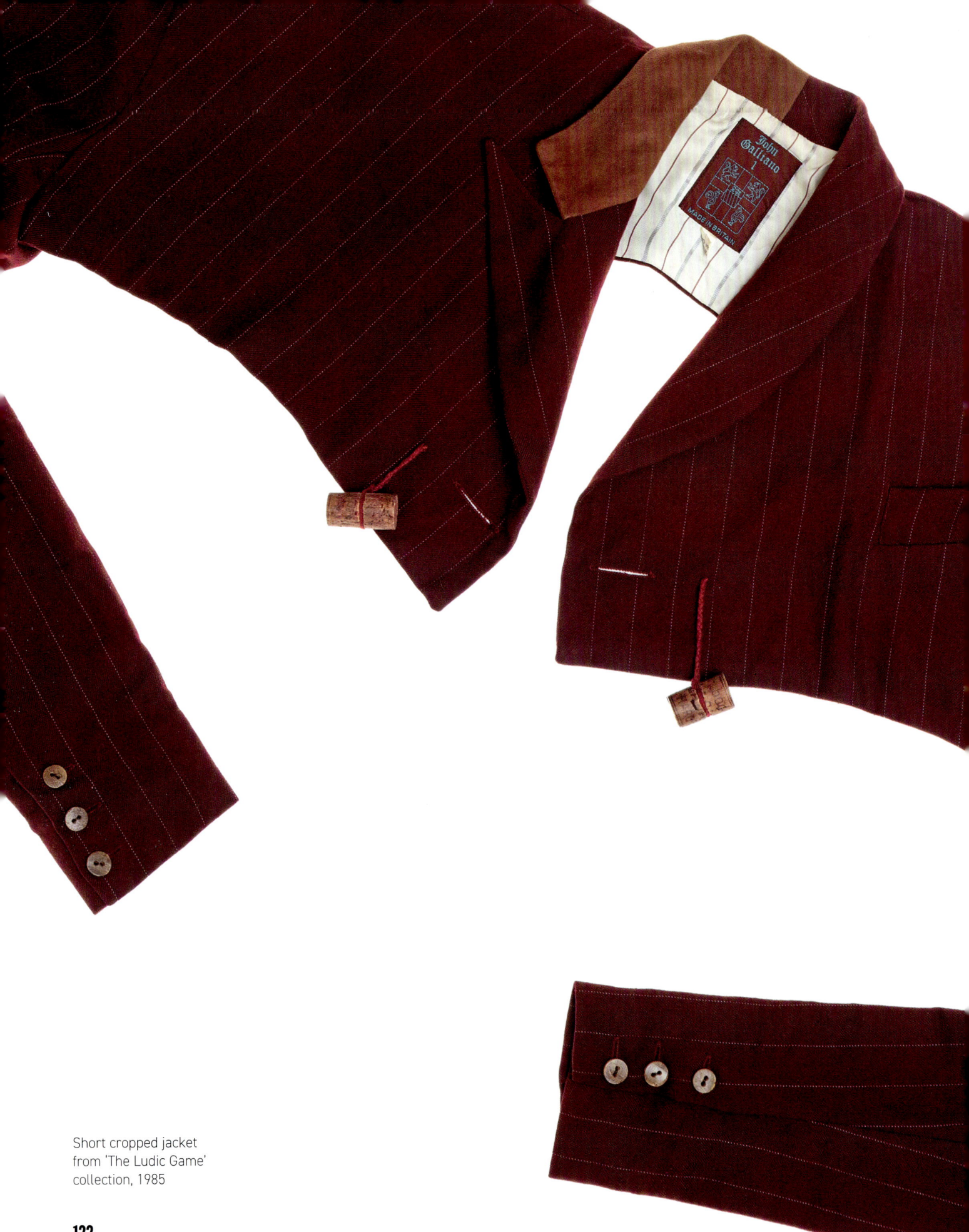

Short cropped jacket from 'The Ludic Game' collection, 1985

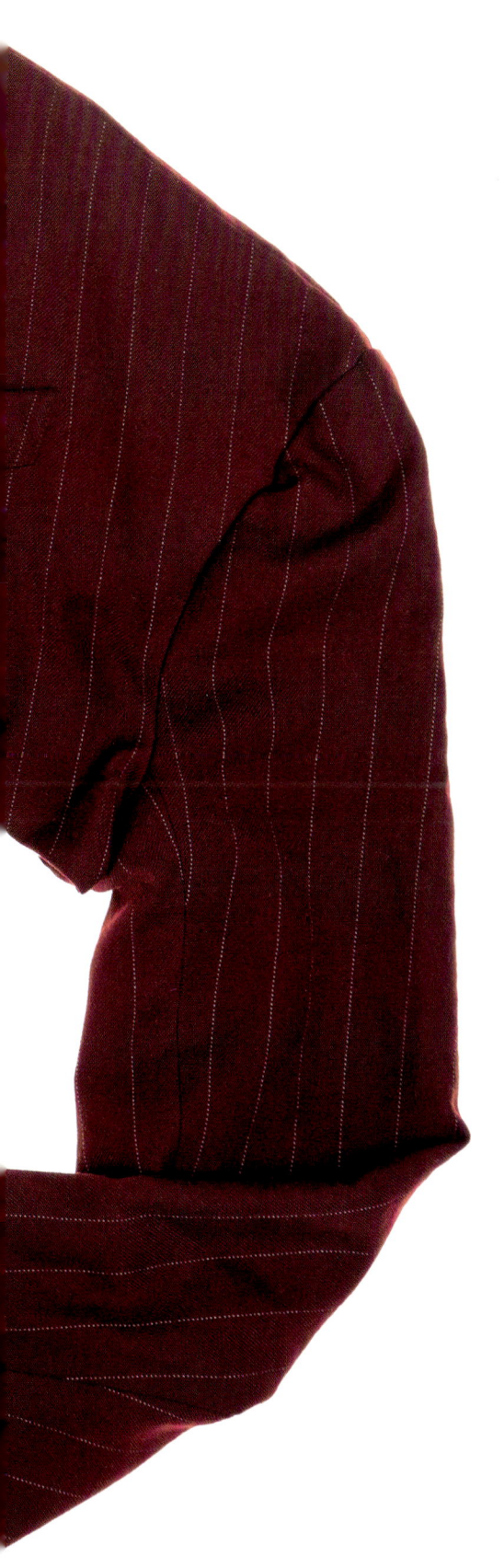

'AS A FASHION MODEL AT ST MARTIN'S I WENT TO JOHN GALLIANO'S DEGREE SHOW AND SHORTLY AFTER I WAS INVITED TO SRI LANKA BY A FRIEND. I WAS TOLD I NEEDED TO DRESS SMART AS HIS MOTHER WAS HOSTING A PARTY FOR THE MINISTER OF CULTURE. I BOUGHT A CROPPED BOLERO JACKET WITH MASSIVELY LONG SLEEVES FROM GALLIANO'S FIRST MENSWEAR COLLECTION. WHEN I ARRIVED, THE OTHER MEN WERE IN TRADITIONAL SUITS, BUT I STRUTTED ABOUT LOOKING LIKE A FASHIONISTA.

THE NEXT MORNING MY FRIEND TOOK OUT A MASSIVE STACK OF RUPEE NOTES SAYING HIS MOTHER HAD ASKED HIM TO GIVE THEM TO ME. I ASKED "WHY?" – APPARENTLY SHE WAS VERY UPSET THAT A FRIEND OF HER SON'S WAS SO POOR HE COULD ONLY AFFORD HALF A JACKET!'

Michael Petry, contemporary American artist working in London

THE PARISH NOTICEBOARD

In many ways club flyers were our internet, some years before the actual internet existed. Finding out what was going on in London clubland came via three sources – word of mouth, *Time Out* magazine and flyers. That was it.

For me, flyers were the most exciting and crucial source of information for finding out what clubs were running in mid-1980s London. In straitened times I would peek a look at the Nightlife section of *Time Out* in Selfridges' magazine department, but I rarely bought it.

As a new arrival to London, I was yet to know who any of the faces in the scene were, only glimpsing them in pages of *i-D* and *The Face*.

I was at the Courtauld Institute studying history of art from 1984 to 1987. Coming from a cloistered – literally – boarding school I despised, London's clubs were a kaleidoscope of vivid sights and sounds I was hungry to immerse myself in. As a result, I would hoover up flyers from clothes and record shops across the West End – and it was the West End then, as the cultural move eastwards had not yet begun in earnest. The hunt to find them was part of the thrill.

Flyers would be found mainly in shops in Soho, with outliers such as the Duffer of St George in Portobello Road, the BodyMap stall in Camden Market, PX and Jones in Covent Garden, Worlds End on the King's Road and the handful of shops in Kensington Market not catering to goths or tourists, with Hyper Hyper across the road selling clothes by Leigh Bowery and Rachel Auburn. In Soho, digging out short-lived fashion shops such as Site, Kunst and John Crancher's Anarchy provided a good range of flyers for club nights my friends and I wanted to go to, as they sold clothes worn by those at the clubs. My favourite record shop – possibly of all time – was Record Shack in Berwick Street, where I tried to peek over DJ Mark Moore's shoulder as he was replenishing his playlist for later that night. You could rest assured that Taffy's 'I Love My Radio' would deliver if he had it in his stack.

Flyers were also key in offering discounted or guestlist entry – every penny counted in student days. But mainly they laid out what you were getting, who was DJing and where and when. Jeffrey Hinton, Mark Moore and Martin Confusion were a quality kitemark for all things Hi-NRG. I was a regular at John Crancher and Sandeep's Anarchy but once it left its spiritual home of Studio Valbonne in Kingly Street, it was hard to keep up with its short-lived locations around Soho. Rather wonderfully, Anarchy's best era was when it ran on a Sunday night, so you could spot likely attendees flamboyantly standing out on the relatively quiet streets, when everybody else was responsibly preparing for the week ahead.

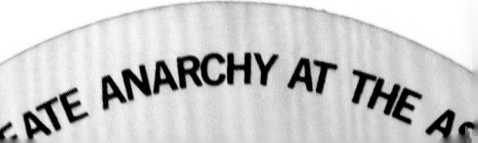

'As a new arrival to London, I was yet to know who any of the faces in the scene were, only glimpsing them in pages of *i-D* and *The Face*.'

The look of the flyer was key. If the flyer looked rubbish, that wouldn't be a good sign. With Anarchy, much of the flyer graphics referenced punk in the cut-up text and circled 'A' symbols. By the early 1980s, punk style was the preserve of a pretty grim bunch, so in some ways this took it back to its fashion foundations. The glassine paper used for their flyers was another Anarchy identifier.

Flyers for The Bell in King's Cross were refreshingly unpretentious, suiting its clientele, which despite featuring all the gay pop stars of the day, was pretty studenty. On Wednesdays when you left The Bell at closing time you were given a flyer for Pyramid at Heaven, so hordes of us would simply get the tube to Charing Cross to continue the night's festivities.

The elegant graphics of Amen and Sacrosanct suggested more sophisticated nights out, although the reality was a lot more chaotic and fun.

So flyers were the parish noticeboard of mid-1980s clubbing. Mine are stuck in scrapbooks and have curiously never attracted the same attention as rave flyers, which appeared only a few years later. I was more cut out for small basements in Soho wearing unsuitable outfits than for damp fields off the M25, so these flyers capture this short era before clubbing exploded.

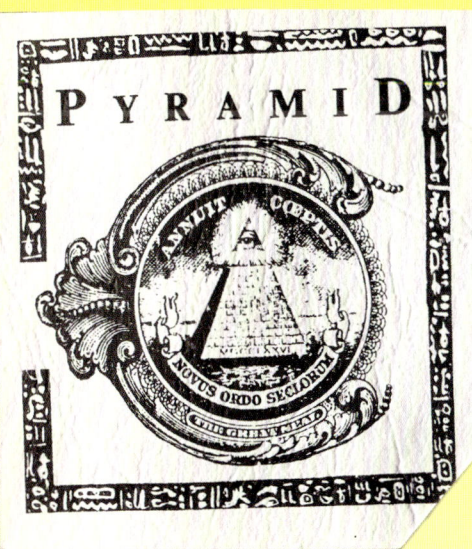
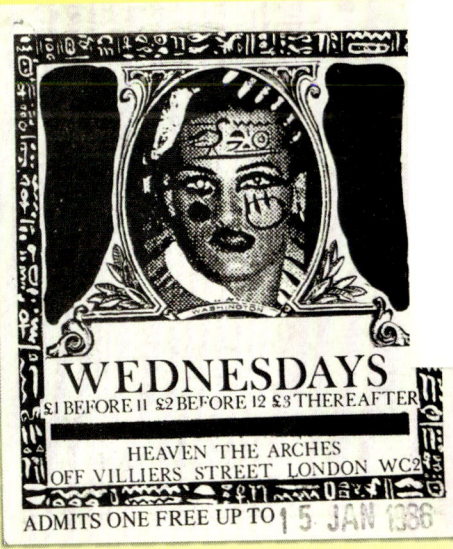
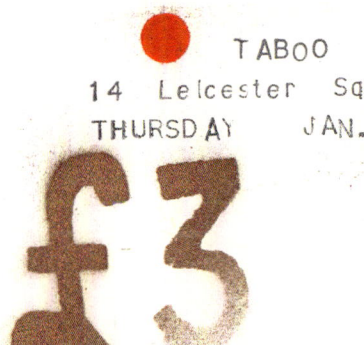

DANIEL SCOTT
PUBLISHER & WRITER

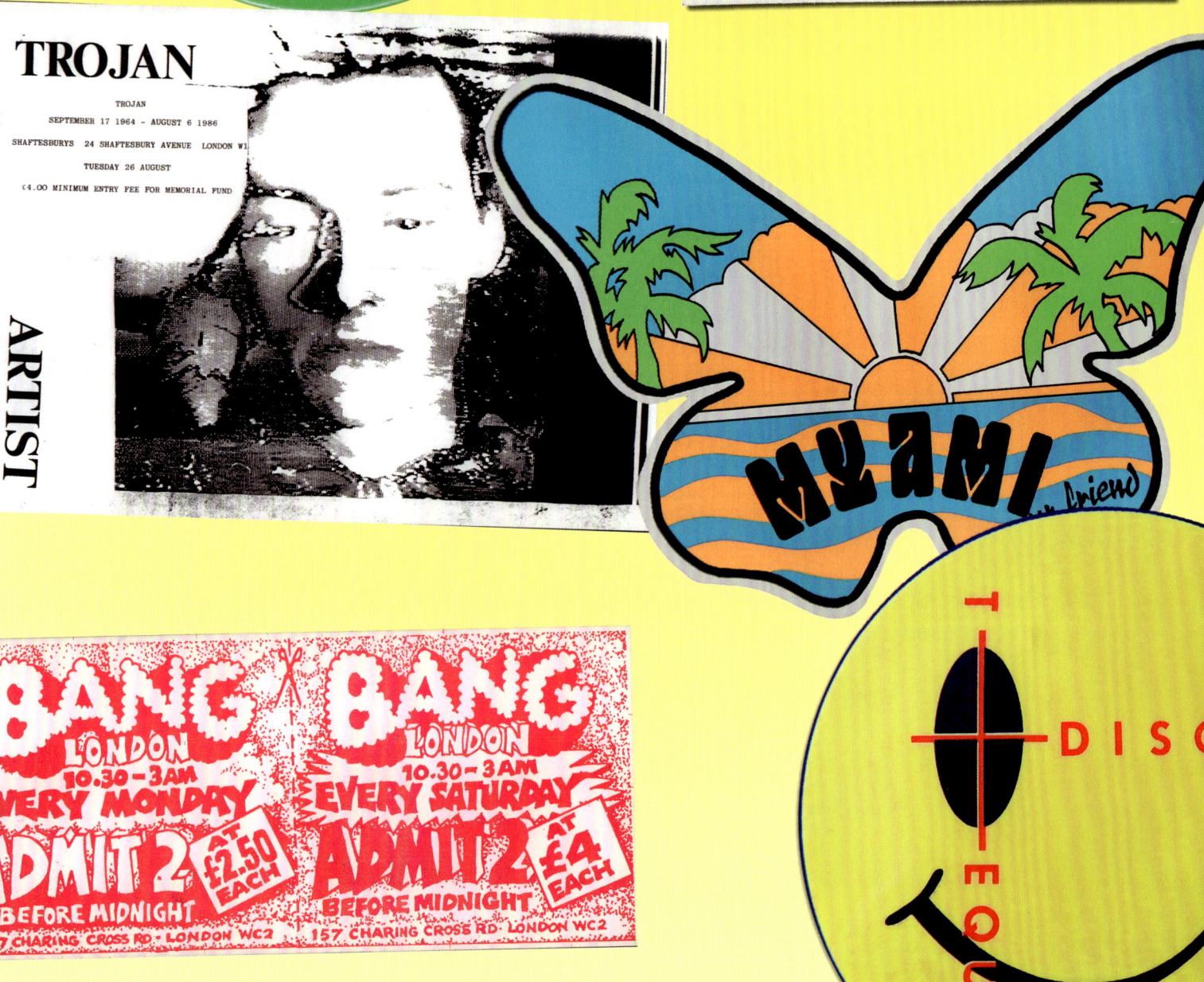

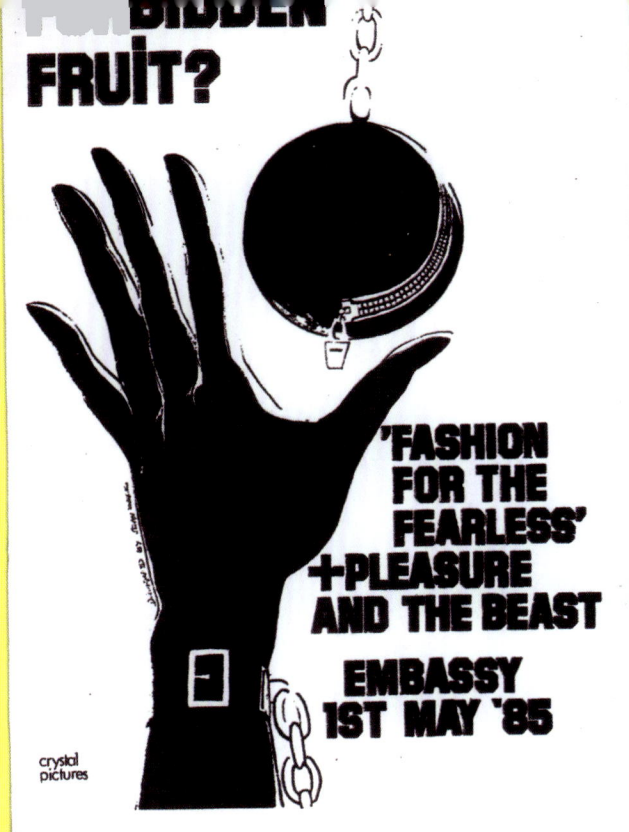
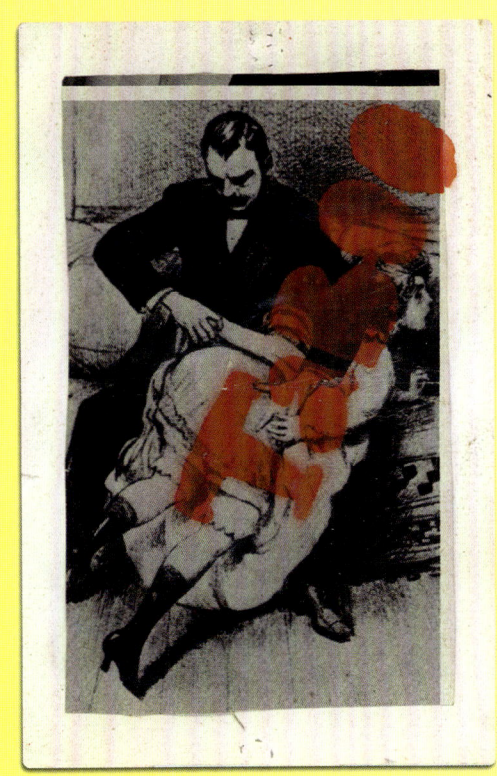
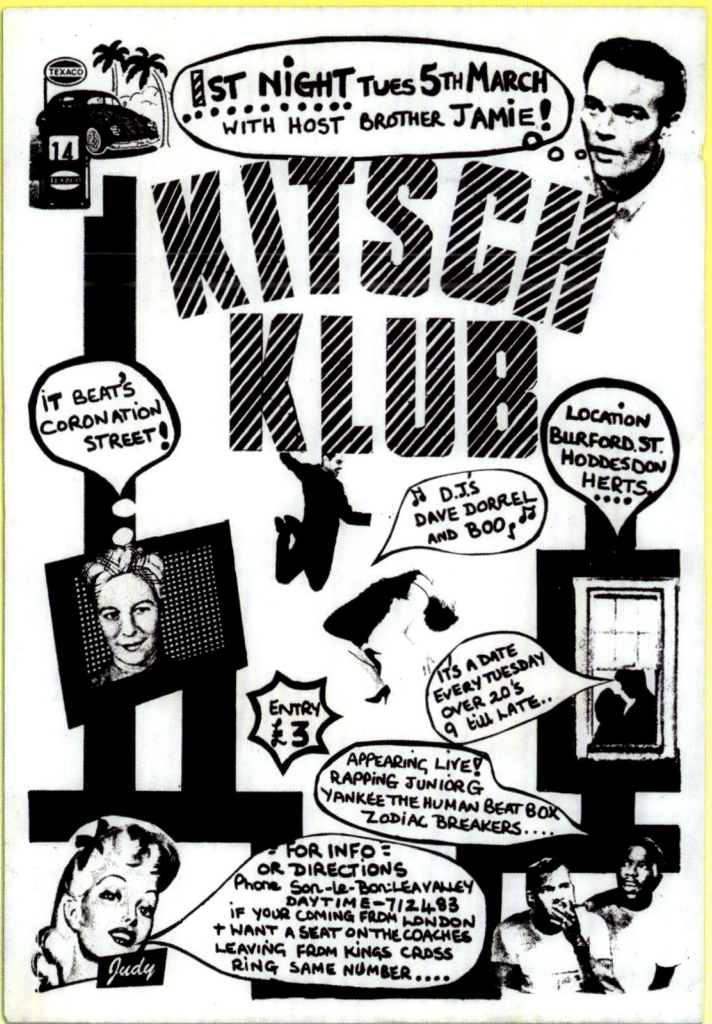
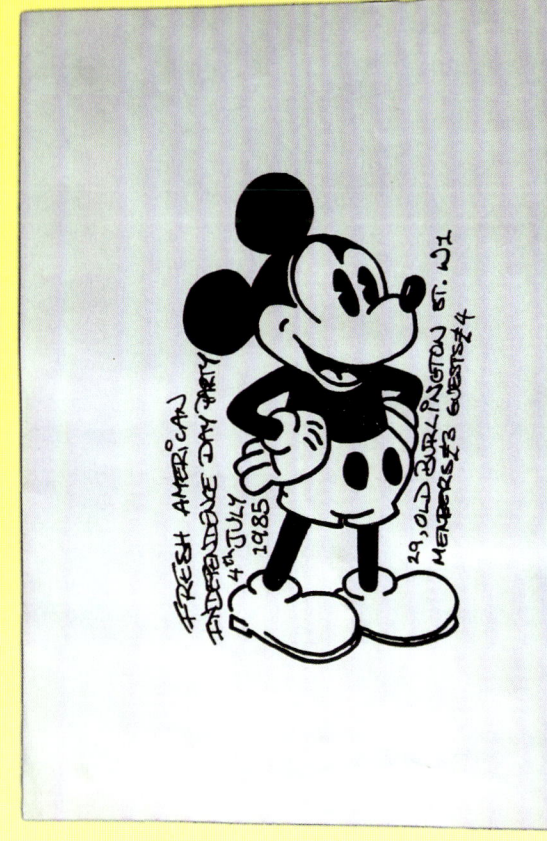

PAM HOGG

The ultimate outlaw, Pam Hogg moved from Glasgow and grabbed London clubland by the scruff of the neck with her mini collections. Her early designs were stocked at Harrods in London and Bloomingdale's in New York, plus boutiques in Paris, Italy and Tokyo. Her popular unit in Kensington Market's Hyper Hyper secured her first catwalk show in 1985.

Over the next five years Hogg launched a Soho boutique and produced a further six catwalk shows, cementing her status as a star of the London fashion scene.

Hogg continues to create, making music and art, and her recent fashion collections are as original, provocative and powerful as ever.

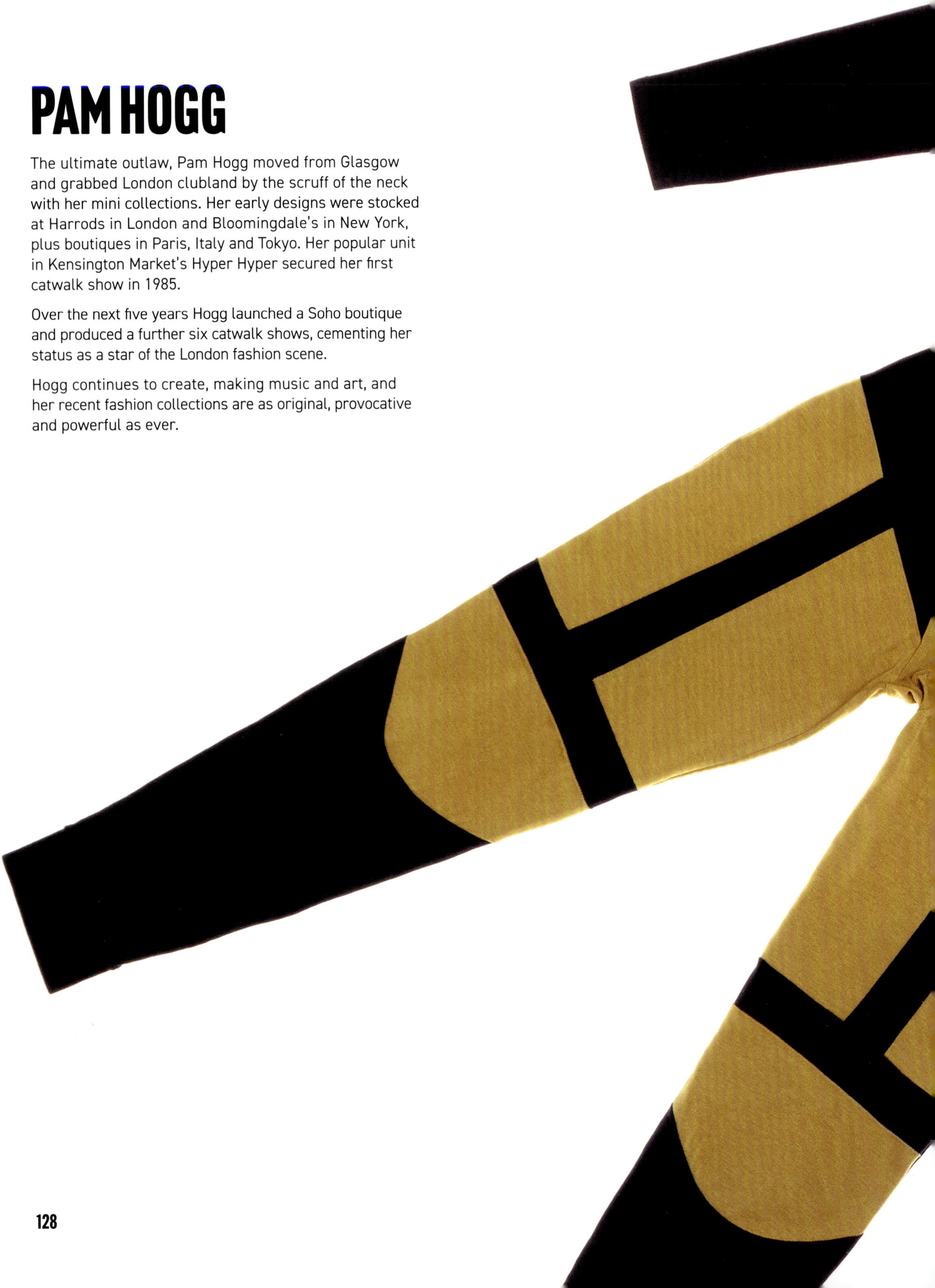

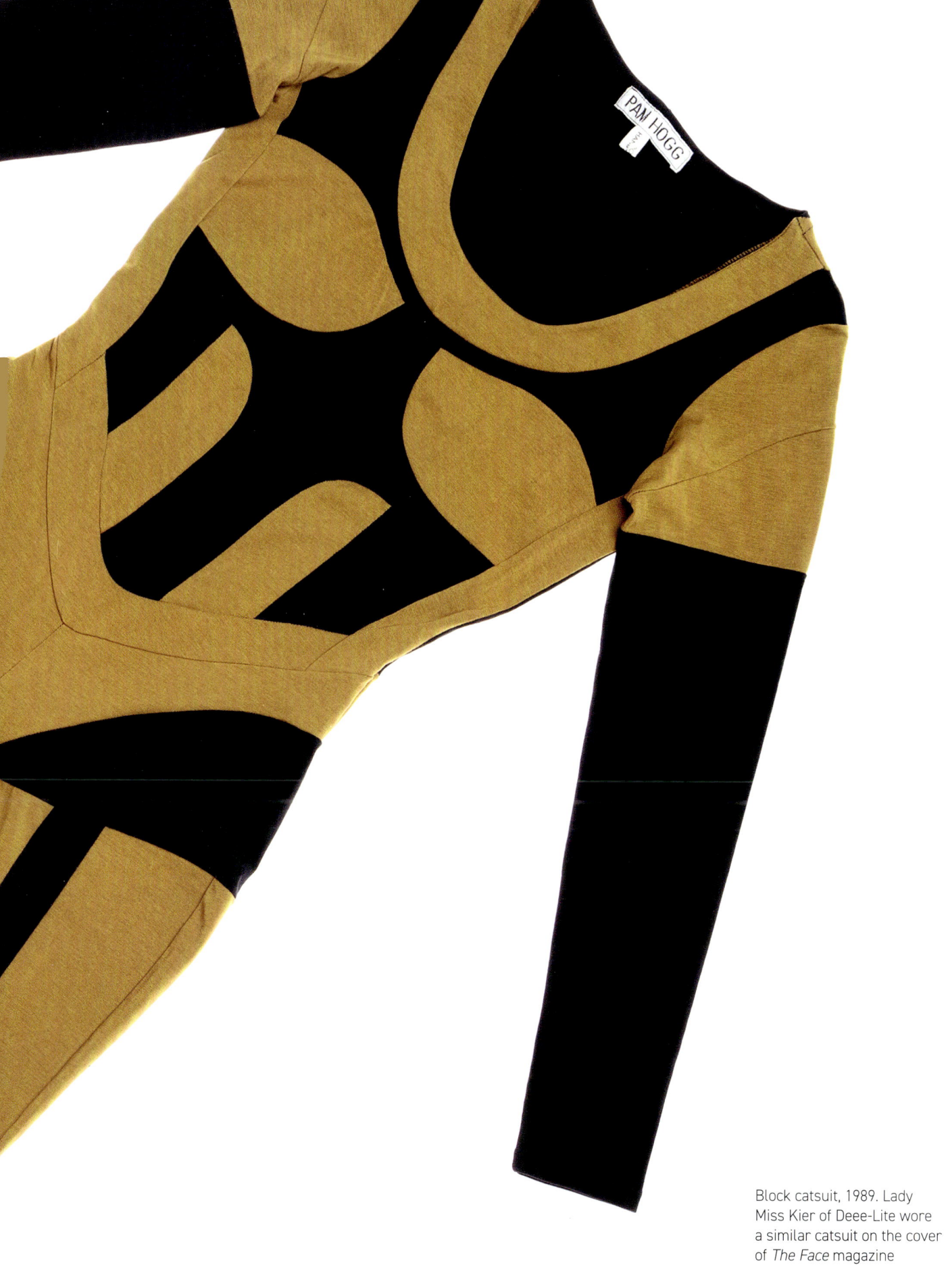

Block catsuit, 1989. Lady Miss Kier of Deee-Lite wore a similar catsuit on the cover of *The Face* magazine

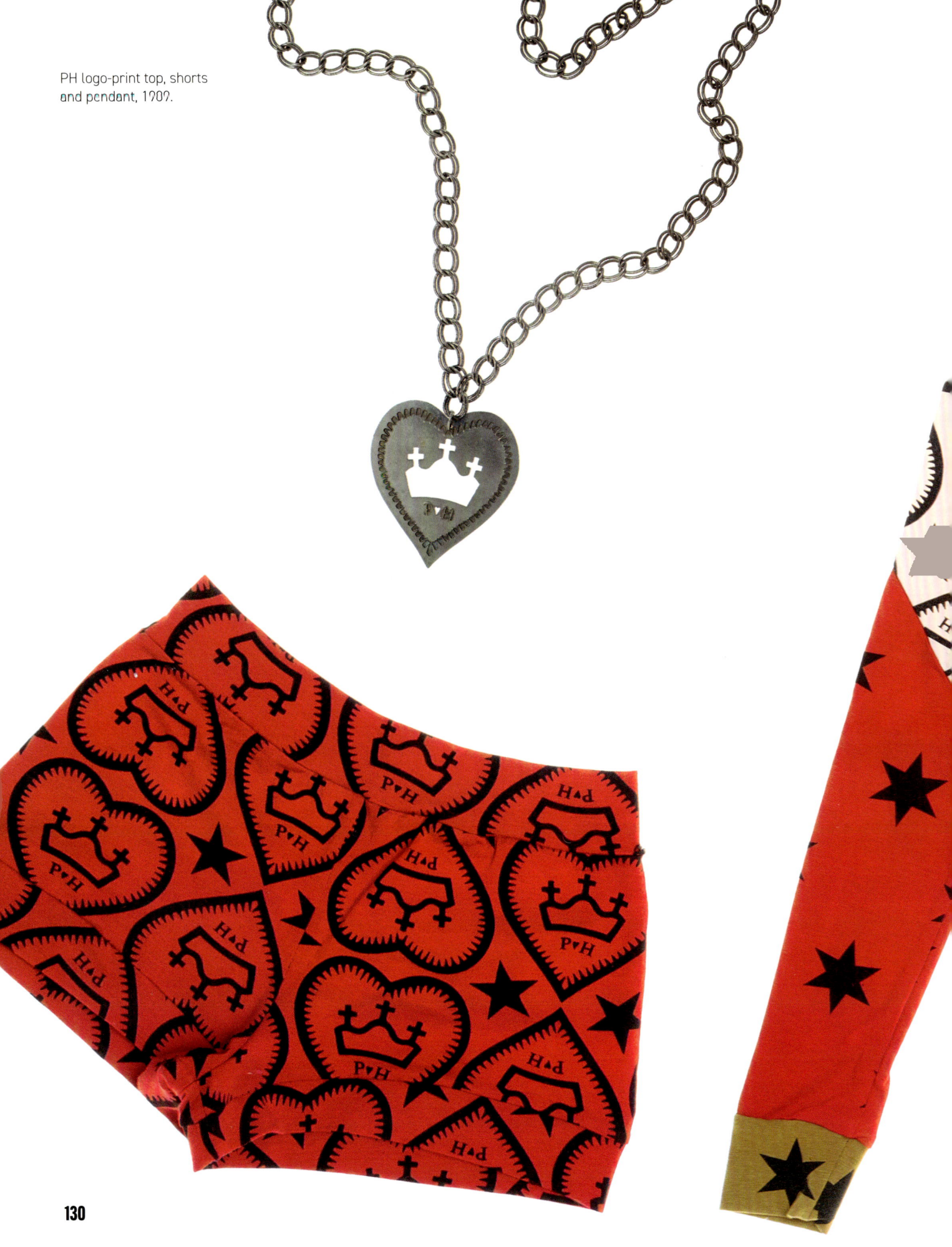

PH logo-print top, shorts and pendant, 1982.

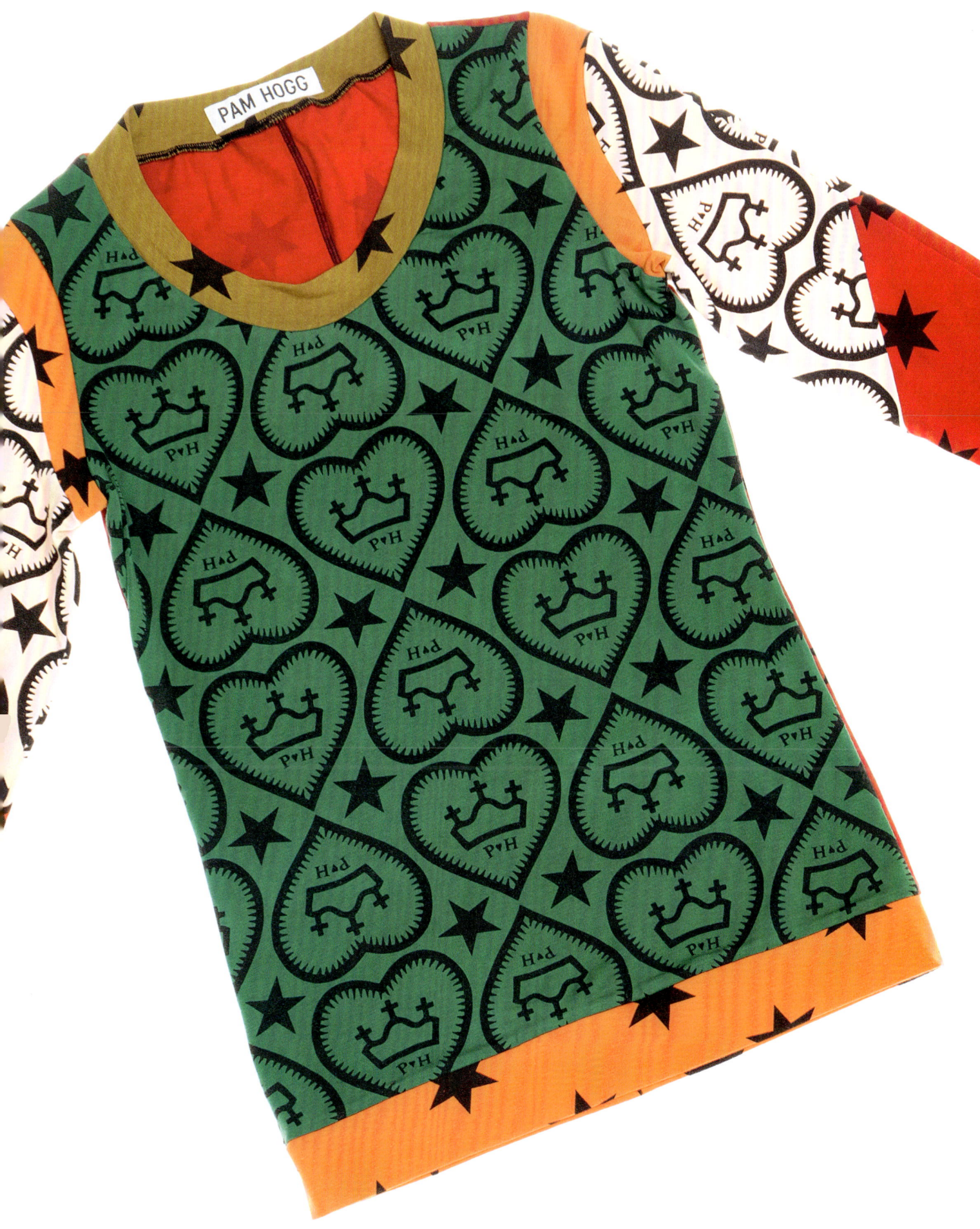

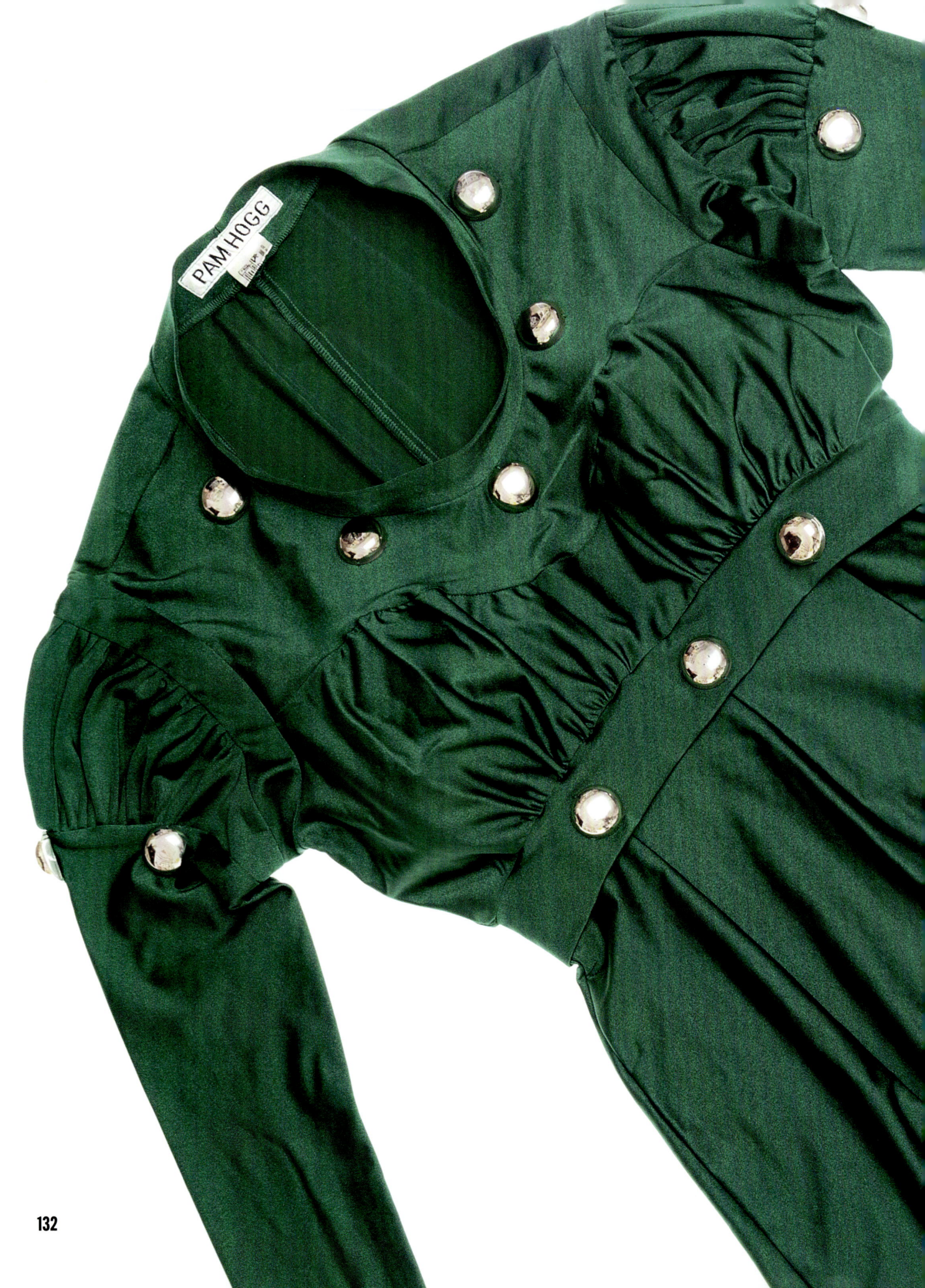

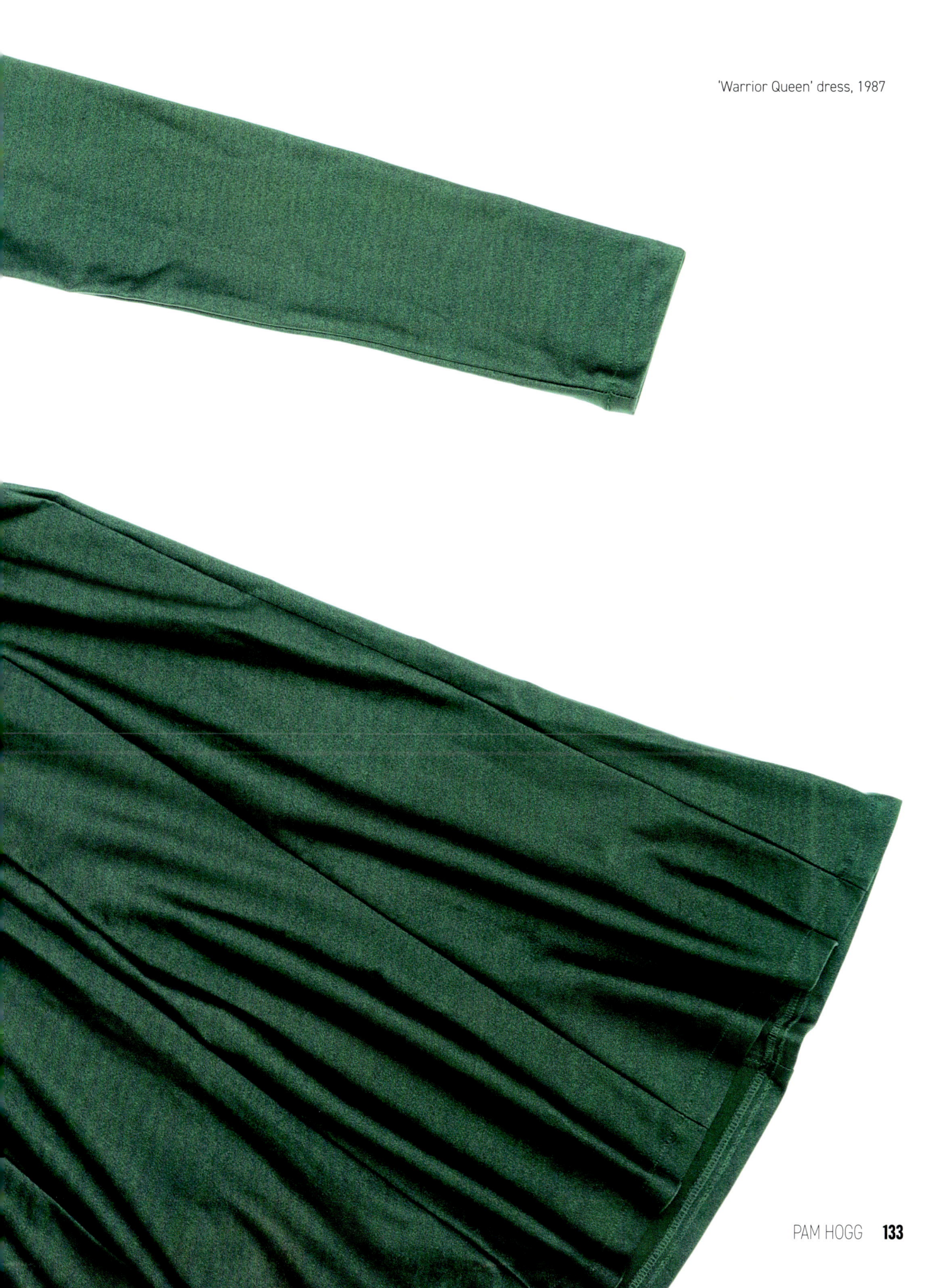

'Warrior Queen' dress, 1987

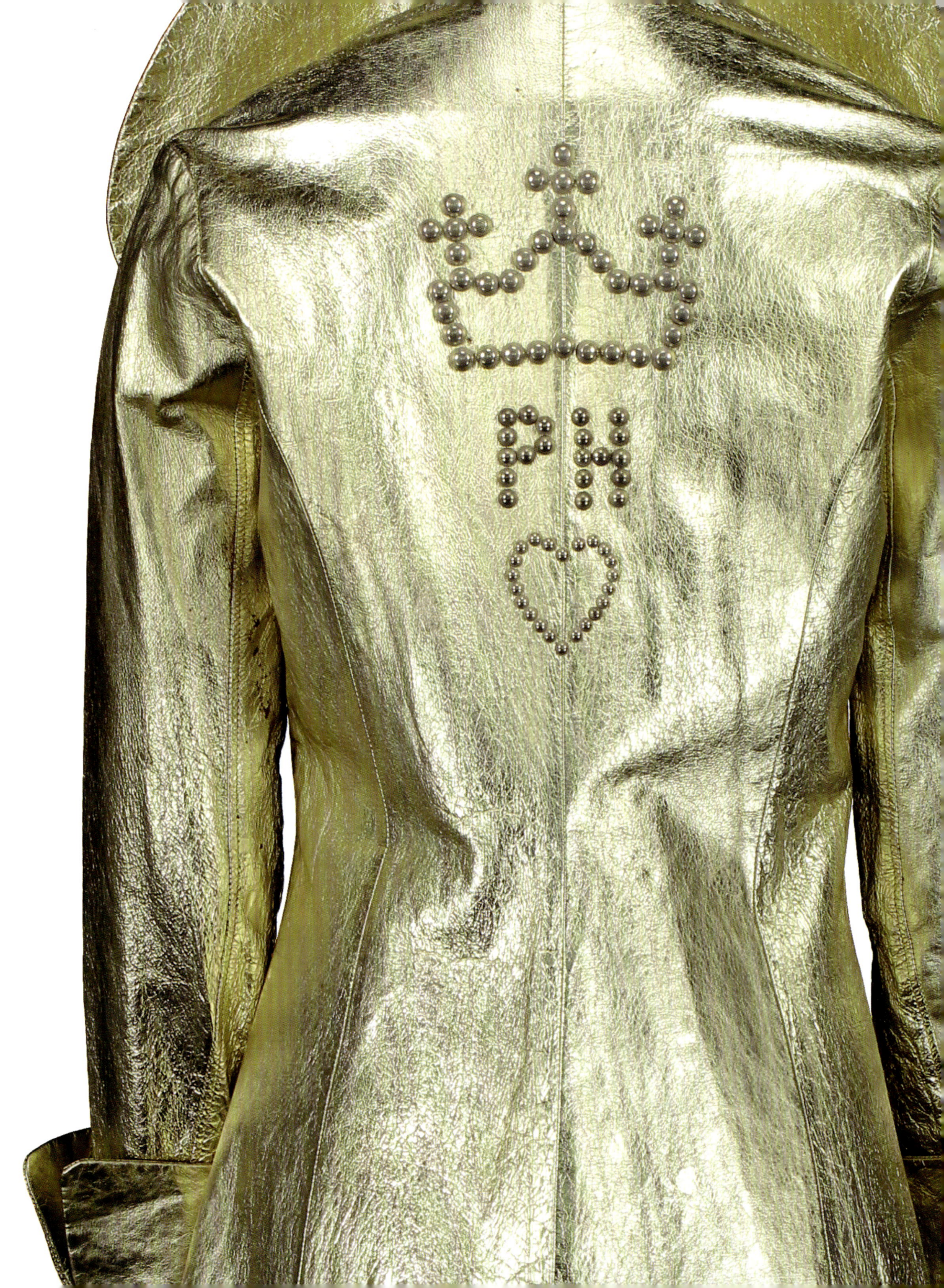

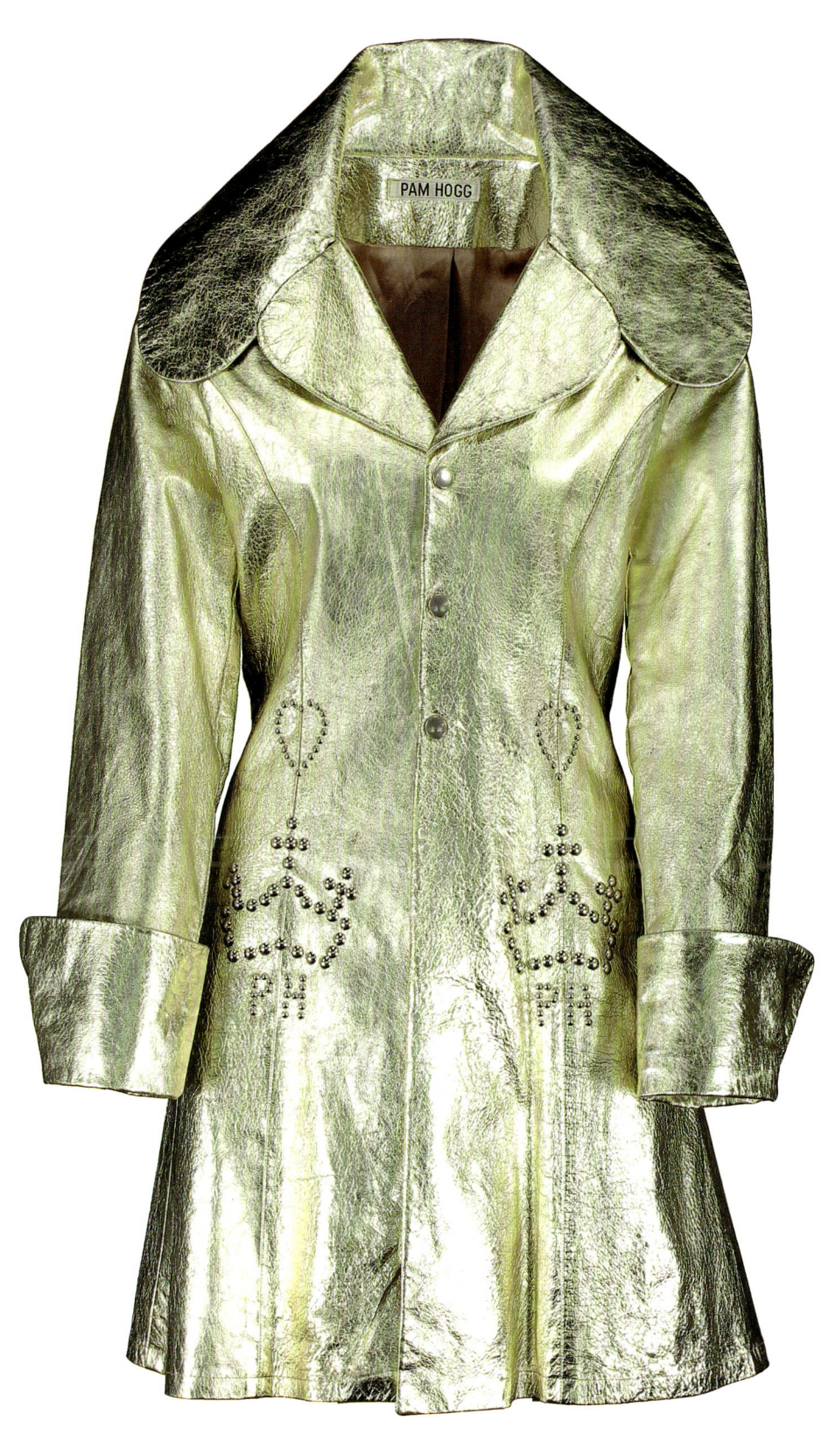

'Lust for Life' gold leather coat, 1989

DEMOB

The Beak Street store Demob was founded in 1982 by Chris and Sue Brick, selling designs by Robin Archer and Franceska King.

Stephen Mahoney, who ran a Friday club night at Le Beat Route with Ollie O'Donnell, worked at the store and introduced other designers including Willie Brown, Richard Ostell and Elmaz Hüseyin.

The Demob look was an eclectic mix of oversized utility and contemporary fashion, which attracted musicians Spandau Ballet and David Byrne along with artists Peter Doig and Jean-Michel Basquiat.

Chris Brick also organised parties in abandoned warehouses and the shop's basement, which became a studio for the band OUT.

At the back of the shop was Demop, a barber where John Egan and Steph Avery would cut hair to complete the look.

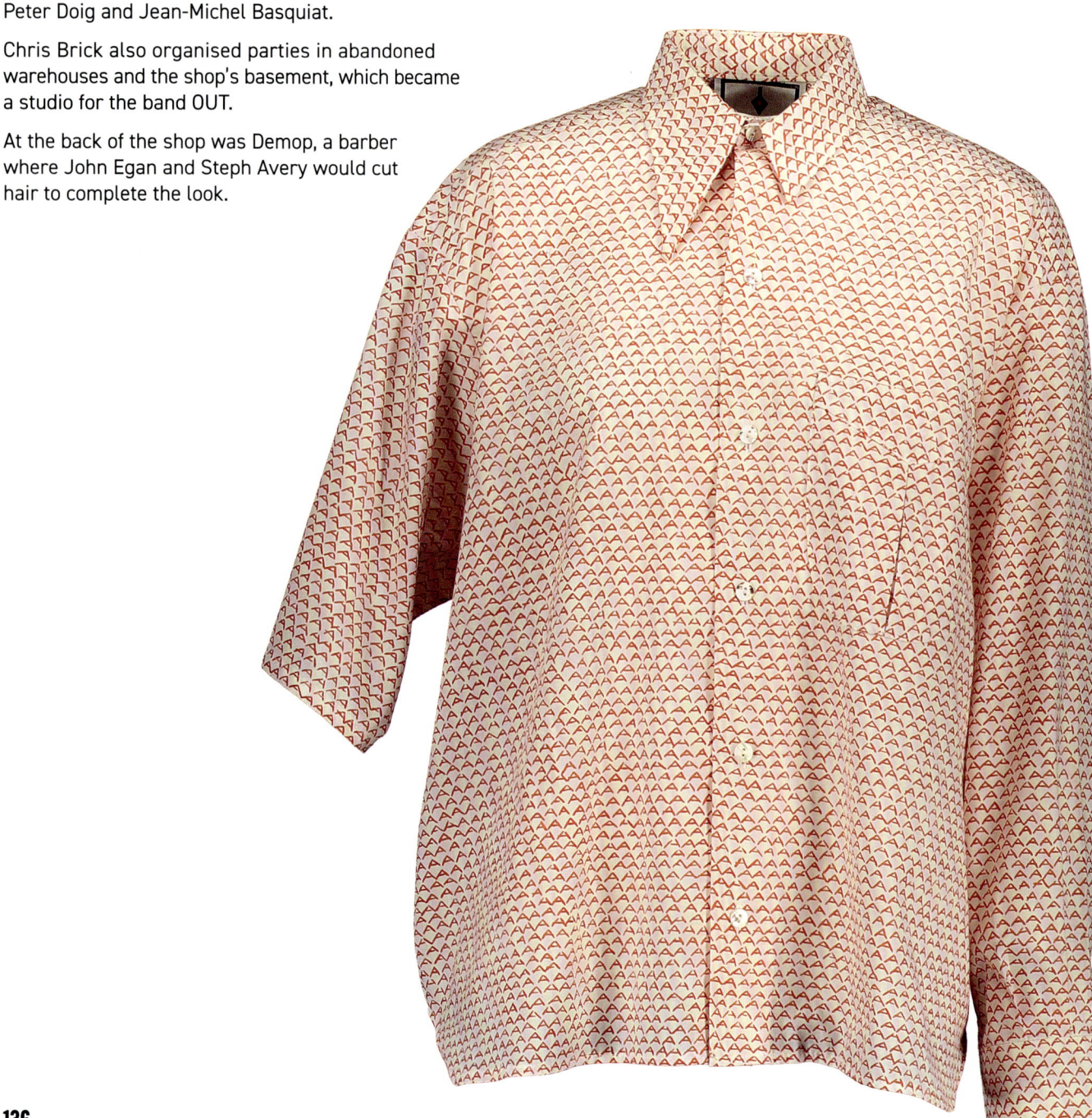

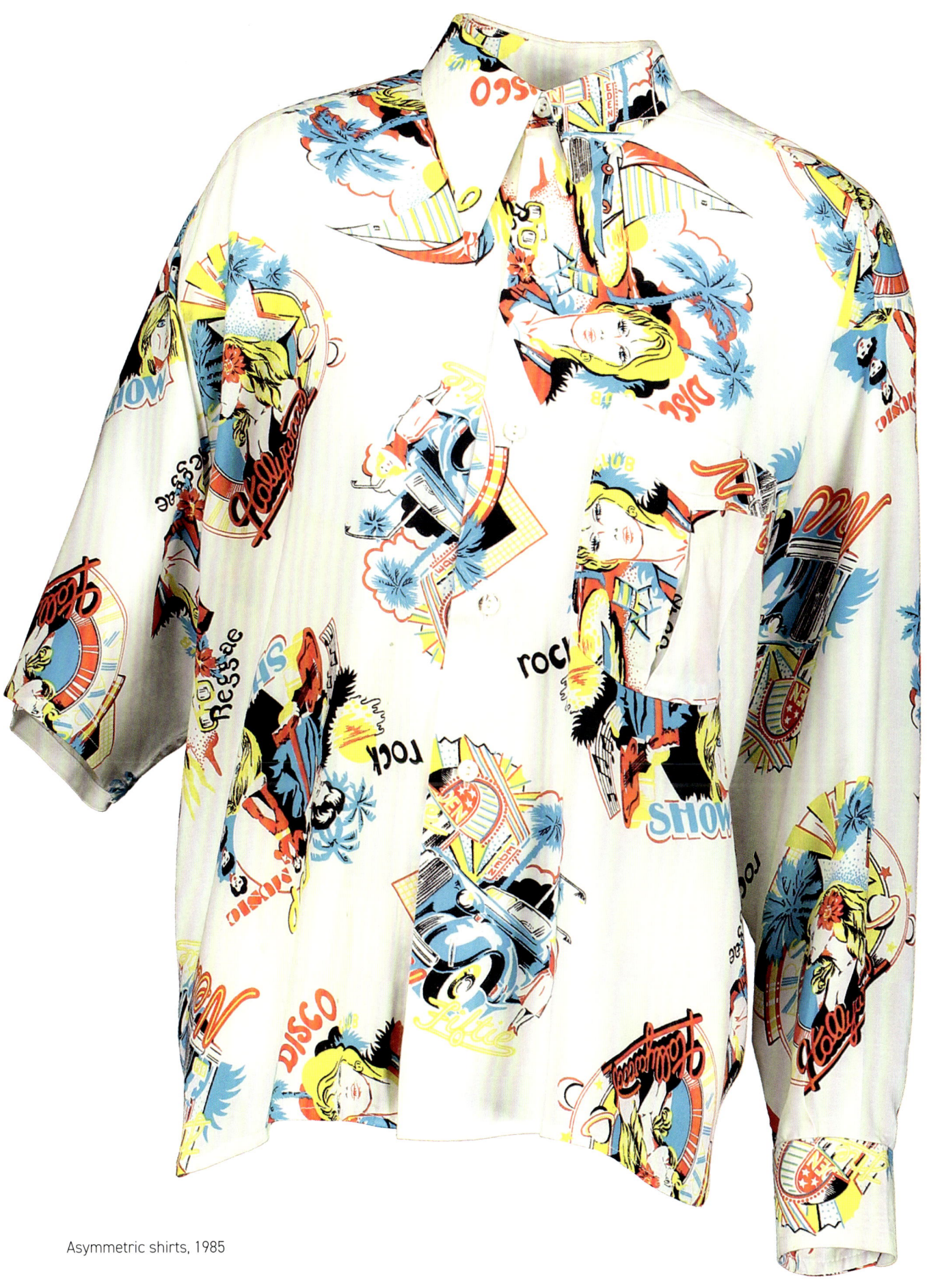

Asymmetric shirts, 1985

DEMOB

IN CONVERSATION WITH

MARK MOORE

Producer, DJ and early pioneer of house music.
Founder of the band S'Express.

Interview by Martin Green

MG: **When were you first aware of Leigh Bowery?**
MM: I used to see Leigh around at all the usual nightspots, places like Cha Cha in the back of Heaven, The Bell pub and Asylum and Pyramid at Heaven. He gradually transitioned from a quieter look into the more extreme Leigh Bowery look. It was a bit like watching a plant grow and suddenly it's in full bloom with loads of flowers, but you don't notice until one day you look up and think how beautiful it is. Taboo was where I remember Leigh being an exotic plant and the club being a glorious botanical garden.

One of the nights I was DJing at Heaven ended up being the same night as Taboo was on, so whenever I did the early shift at Heaven I would walk down to Leicester Square and party at Taboo afterwards. I'd hang out with Nicola Bateman and one night we decided we would 'get married'. We did a quick ceremony in the club and always referred to each other as husband and wife. In 1994 Leigh and Nicola were married for real, so Leigh Bowery stole my pretend wife.

Leigh was meant to be in the S'Express 'Hey Music Lover' video. We talked about it and storyboarded the whole thing, and we were both really excited. On the day, I woke up to an answerphone message from Leigh saying he couldn't make it with no explanation as to why. I hastily rung around to get a replacement for the opening scene and got David Cabaret to do it.

David always looked amazing and was a hired podium dancer at Pyramid. It all went well and the single went to number six in the charts, however David Cabaret upped all his fees at Heaven as he was now a star and the management berated me for creating a monster! Meanwhile Leigh didn't talk to me for ages and told everyone I was evil and that I had hired a Leigh Bowery clone for

'He gradually transitioned from a quieter look into the more extreme Leigh Bowery look. It was a bit like watching a plant grow and suddenly it's in full bloom with loads of flowers, but you don't notice until one day you look up and think how beautiful it is.'

the video. He chilled out a bit later after he decided that David was indeed his own creature and not a clone – but this was after he spat in David's face in a club. Leigh also got very excited when I worked with Philip Glass, as he was a fan, so that made him talk to me again: 'Oh Mark, not only have you conquered the music world, you've now conquered the art world too!'

MG: **When did you first develop an interest in clothes and how they could provoke?**

MM: Punk rock changed everything as it was anti-fashion and do-it-yourself. Ugly became beautiful and the old rules were set on fire. Fashion was now for little old ladies; style and attitude were what was important. Walking into Vivienne Westwood and Malcolm McLaren's shop Seditionaries was like entering the mothership, and there was no looking back. I love that you could be arrested for wearing clothes like the two cowboys T-shirt. Clothes were now dangerous. The police would often raid Seditionaries and Boy on the King's Road. Why don't clothes shops get raided now?

MG: **S'Express had a highly distinctive look. How did this come about and where did you find the clothes?**

MM: The S'Express look was inspired by *The Jackson 5ive* and *Josie and the Pussycats* cartoons from the 1970s. Sly and the Family Stone plus Parliament-Funkadelic were also big influences. Pretty much everyone like Chilo, Linda Love and Michellé would find clothes in second-hand shops and turn up with bags of the stuff. We'd dress each other up saying, 'Oh this will look great on you', rummaging through mounds of garments. Friends like Amelia Ayewan made clothes for me as well, which were used for our first few *Top of the Pops* appearances. We had no idea that bands usually got a stylist to sort out their looks.

MG: **What's the story behind your fabulous John Crancher jacket with the Dave Baby print?**

MM: I met John Crancher when he was working in the Our Price record shop in Leicester Square. Strangely, it was located next door to where Taboo would end up being a few years later. Me and my friend Judy thought he looked great and would go in and chat and buy records from him before going to Blitz or Hell. We got him to come with us eventually, as he wasn't really into clubbing. He then started going out with Sal Solo, the singer from Classix Nouveaux, who lived in Finchley Central when I was living in North Finchley, so he would come round a few times.

When he announced that he was going to design clothing we all went to his new stall in Kensington Market. Jessica, a beautiful roadie for Sigue Sigue Sputnik, was either working at the stall or had her own next to it. I remember her saying quietly under her breath, 'Oh my god, John's clothes are awful.' He had things like a rectangle of black leather with a hole in the middle so you could put your head through it. And that was it! I don't think anyone bought anything. But then as the days went on, I remember buying stuff, Seditionaries-inspired bondage tops and the likes. The clothes just got better and better. That Crancher satin bomber jacket with the Dave Baby print is one of my favourites. Unfortunately, if you get it wet in the rain the print starts to drip off!

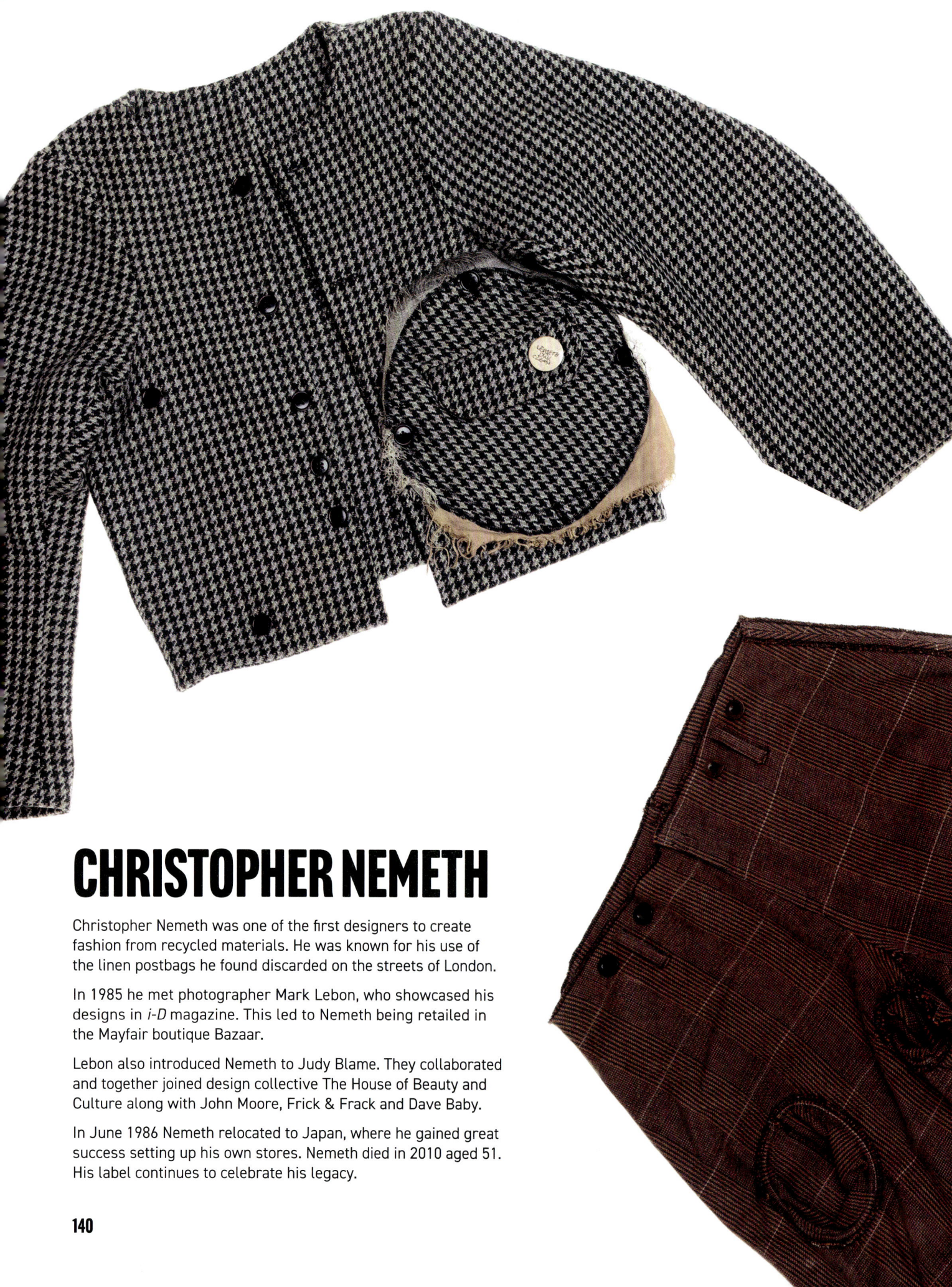

CHRISTOPHER NEMETH

Christopher Nemeth was one of the first designers to create fashion from recycled materials. He was known for his use of the linen postbags he found discarded on the streets of London.

In 1985 he met photographer Mark Lebon, who showcased his designs in *i-D* magazine. This led to Nemeth being retailed in the Mayfair boutique Bazaar.

Lebon also introduced Nemeth to Judy Blame. They collaborated and together joined design collective The House of Beauty and Culture along with John Moore, Frick & Frack and Dave Baby.

In June 1986 Nemeth relocated to Japan, where he gained great success setting up his own stores. Nemeth died in 2010 aged 51. His label continues to celebrate his legacy.

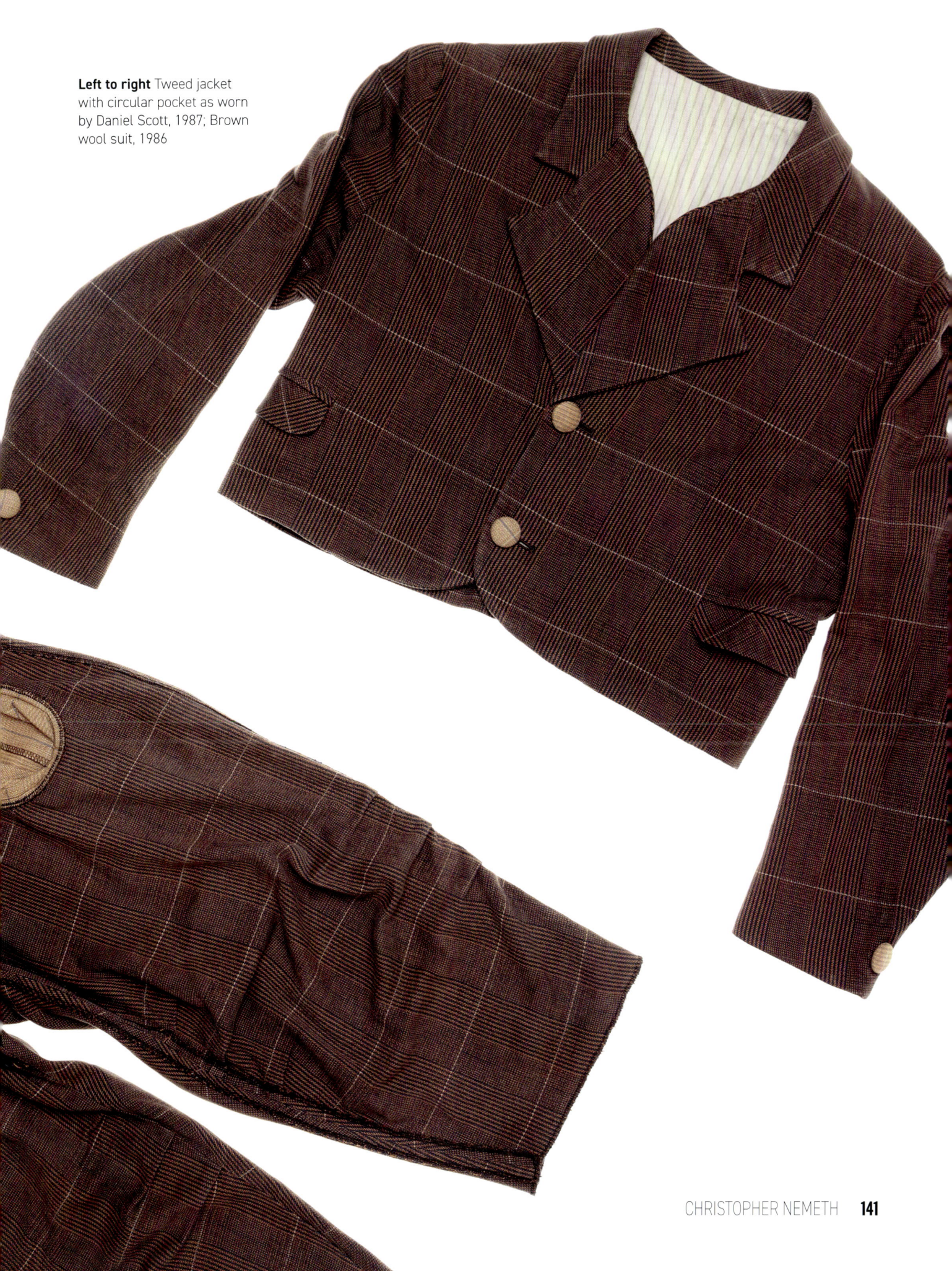

Left to right Tweed jacket with circular pocket as worn by Daniel Scott, 1987; Brown wool suit, 1986

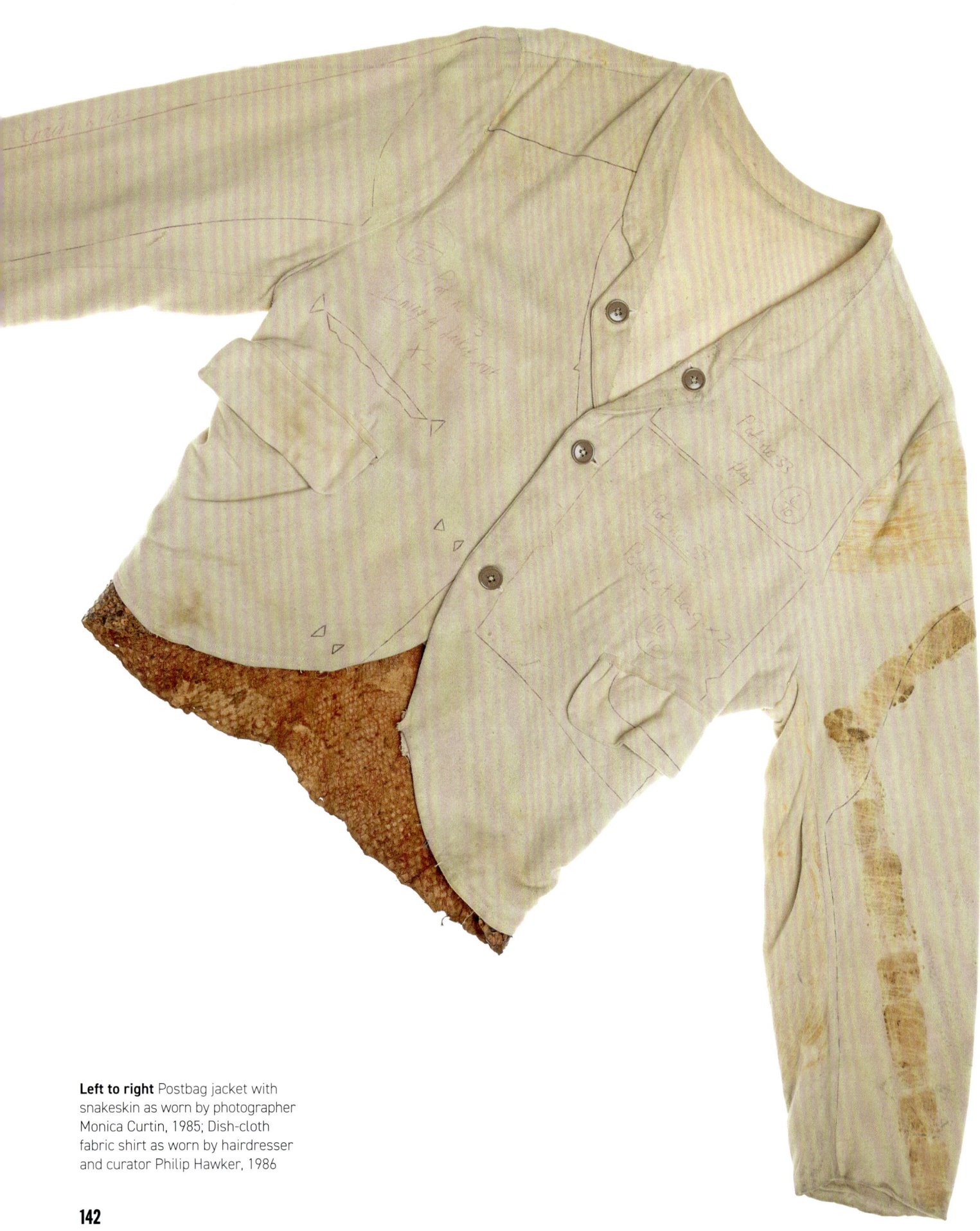

Left to right Postbag jacket with snakeskin as worn by photographer Monica Curtin, 1985; Dish-cloth fabric shirt as worn by hairdresser and curator Philip Hawker, 1986

'IN 1984 I TRAVELLED FROM NOTTINGHAM TO LONDON AND MET CHRIS IN HIS POKEY STUDIO WHICH LOOKED LIKE AN EPISODE OF "HOARDERS", WITH WEIRD AND WONDERFUL EXPERIMENTAL CLOTHING ALL OVER THE PLACE. MY "INTERVIEW" WAS TO MAKE A SIGNATURE NEMETH JACKET IN OLD TAILORING FABRIC WITH POSTBAG-SACKING BACK AND SLEEVES. I GOT THE JOB. I WORKED FOR HIM UNTIL HE MOVED TO JAPAN, AND I LOVED HIS ENERGY - HE WAS SWEET AND SUPER CHARMING (I HAD A BIT OF A CRUSH ON HIM).'

Richard Kemp, designer at Rabens Saloner in Copenhagen

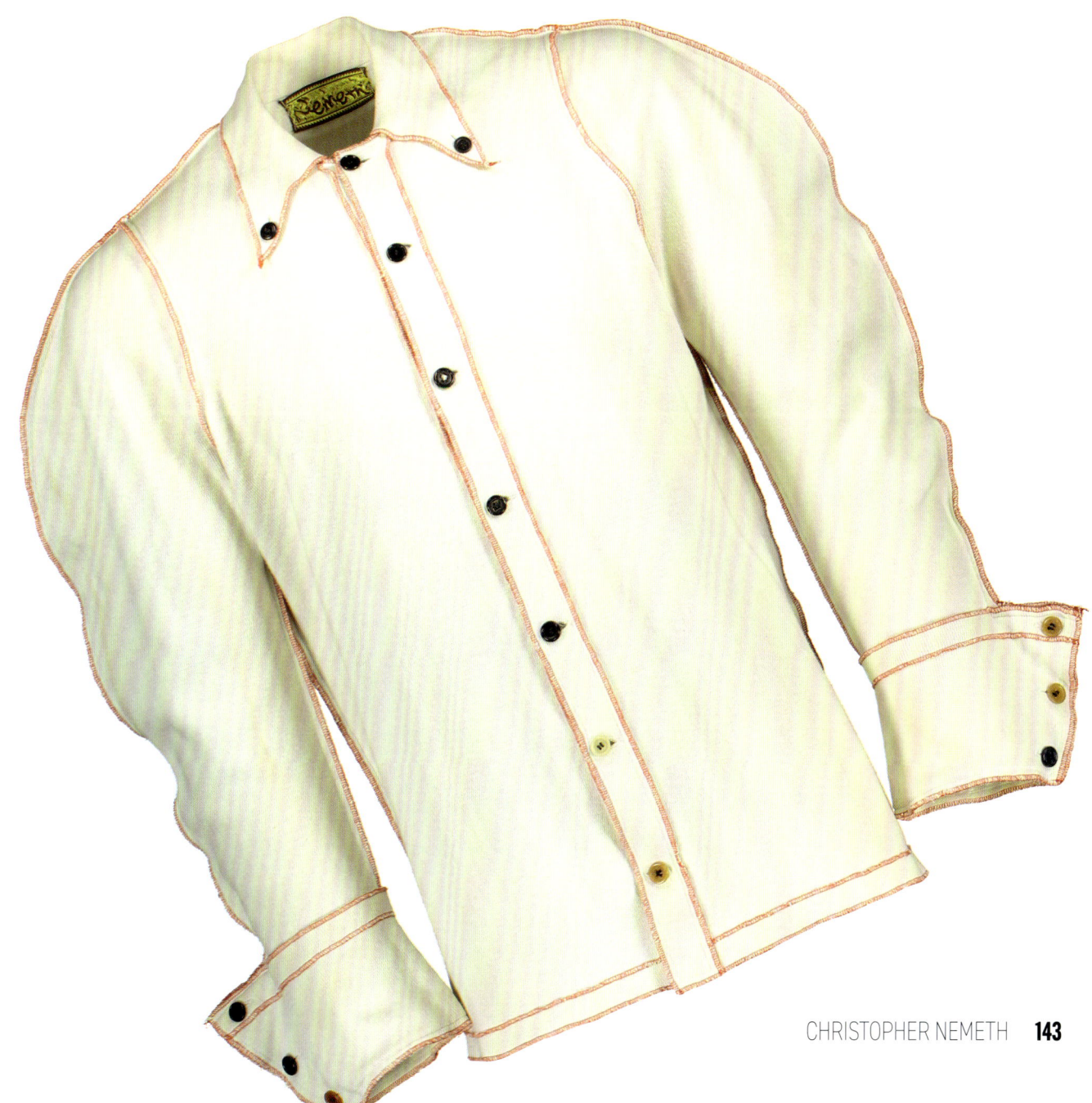

NOCTURNE

David Mumford and Eric Holah met at a punk rock party in Banbury in 1977 and became partners. Both had a strong interest in fashion and were initially taught how to sew by Holah's mother, Mary.

In 1980 they moved into a London squat, set up a makeshift studio and opened a stall in Kensington Market. Their 'Nocturne' collection consisted of simple, reversible geometric cotton shapes, splashed and hand-painted with bleach. Scraps of fabric were torn into strips and knitted into jumpers.

Michael and Gerlinde Costiff brought Susanne Bartsch to Nocturne, who then invited them to be part of the New London in New York fashion shows in 1983. At this point Mumford's then-partner Stephen Tucker joined and a year later Eric Holah started working with his brother David at BodyMap.

Mumford and Tucker continued Nocturne, opening a shop in Kensington's Hyper Hyper, and they went on to create an outfit for Diana Ross's 'Chain Reaction' video. In 2017 Mumford started the upcycling brand and boutique Frock.U at Brick Lane's Truman Brewery.

Eric Holah collaborated with David Mumford until he died in 2018. Stephen Tucker died in 2016.

Jumper hand-knitted from mixed torn fabrics, 1982, belonging to David Holah from BodyMap

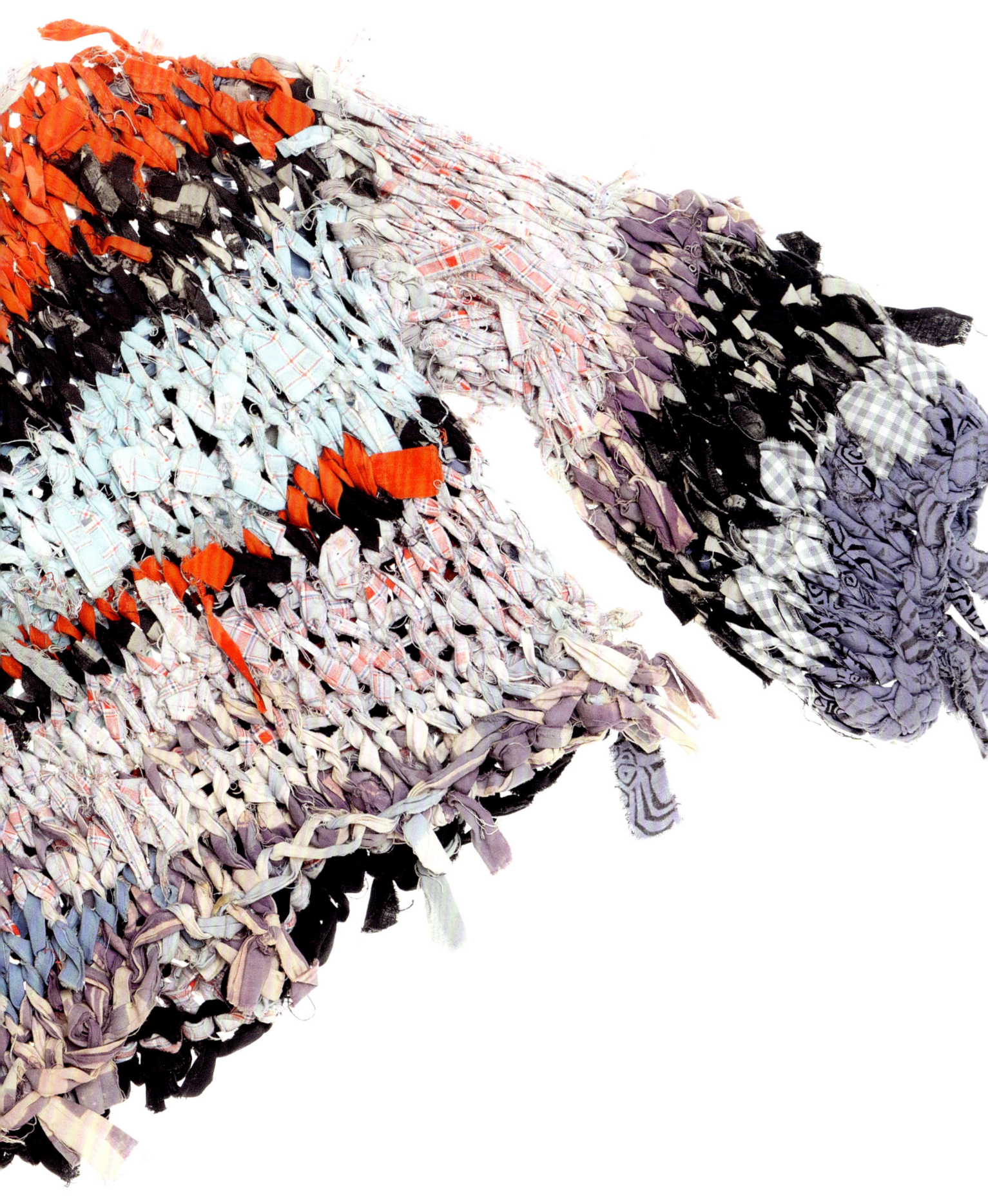

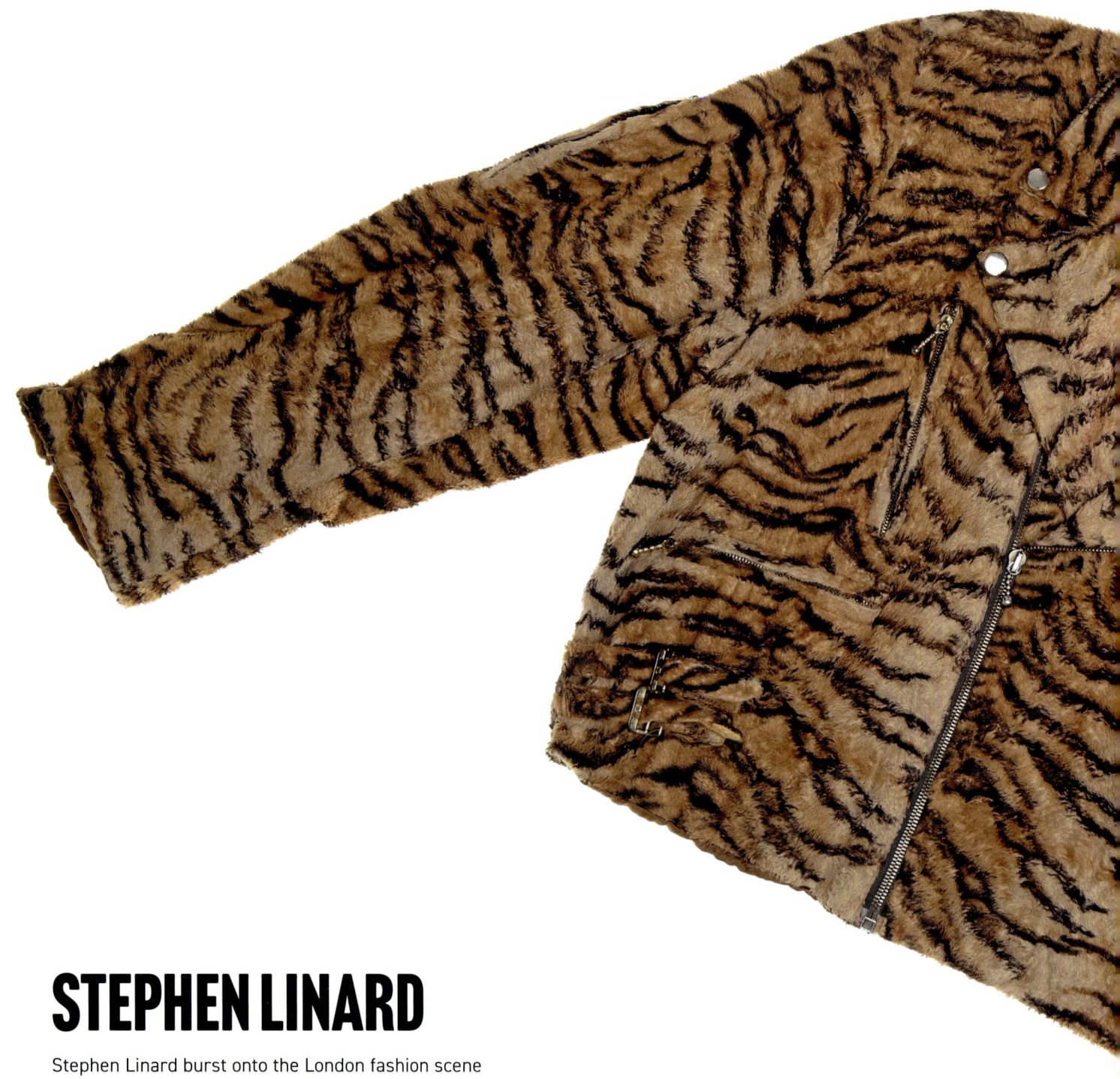

STEPHEN LINARD

Stephen Linard burst onto the London fashion scene with his enormously successful St Martin's graduate show 'Reluctant Emigrés' in 1981 and went on to make clothes for Boy George, David Bowie and Spandau Ballet. A habitué of London's Blitz nightclub, Linard belonged to a crowd who bid to outdo each other in flamboyance every night of the week.

His clothes were elegant, romantic, theatrical and beautifully tailored. He produced his own label, designed for Jun Co. in Tokyo, and until recently was a key player on the design team at Drake's on Savile Row.

An absolute New Romantic legend, Linard died in March 2024.

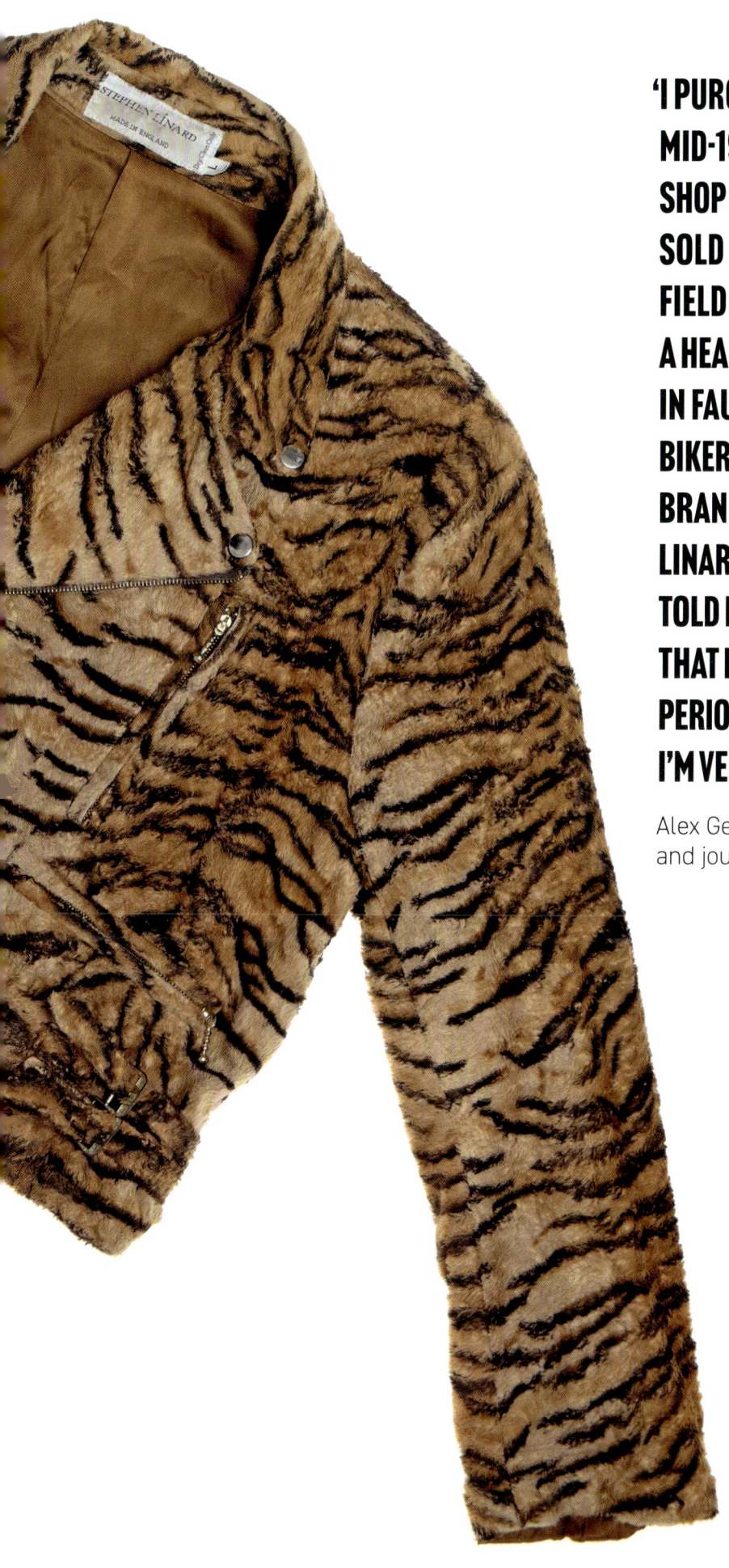

'I PURCHASED THIS JACKET IN THE MID-1980S IN A BERWICK STREET SHOP NAMED KUNST, WHICH MAINLY SOLD GARMENTS FROM YOUNG LEFT-FIELD DESIGNERS. I SNAPPED IT UP IN A HEARTBEAT. IT IS PERFECTLY DESIGNED IN FAUX FUR TO INTERPRET THE ORIGINAL BIKER JACKET WORN BY MARLON BRANDO IN "THE WILD ONE". STEPHEN LINARD WAS VERY FLATTERED WHEN I TOLD HIM SHORTLY BEFORE HE PASSED THAT IT'S THE ONLY THING FROM THAT PERIOD THAT I KEPT IN MY WARDROBE. I'M VERY GLAD I DID.'

Alex Gerry, clubland portrait photographer and journalist

IN CONVERSATION WITH
DAVE SWINDELLS

Nightlife Editor at *Time Out* from 1986 to 2009.
Photographer of the London club scene since the mid-1980s.

Interview by Martin Green

MG: **When was the first time you photographed Leigh Bowery and did you have a favourite look of his?**

DS: It was in December 1984 at Dodo's, an ace monthly Monday-nighter at Busby's. Leigh was walking down the stairs from behind the DJ box but someone was trying to block his way. I quickly grabbed a shot as I'd been excited by photos I'd seen of Leigh and Trojan in *The Face* and *i-D* and impressed by the looks they created.

Leigh is all smiles in the photo, but as was quite often the case people were annoyed with him, and flamboyant club kid Garrigan is looking offended. Leigh could be incredibly charming and considerate, but after a few drinks accidents would happen, or he'd inadvertently make them happen. He was big and strong and could drink like a sailor who was always on shore leave. Dead or Alive's 'You Spin Me Round (Like a Record)' would definitely have been playing that night, not that Leigh needed any encouragement; it was standard behaviour for him to spin around the dancefloor without being too concerned about other people (or their drinks) that happened to be in the way.

The dripping-wax look at Taboo was sensational, but it was always a thrill to see what he would do next and I loved taking photos of him dancing at Jungle and Daisy Chain, and some years later at Casablanca and Kinky Gerlinky.

MG: **What was your experience of Taboo?**

DS: I first went to Taboo in the spring of 1985 with a friend, David Somerville, who was at Chelsea School of Art. I'm sure I only got in because David knew Tony Gordon (who ran the club and had invited Leigh to host it) and David had been going since the opening week. So he knew the meeter-greeter Marc Vaultier (aka Mark Golding) and that meant we swerved the mirror being held in our face and the 'Would you let yourself in?' grilling at the door.

We didn't stay more than an hour that night as it just felt so bizarre; everyone we met seemed to speak in a performatively camp mockney drawl, with extra-long vowel sounds: 'How are yooooouuu?' It was hilarious and disconcerting but also fascinating, with Leigh as the larger-than-life locus around which the night whirled. It was 'Where's Leigh?' or 'Is Leigh coming?' His appearance and his look would supercharge the night, and definitely added to its unpredictability as he loved to challenge perceptions and embrace a little chaos. Here was a weekly night that was linked by myriad relationships with every gay, gender-bending (a mid-1980s way of saying non-binary) and underground club that had existed in London since the Blitz and the New Romantics, yet which still appeared to operate according to its own rules. So that meant dressing up as though your life depended on it, dancing like no one was watching and acting as though there were no rules.

That was especially true when a few dozen of the regular Taboo crowd began taking ecstasy. I wasn't part of that crowd, but the story I heard was that someone had brought back half a suitcase of MDMA from New York (where it had not yet been certified by the US Drug Enforcement Administration, a ban which came into effect in July 1985). For a while the result was a kind of devil-may-care anarchy.

One night in particular comes to mind, when Leigh lifted BodyMap's David Holah onto his shoulders and started dancing and spinning around. Inevitably, sooner or later he tripped or fell to the floor and that was the cue for a pile-on. There was a heap of people rolling around and jumping on top of each other, laughing hysterically, and even the DJ ran from the booth to join in. When the record finished the needle slipped off the vinyl and the only sound was a muffled whirring as it dragged across the record mat, along with some whooping and screaming from the ecstatic dancers as they gradually untangled themselves from the pile of bodies.

Eventually Jeffrey Hinton or Rachel Auburn got back to the decks and put on another record, and ten minutes later the same thing happened all over again! This was by no means a typical Taboo event but it happened; I just wished I'd had a camera with me. I wasn't there every week, but I'd be drawn back by the energy and the feeling that anything might happen. The 4th of July, when a troupe of the Neo Naturists appeared in the club – sporting red-white-and-blue body paint and fresh from performing on stage at Heaven at an American Independence Day party – was another thriller. Michael Clark was chatting to Christine Binnie of the Neo Naturists, Andrew Logan was dancing with Molly Parkin and the pop artist Duggie Fields was throwing shapes, John Galliano was wearing a Judy Blame hat and Judy Blame was there with Christopher Nemeth.

In the summer of 1985 *i-D* columnist Alix Sharkey described the night as 'London's sleaziest, campiest and bitchiest club of the moment… stuffed with designers, stylists, models, students, dregs and the hopefully hip, lurching through the lasers and sniffing up amyl.' Is that what it felt like? Well, yes, for a while. But Taboo ran for about a year and a lot happened in that time. It was both more fun and potentially darker than that, especially in 1986 when stories emerged about the tragic deaths of Trojan and Mark Vaultier.

Taboo really embraced disco-dancin' diversity with Jeffrey Hinton and Rachel Auburn on the decks, so it was very different to the pure Hi-NRG you'd hear at many gay or polysexual nights. You would hear all the new Madonna tunes, lots of Donna Summer and Janet Jackson and Wham's 'I'm Your Man', classic and trash disco, some funky stuff, hip-hop and reggae in the mix as well as occasional film soundtrack tunes (Jeffrey loved Bollywood, Leigh loved *Saturday Night Fever*).

Taboo didn't feel Fellini-esque in the sense that every single person looked remarkable or fantastical, as there were always some 'straights' who were allowed in, partly to ensure that the club actually earned some door money.

It was really sad when Taboo suddenly came to an end, but not at all surprising that the next weekly club to attract a lot of the Taboo crowd was called Vive l'Anarchie, which was soon shortened to Anarchy.

MG: **What was life like for you during the mid-1980s, writing about clubs, photographing clubbers and being out almost every night?**

DS: When I moved to London in the summer of 1984 I didn't know much about London or nightlife photography, but I was determined to find out, and there was a dynamic West End scene to discover. But first I needed to pay the rent, so my brother Steve (who hosted a predominantly gay club called The Lift and had introduced me to The Wag, Heaven and the Mud Club), helped me get a job working the cloakroom and behind the bar at Fouberts, where Philip Sallon's Mud Club, the Kit Kat club hosted by Simon Hobart and Steve's Lift night were some of the resident one-nighters.

In the mid-1980s many of the clubs in the West End were relatively tiny; there were bijou mirror-tiled discos or flock-wallpapered dives in the backstreets of Soho that might hold 120 to 200 people at a squeeze. There were also venues like Heaven and Busby's that held 1,000 or more, alongside former theatres like The Lyceum and The Astoria where more ambitious nights happened at weekends, but those smaller spaces were ideal for emerging one-nighters and made it possible to go to five clubs in a night and still be home by 4.30 a.m. after a night-bus ride to north London! When Fouberts closed, the owners took over The Embassy on Old Bond Street in Mayfair, so that was a swanky change. I was just starting to capture the characters and moves that I was seeing in clubs, and I was so excited by this that I would take photos while I was collecting the empty glasses around the club – until I got fired for not doing my job.

Luck played a big part in me landing a small role taking club photos for *i-D* early in 1985, so I was back at The Embassy the following week to take snaps at the thriving Helter Skelter night. Working for *i-D* gave me all-important access and a licence to roam, heading off to the Fridge in Brixton or the Flim Flam in New Cross, getting lost with half of London's trendies searching the deserted streets behind King's Cross before we finally found the Circus warehouse party at Bagley's. Clubs might close at 3 a.m., but there were occasional boat parties and warehouse events around Old Street to carry on at, and all-night film fiestas at the Scala cinema. When I became the Nightlife Editor at *Time Out* in 1986 ('How would you beat Leigh Bowery to the hottest new club?' asked the job advert) I was well aware that I was writing for weekend clubbers rather than the Soho Boho crowd and that it was vital to cover all sorts of scenes as well as the super-trendy West End club nights. So I was lucky, as I could be hearing Giles Peterson and Coldcut playing at the Special Branch's Doo at the Zoo (yep, it was at London Zoo) one night and photographing breakdancers at Legends or Bananarama with Vaughn Toulouse and Gary Crowley at The Wag Club the next. I can't quite believe that I had all that freedom now!

MG: **During this period everyone was dressing up with different looks every night. What were your reactions?**

DS: There *was* a lot of dressing up, but not everyone was in different looks every night. There were plenty of style tribes whose appearance was defined by dedicated lifestyles rather than daily transformations. There were the ones you'd expect, like the skinheads and the punks and the 1950s-faithful rock'n'roll fans. There were also gay male 'clones' sporting a uniform of leather trousers, peaked caps and moustaches, and the Dirtbox warehouse party crowd in their flat-tops, faded 501s and vintage Americana from Flip in Covent Garden. Then there were the indie kids and Smiths fans moping about with long coats and floppy hair.

Nearly every style tribe had their own club nights or live gigs (the fetish scenesters in leather and latex were still mostly hidden and underground in the mid-1980s, although *Skin Two* magazine got going in 1984) and counterintuitively, the goths looked like they were having the most fun, as they had clubs like the Batcave, the Kit Kat, Alice in Wonderland, Astral Flight and Helter Skelter to party in, and designers like Jane Khan of Khaniverous. Jane Khan always looked amazing. I photographed

'There *was* a lot of dressing up, but not everyone was in different looks every night. There were plenty of style tribes whose appearance was defined by dedicated lifestyles rather than daily transformations.'

her at Taboo and the Mud Club, where Philip Sallon was one of many club hosts who demanded some kind of sartorial effort otherwise punters weren't getting in (he turned me away on my 21st birthday, which was fair enough as I hadn't dressed up). Taboo, Anarchy, The Café de Paris, Sacrosanct, *i-D* parties, City of Angels at Raw and the goth clubs were some of the nights with similar expectations, but it's obvious from looking back at the photos that there was a lot of latitude allowed, and that attitude was almost as important as attire.

MG: **What do you think were the elements that came together to create such an incredibly vibrant club scene in the 1980s?**

DS: London did have a thriving scene but even in 1985 it sometimes seemed like a provincial outpost compared to what we heard about the round-the-clock nightlife in New York City. Clubs across the capital were still obliged to close at 2 a.m., although they could carry on right through until 3 a.m. in the West End! During the next few years though, a host of elements came together that made London arguably the leading clubbing city of the 1990s, with world-class clubs open all night long.

One-nighter clubs (originally inspired by 'Bowie Night' parties such as Club for Heroes and the Blitz) enabled regular partygoers to become party-throwers, presenting specialist nights for their musically like-minded mates. Some of these were fairly niche, such as the b-boys and fly-girls who threw shapes on the lino in Covent Garden Market and at West End club sessions, which, like most clubs in Soho, attracted dancers from across the city. From 1982 onwards promoters like Dirtbox, Demob and the Lift began to put on illegal, all-night warehouse parties, often in the (relatively) quiet streets around Old Street or behind King's Cross station, and the mobile sound systems that they hired were often the same ones used to deliver drum-and-basslines to reggae all-nighters, 'blues' jams and lovers'-rock house parties – and best known for firing up the Notting Hill Carnival.

During the mid-1980s a whole set of parallel scenes and networks gradually began to cross-pollinate and coalesce, from the social networks provided by record shops, fashion boutiques and bars (great places to drop club flyers) to the myriad pirate radio shows championing every type of dance music from funky rare grooves and bhangra and Chicago house to Ghanaian highlife. The style press of *i-D*, *The Face* and *Blitz* magazines showcased street fashion and 'underground' club scenes while London listings magazines *Time Out* and *City Limits* introduced the city's great diversity of gigs, clubs and music long before the internet was even dreamed of.

As cheap new musical technology allowed wannabe producers in Chicago and Detroit to create house and techno, the same thing was happening in London and Manchester with DJ producers like S'Express, Bomb the Bass, Coldcut, M|A|R|R|S and Bang the Party releasing international dancefloor hits from late 1987. London clubbers weren't just avid consumers of US dance music; they were about to create whole new dance music styles of their own.

DAVID CABARET

As a London-born teen David Cabaret frequented the clubs that were a melting pot for many creatives in the 1980s and became a recognisable face on the scene.

Cabaret was known for his experimental and highly detailed looks, which often featured in *The Face* and *Time Out*. His shape-changing sci-fi-influenced 'bumps and spikes' outfits instantly gained attention in 1988's clubland, and Cabaret was the first to cover his entire body and shoes with a total look made from one choice of fabric.

He featured prominently in the video for 'Hey Music Lover' by S'Express and is on the cover of *The Sound Gallery* album.

Cabaret has worked in film and theatre costume for several decades and in 2002 was assistant designer and head maker on Boy George's *Taboo the Musical*, replicating the outfits of Leigh Bowery and others in the Taboo gang.

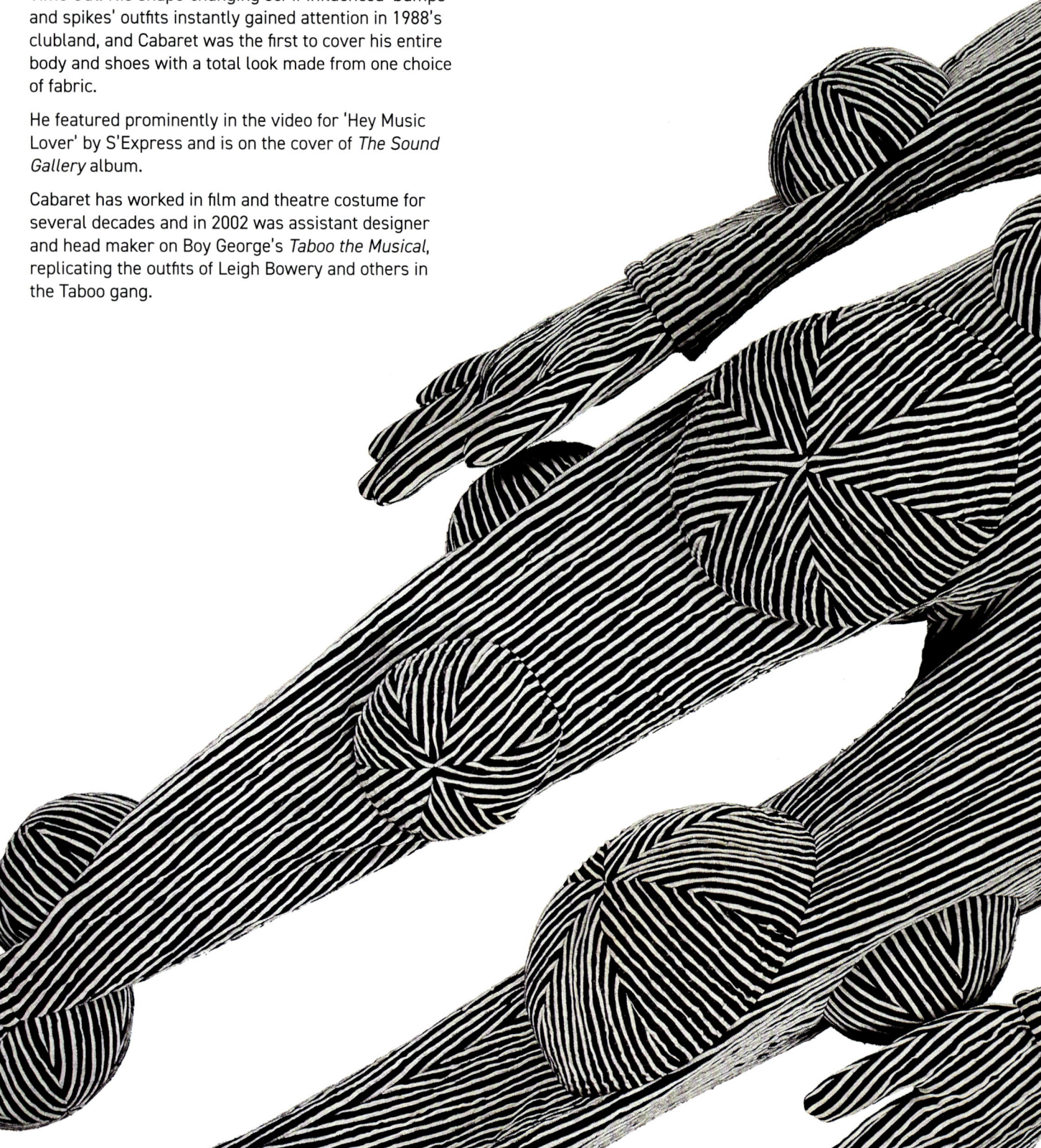

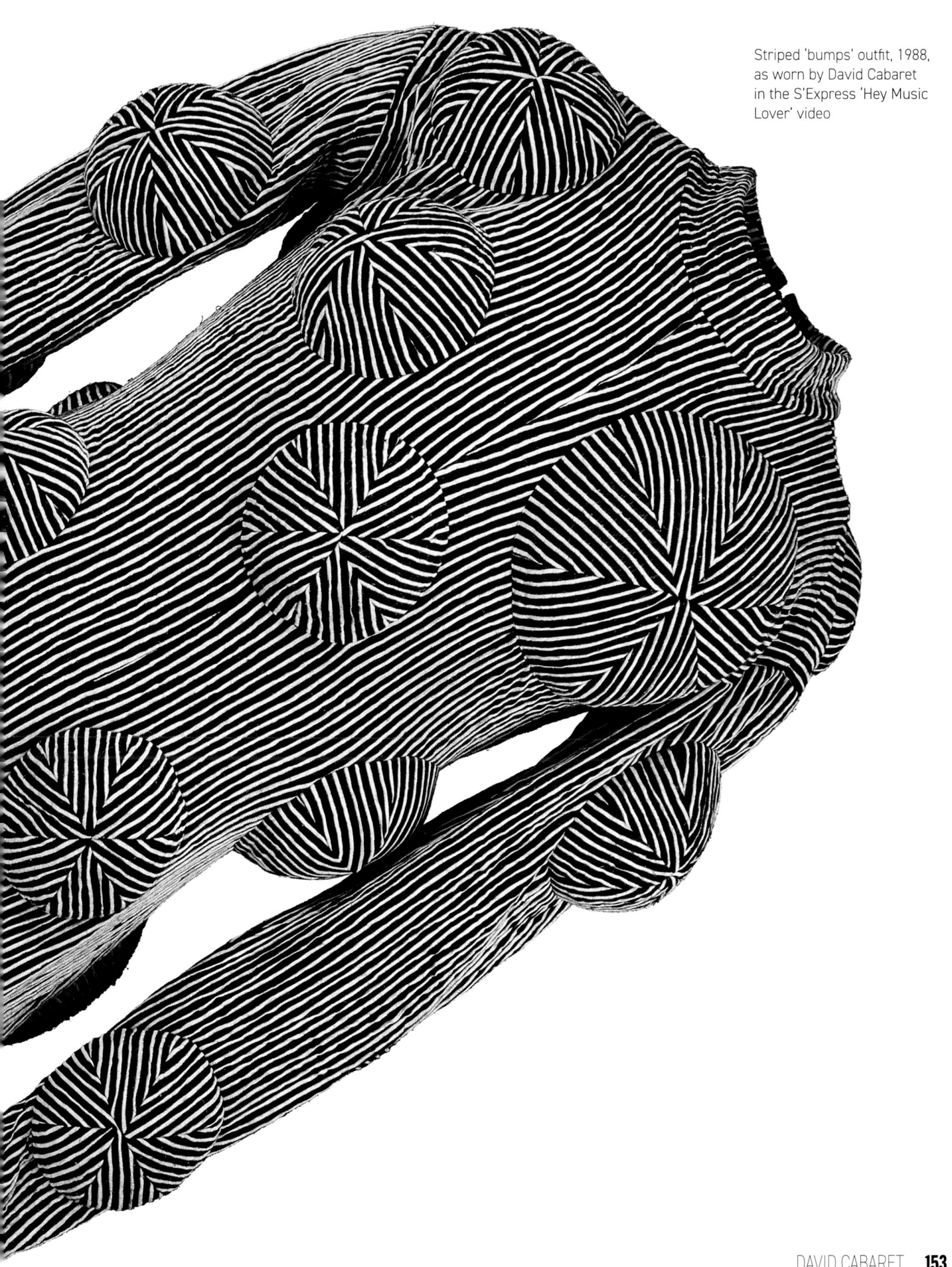

Striped 'bumps' outfit, 1988, as worn by David Cabaret in the S'Express 'Hey Music Lover' video

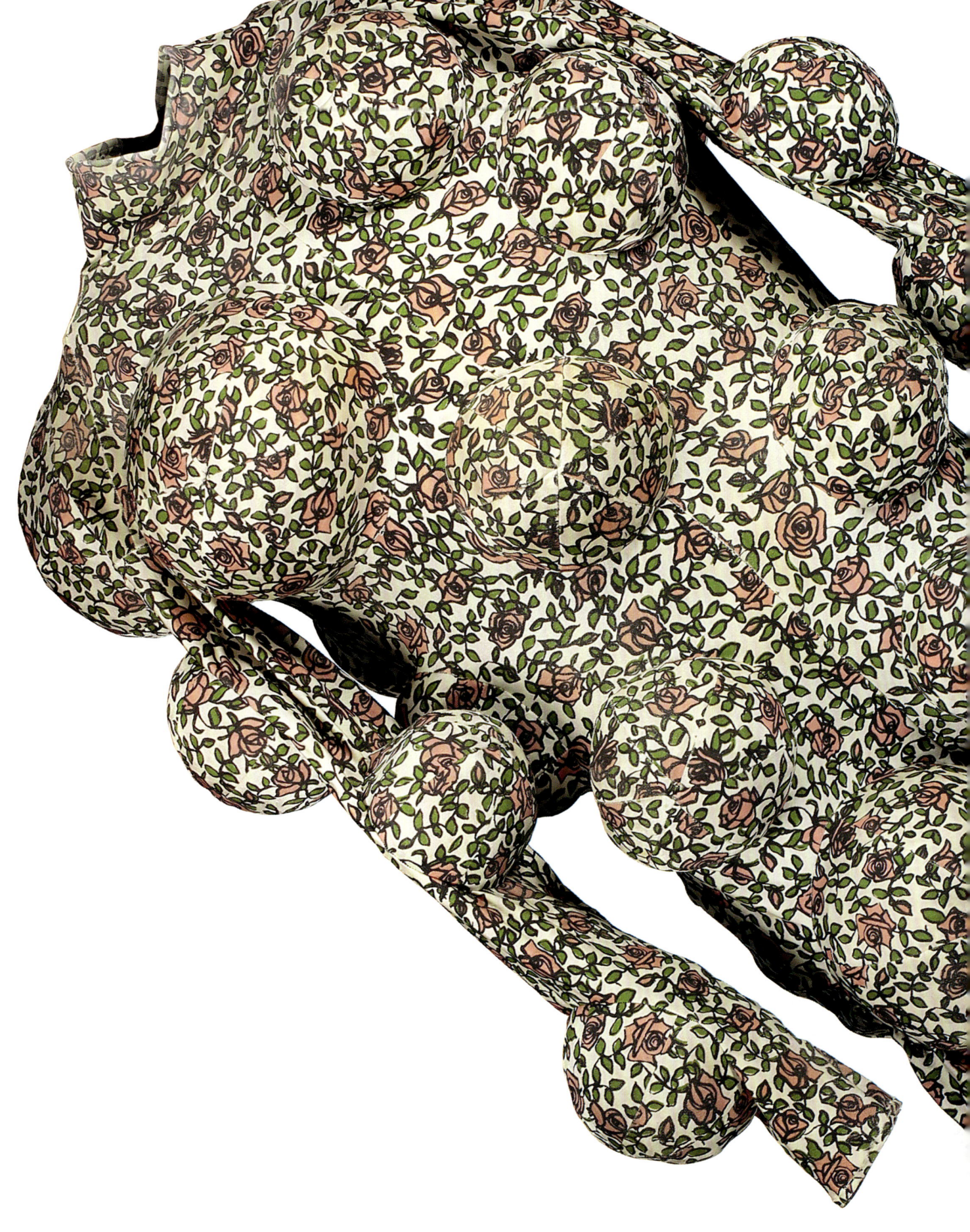

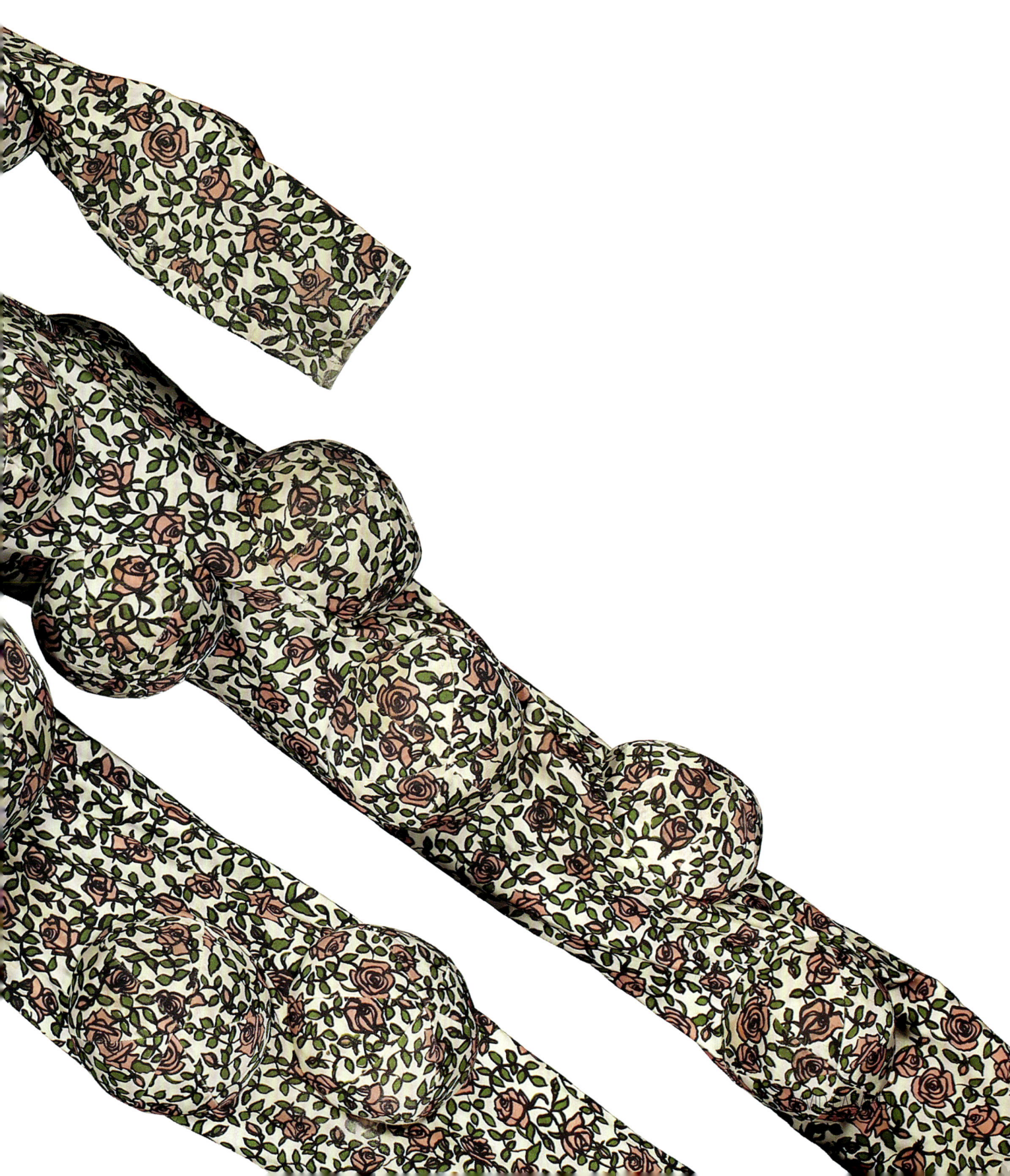

Floral 'bumps' outfit as worn by David Cabaret, 1988

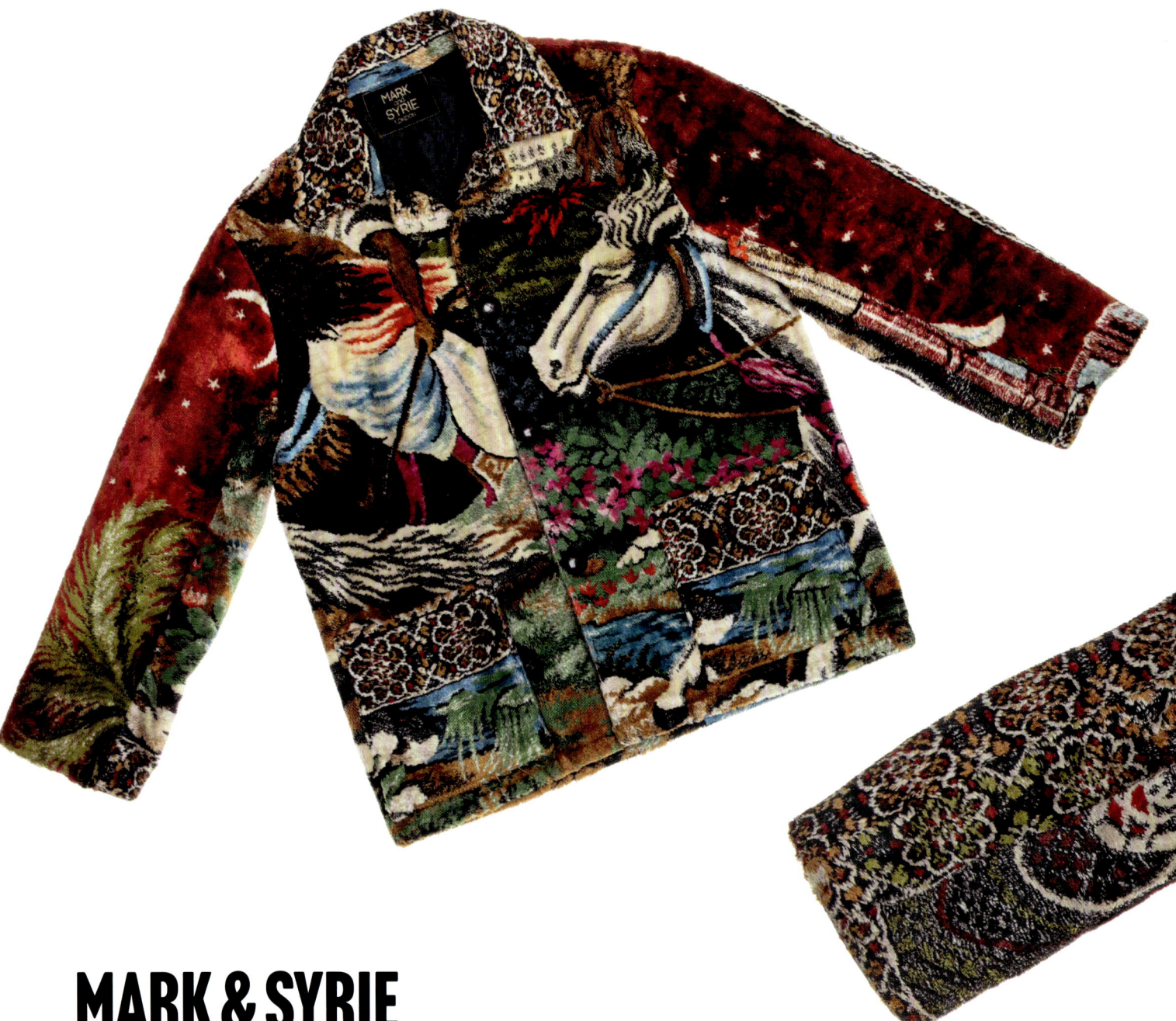

MARK & SYRIE

Self-taught British fashion designers Syrie Panton and Mark Lowings were pioneers of repurposing materials. Their coats made from recycled carpets and beer towels, and suits fashioned from souvenir tea towels, grabbed attention as they reworked fabrics to create a contemporary fashion uniform.

From fly-pitching at Covent Garden to debuting at London Fashion Week in 1984, Mark and Syrie were soon exhibiting at the Victoria and Albert Museum and the Louvre. Naomi Campbell made her catwalk debut in their show at Cambridge Theatre and the brand's retailers included Liberty, Browns and Paul Smith in the UK, and Bloomingdale's and Macy's in the US. In print their designs featured in *The Face*, *i-D*, *Blitz*, *Vogue* and *Harper's Bazaar*.

Mark Lowings died of AIDS in 1994. He was 35.

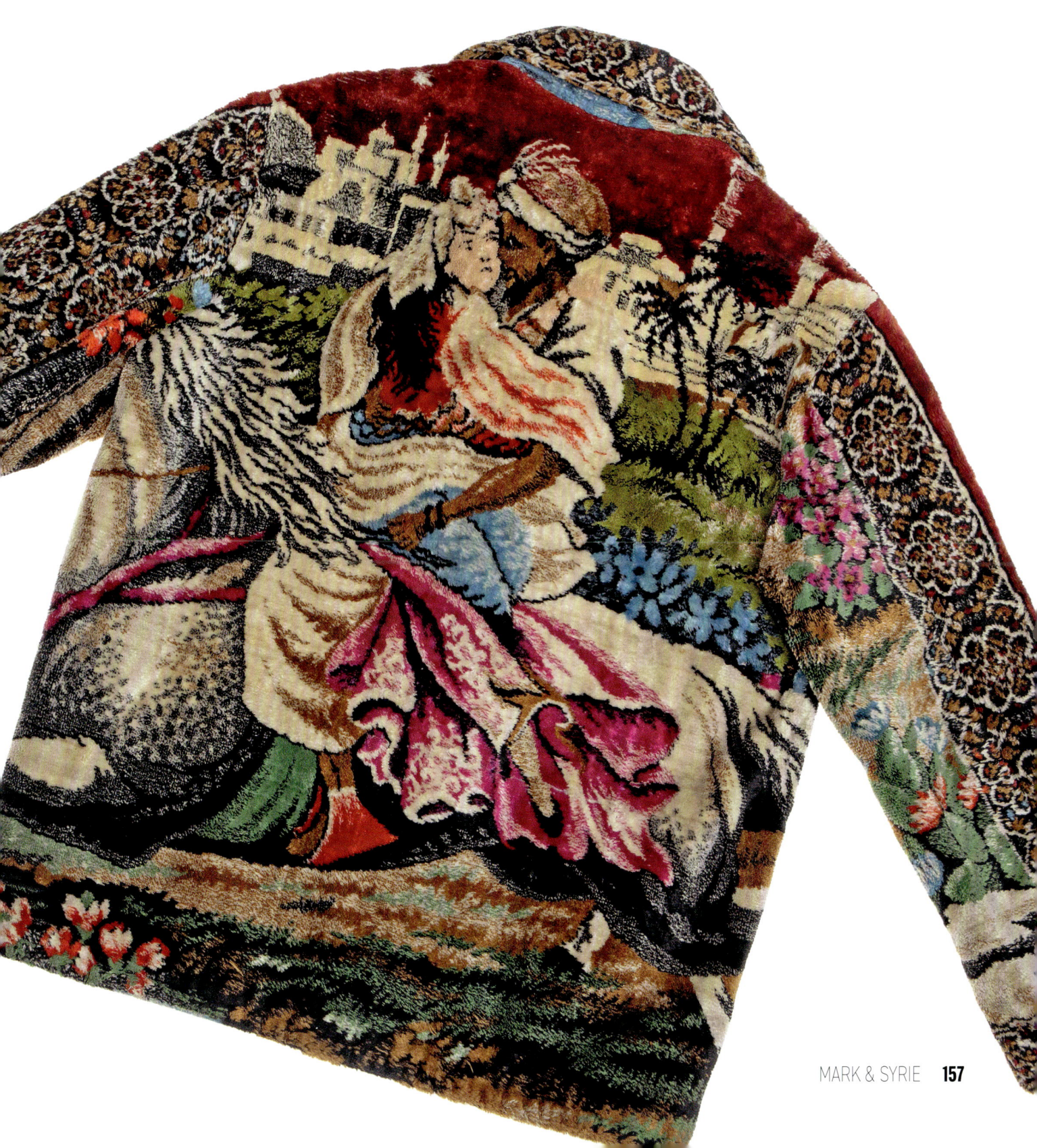

Turkish-carpet jacket from the 'Workman and Cats' collection, 1985

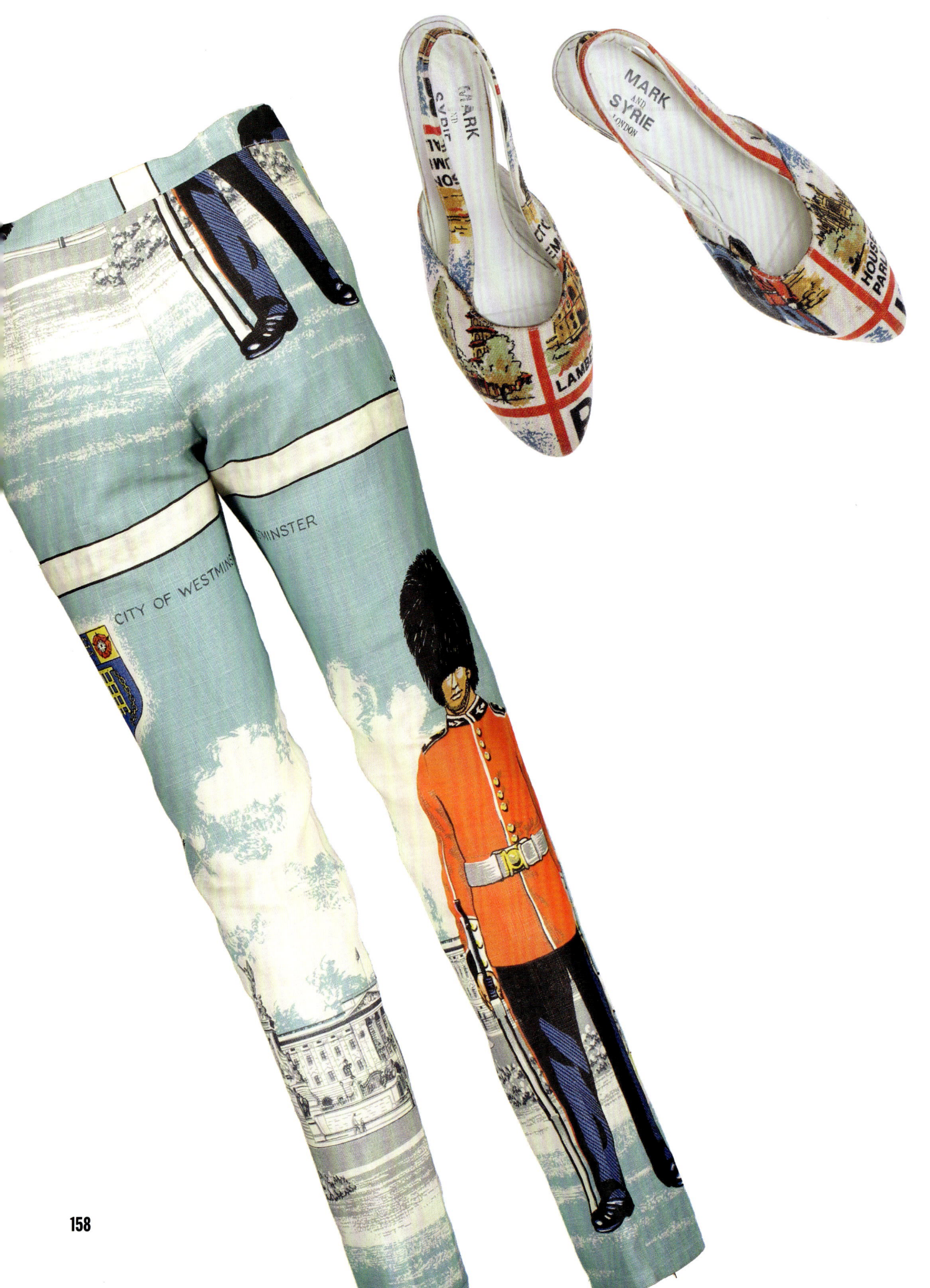

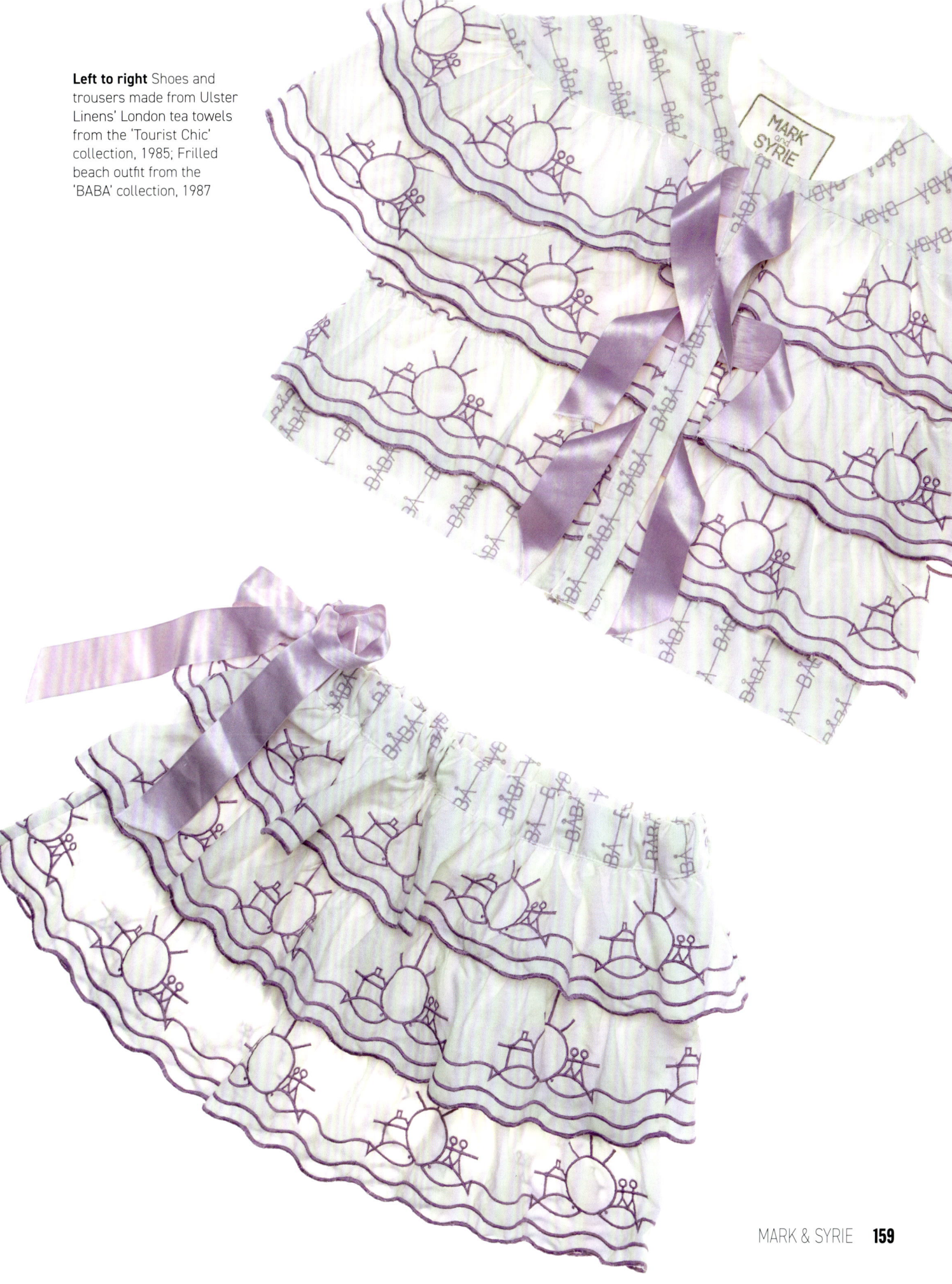

Left to right Shoes and trousers made from Ulster Linens' London tea towels from the 'Tourist Chic' collection, 1985; Frilled beach outfit from the 'BABA' collection, 1987

CLOTHES FOR LONDON WARRIORS

Mark and I grew up in working-class suburbia, where the pallets of our lives were limited. Kindred spirits in parallel realities.

Our journey began when we met in 1982 on a train platform in Belgrade and then stayed in a Victorian tenement when Clerkenwell still needed a public bath house. We were compelled to create. The idea of fashion as produce, creating for livelihood, emerged, and fly-pitching a rail of clothing we made from curtains in Covent Garden offered the marketplace. Passersby stopped and spent money, followed by fashion editors, stylists, artists and socialites – our circle widened and we never got arrested.

Next stop was a squat in Hackney. While journeying through the undiscovered hinterlands of Dalston, Brick Lane and Whitechapel we came across Ravi's carpet shop. The flamenco dancers, Cornish galleon and other velvety picturesque wall hangings displayed in 1970s restaurants through our eyes could be worn as a donkey jacket – what a juxtaposition! And our first 'Workman and Cats' collection was born.

We loved the City of London. How about we concoct new city attire, a pinstripe wool tribal dress photographed against the muddy banks and groynes of the Thames? Dogtooth cloth, braces, starched Eton collars, dress studs and cufflinks. Deconstruct traditional male outfitters to be reformed as a sassy dress. We can extemporise outside of class and prevalent frames of reference.

Next, expeditions to the outer reaches of London.

Vibrant Southall with rooms and rooms of exotic fabrics reimagined as sari trousers. All history and cultures coming together for a new London look. Clothes for London Warriors at the 1985 Individual Clothes Show. Thanks to Vivienne Westwood for the commendation in *The Face* magazine.

Our most memorable move was to Lascelles Tea Shop off Carnaby Street, run by the inimitable and free-spirited sisters Joyce and Barbara. We lived in a bathroom and slept on the floor, serving up the tea and scones in between fashion creation. The innovation of 1960s Carnaby Street had faded to tourist gimcrack, but this too was revalued and loved within our 'Carnaby Tourist Chic' collection. Linen tea towels were handblocked by Ulster Linen and familiar London sites were transposed into uniforms for a changing of the fashion guard. Charm necklaces comprising red buses, black taxis and horse guards in perpetual motion across tourist headscarf blouses.

By this time the Update State conception of our work had fully formed and we had our own studio above a sex-worker's room in D'Arblay Street, Soho. We had arrived.

In 1986 we explored our version of couture for a night on the town. Ruched velvet cummerbund-inspired

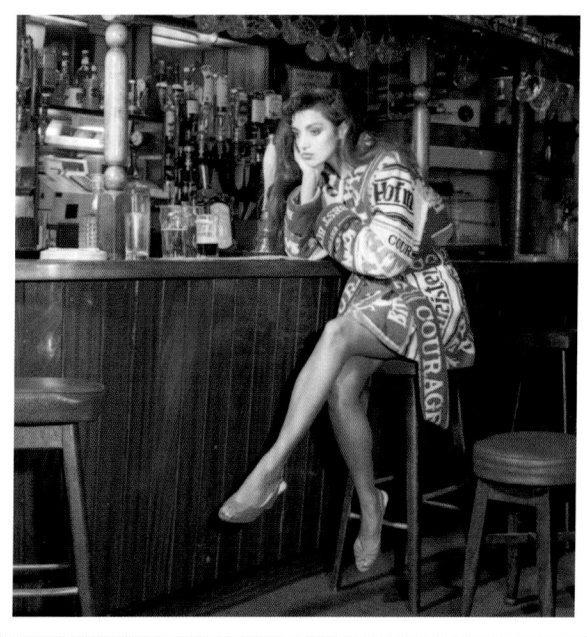

skirts, white harem pants from pleated dress-shirt fabric, a denim double-breasted suit, marabou wraps and 'chocolate' jewellery interspersed with crystals. The Cambridge Theatre bar provided a gilded backdrop for this reworking of the black-tie dress code and a young Naomi Campbell walked to illuminate the room.

Looking back on this journey our work was about finding, repurposing and reinventing, and comprised elements of upcycling, including ourselves. It was a dialogue and love story within an inclusive London. Clothes comprised a form of authentic expression. Never mind the broken glass, live for the look.

Our final collection 'BABA' can be understood against the summer of love and the house party scene. Pure embroidered colours capturing a spiritual life in the garden of a non-fallen world: depictions of the sun, love, nature, the beach. An age of innocence. Fruit tea-towel jackets, gingerbread-people jeans, childlike frilly skirts for gazelle legs. 'BABA', or 'Before Alpha Beta After'. 'As it was in the beginning and so shall it be in the end.'

Mark travelled to New York. We travelled around India, worked in Liverpool and then opened a homeless shelter. Mark died in 1994, AIDS being the spectre that ravaged our lives, stealing talent from our generation, breaking hearts and futures. I protected our enfant (the most miraculous of our creations) from the ash clouds of stigma and the government's tombstones of discrimination. I disappeared in view.

Over the subsequent years I developed a life of activism and philanthropy, fashioning services with and for young people who, like Mark and Syrie, want or need to escape, to find, to reinvent and rematerialise.

SYRIE PANTON

DESIGNER & PHILANTHROPIST

Black nylon vamp jacket, 1982

DEGVILLE'S DISPENSARY

During the early 1980s Martin Degville designed and sold clothes with designer Jane Farrimond in YaYa, a shop in the basement of Kensington Market. It was there that his distinctive look was spotted by Tony James and Neal X, who asked him to join their new band, Sigue Sigue Sputnik.

Prior to YaYa, he ran Degville's Dispensary in Birmingham, with Boy George as his shop assistant. Both were fierce, outrageous, visually striking and destined for pop stardom.

Degville styled the members of Sigue Sigue Sputnik, fusing punk, glam and cyber goth, which created a global impact when their first single 'Love Missile F1-11' exploded into the charts.

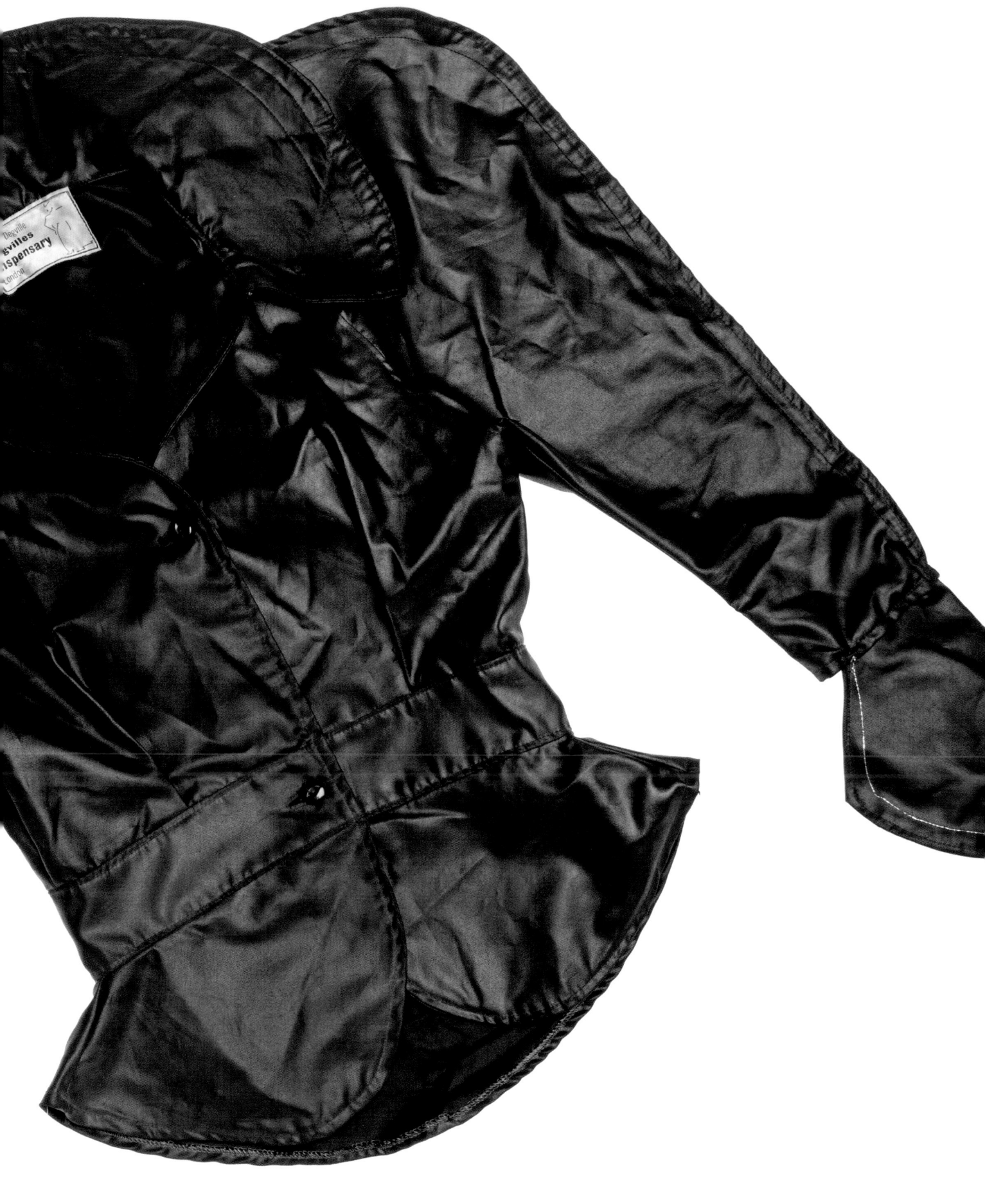

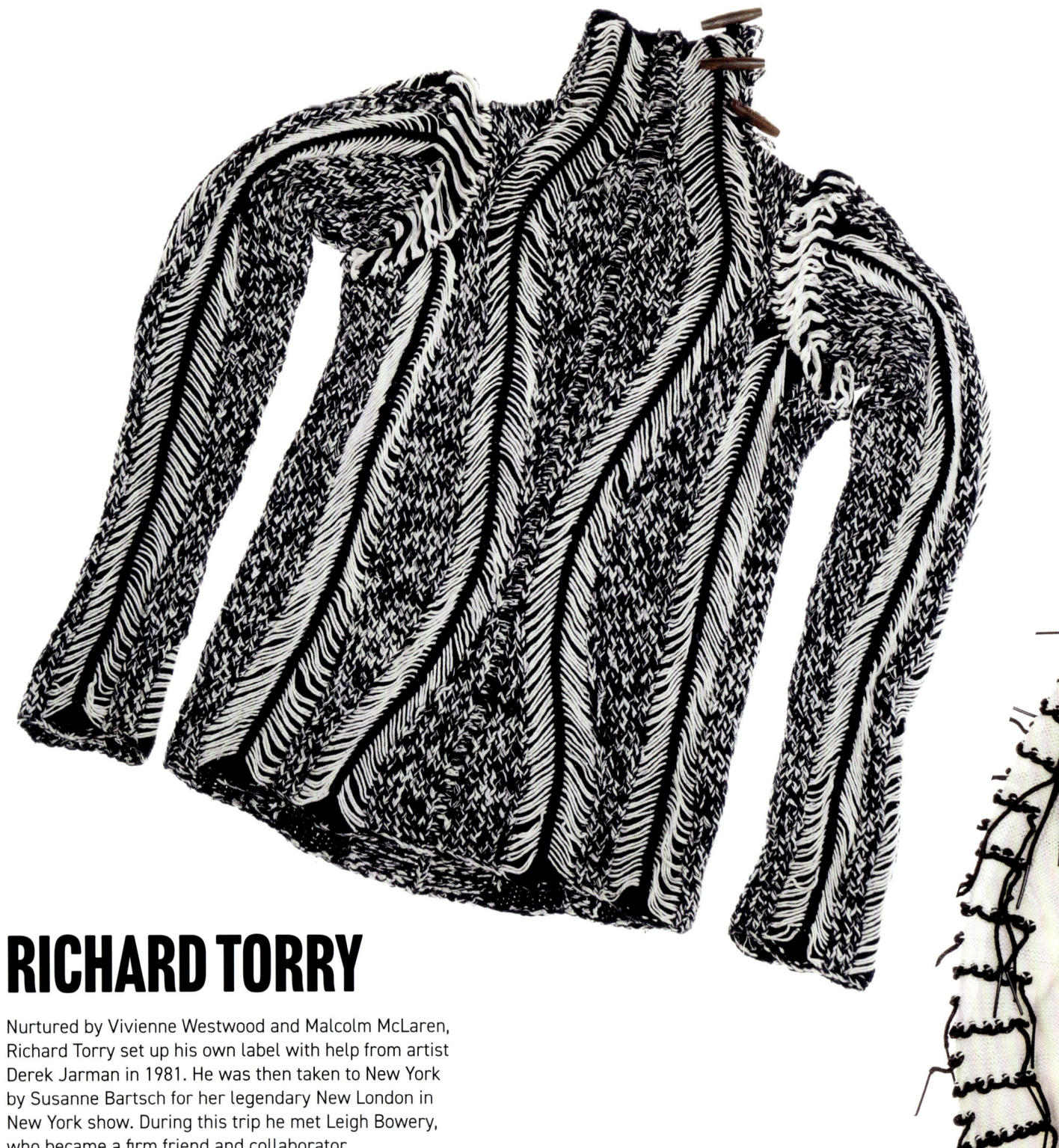

RICHARD TORRY

Nurtured by Vivienne Westwood and Malcolm McLaren, Richard Torry set up his own label with help from artist Derek Jarman in 1981. He was then taken to New York by Susanne Bartsch for her legendary New London in New York show. During this trip he met Leigh Bowery, who became a firm friend and collaborator.

His wildly creative label became famous for knitwear and was backed by Japanese designer Hanae Mori. This period saw Torry dividing his time between London and Tokyo. In 1986 he became one of the original members of design collective The House of Beauty and Culture in Dalston.

In 1991 Torry decided to focus on his true passion, music, and a year later formed the ultimate art-band, Minty, with Leigh Bowery.

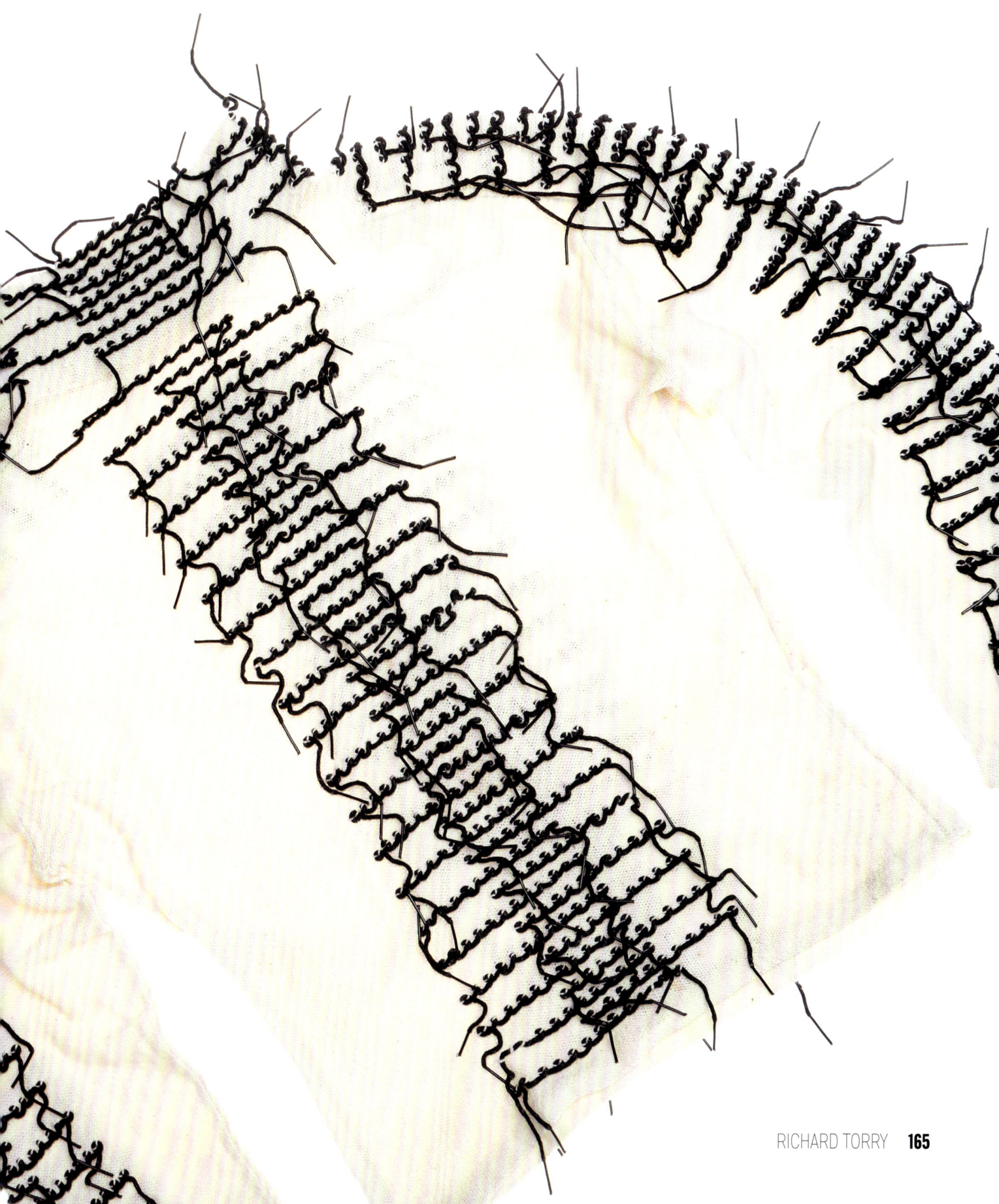

Left to right Herringbone hand-knitted sweater, 1986; Shoelace sweater, 1986

RICHARD TORRY 165

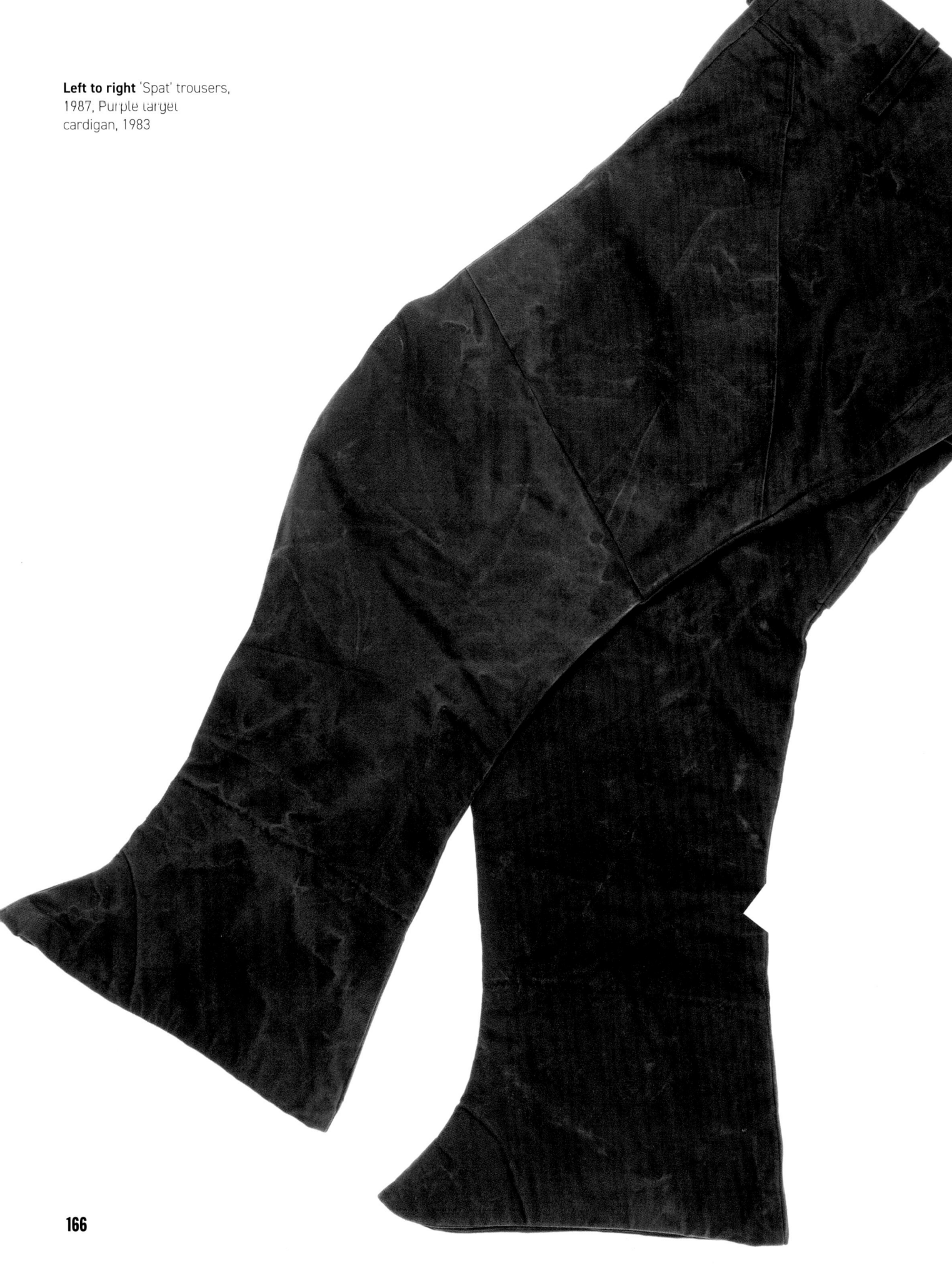

Left to right 'Spat' trousers, 1987, Purple target cardigan, 1983

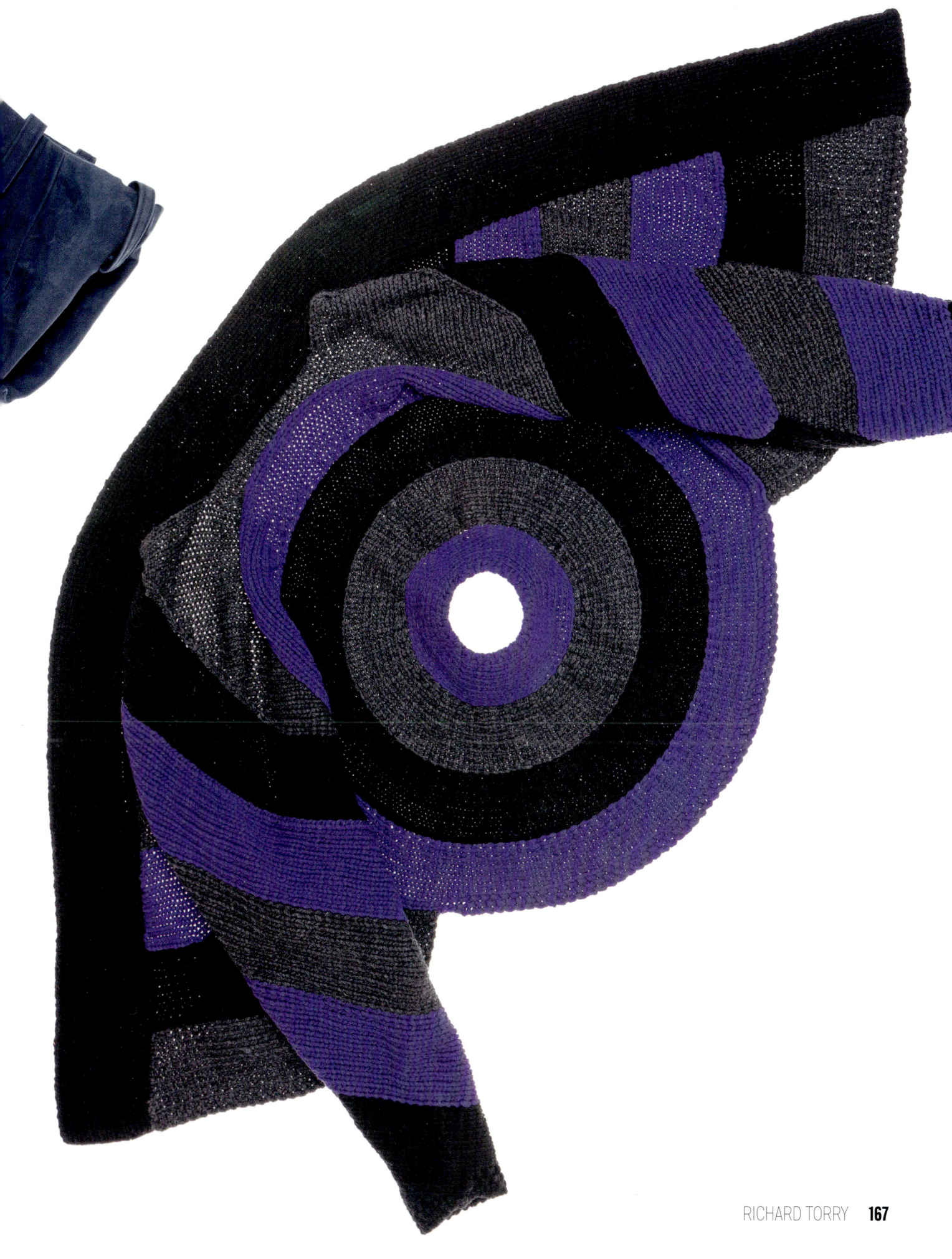

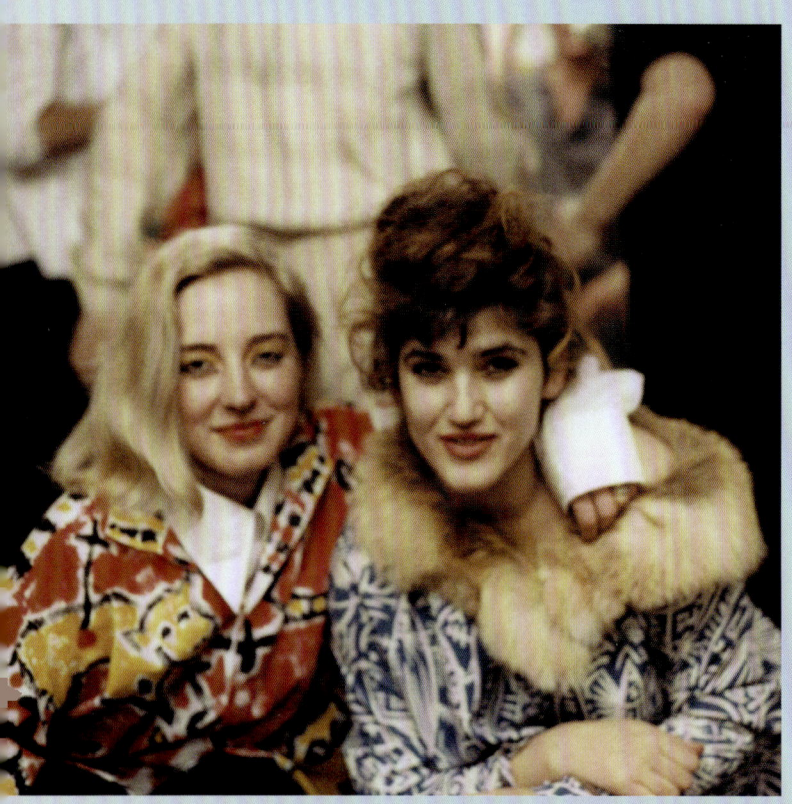
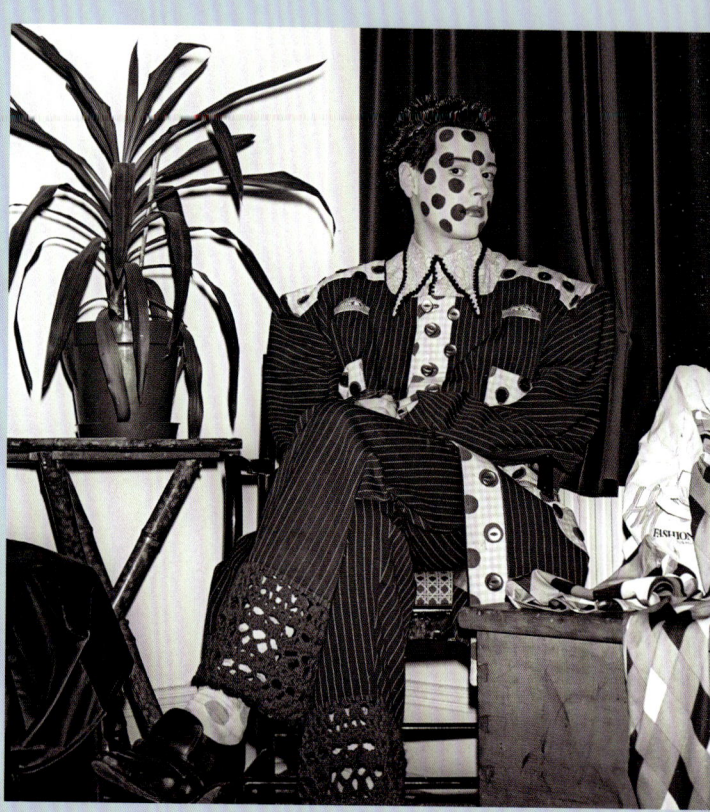
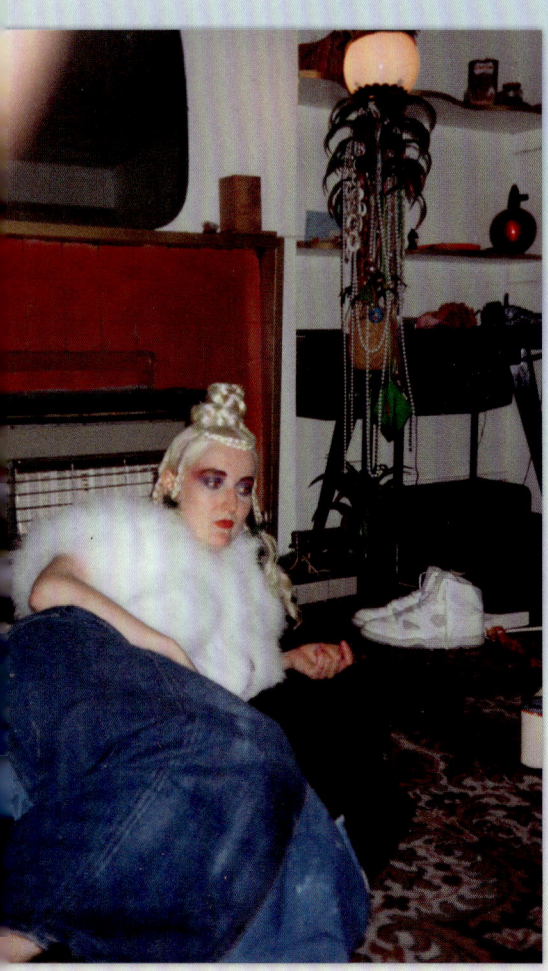
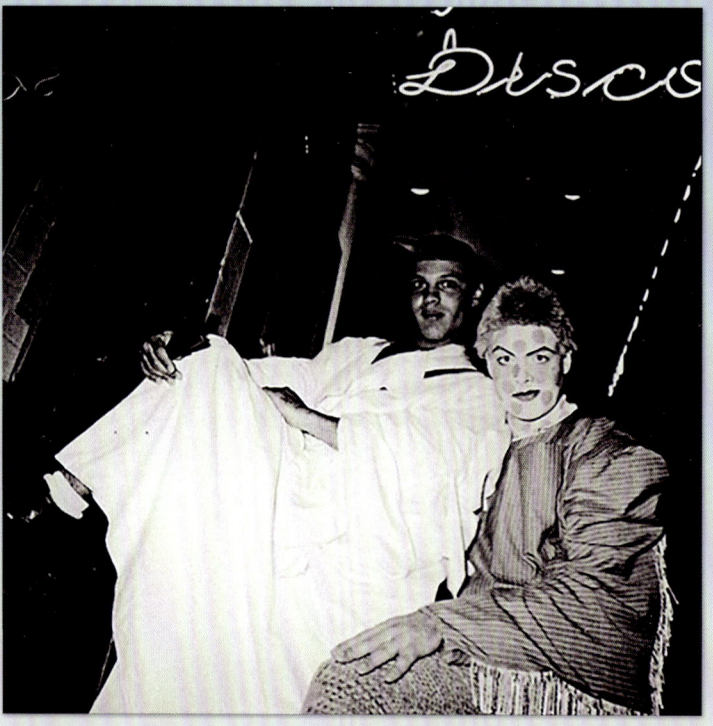

Clockwise from top left Sue Came and Elmaz Hüseyin; Trojan; Mr Pearl and Mike Nichols; Sue Tilley; Grayson Perry; Hilde Smith and Caroline Houghton styled by Iain R Webb; Leigh Bowery (right) outside Taboo; Gaynor Prior

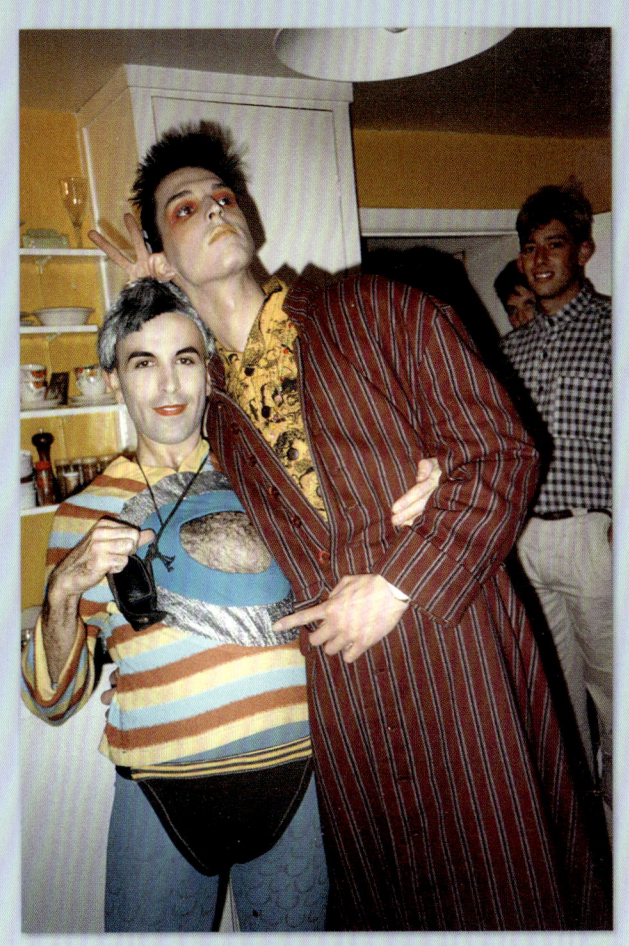
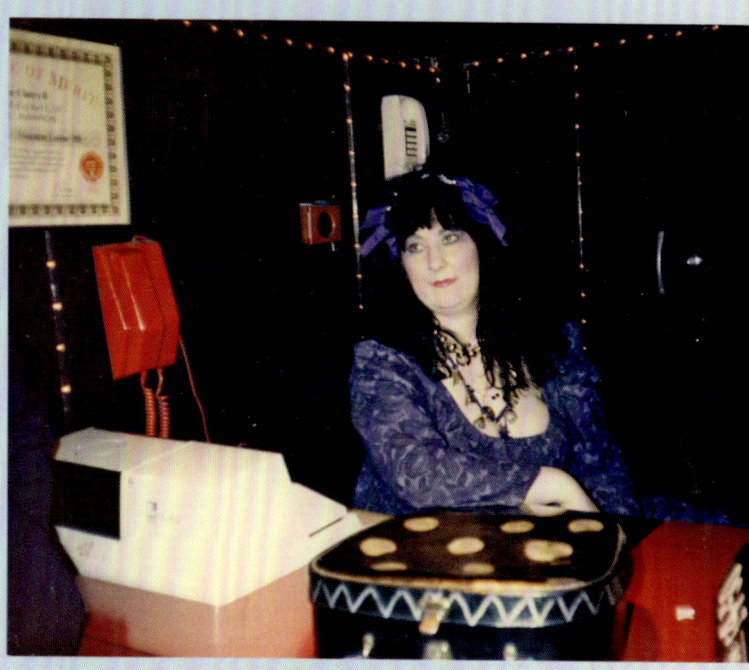
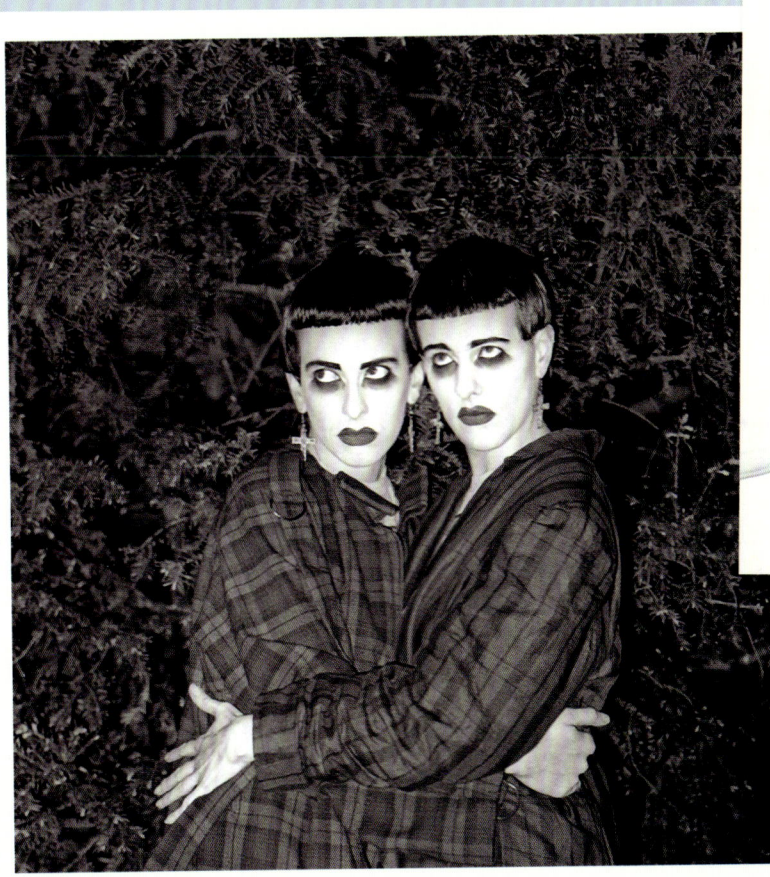
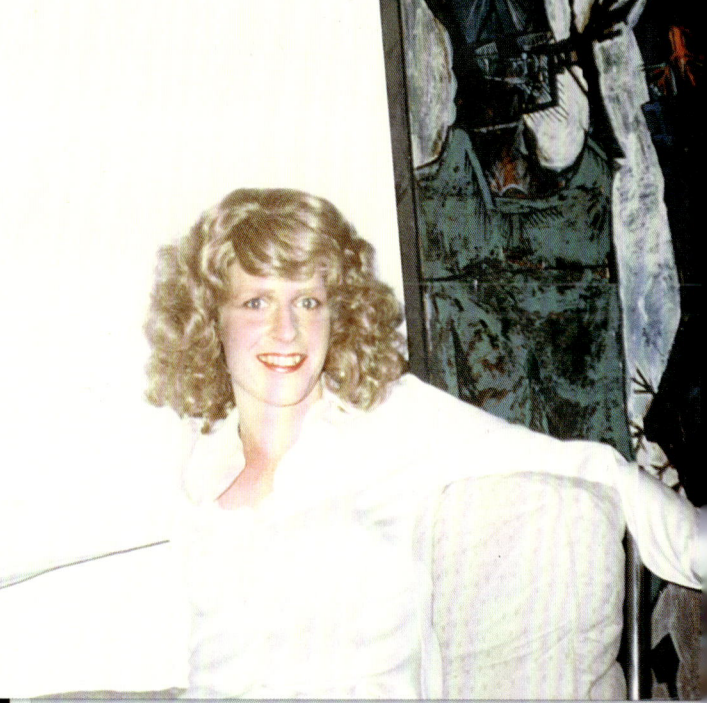

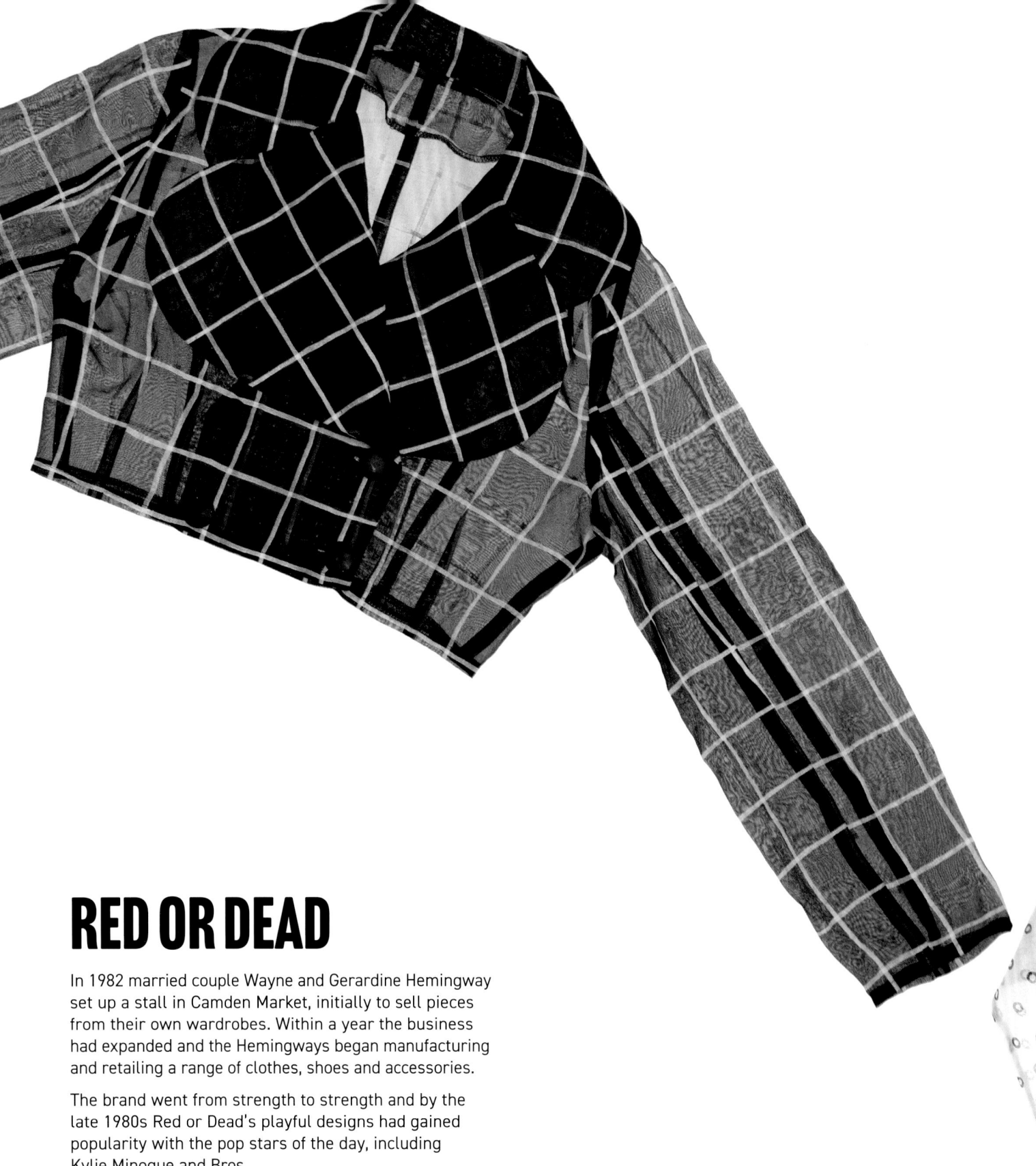

RED OR DEAD

In 1982 married couple Wayne and Gerardine Hemingway set up a stall in Camden Market, initially to sell pieces from their own wardrobes. Within a year the business had expanded and the Hemingways began manufacturing and retailing a range of clothes, shoes and accessories.

The brand went from strength to strength and by the late 1980s Red or Dead's playful designs had gained popularity with the pop stars of the day, including Kylie Minogue and Bros.

Although the Hemingways were at first snubbed by London Fashion Week on the grounds that 'designer fashion' should be elitist, the organisers later relented and Red or Dead was voted Streetstyle Designer of the Year for three consecutive years.

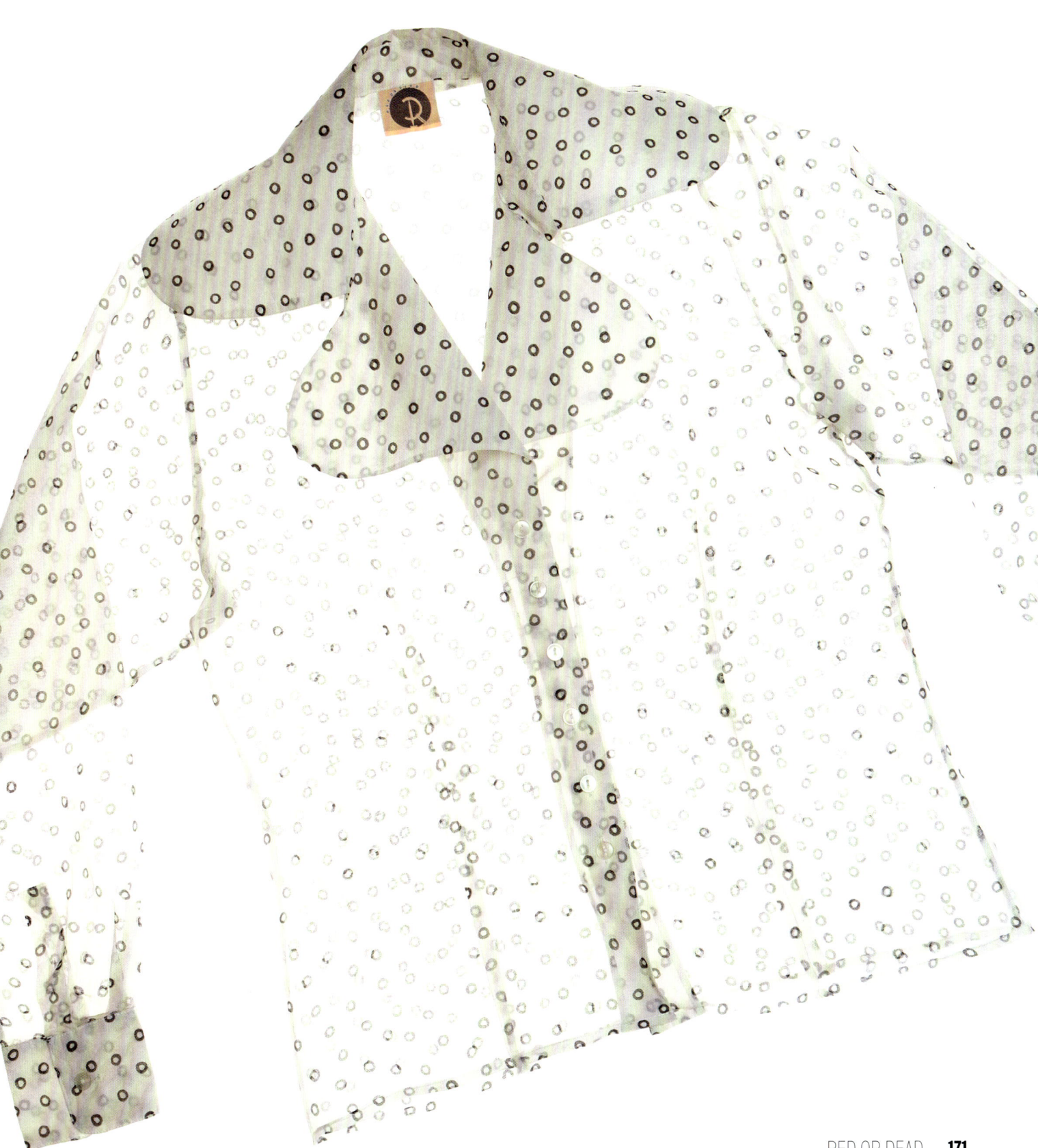

Left to right Black and white check women's shirt, 1988; Round-collar shirt, 1988

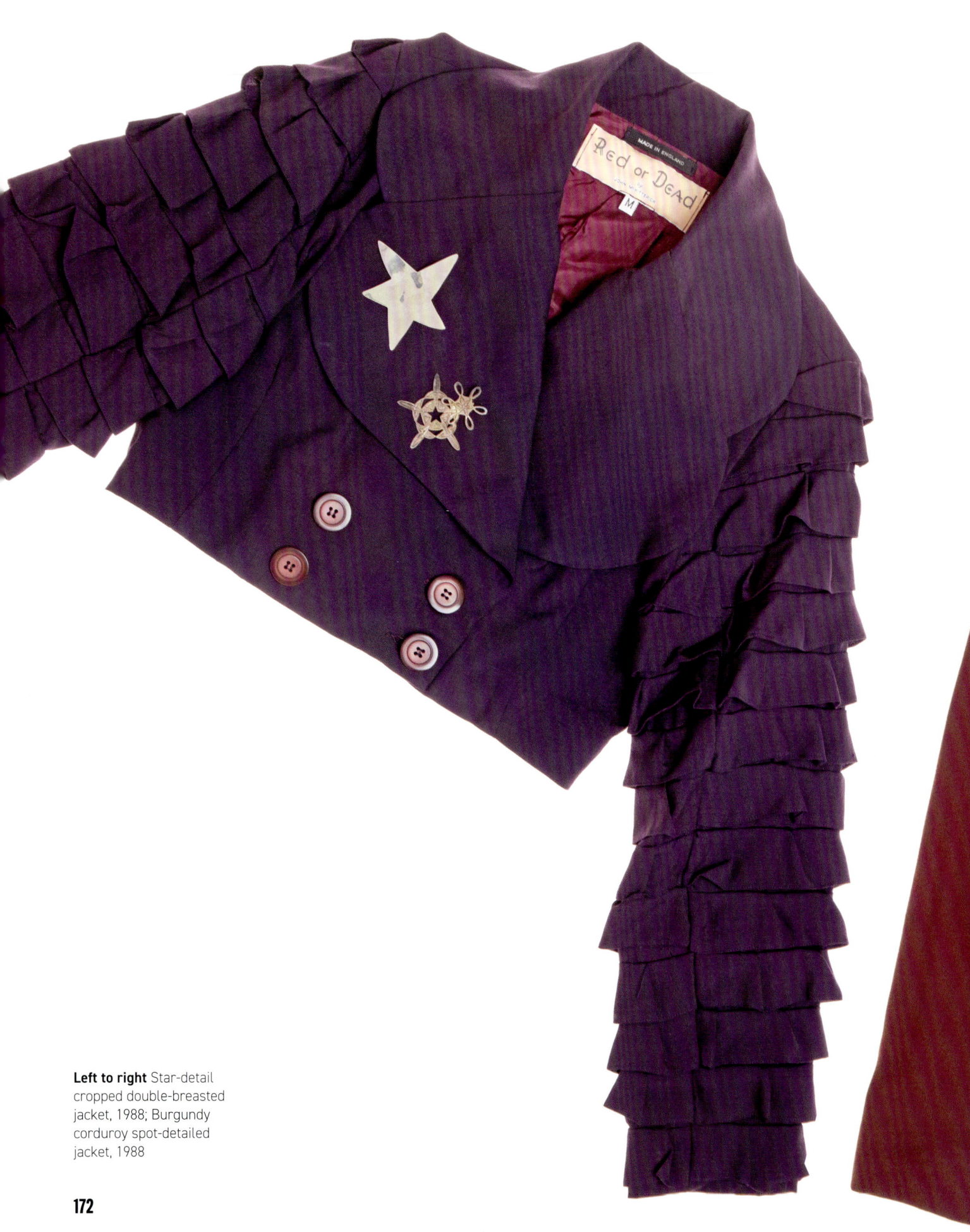

Left to right Star-detail cropped double-breasted jacket, 1988; Burgundy corduroy spot-detailed jacket, 1988

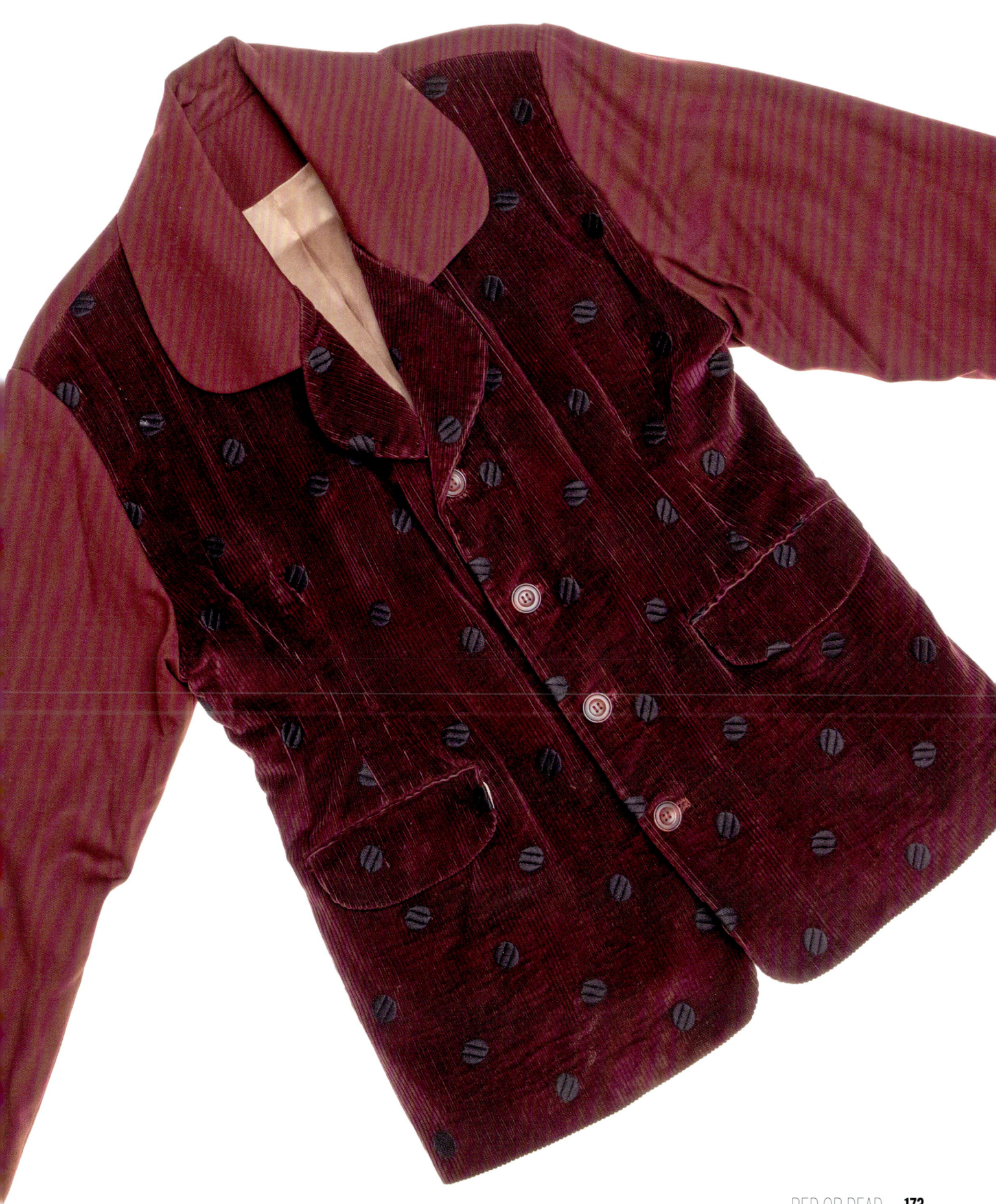

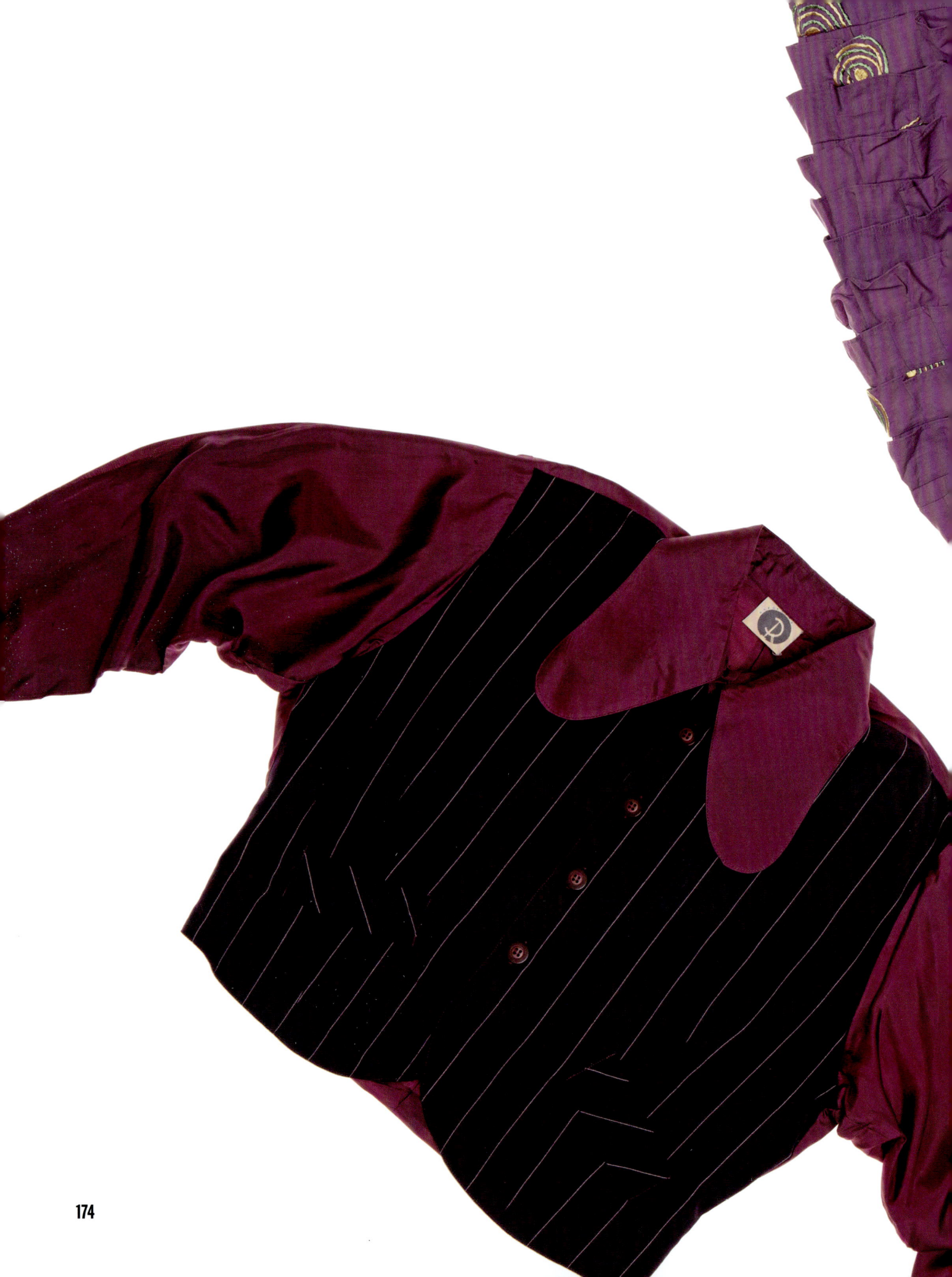

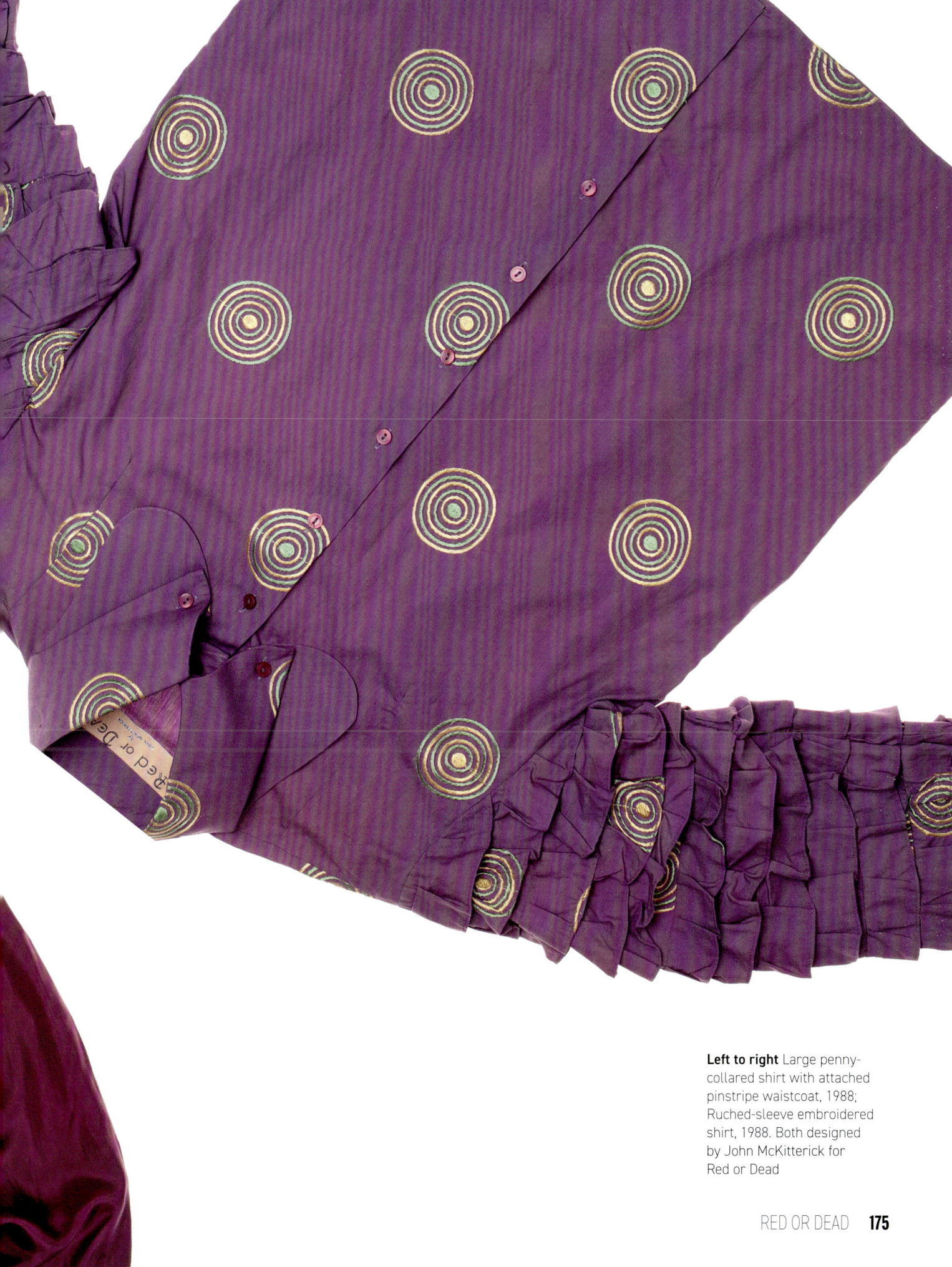

Left to right Large penny-collared shirt with attached pinstripe waistcoat, 1988; Ruched-sleeve embroidered shirt, 1988. Both designed by John McKitterick for Red or Dead

IN CONVERSATION WITH

WAYNE & GERARDINE HEMINGWAY MBE

Designers and founders of globally-successful clothing brand Red or Dead.

Interview by Martin Green

MG: **You've DJed and been involved in clubs for decades. How did you discover nightclubs in the 1980s and how did they manifest themselves in your creative practice?**

WH: Gerardine and I met in a Northern Soul nightclub and we learnt our trade by going out. It was life back then for us and a lot of people like us – you lived to go clubbing. I can't remember anything else in my life that was as important as going dancing and obviously the byproduct was to look the best, like a competition.

GH: For me it was to have a different outfit every Saturday night. I'd either go and buy fabric at the markets and make myself a new outfit or add something to an old outfit to make it look different.

WH: I wanted to look different every week. I still don't know whether it was for myself or just to show that I could. I did it with second-hand clothes and army surplus in Blackburn. Right from punk times, I had to be different every single week – like Gerardine said, it couldn't be the same outfit. It was pushing ourselves that taught us to be designers. Neither of us trained.

GH: A lot of it stemmed from our background because we were working class. We couldn't afford to go and buy clothes every week, so Mum made nearly all our clothes and my aunties used to knit all our cardigans. So picking up a sewing machine and having a go was second nature.

WH: Then we both moved to London. I only came for two reasons: one was to be in a band and the other one was to go dancing. I'd started to come down to London in 1976 as a teenage punk.

MG: **Did you go to college?**

WH: I got a 100 per cent grant from Blackburn Council. That must be hard to understand for today's young generations, the concept that you were paid to go to university by the public sector. I studied geography and town planning, and the only reason is because they offered me a place if I simply got an E grade at A-Level. I only had to get one E (I got an A!) to get to UCL and live in the centre of London, and the first thing I did at university was form a band.

MG: **How did you become fashion designers?**

WH: We started selling second-hand clothes in Camden Market. We spent every spare second going around every jumble sale and occasionally auction as there weren't many charity shops. We soon became the biggest sellers of second-hand in London and we were learning about the history of fashion because we were handling fashion items every day of the week.

GH: Also, whenever I made something for myself I'd make a few more for the market.

WH: We'd no plans to have a label. We had no plans full stop!

MG: **How did Red or Dead start?**

GH: I rented a unit in Kensington Market and sat making clothes every day in there. Macy's New York came in and placed a big order, but my clothes had no labels so we had to come up with a name, and Red or Dead was it. The story of the name is well documented.

WH: Gerardine rang and said we've had an order, and this was the first from a shop. We'd never heard of Macy's. How were we going to make the clothes? My mum got an *Exchange and Mart* newspaper and bought some old nurses' uniform sewing machinery. We took a unit, one of Gerardine's sisters left her job because she could sew, and they basically set up a factory in Blackburn. That was the start of Red or Dead.

GH: Jean Paul Gaultier used to come to our stall whenever he was in London. He'd take second-hand stuff and buy a sackful of Dr. Martens. I remember Marc Almond coming in all the time too.

MG: **When did you start producing collections?**

WH: We probably started about 1985, but we didn't do catwalk until spring–summer 1989, which was in late 1988. So we probably had three years of practising, then we opened a shop on Rupert Street. Then Neal Street was the first one with lots of clothing – we were the first fashion store on Neal Street. Across from us was a kite store. There was an appliance repair shop. It was just like a street with no style and no fashion. The Red or Dead footwear had really taken off already.

MG: **How did you get into footwear?**

WH: We started to pair Dr. Martens with Gerardine's clothing to give it that kind of harder look. So you had the kind of more feminine clothes and we bought Dr. Martens to sell with it. And it started to sell – Demi Moore wore a pair with a dress on the front of *Vogue*. I realised that they were going to be massive and I found all of the old wholesalers in the UK and just bought up every pair I could find. We also opened in Manchester and Liverpool and then started wholesaling Dr. Martens all around the world, from America to Japan to Europe to everywhere.

Because it became such big business and we couldn't get enough Dr. Martens, we needed to do clumpy shoes of our own and the demand for these was mainly from women. This was the first time I remember women had worn big flat clumpy shoes. This was 1985.

MG: **How did you begin working with Taboo DJ Jeffrey Hinton?**

WH: We worked with Jeffrey from day one on the music soundtracks for our catwalk shows. He has always shared the wit we put into the collections and is a kindred spirit in not taking fashion and style too seriously.

MG: **Were you still going to nightclubs then?**

GH: Yeah, but not as much as we did in the 1970s and early to mid-1980s – we had our first two children in 1986 and 1987.

WH: Everybody in the Red or Dead shops was into clubbing. So I would go out with all the crew, basically. We were all going out dressed in the collections. It was a group of us. Mixed, gay and straight. We just danced, danced, danced. And that was when The Wag Club was still going. Back then, club culture and street fashion went completely together, totally hand in hand.

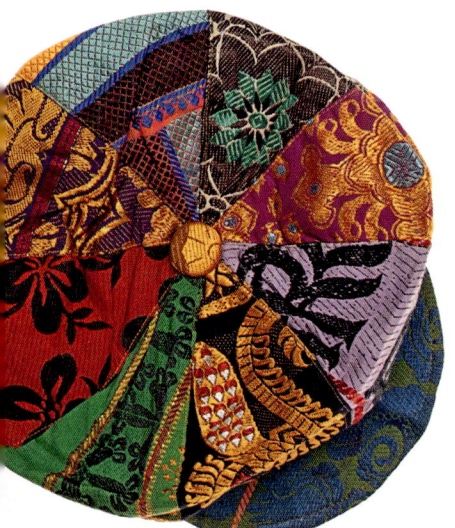

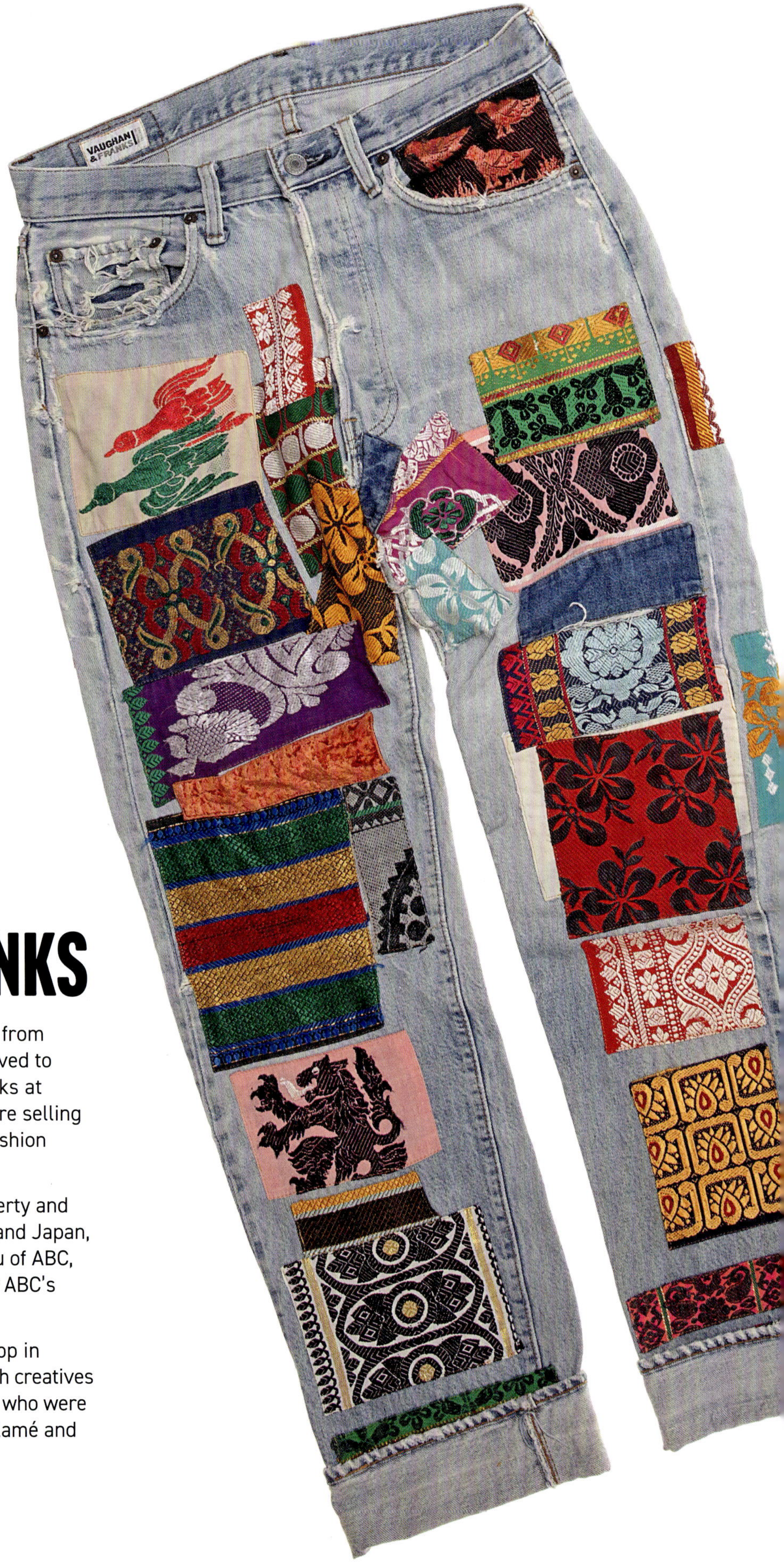

VAUGHAN & FRANKS

David Vaughan and Bunty Franks graduated from Nottingham Trent University in 1980 then moved to London to set up their label Vaughan & Franks at Kensington Market. Within two years they were selling to Browns and were included in the store's fashion show promoting young British designers.

They designed collections for Joseph and Liberty and attracted buyers from America, Italy, France and Japan, along with performers including David Yarritu of ABC, who wore their 'cosmos' shirt in the video for ABC's 1985 hit 'Be Near Me'.

In 1984 they opened a Vaughan & Franks shop in Nottingham, which swiftly became popular with creatives and followers of the alternative fashion scene, who were drawn to their fusion of vintage Indian cloth, lamé and hand-bleached patterns on denim.

Denim patchwork customised ensemble with Indian fabric, 1988

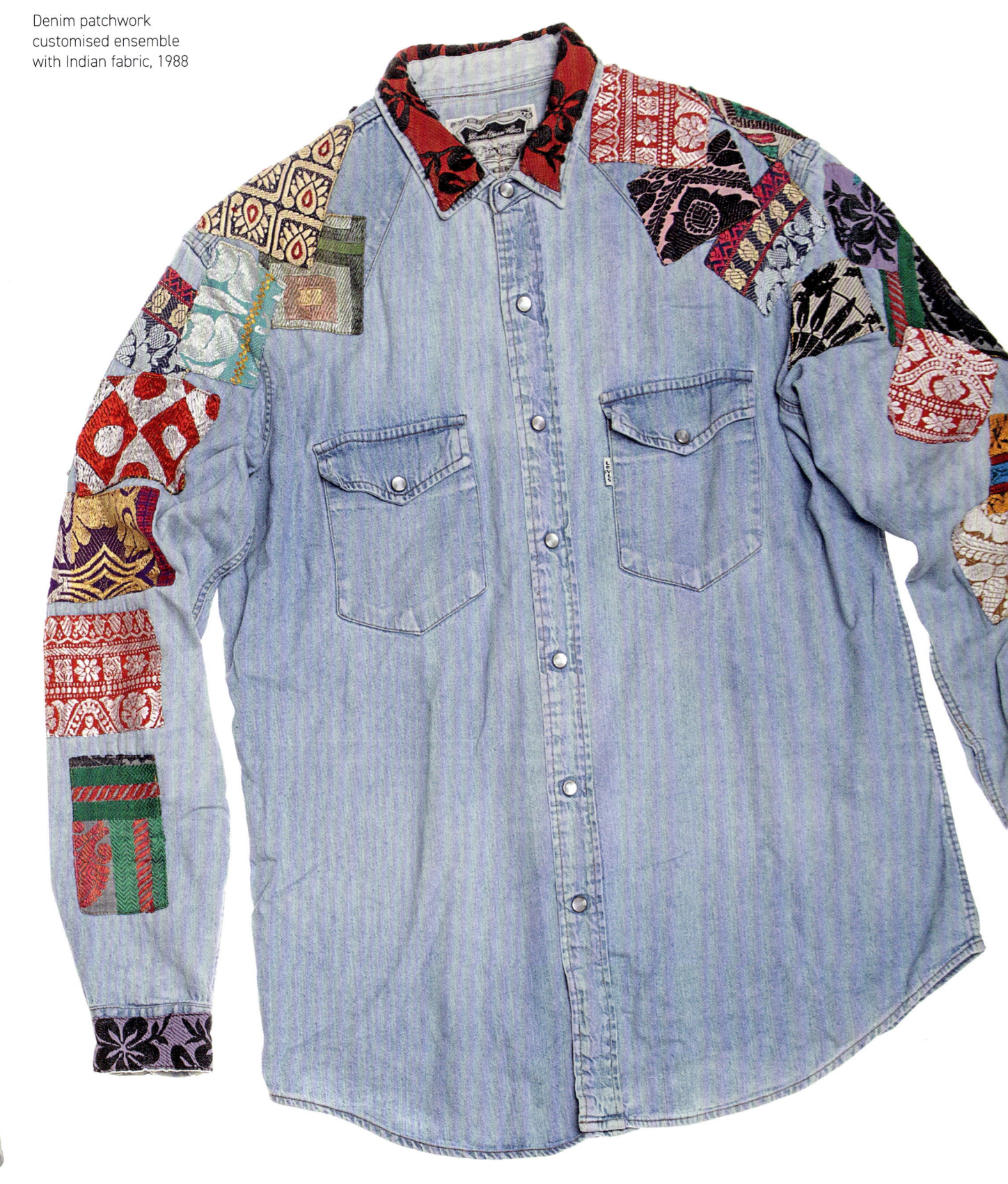

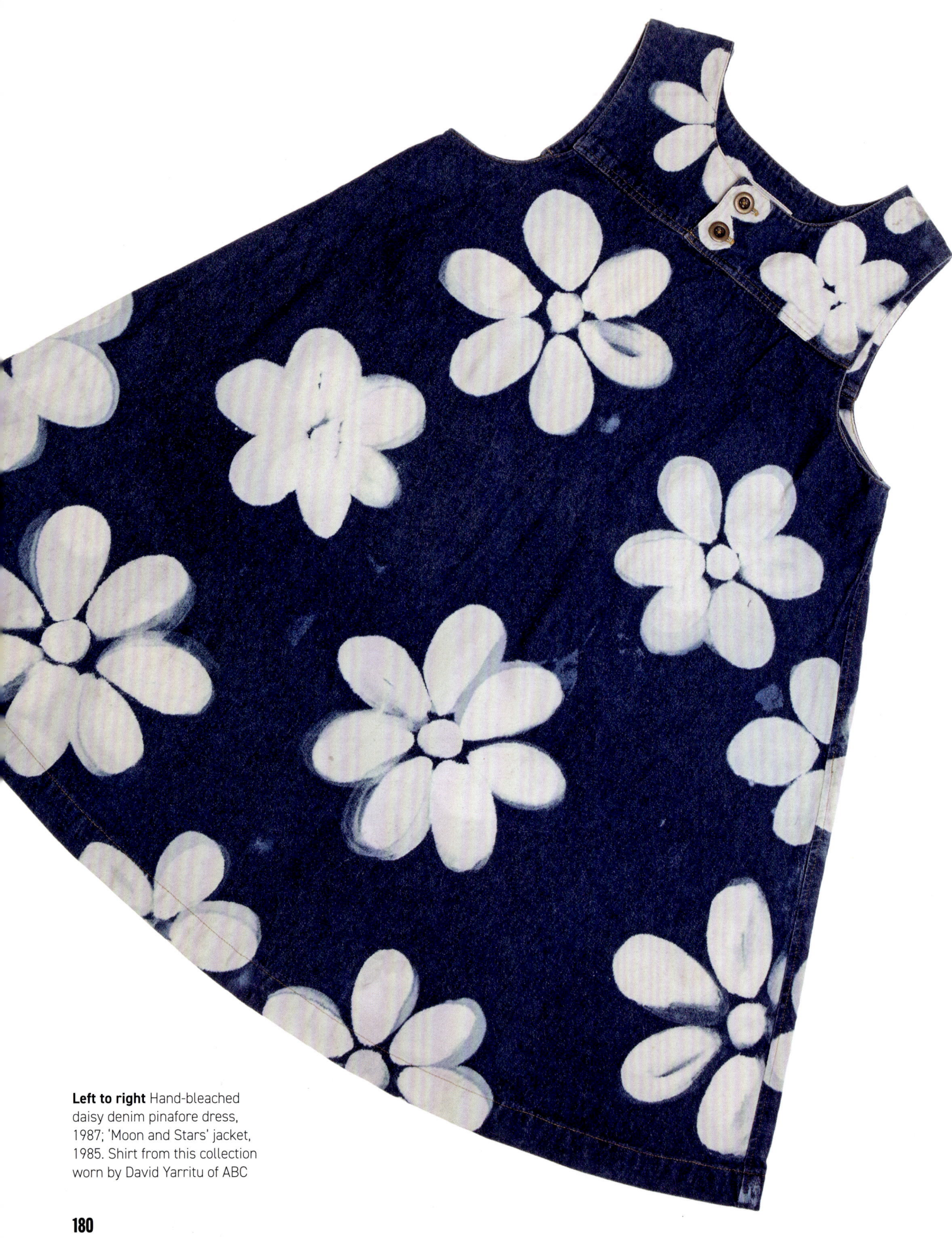

Left to right Hand-bleached daisy denim pinafore dress, 1987; 'Moon and Stars' jacket, 1985. Shirt from this collection worn by David Yarritu of ABC

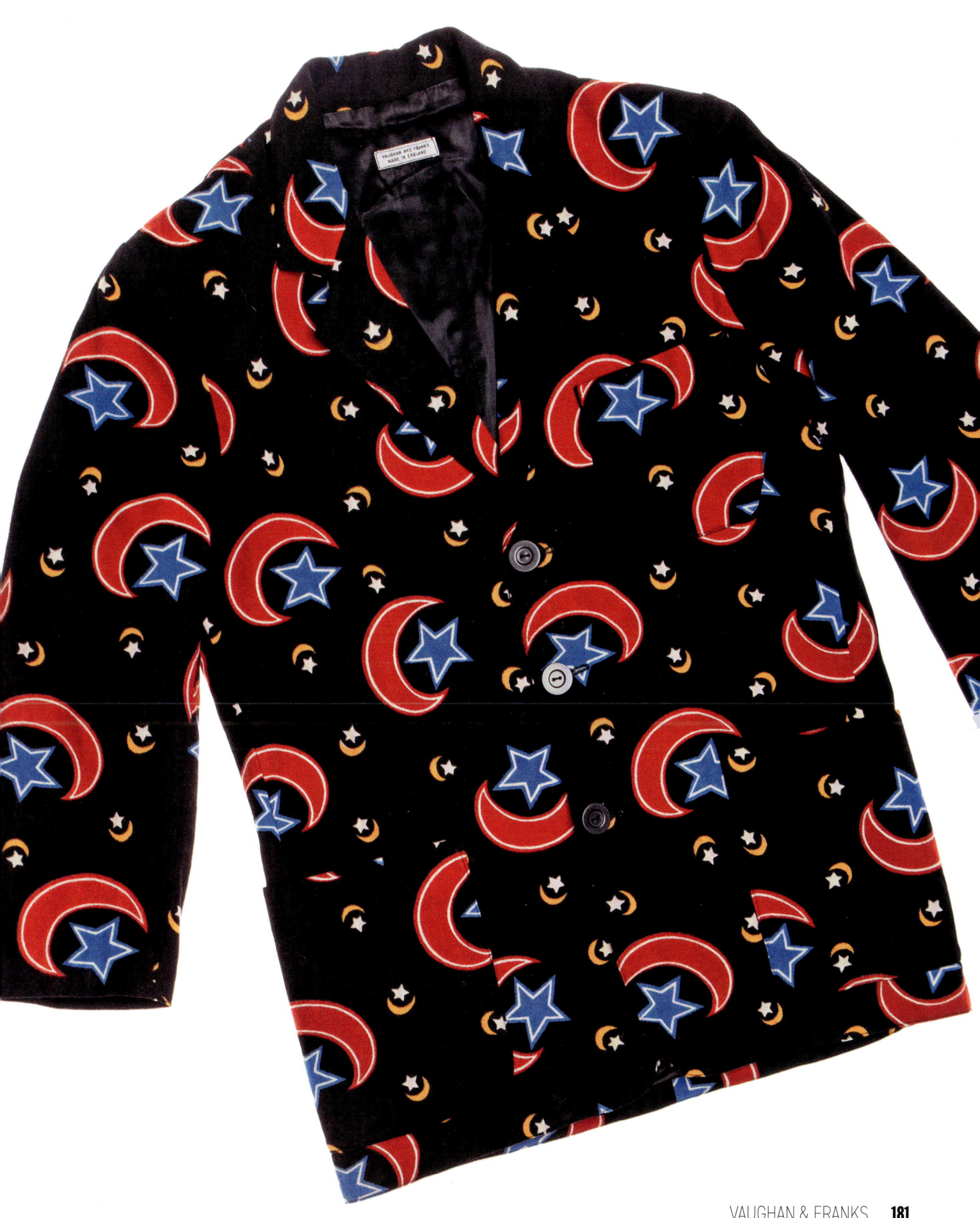

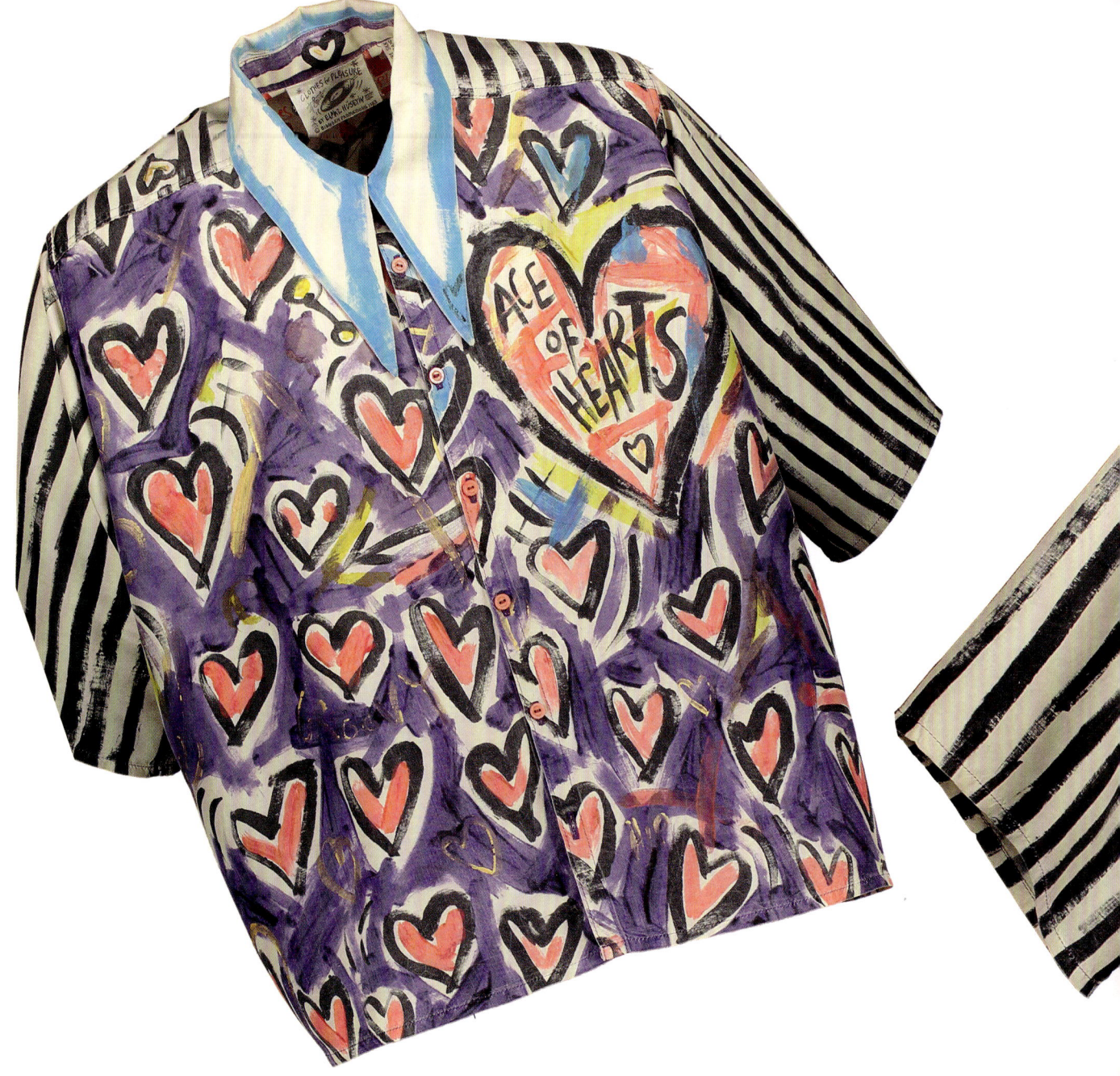

ELMAZ HÜSEYIN

After graduating from St Martin's School of Art in 1982, Elmaz Hüseyin and college friend Sue Came rented a studio in Wapping to hand-paint vibrant second-hand shirts and dresses, which they sold to BOY on the King's Road.

During the same period, Hüseyin illustrated record sleeves for the band Second Image. Then in 1984 she moved towards tailoring and created an influential 1970s inspired collection of big collars and cool cutting, which Susanne Bartsch showed in New York. This led a glam renaissance epitomised by ABC, who wore her outfits during their iconic *Zillionaire* period.

Hüseyin settled in New York and became a creative director and a designer for various fashion brands. She died in 2019.

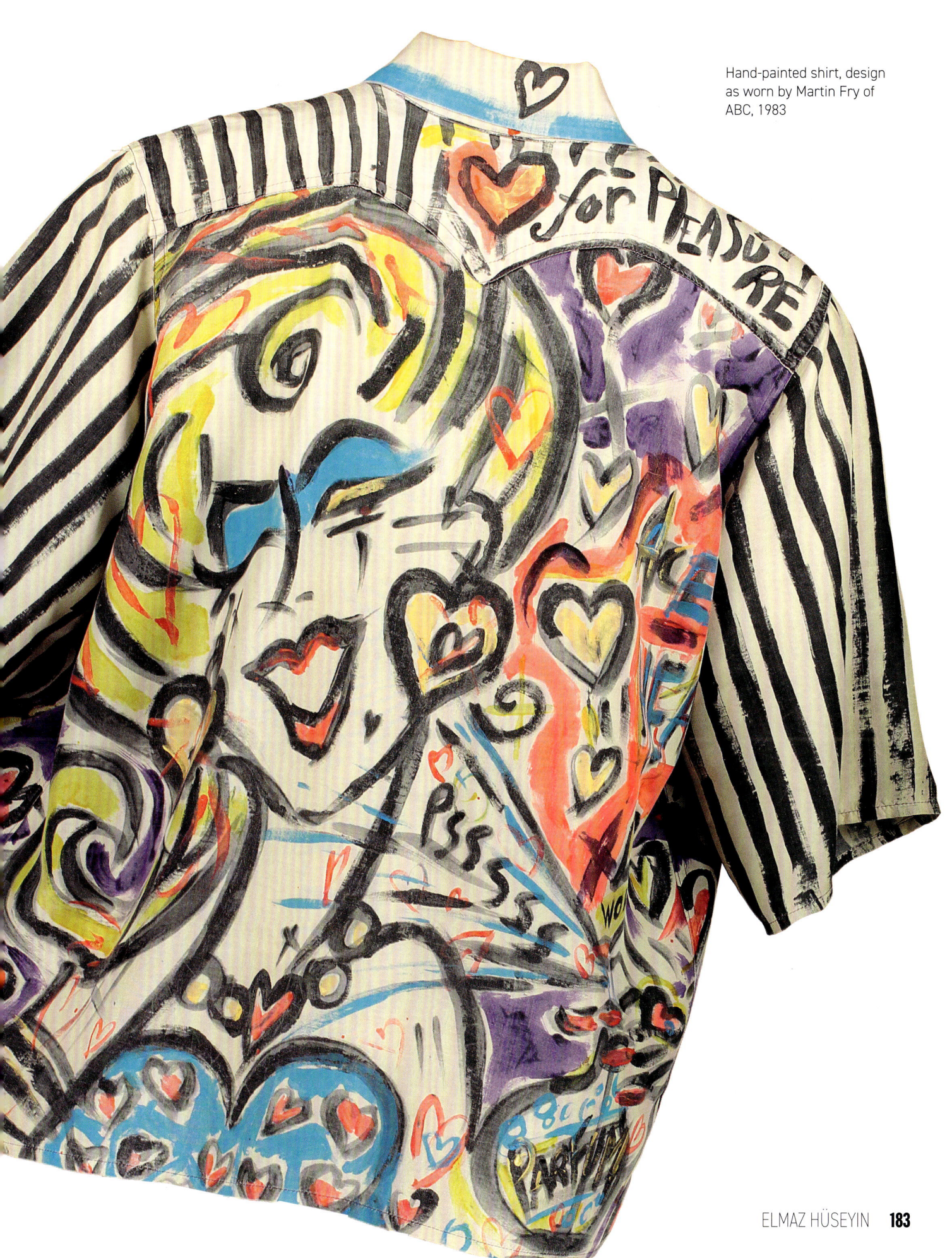

Hand-painted shirt, design as worn by Martin Fry of ABC, 1983

ELMAZ HÜSEYIN

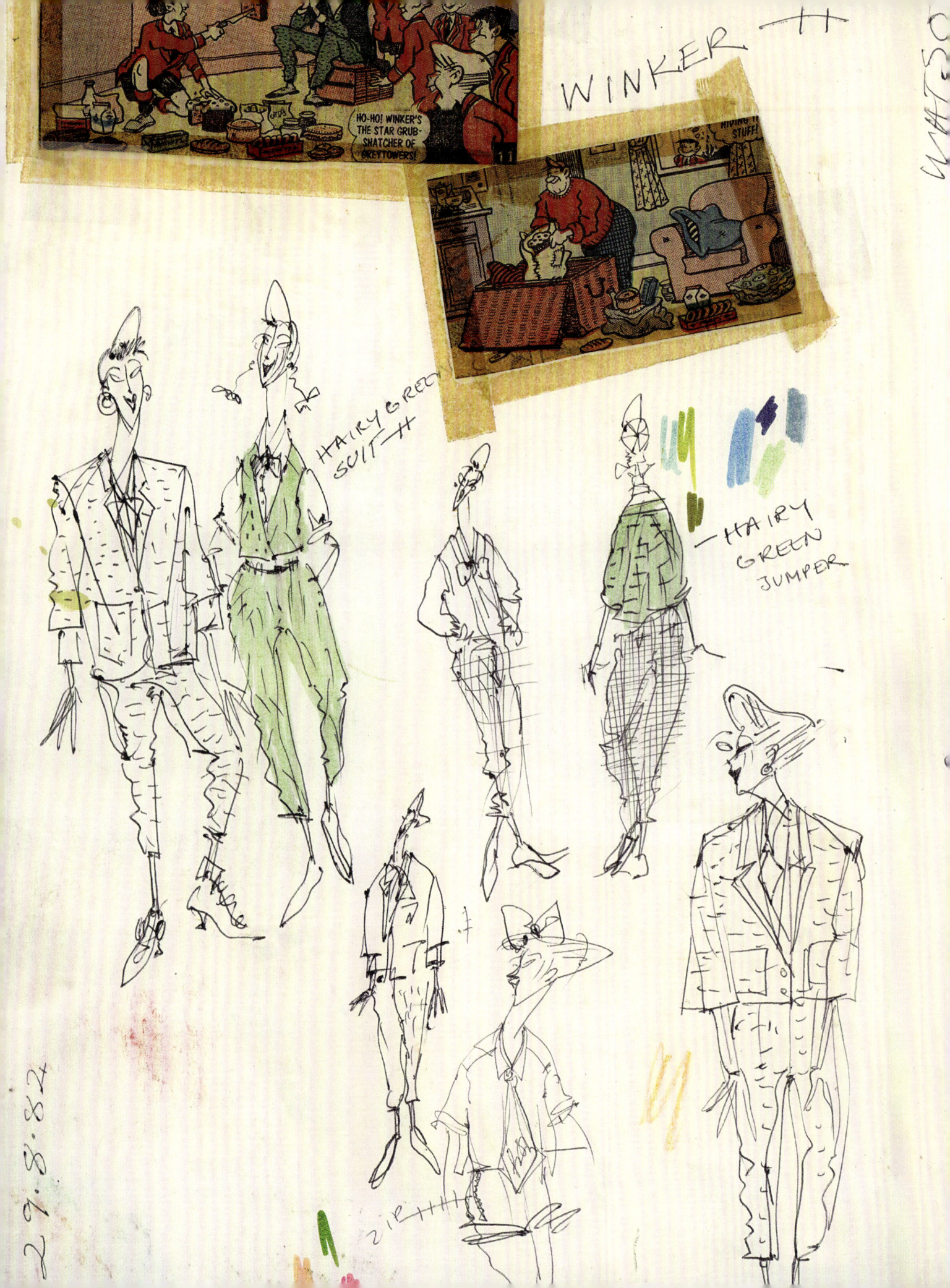

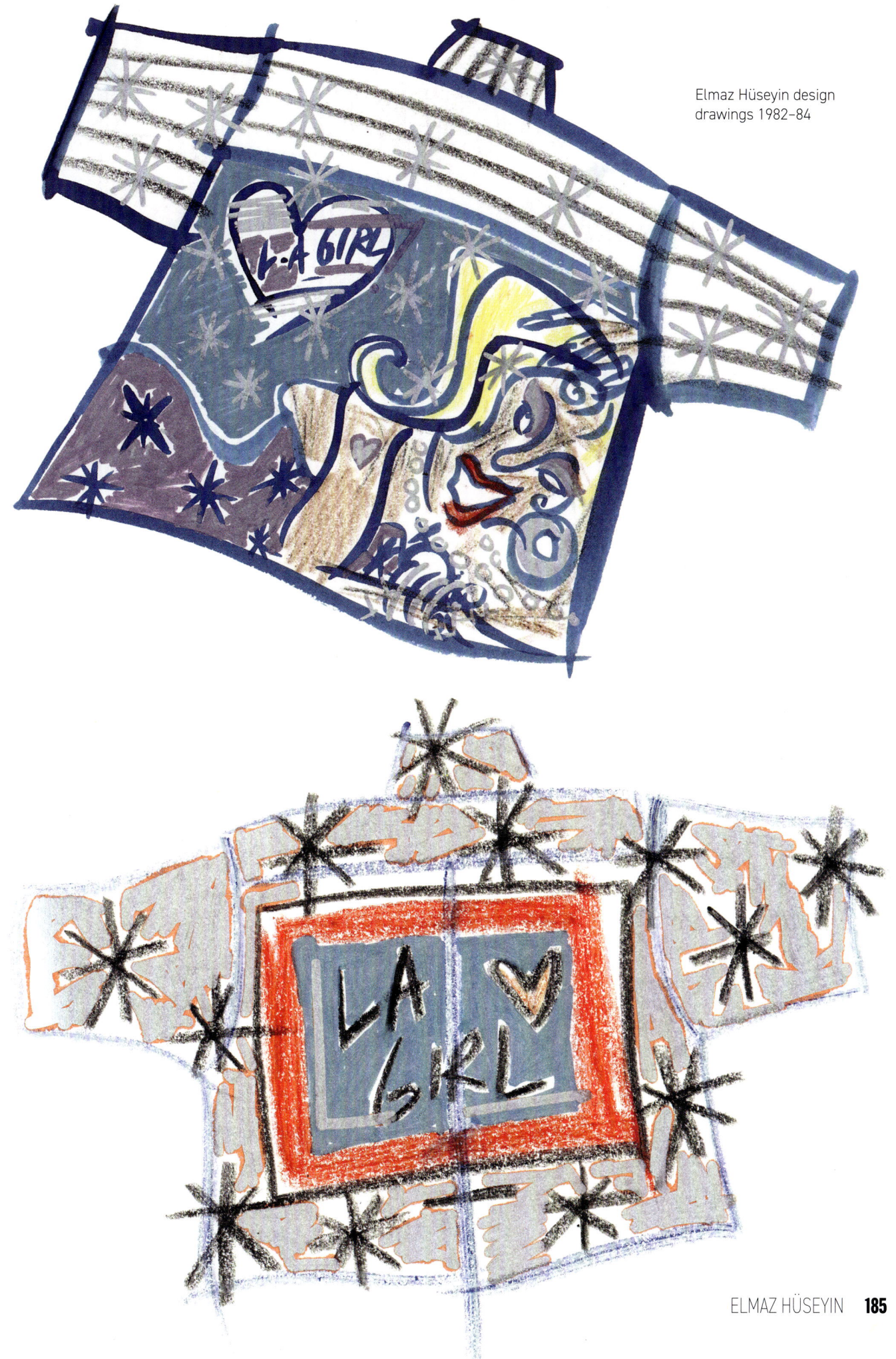

Elmaz Hüseyin design drawings 1982–84

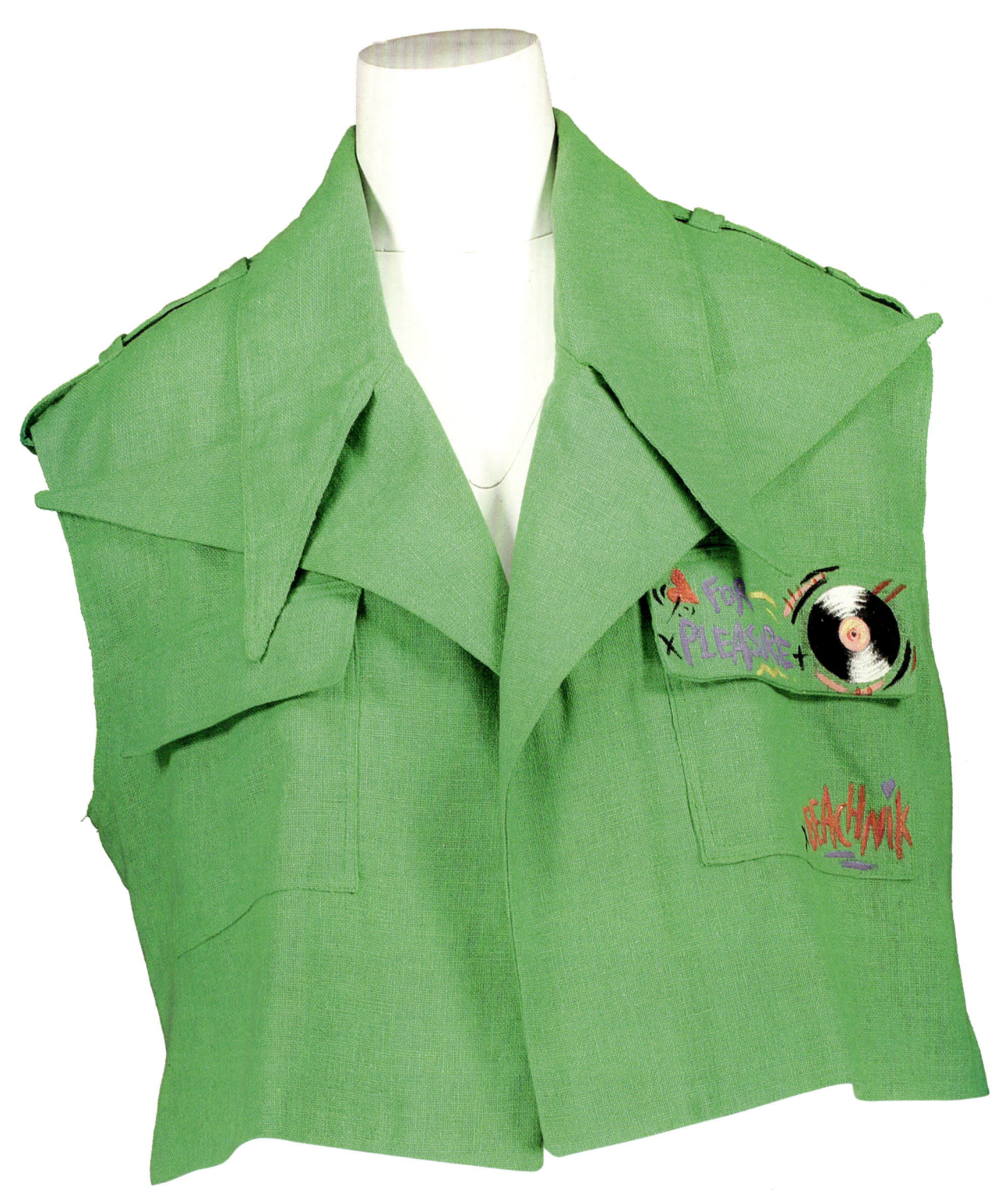

Left to right Green towelling beach suit jacket, 1984; Red belted trench coat with faux-fur collar, 1984

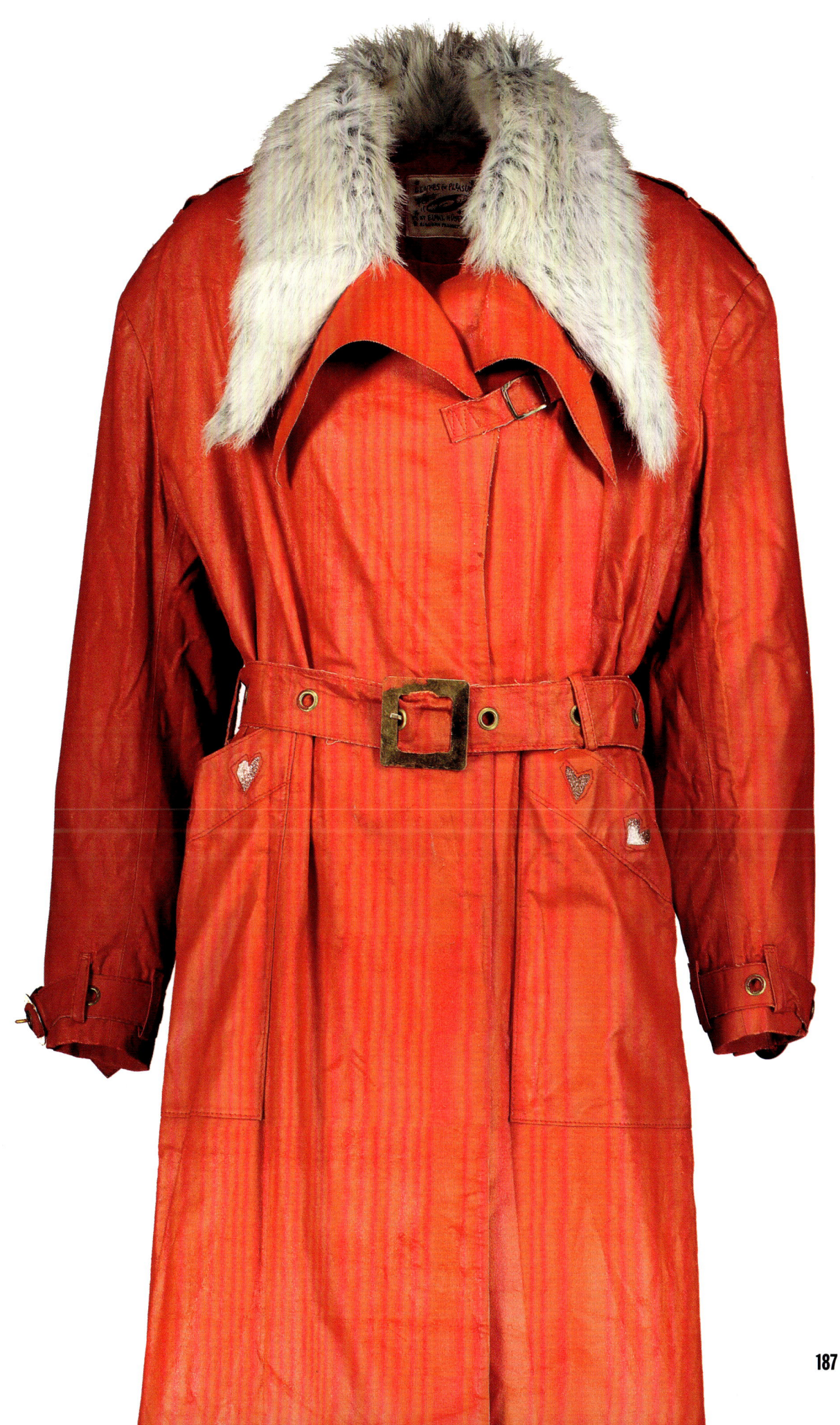

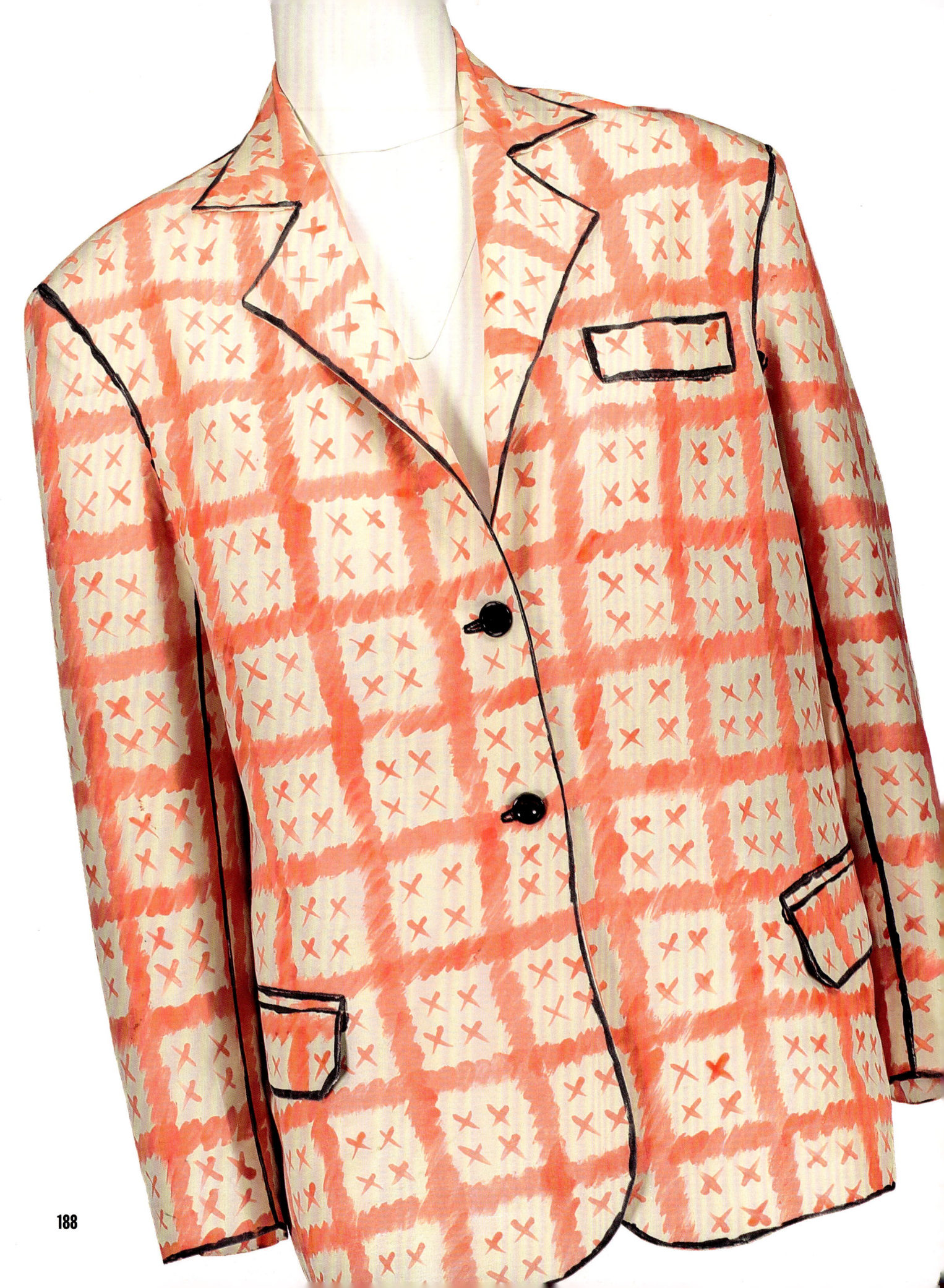

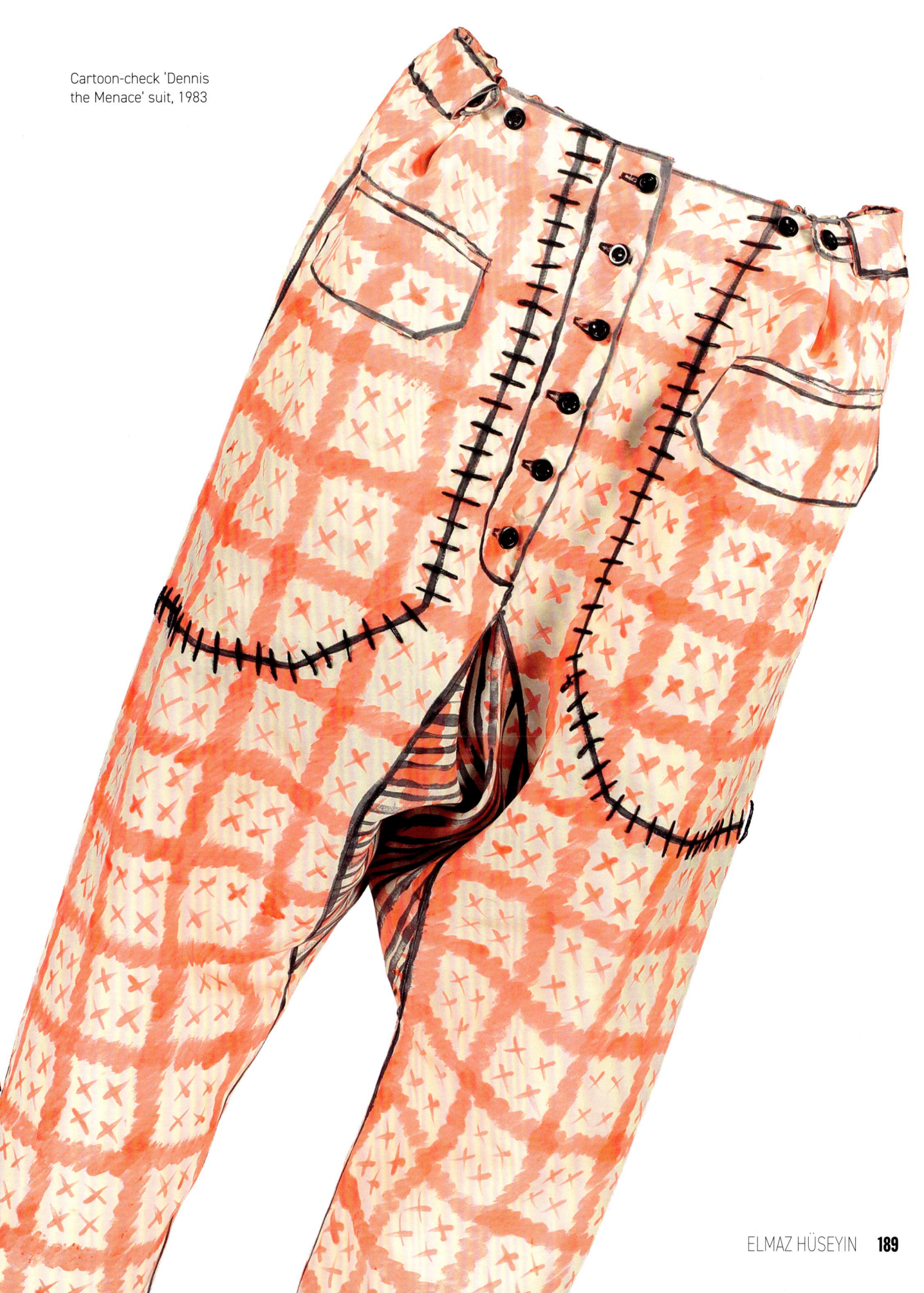

Cartoon-check 'Dennis the Menace' suit, 1983

ELMAZ HÜSEYIN

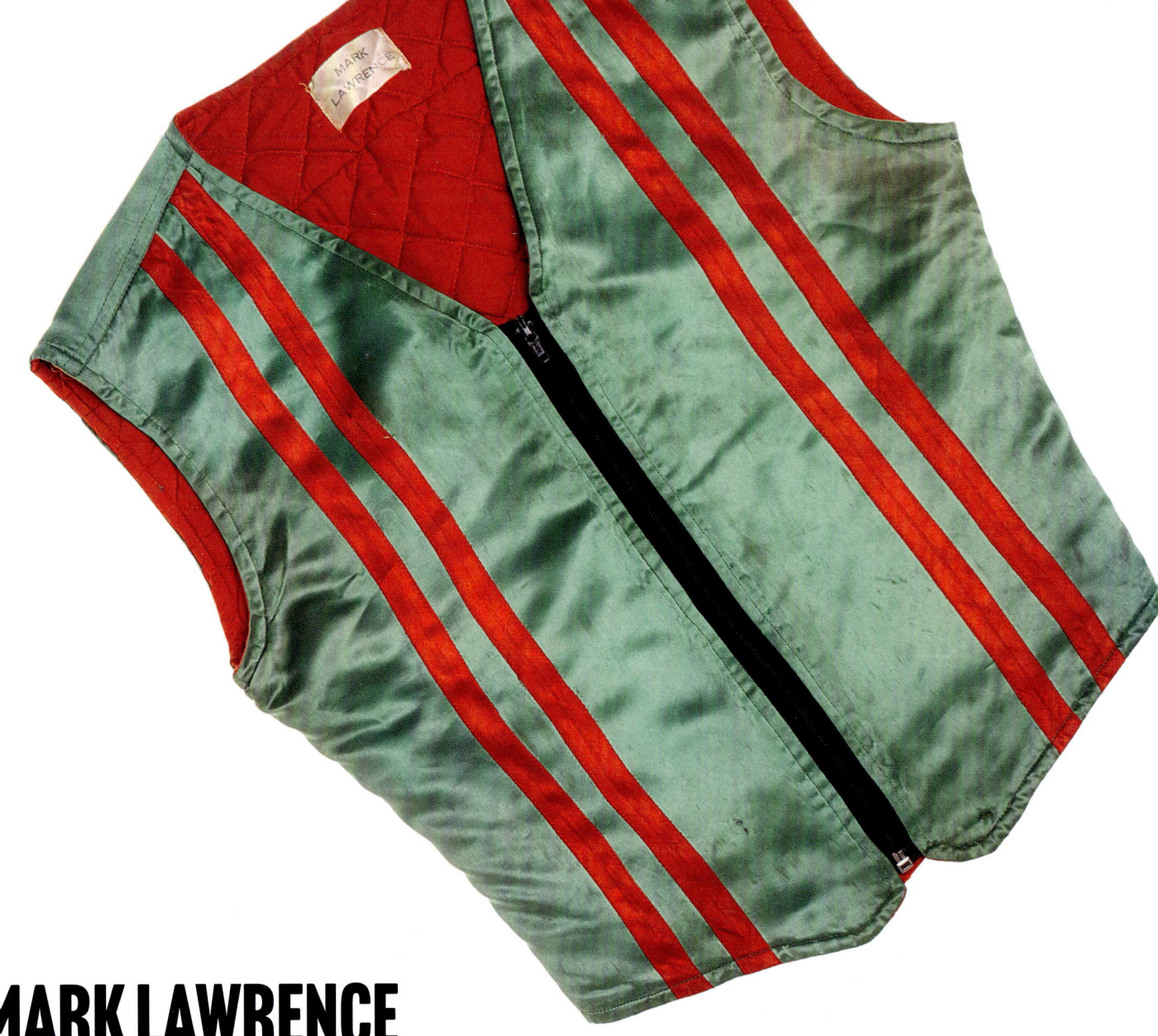

MARK LAWRENCE

Born in 1965, Mark Lawrence was an expert tailor and perfectionist who studied for a while at St Martin's School of Art before deciding it wasn't for him. He helped cut John Galliano's first collection before setting up his own label.

In 1985 he debuted his collection of male and female Tonic suits with high-contrast bound seams, which were a big hit with Browns, leading him to become a prolific maker for many club-goers and fashion friends.

He also ran the door at Leigh Bowery's Taboo along with Marc Vaultier, and in his spare time turned his hand to modelling and DJing. He took part in many editorial shoots, including a *Blitz* magazine cover, and modelled for Jean Paul Gaultier on the runway in Paris.

He was a much-loved personality who DJed at many clubs, including Daisy Chain and Disco Hospital among others. Lawrence died of AIDS in 1995 aged 30.

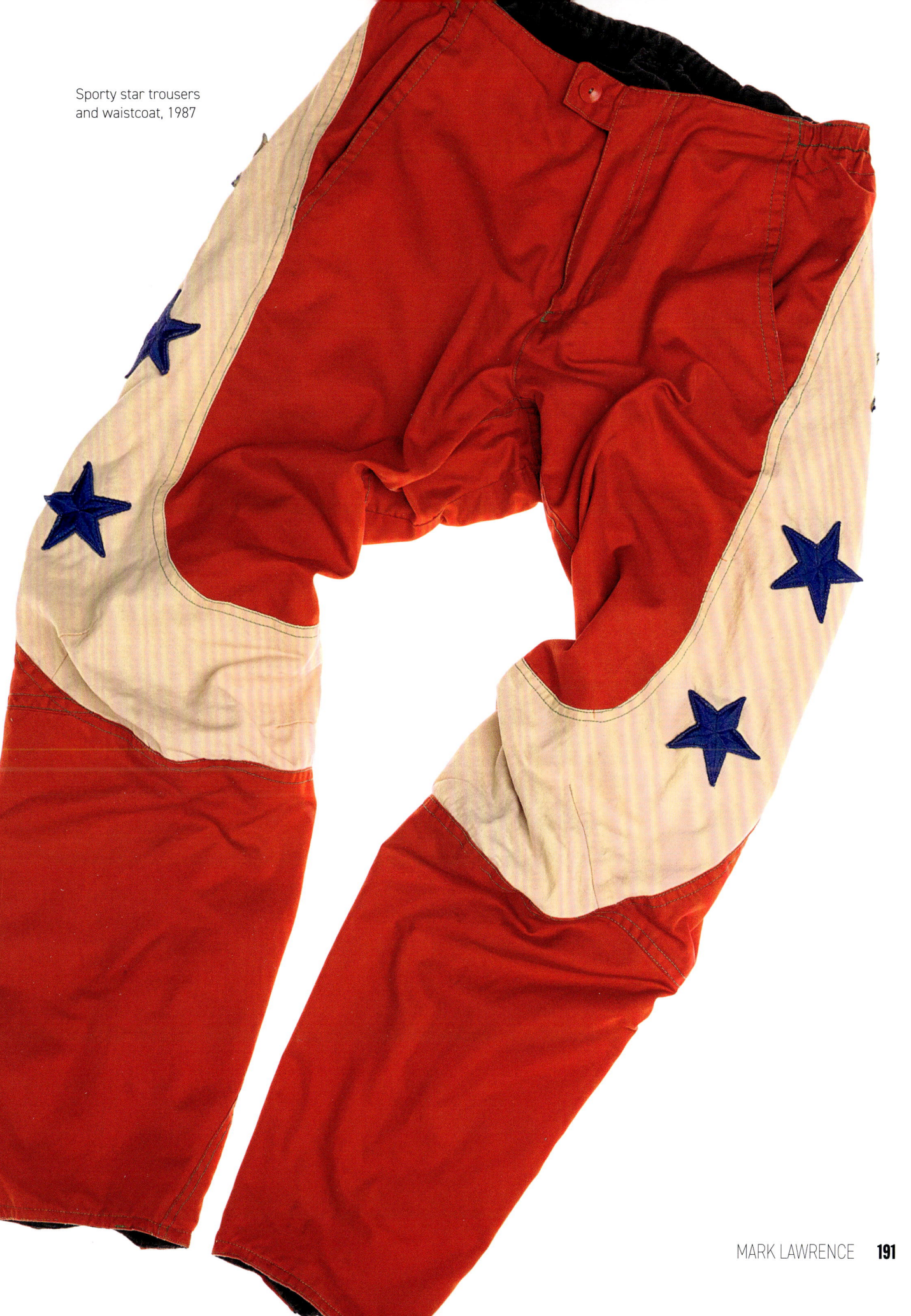

Sporty star trousers and waistcoat, 1987

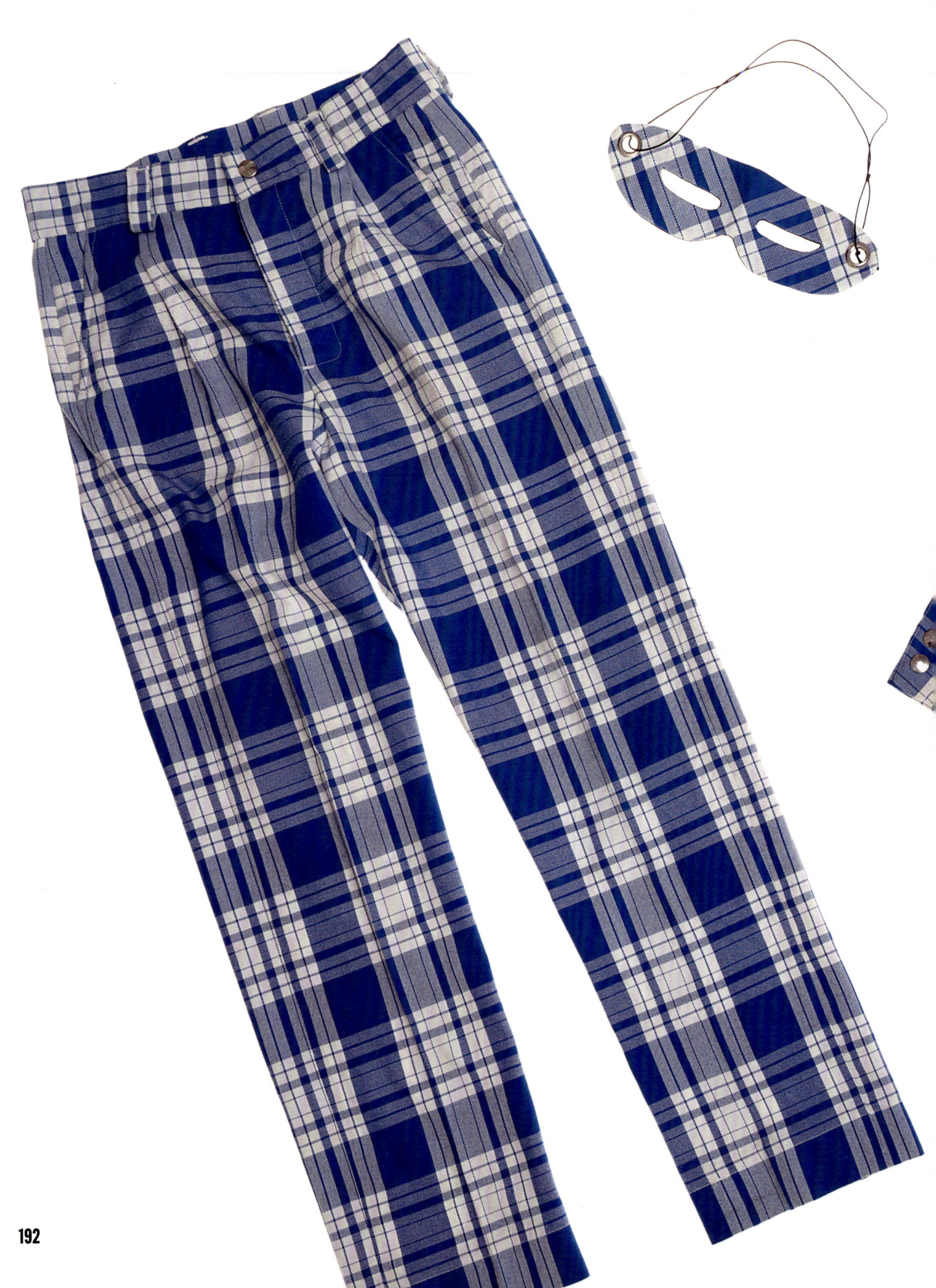

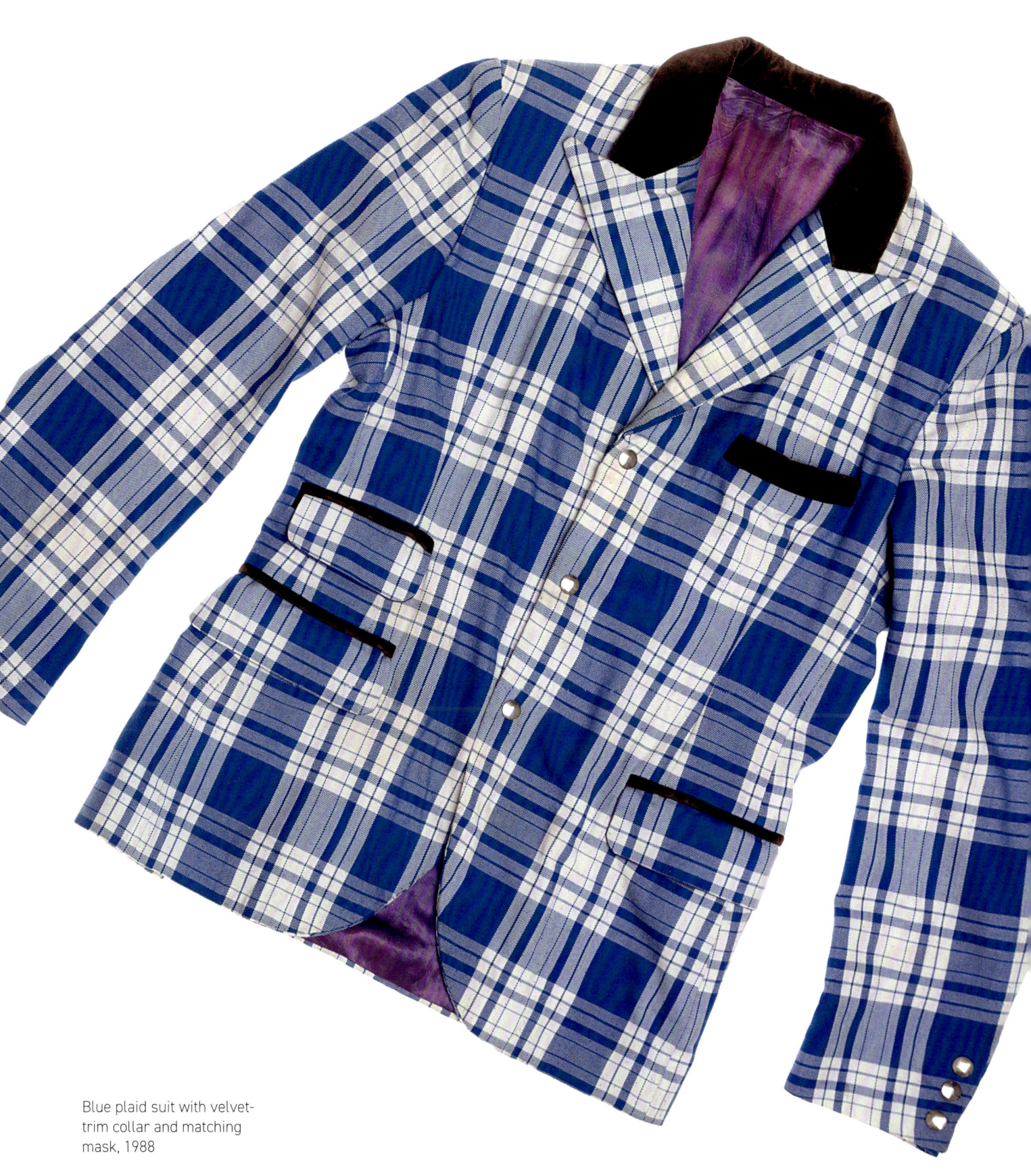

Blue plaid suit with velvet-trim collar and matching mask, 1988

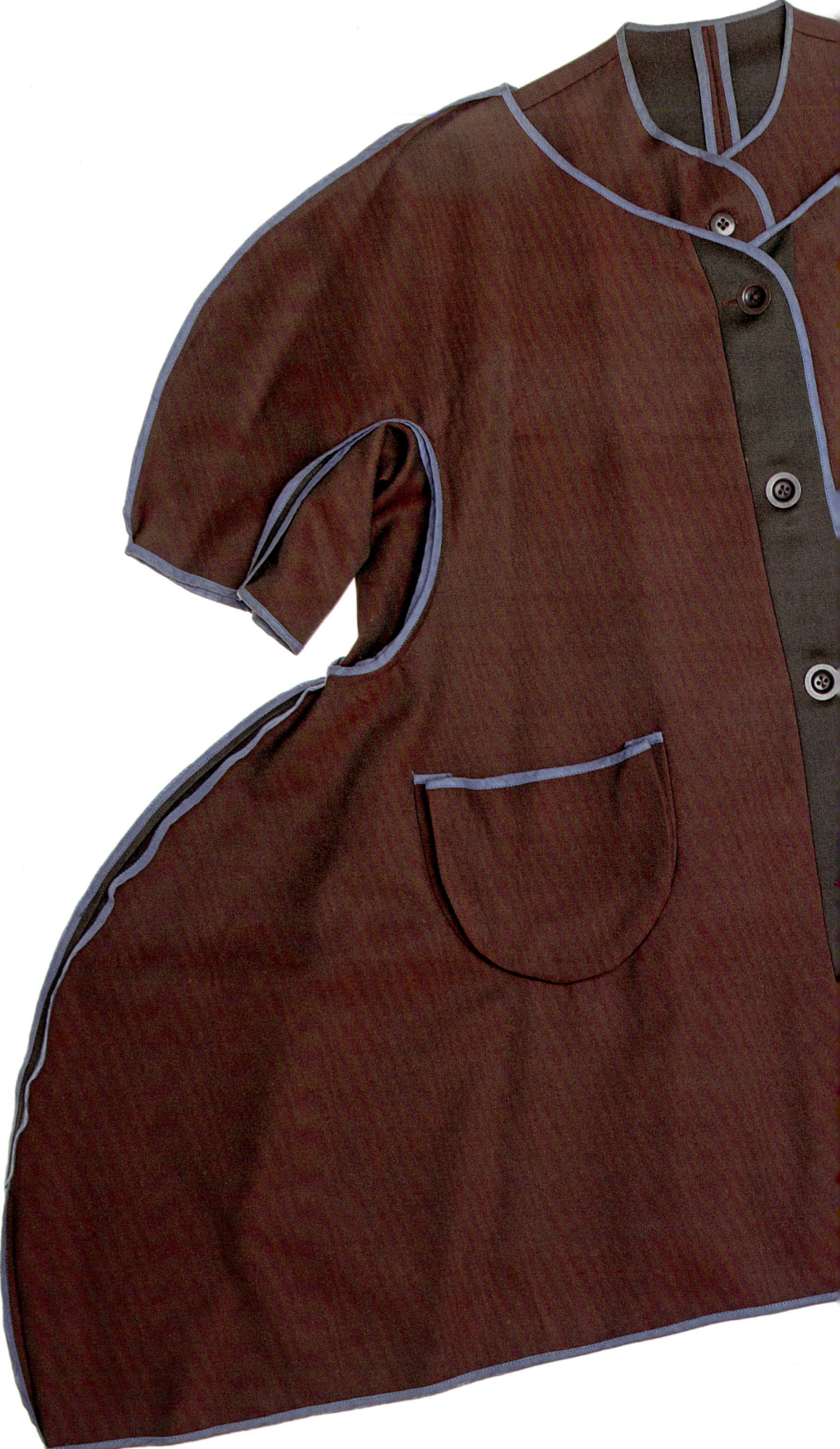

Blue-edged two-piece suit, 1985, as worn by Scarlett Cannon in the Lanah Pellay 'Pistol in my Pocket' video, filmed at Taboo by John Maybury

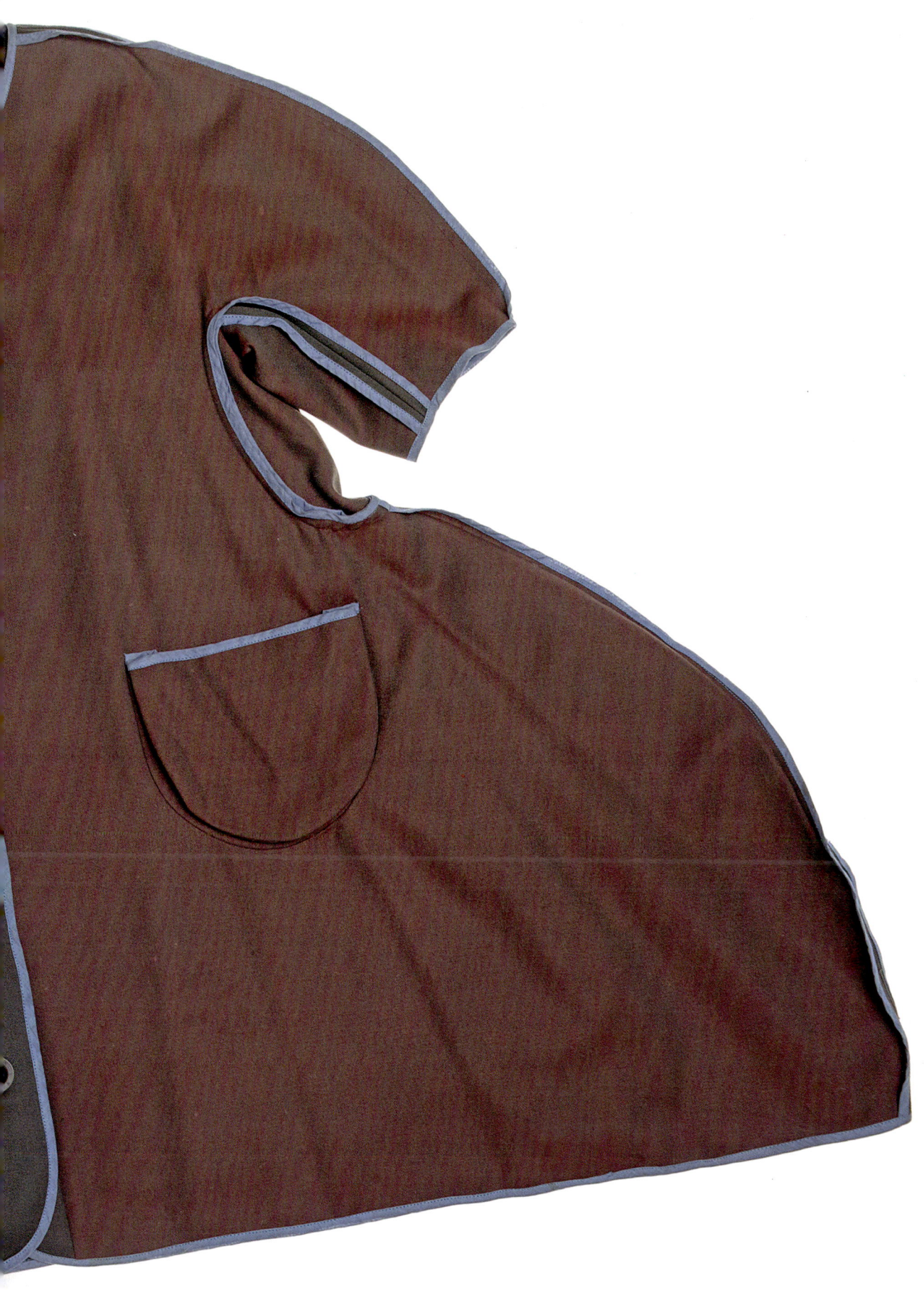

THE AFTERPARTY

CLAIRE LAWRIE

In 1982 I was 15 years old and 6ft 2in tall with a purple Mohican, making my way home from a Siouxsie and the Banshees gig. Sat across from me, a tall skinny boy with blue hair was showing off. His eyeliner smudge was perfectly imperfect. We exchanged dirty looks but soon became best friends.

A few months later, while celebrating blue-haired Mike's 18th birthday with a group of friends, we endured a nasty queer-bashing on Earl's Court high street which left me with 45 stitches in my leg. Undeterred and by then very much bonded, I moved permanently out of the suburbs south of London, where I grew up, and began to stay at Mike's and other friends' bedsits in Earl's Court.

The first nightclub I went to was called The Padded Cell, in Green Park, run by a couple of Numanoids. In those days you could get banned, like my friend David did, for wearing the wrong clothes – he was a buffalo boy and that was unforgivable at The Padded Cell. I saw Tasty Tim there with his friend Flanagan, both stunning, in Flanagan's loose muslin wear.

Clothes were so important; you made your own, or went to Laurence Corner in Camden, jumble

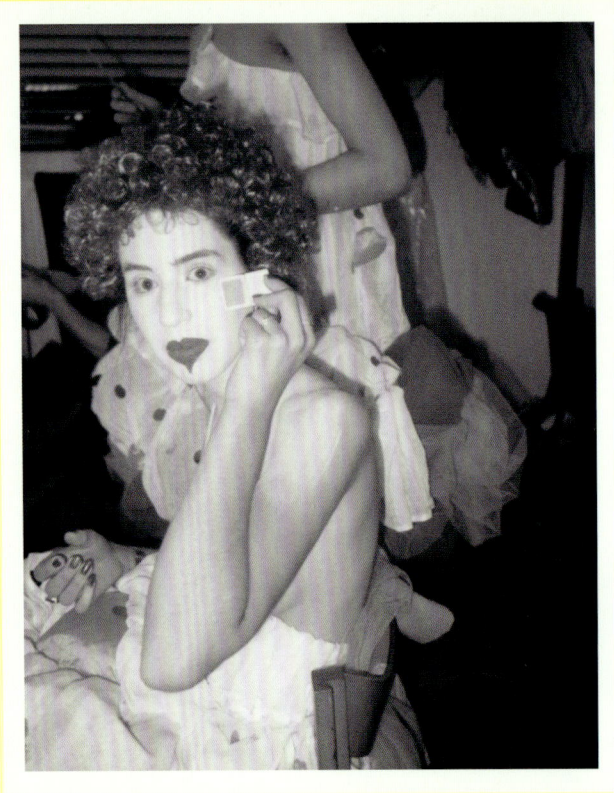

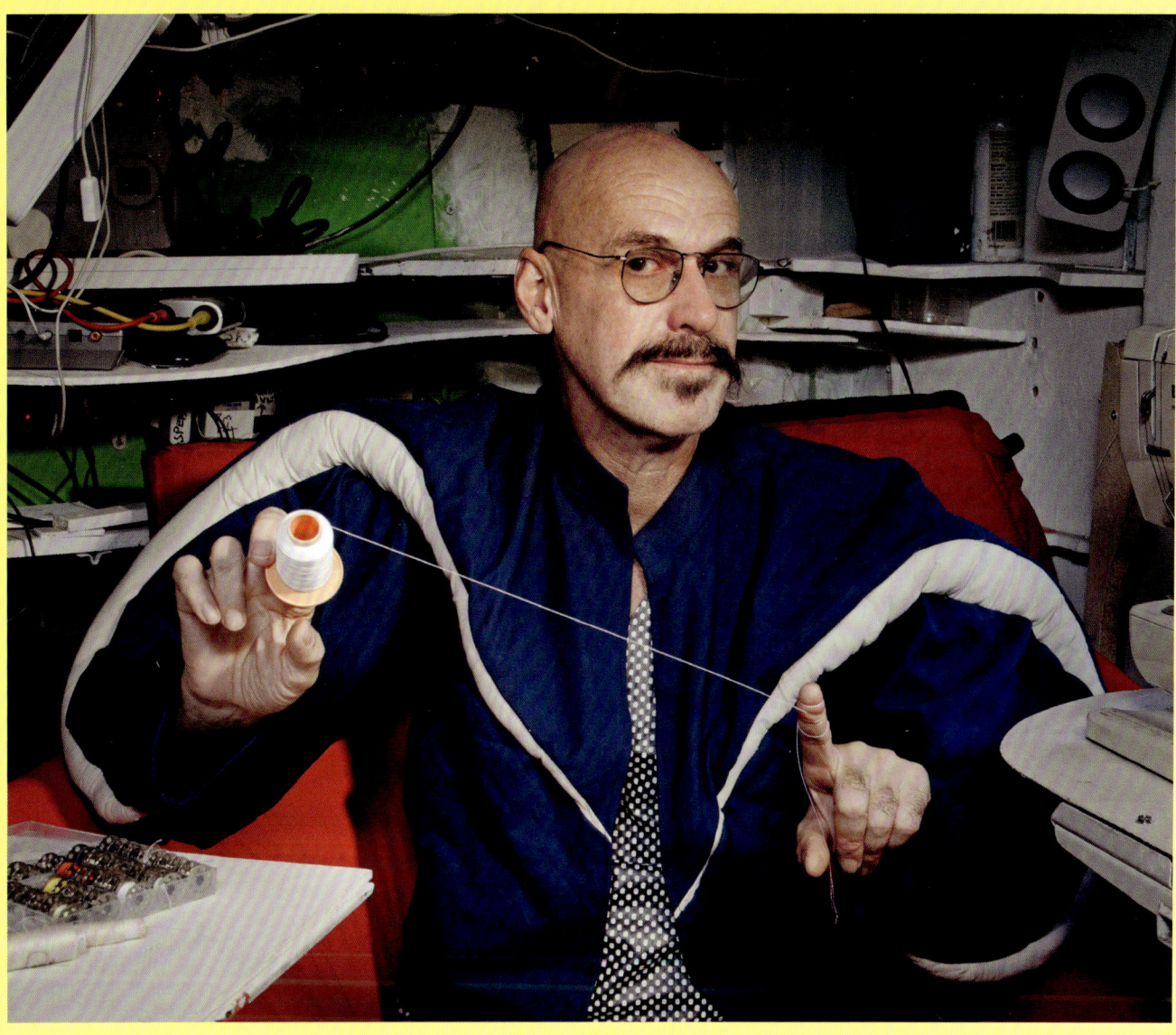

ABOVE
Richard Torry wearing his own designs

sales and markets. Sometimes a designer would give you something, friends would make you something, or you would save up for that one thing. Hair was key – you bleached it until it stretched in your hands, ironed it, crimped it, went to Cuts or Antenna, backcombed it, dyed it, shaved it off and started again. But for me, shoes were everything – it was shoes that you looked at first and they said it all.

A lot of people lost friends and lovers to HIV and drugs. I realised then that life is fragile and now some of that grief has been expressed through making. With no phones, rarely a camera, let alone the internet or social media, we had more time to play, and I drew from that while shooting these portraits. The clothes the sitters wear are not only evidence of their youthful figures, but also hold meaning in every fold; testament to their skills, to friendship and to resilience. They celebrate with much love those who wear the clothes and acknowledge the talented friends that left us far too soon.

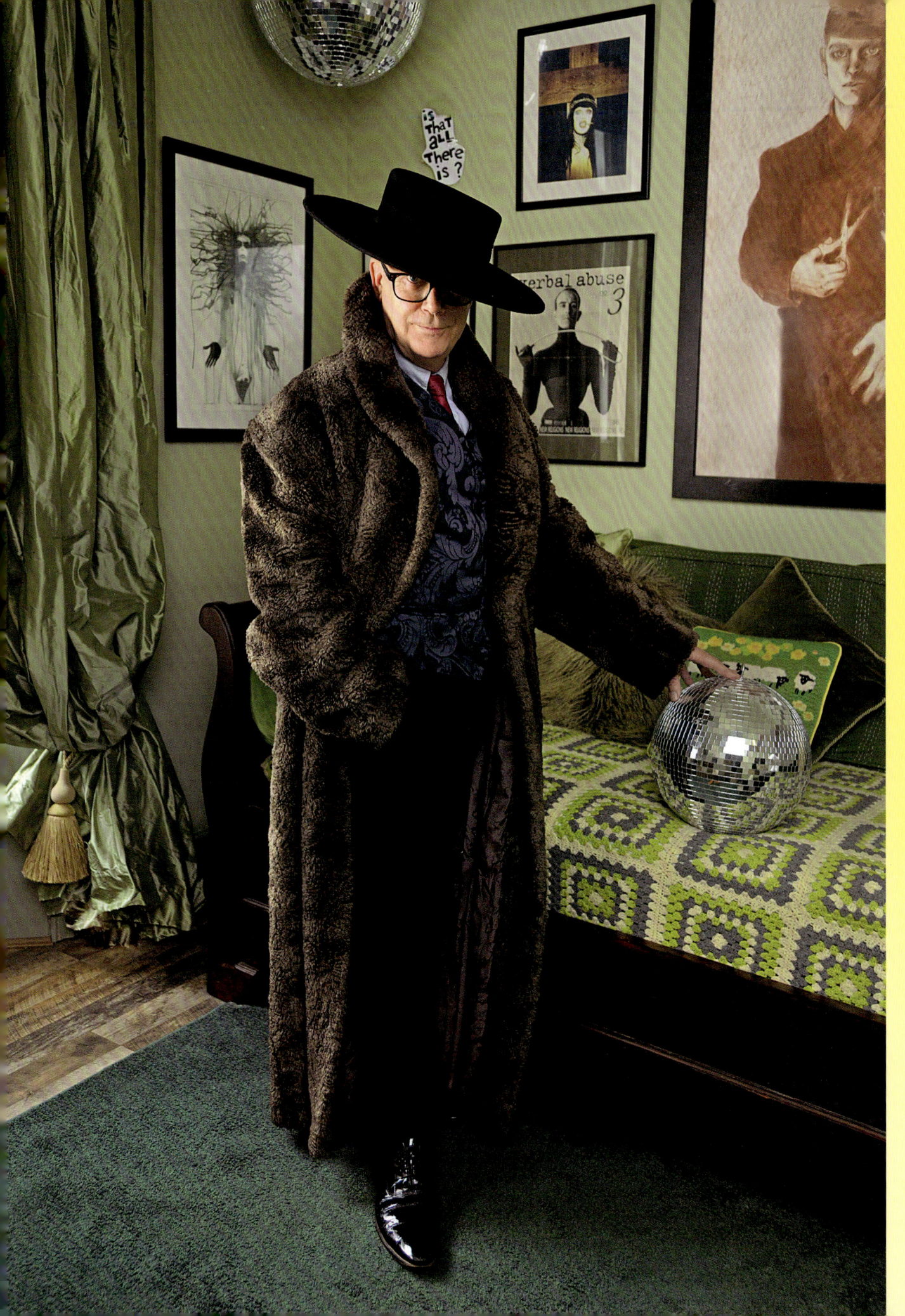

OPPOSITE
Dean Bright wearing his own designs

RIGHT
Scarlett Cannon wearing Mark Lawrence

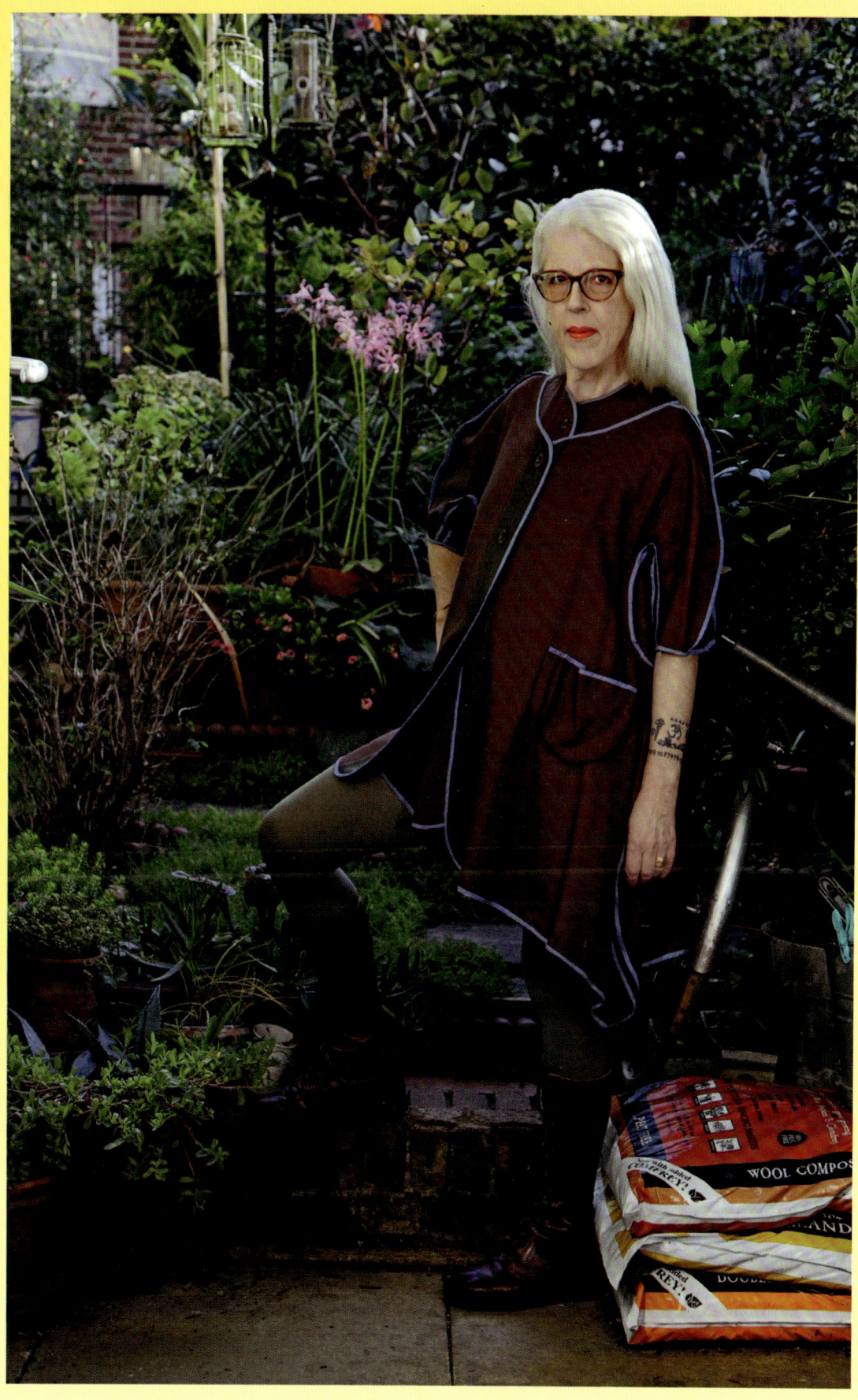

THE AFTERPARTY 199

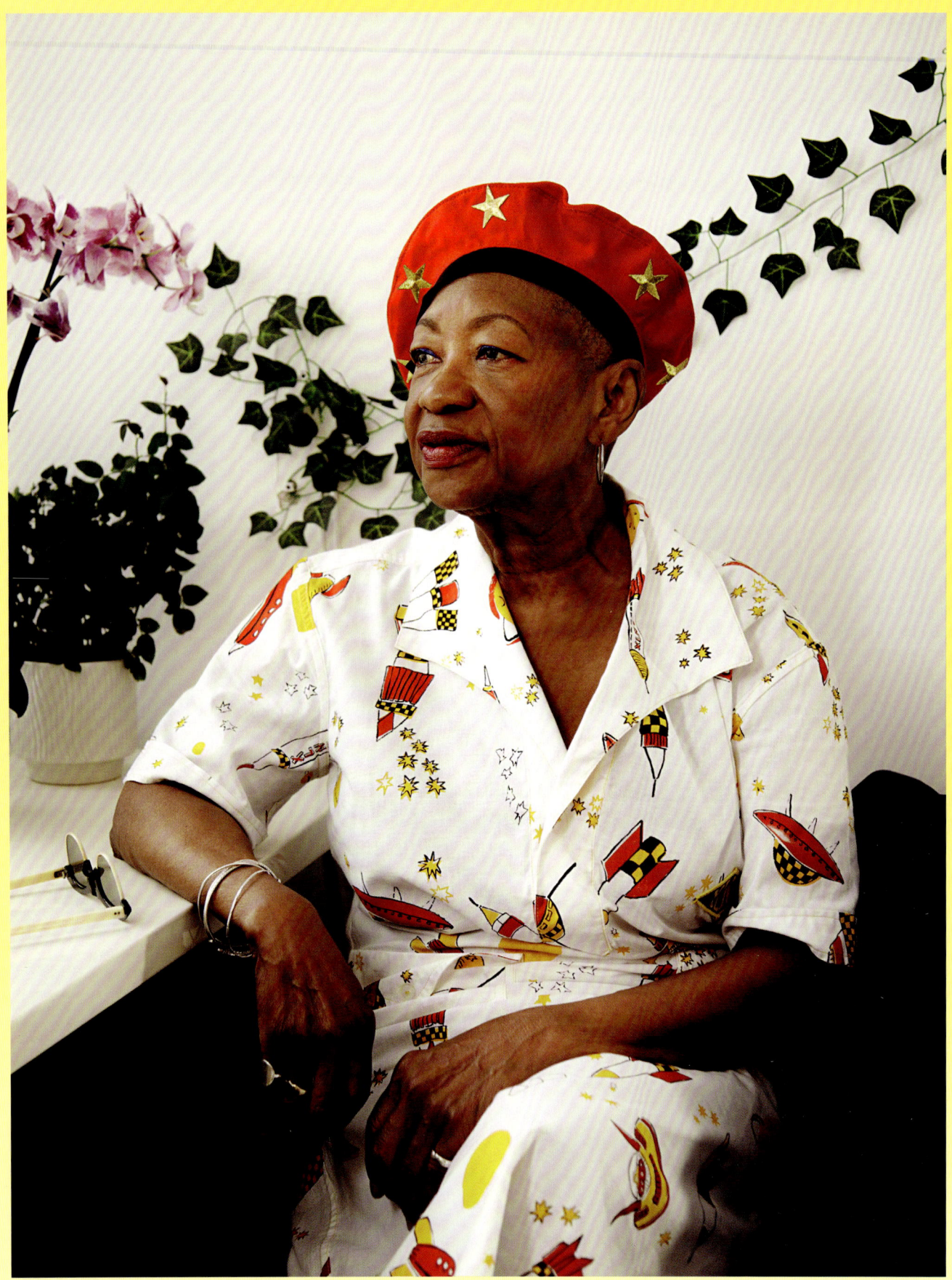

OPPOSITE
Joan Burey wearing a Demob dress and a Bernstock Speirs hat

BELOW
Mark Moore wearing Sybil Rouge

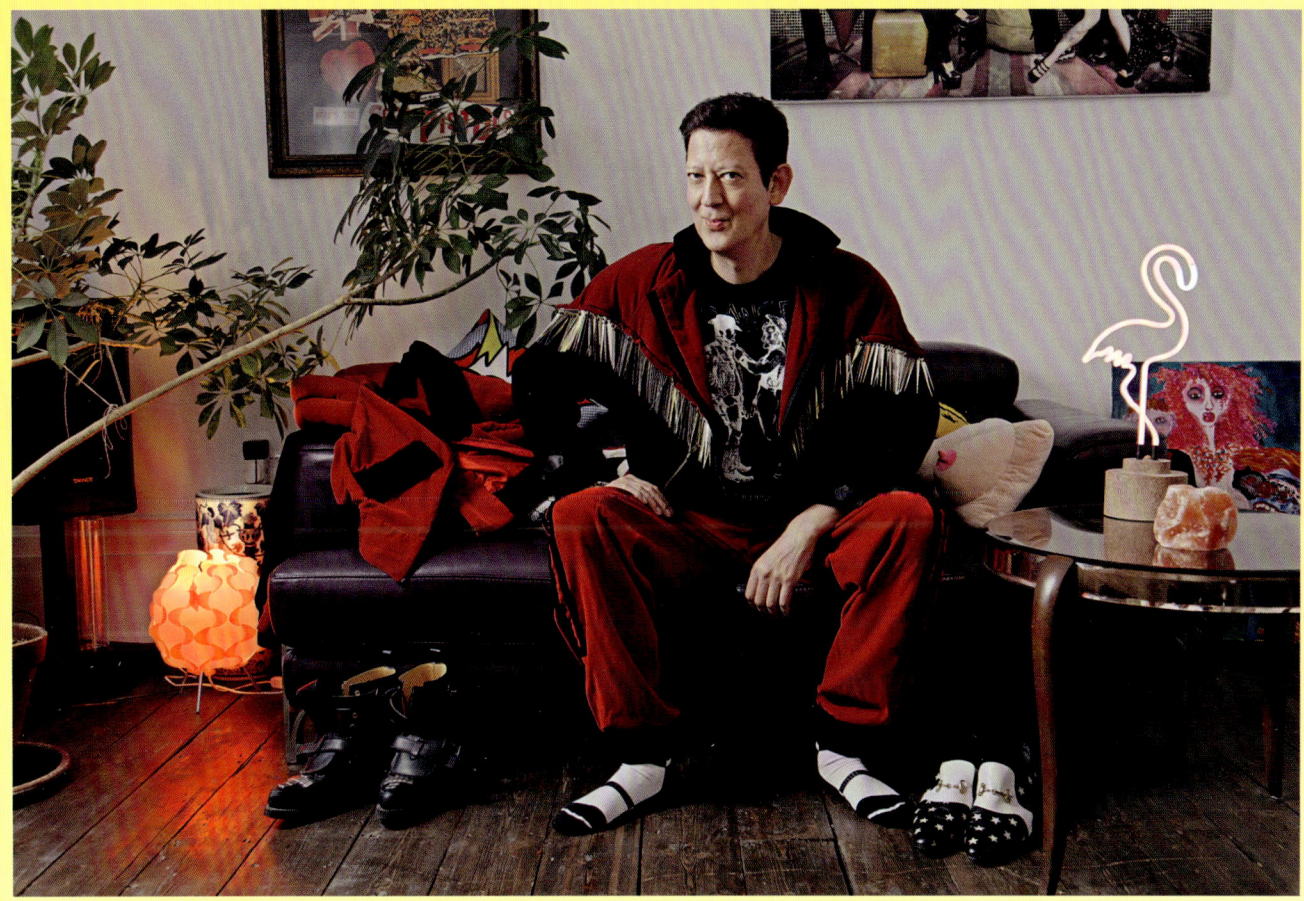

'With no phones, rarely a camera, let alone the internet or social media, we had more time to play, and I drew from that while shooting these portraits.'

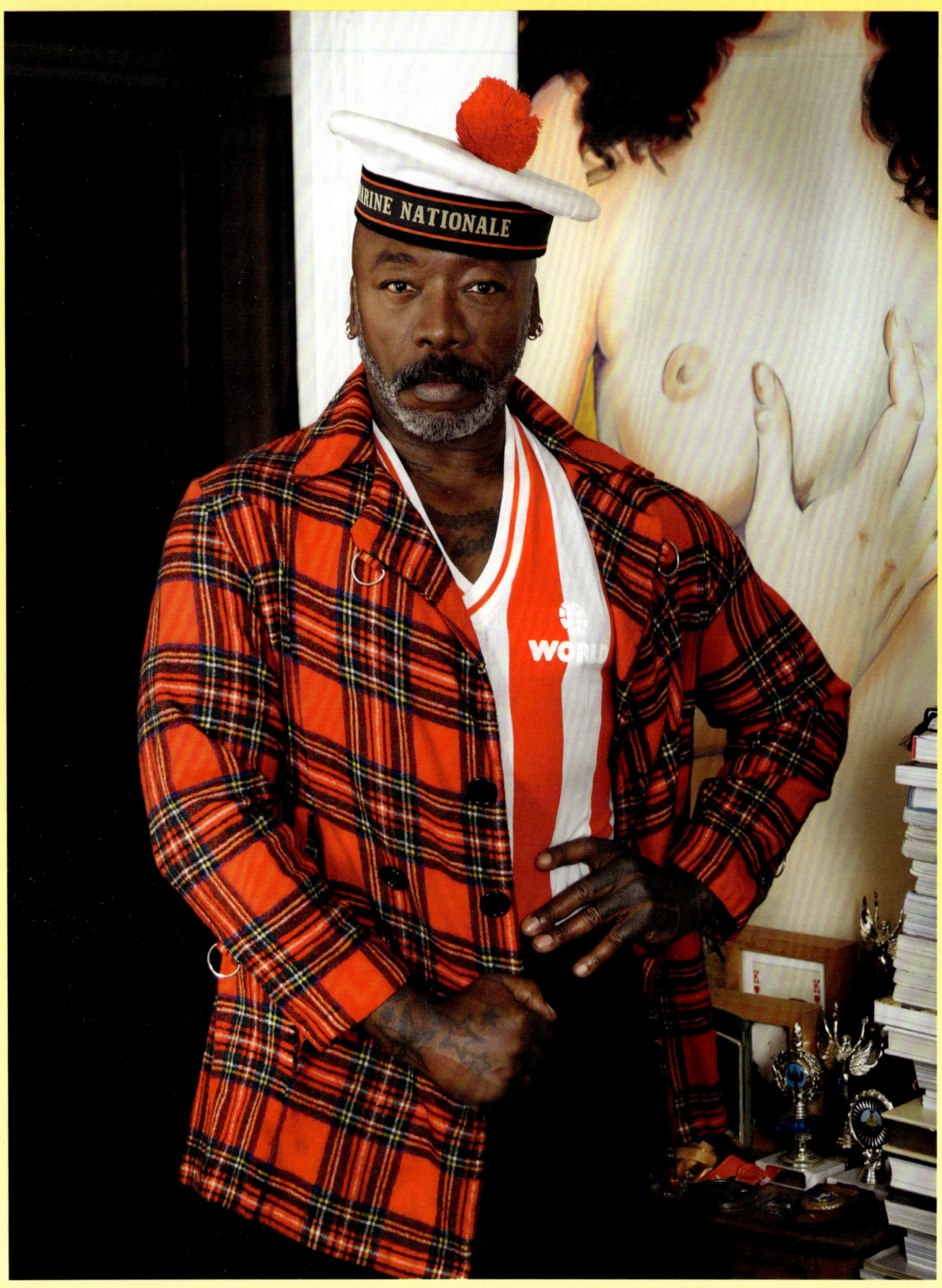

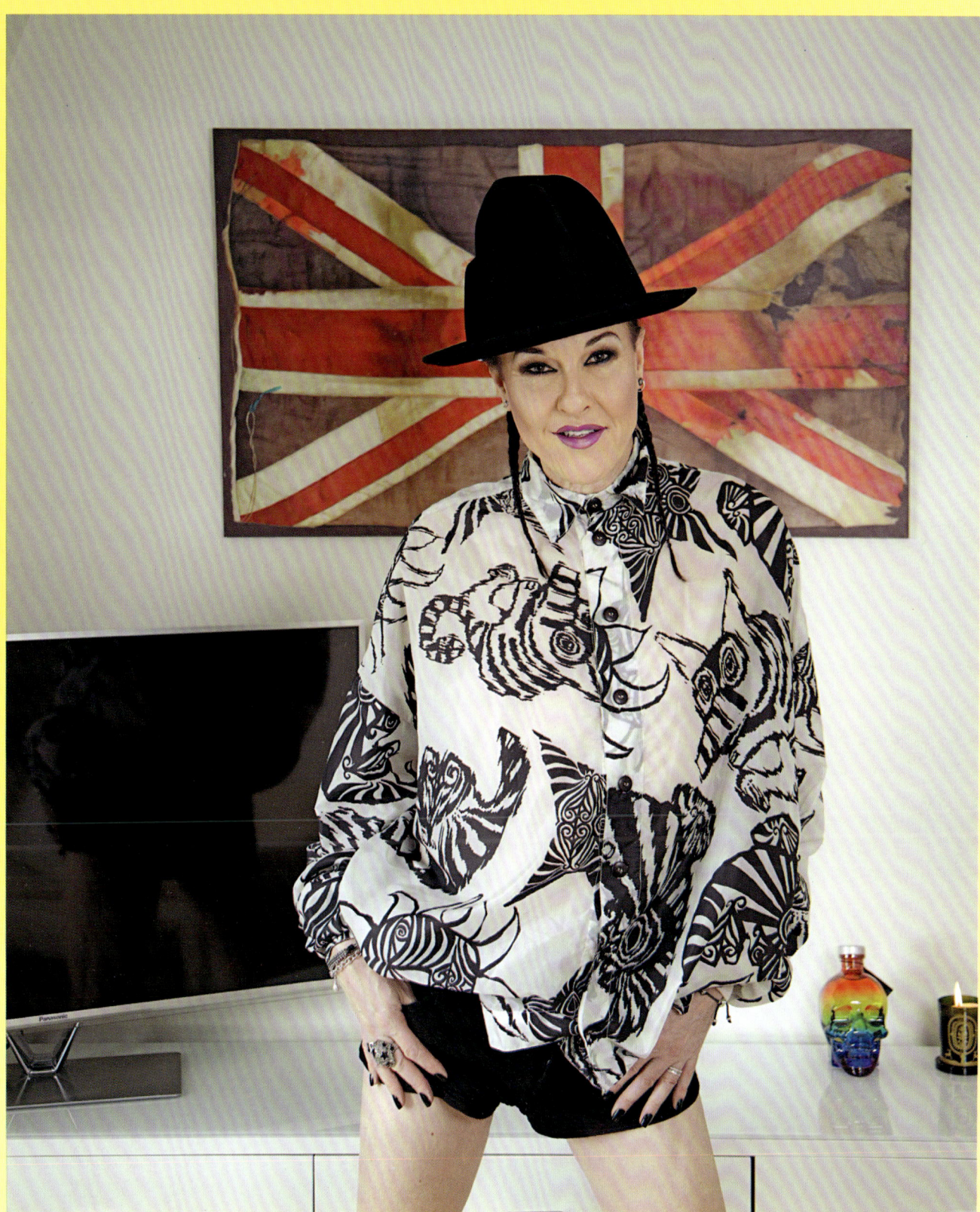

OPPOSITE
Roy Inc wearing
Pam Hogg

ABOVE
Maur Valance
wearing BodyMap

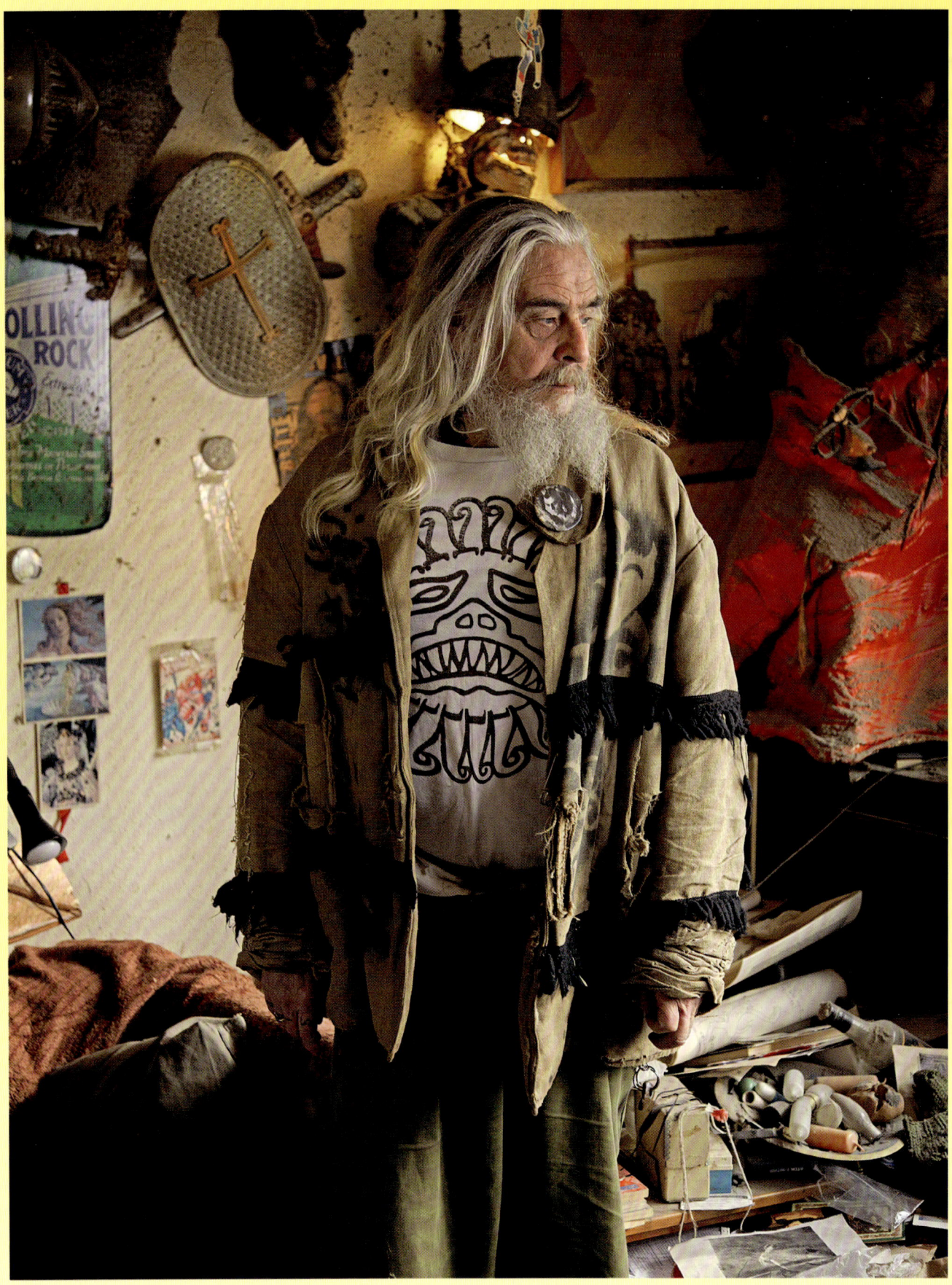

OPPOSITE
Dave Baby wearing Christopher Nemeth

RIGHT Michael Costiff wearing Mark Lawrence

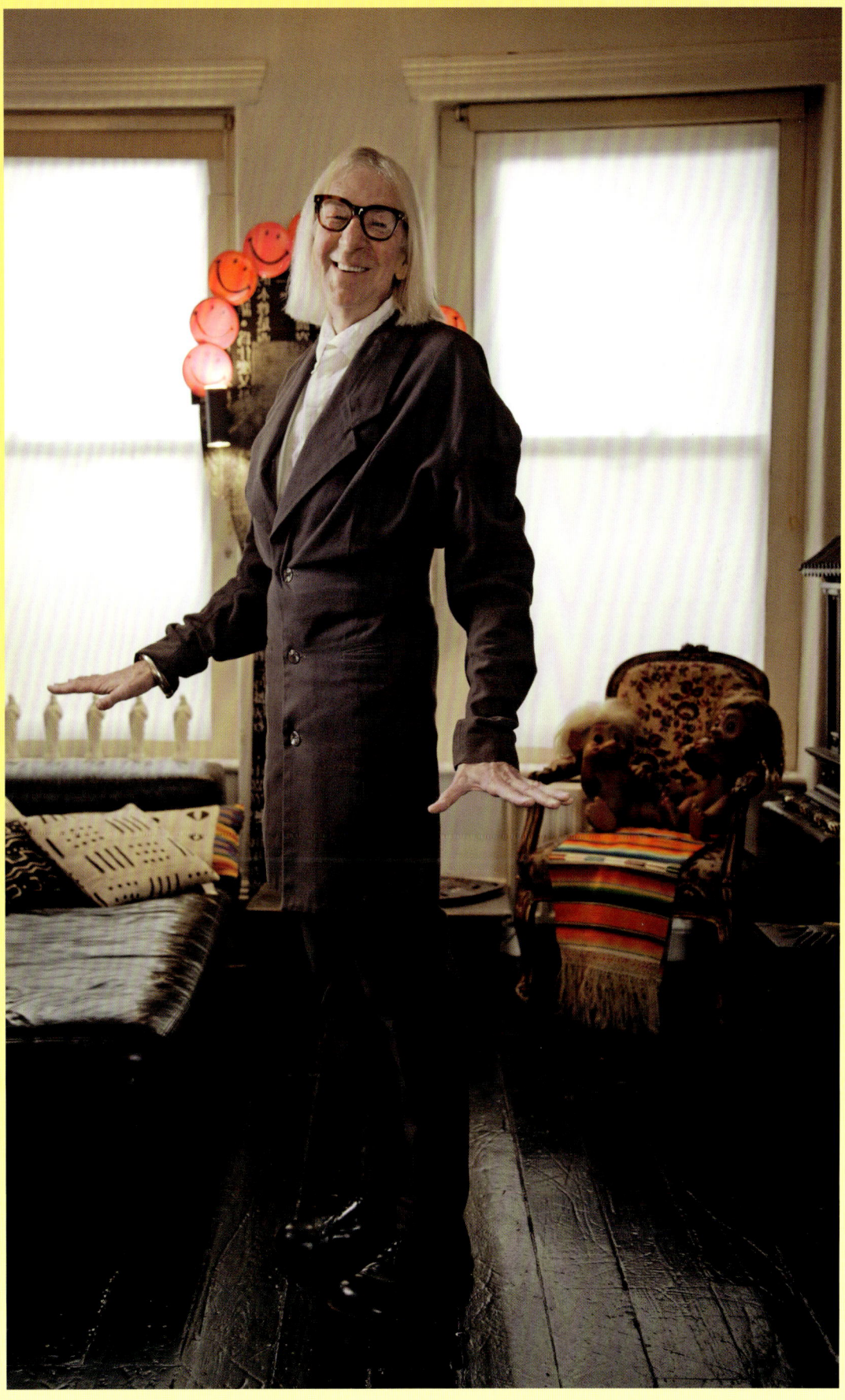

THE AFTERPARTY

AUTHOR BIOGRAPHIES

Martin Green was a regular on the 1980s club scene and went on to run the legendary club night Smashing. He has curated over 40 exhibitions, including *Outlaws: Fashion Renegades of 80s London* at the Fashion and Textile Museum. Green has compiled 30 albums and has a show on Soho Radio. He has co-ordinated fashion-show music for Katharine Hamnett, Pringle, Pucci and Ghost and has DJed at countless afterparties including events for Pulp, Prada and Paul McCartney.

NJ Stevenson began her fashion curatorial career in 2008 and has since worked on many projects with venues including the Fashion and Textile Museum, University of the Arts London and the Southbank Centre. Stevenson is widely published and is a lecturer at the London College of Fashion. She first met co-author and co-curator Martin Green on the London club scene in the early 1990s.

ACKNOWLEDGEMENTS

Martin Green and NJ Stevenson would like to thank our exhibition's artistic director David Cabaret and creative consultant James Lawler of DuoVision Arts for their hard work, impeccable taste and vast knowledge.

We must also thank Dennis Nothdruft and the team at Fashion and Textile Museum and David Graham at B.T. Batsford Ltd for believing in *Outlaws* and making it happen.

Anna Danby and Oliver Craske at Scala Arts & Heritage Publishers alongside art director Eoghan O'Brien brilliantly created this book in an incredibly short time. They deserve a standing ovation.

Thanks to Dominic Harris who expertly photographed the clothes and to lenders Peter Doig, Mark Moore, Gaynor Prior, Joan Burey, Maur Valance, Eliz Hüseyin, Sue Smallwood, Helen Carey-Cunningham, Helen David, Daniel Scott, Michael Murphy, Alex Gerry, Andrew Newman, Bibabibitch, Richard Torry, Monica Curtin, Dean Bright, Michael Petry, Emma Day, Steven Moore, Marcus Wayland, Michael Hardy, Les Child, Steph Avery, Leslie Chilkes, David Holah, Stevie Stewart, Scarlett Cannon, Roy Inc, David Vaughan, Juliana Sissons, Annie La Paz, Cathy Ward, Mark and Cleo Butterfield of C20 Vintage Collection and Roger Burton at Contemporary Wardrobe.

Additional clothing photographs were produced at Westminster University Menswear Archive courtesy of Andrew Groves and Robert Leach.

Personal photos were generously provided by Louisa Buck, Joan Burey, Dean Bright, Scarlett Cannon, Maur Valance, Gaynor Prior and Eliz Hüseyin with original club flyers from The Mott Collection and Daniel Scott's archive.

We would especially like to thank contributors Iain R Webb, Peter Doig, Holly Johnson, Mark Moore, Wayne and Geradine Hemingway MBE, Syrie Panton and Dave Swindells.

In addition valuable insights were given by Steven Philip, Corinne Drewery, Dave Baby, George Gallagher, Sue Tilley, Rachel Auburn, Nicola Bowery, Matthew Glammore, Gregor Muir, Fiontan Moran, David Harrison, Michael Costiff, Winn Austin, Sue Came, Michael Hardy, Toby Mott, Mike Nicholls, Richard Kemp, Lanah Pellay and Stephen Mahoney.

Special thanks must go to Corinne Charton for lending us Jalle Bakke's precious work diaries and Claire Lawrie for creating superb contemporary photographic portraits of 1980s renegades in their original clothes.

Finally we would like to thank Will Hodgkinson, Jonny Trunk, Whitaker Malem, Tris Penna and Daniel Scott for their encouragement and support.

Outlaws is dedicated to those bright and brave young creatives who lost their lives way too early, but left us with a legacy of unbridled brilliance.

This edition © B. T. Batsford Ltd., 2024
Text © the authors 2024

First published in 2024 by
Scala Arts & Heritage Publishers Ltd
43 Great Ormond Street
London WC1N 3HZ, UK
www.scalapublishers.com

An imprint of B. T. Batsford Holdings Ltd.

ISBN 978-1-78551-601-6

Copy-edited by Emma Bastow and Beth Holmes
Designed by Eoghan O'Brien and Sanya Jain
Printed in Turkey by Elma Basim

10 9 8 7 6 5 4 3 2

All rights reserved. No part of this book may be reproduced, stored in a retrieval system or transmitted in any form or by any means electronic, mechanical, photocopying, recording or otherwise, without the written permission of Scala Arts & Heritage Publishers Ltd.

Photography credits:
© Dave Swindells: front cover and pp. 6, 13, 15, 16, 22, 24, 25, 26
© Dominic Harris: clothing photography
© Alamy: pp. 19, 21, 27
© Fritz Mason/Solomon: p. 61
© David Levine: p. 102 (ABC)
© Pete Moss: pp. 161, 168 (top right & bottom right), 169 (bottom left)
© Claire Lawrie: pp. 197–205

Other images courtesy of Louisa Buck, Joan Burey, Dean Bright, Scarlett Cannon, Maur Valance, Gaynor Prior and Eliz Hüseyin. Original club flyers courtesy of The Mott Collection and Daniel Scott.

Every effort has been made to acknowledge correct copyright of images where applicable. Any errors or omissions are unintentional and should be notified to the Publisher, who will arrange for corrections to appear in any reprints.

Cover photography © Dave Swindells
Top, from left Mark Natham, Dencil Williams, Marc Vaultier and Trojan at Taboo, 1986
Bottom, from left Leigh Bowery and Nicola Bateman at Taboo, 1986

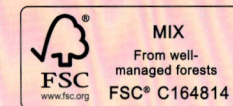